The Biblical Seminar
10

RUTH

RUTH

A New Translation with a Philological Commentary and a Formalist-Folklorist Interpretation

2nd Edition

Jack M. Sasson

Sheffield Academic Press

First published by The Johns Hopkins University Press
Baltimore and London, 1979
in the series The Johns Hopkins Near Eastern Studies

Second edition (with corrections) published 1989
by Sheffield Academic Press, reprinted 1995

Published by Sheffield Academic Press Ltd
Mansion House
19 Kingfield Road
Sheffield S11 9AS
England

Printed on acid-free paper in Great Britain
by The Cromwell Press
Melksham, Wiltshire

British Library Cataloguing in Publication Data

A catalogue record for this book is available
from the British Library

ISBN 1-85075-213-3

to S.D.S.

... וְאַתְּ עָלִית עַל־כֻּלָּנָה

Proverbs 31:29

CONTENTS

Preface ix
Foreword to the Second Edition xiii
Abbreviations xvii

1. Translation 1

2. The Book of *Ruth* 8
   The Text of *Ruth* 8
   Canonical Status of *Ruth* 11
   Liturgical Use of *Ruth* 12

3. Philological Commentary 14
   In Moab (1:1-6) 14
   The Parting (1:7-14) 22
   The Pledge (1:15-19a) 28
   Back to Bethlehem (1:19b-22) 31
   A Plan (2:1-7) 38
   Boaz and Ruth: The First Encounter (2:8-13) 48
   Boaz Responds (2:14-18a) 54
   The Report (2:18b-23) 57
   Naomi's Plan (3:1-5) 63
   Ruth and Boaz: The Second Encounter (3:6-15) 71
   Nothing to Do But Wait (3:16-18) 99
   Legal Discussions (4:1-12) 102
   Birth of Obed (4:13-17) 157
   The Ancestry of David (4:18-22) 178

4. An Interpretive Synopsis 191

5. Interpretation 196
The Literary Genre of *Ruth* 197
The Narrative Style of *Ruth* 216
The Contexts of *Ruth* 225
A "Political" Context for *Ruth*? 232
The Dating of *Ruth* 240
Conclusion 251

Bibliography 253
Indexes 273
Biblical References 275
Citation of Scholars 284
Subject Index 289

PREFACE

This book is dedicated to my wife, Diane, who helped shape many of the ideas expressed in the following pages. Because of her involvement in all stages of this book's formulations, she will certainly find superfluous the few remarks I will presently make. But it may be appropriate to offer the reader a few words at the outset in order to explain matters of content and organization lest they be judged idiosyncratic.

Two summers ago (1976), my most ambitious plans concerning *Ruth* were limited to writing a paper that would chart the manner in which Ruth persuaded Boaz to become Naomi's redeemer. The article would have highlighted the brilliant artistry of a narrator who managed to propel events by concentrating almost exclusively on the dialogue of the protagonists as presented in chapters 2 and 3. But as I began to consult the commentaries and to research the scholarly discussions on *Ruth*, it became obvious that their understanding of what transpired between Boaz and Ruth differed appreciably from mine. In particular, there seemed to be a pervasive tendency to rely too much on a *deus ex machina*, so to speak, to unravel the plot of the tale. Moreover, passages crucial to my thesis were translated in a manner that could bear different renderings. It soon became clear that a new translation had to be prepared and defended before my thesis could be promoted.

The translation and the annotations contained in the Philological Commentary were, therefore, the first to be written. I tried not to be so slavish in my attachment to the Hebrew text that my translation would turn wooden and lifeless. Above all, what I assessed to be the flavor of the Hebrew text became my guideline. *Ruth* is a remarkable tale in which richly elaborate statements were juxtaposed to others noteworthy for their dignity, simplicity, and curtness. A number of lines almost broke the bounds, always artificial, between prose and poetry. A few even matched the best poetic lines of the Old Testament. Yet, it will be noted, I have refrained from presenting any of my translation in verse. I sought to keep in mind that the tale was, after all, about common people who, unknowingly, achieve uncommon ends. Whereas Hebrew poetry could unobtrusively be placed in the mouth of even the most uncouth, a modern English translation that does so imitatively might confer upon the characters status and refinement irrelevant to the Hebrew narrative.

Some liberties have been taken in order to permit the English rendering to flow as naturally as does the Hebrew. I have inserted, in many cases, personal names in the place of pronouns, broken down, in a few instances, the confines of individual verses, treated the ubiquitous conjunction *waw* in a manner that suited the context, and altered the sequences of words and idioms when clarity could thereby best be achieved. In one passage, 4:4, I have inserted between brackets a whole sentence in order to preserve the integrity of a Hebrew verbal form. It is hoped that the gains obtained by such interferences will outweigh the merits of a literal translation. I have, however, been scrupulous to explain any deviation from the Hebrew in the Philological Commentary.

Necessarily, the Commentary reached large proportions. There, I tried not only to explain renderings that differed from those of other translations, but to turn this section into a repository of the philological and interpretive discussions current in *Ruth* scholarship. I trust that I have been fair to the views of others; but I should be quick to admit that I could not assemble all opinions within these pages. A large amount of space in the Commentary was devoted to analyzing the art of the storyteller as he constructed a tale in which verses depended on preceding verses, and words bore multiple nuances. For this reason, as the Commentary reaches the end of chapter 2, the annotations perceptibly expand.

By November 1976, I had finished the two sections introduced above. I have benefited from the suggestions offered by those who read various portions of the Commentary: Professor William F. Stinespring (Duke University), Dr Thomas L. Thompson, Professor David J. Halperin (University of North Carolina), and Professor Baruch Levine (New York University). Professor Cyrus H. Gordon (New York University) responded quickly to one of my queries.

In introducing the Interpretation segment, I thought it imperative to locate *Ruth* within a literary category more firmly than has heretofore been done. I therefore turned to the methods of V. Propp, well known to folklorists, as providing a fruitful avenue of research. A confession may be in order at this point, however. Congenitally skeptical of most approaches that resolve problems by invoking the subconscience of mankind, I had, at first, been reluctant to decipher Propp's code. My skepticism was heightened by the literature, mostly French, that sought to 'improve' Propp by subjecting his approach to structuralist formulations. I returned to Propp's original model in order to determine whether his functions were applicable to *Ruth*. I was persuaded of the validity of the approach and its application to Ancient Near Eastern texts when a verbal form, which had been commonly emended by modern scholars, fitted Propp's scheme only when the original Hebrew was preserved.

I leave it to others to decide on the merits of formalistic analysis. But I should like it to be recorded here that Propp's categories will doubtless have to be refined and perhaps redefined if better and more complete application to Biblical and other Near Eastern texts is sought. *Ruth* is obviously neither a folktale nor a fairy tale of nineteenth-century Russia. But I do not think it would be sound methodology to restructure an approach before it is tested in the form first proposed.

The remaining segments of the interpretation do not rely exclusively on conclusions derived from application of Propp's technique; for many scholars do regard *Ruth* as a folktale. My aim was to entertain those queries that can be posed to a text once its genre is established. I found it distressing that those who label *Ruth* with folkloristic terminology nevertheless proceed to extract from it information of legal and theological import. I tried, therefore, not to abuse the limitations inherent in the folktale genre by strictly delineating the agenda of discussion to topics that could be fruitfully pursued. Those who are not persuaded by the wisdom of a folkloristic approach should be assured, however, that I found it prudent not to recast the findings obtained in the Commentary to accord with those of the Interpretation. Thus, while minor divergences might be noted in the methods pursued in these two sections, the conclusions obtained by application of both a philological and a folkloristic approach will be quite consistent.

I have had occasion to discuss the methods and implications of a folkloristic approach with friends and colleagues. Dr Thomas Thompson and his wife Dr Dorothy Irvin, Mr Norman Dunbar, Professor Charles Long, Professor John H. Schütz, and Professor Ruel Tyson have placed me under obligation by sharing some of their insights with me.

The section on the text of *Ruth* was written last. The manuscript was typed partly by Ms Bonita Samuels of the Institute for Research in Social Science at the University of North Carolina, and partly by our family friend, Ms Mary Ellen Powell. I am well aware of the difficulties of preparing a good manuscript from badly typed and edited pages with a polyglot vocabulary, and thus cannot be grateful enough to them. The Institute and its director, Dr Frank Munger, were kind enough to extend to me many services that facilitated the production of this volume. My research assistant, Mr Norman Dunbar, graduate student at Duke University, was charged with checking the manuscript and with preparing a final copy of the Bibliography. I frequently hounded him; but he bore the brunt gracefully.

Delbert Hillers was one of two readers of the manuscript when it was submitted to press. I am beholden to him for his care and attentiveness in reading it and was most happy to accept and incorporate almost all the suggestions he offered. It is a pleasure to thank Hans Goedicke, William P. Sisler, and the governing board of The Johns Hopkins University Press for including Ruth as part of The Johns Hopkins Near Eastern Studies Series. I am indebted to Mr Stanley Steinger for so ably editing my manuscript. I am very grateful to the University of North Carolina's Research Council and to George R. Holcomb, Dean of Research Administration, for financial support. The Pierpont Morgan Library was very kind in permitting me to reproduce an illuminated folio from one of its medieval manuscripts.

I need add that none of those mentioned above is responsible for the weaknesses contained in the following pages.

The final draft of this study was completed in December 1977. Only minor changes were incorporated after that date.

FOREWORD TO THE SECOND EDITION

Copies of *Ruth* began to be scarce within two years of publication. Shortly afterwards, the Johns Hopkins University reported it to be out of print. It is with pleasure, therefore, that I greet this reissue and hope that the commentary will find a wider circulation. Because this is a reissue of a previous publication, I have had opportunity to correct only some of the more glaring and embarrassing typographical errors in that edition.

In offering a philological commentary to Ruth, I had sought to clarify the tale's sequence of events and to explain its plot. I wanted to detail how, at her own initiative, Ruth loses control over her own fate when she pledges herself to Naomi and I have done so by annotating Chapter 1. Commenting on Chapter 2, I showed how Ruth, albeit a foreigner (*nokriyyâ*) with minimal rights and opportunity in Bethlehem, nevertheless persuades Boaz to accept her as a maidservant (*šipḥâ*), thus securing his protection. In Chapter 3, I discuss a number of interrelated topics. I suggest that Ruth convinces Boaz to take her into his personal service (*'āmâ*) as well as to become a redeemer (*gō'ēl*) for Naomi. In this way, Ruth hopes to retain links to Naomi through a common reliance on Boaz. Boaz, instead proposes to marry Ruth because her marriage to Mahlon had already made her a 'wife of a notable (*'ešet ḥayil*)'. Boaz also pledges to become Naomi's redeemer.

The fourth and last chapter required a highly nuanced exegesis. There, I first demonstrated how Boaz cleverly forces the potential redeemer to give up redemption of Naomi's land by publicly pledging to acquire Ruth in order to perpetuate Mahlon's memory. In explaining how Boaz's strategem works, I defended the integrity of the *ketiv qnyty*, 'I am acquiring' in 4:5. Secondly, I explained how, with the birth of Ruth's son, Elimelech's estate comes to have an heir, Naomi acquires a comforter and Boaz obtains a male offspring. Finally, I disproved the oft-stated contention that the genealogy at the end of Chapter 4 is a later insertion into the text of *Ruth*. (For a handy overview of these arguments, see my contribution in R. Alter and F. Kermode, *The Literary Guide to the Bible*, 1987).

I have not kept up with the scroll's bibliography as much as I would have liked. The reviews of this book that I have seen cover a wide spectrum, with favorable, even (to my mind) complimentary, evaluations more numerous than those critical. Honesty requires me to admit, in sorrow more than in resentment, that an assessment by a classicist must be classified as disparaging. Yet, I have noticed that in the more recent major treatments of Ruth (examples cited below), some of my proposals have increasingly found favor and are becoming part of the received lore. And in this business of biblical studies, where really new insights (as contrasted to old ones unknowingly resurrected or shamelessly appropriated) are rather scarce, I have to be pleased with my contribution.

It goes without saying that I learned much from my critics and from recent Ruth expositors. Thanks largely to their efforts, I can now formulate better a number of comments to individual words or phrases and can feature a number of clever plays on words. One critic convinced me that I foolishly undervalued the way names in Ruth control themes as well as specific segments of the plot. Additionally, there are a number of idioms that I can document more fully now in cuneiform texts (e.g., compare 3:9 with ARM 26:251:17-18).

While full reflection on all thee improvements will have to await another occasion, I confess here that my critics have also made me regret some lines I had written. To begin with, I now doubt the wisdom of having featured the work of Propp even as modestly as I had, mostly because it has attracted to itself a larger amount of attention than it deserves. This is not to say that I renounce the use of Propp to understand ancient narratives better, but that I should have been more careful in packaging it for readers of my book. I certainly did err when I linked the translation I had reached (pp. 1-6) to Proppian symbols because philology was my sole guide in achieving that rendering. It would therefore have been far wiser to restrict any reference to Propp and his methods to the 'Interpretation' section of the book. I used Propp functionally, simply to corroborate what many scholars had previously suggested, that Ruth is a piece of historicizing fiction and that it is strongly reminiscent of folk tales. I had wanted to 'nail down' such assessments firmly, and Propp's anatomical dissection of fairy tales gave me a fairly refined technique with which to work. I was far more interested in restricting our use of Ruth to reconstruct Ancient Israel. If, as so many scholars continue to say, Ruth resembles or imitates a folktale, then the tale should not be mined for evidence on Israel's political or legal past because this sort of literature does not ordinarily retain accurate memory of specific moments of a given culture; rather it tends to blend and even telescope past events into patterns of exemplary behavior. Moreover, if Ruth is a tale rather than an accurate chronology of past activities, then we should stop treating it as an imperfect retelling of history, charging the teller with dropping crucial incidents from the narrative simply because they were common knowledge to an ancient audience. Instead, we have to deem what is currently available to us as repository of *all* the information needed to unravel the tale's plot and recover its themes.

I had hoped that readers would find useful how I chart *Ruth's* literary quality and reconstruct its cultural contexts, whether or not they approve of my Proppian analysis. Finally, I was particularly keen to show that the search for a date for the scroll's redaction is not a fulfilling exercise.

I would revise one other stance I took in *Ruth*. On pp. 220-22 and also on p. 249 I wrote about the marginal value of Ruth for our understanding of Hebrew theological ideology or religious convictions. I think I was then insensitive to the manifold issues and perspectives that the topics raise. To begin with, I should have distinguished between the religious and the theological in Ruth and then also recognized that these categories play differently whether Ruth is assessed as an independent tale or as part of sacred Scripture. Had I been alert to these distinctions, I would certainly have refrained from blanket censure of efforts to uncover the workings of a providential God.

Finally, further reflection on the translation I have given permits me to suggest refinements or promote alternate renderings [differences in *italics*]:

1:15-16	Naomi said: 'Well now, your sister-in-law has returned, to her people and her god; follow her example'. To this, Ruth replied: 'Do not *urge* me to desert you, to *give up* following you;. . . .
11:3	She went her way *to glean* in the field behind the reapers,
:13	. . . Yet, *I could not be like* one of your maidservants'.
:18	Her mother-in-law saw how much she had gleaned. *When Ruth brought out to give her the leftovers from her filling meal, Naomi asked*: 'Where did you glean today and how did you accomplish it?. . . '
:22-23	. . . 'It is best daughter, that you join his women and not be *harrassed in* another field'. So she kept close to Boaz's *women*, gleaning until the end of the barley harvests.
III:3-4	Your presence should not be *known* to the man until after he finishes eating and drinking. Then, as he lies down and *you come to know the place where he is stretching out*, approach him, bare his *legs* and lie down.
:7	Approaching quietly, Ruth bared his *legs* and lay down.
:12-13	Now, since there is a redeemer with rights prior to mine—despite the fact that I am most certainly a redeemer—spend the night here; in the morning, we shall see: should he decide to redeem for you, well and good;. . .
IV:10	. . . As to Ruth of Moab, wife of Mahlon, I have also *aquired* her, in order to perpetuate the memory of the deceased over his estate;. . .
:18	. . . Perez *fathered* Hezron;. . .
:22	. . . and Jesse *fathered* David.

It remains for me to thank Philip R. Davies for advocating the reprint of *Ruth*, David E. Orton for shepherding its production, and the officers of the Judaica program at UNC for subsidizing its publication.

August, 1989

Recent Discussion on Ruth

Berlin, Adele
1983 *Poetics and the Interpretation of Biblical Narrative*. Sheffield: Almond Press.

Brenner, Athalyah
1988 *The Love of Ruth*, '*Who is Dearer to You Than Seven Sons*'. Tel Aviv: 'Oranim' Hakkibutz Hameuchad Publishing House.

Hubbard, Robert L., Jr.
1988 *The Book of Ruth*. [The New International Commentary on the Old Testament]. Grand Rapids: William B. Eerdmans.

Milne, Pamela J.
1988 *Vladimir Propp and the Study of Structure in Hebrew Biblical Narrative*. Sheffield: Almond Press.

Zenger, Erich
1986 *Das Buch Ruth*. [Zürcher Bibelkommentare AT, 8] Zürich: Theologischer Verlag.

ABBREVIATIONS

AB	*Anchor Bible*
AfO	*Archiv für Orientforschung*
AHw	W. von Soden, *Akkadisches Handwörterbuch* (Wiesbaden, 1965-)
AJA	*American Journal of Archaeology*
AJSL	*American Journal of Semitic Languages and Literatures*
ANET[3]	J. B. Pritchard, ed., *Ancient Near Eastern Texts relating to the Old Testament*, 3rd ed. with supplement (Princeton, 1969)
AOAT	*Alter Orient und Altes Testament*
ARMT	*Archives royales de Mari. Transcriptions et traductions*
BASOR	*Bulletin of the American Schools of Oriental Research*
BAH	*Bibliothèque archaéologique et historique*
BDB	F. Brown, S. R. Driver, and C. A. Briggs, *A Hebrew and English Lexicon of the Old Testament* (Oxford, 1929)
BH[3]	R. Kittel and P. Kahle, eds., *Biblia Hebraica*, rev. A. Alt and O. Eissfeldt (Stuttgart, 1962)
BiOr	*Bibliotheca Orientalis*
BJ	*Bible de Jérusalem*
BK	*Biblischer Kommentar*
BZ	*Biblische Zeitschrift*
BZAW	*Beihefte zur Zeitschrift für die alttestamentliche Wissenschaft*
CAD	*Chicago Assyrian Dictionary*
CAH	*Cambridge Ancient History*
CBQ	*Catholic Biblical Quarterly*
CT	*Cuneiform Texts from Babylonian Tablets in the British Museum* (London, 1896-)
CTA	A. Herdner, *Corpus des tablettes cunéiformes alphabétiques découvertes à Ras Shamra-Ugarit de 1929-1939*, BAH, 79 (Paris, 1963)
EB	*Encyclopaedia Biblica* (Jerusalem)
EBI	*Encyclopedia of Biblical Interpretation* (New York, 1962-)

EJud	*Encyclopaedia Judaica*
ET	*Expository Times*
GKC	W. Gesenius, E. Kautzsch, and A. E. Cowley, *Hebrew Grammar* (Oxford, 1910)
HAL	W. Baumgartner, *Hebräisches und Aramäisches Lexicon zum Alten Testament* (Leiden, 1967)
HAT	*Handbuch zum Alten Testament*
HSAT	*Die Heilige Schrift des Alten Testaments*
HSS	*Harvard Semitic Series*
HThR	*Harvard Theological Review*
HUCA	*Hebrew Union College Annual*
IB	*Interpreter's Bible*
ICC	*International Critical Commentary of the Holy Scriptures*
IDB	*Interpreter's Dictionary of the Bible*
IDBS	IDB Supplement
IEJ	*Israel Exploration Journal*
JANES	*Journal of the Ancient Near Eastern Society of Columbia University*
JAOS	*Journal of the American Oriental Society*
JBL	*Journal of Biblical Literature*
JBR	*Journal of Bible and Religion*
JCS	*Journal of Cuneiform Studies*
JESHO	*Journal of the Economic and Social History of the Orient*
JNES	*Journal of Near Eastern Studies*
JPS^2	Jewish Publication Society of America, *The New Jewish Bible*
JQR	*Jewish Quarterly Review*
JRAS	*Journal of the Royal Asiatic Society of Great Britain and Ireland*
JSOT	*Journal for the Study of the Old Testament*
JTS	*Journal of Theological Studies*
KBL	L. Koehler and W. Baumgartner, *Lexicon in veteris testamenti libros* (Leiden, 1953-58)
NEB	*New English Bible*
NKZ	*Neue Kirchliche Zeitschrift*
OTS	*Old Testament Studies/Oudtestamentische Studïen*
PEQ	*Palestine Exploration Quarterly*
PRU	*Palais royal d'Ugarit*
RA	*Revue d'assyriologie et d'archéologie orientale*
RB	*Revue Biblique*
RGG	*Religion in Geschichte und Gegenwart*
RLA	*Reallexicon der Assyriologie*

RSV	Revised Standard Version
TB	Babylonian Talmud
THAT	*Theologisches Handwörterbuch zum Alten Testament*
ThW	*Theologische Wissenschaft*
ThZ	*Theologische Zeitschrift*
TSK	*Theologische Studien und Kritiken*
TWAT	*Theologisches Wörterbuch zum Alten Testament*
UF	*Ugarit-Forschungen*
Ug	*Ugaritica*
UT	C. Gordon, *Ugaritic Textbook*, Analecta Orientalia, 38 (Rome, 1969)
VT	*Vetus Testamentum*
VTS	VT Supplements
ZA	*Zeitschrift für Assyriologie*
ZAW	*Zeitschrift für die alttestamentliche Wissenschaft*

1. TRANSLATION[1]

I —

1 During the time of the Judges, when a famine occurred
in the land, a certain man from Bethlehem in Judah migrated
to Moabite territory together with his wife and two sons. α
2 The man's name was Elimelech, his wife's Naomi, and those of
his two sons Mahlon and Chilion. They were members of the
Ephrathite clan, from Bethlehem in Judah. They came to settle in Moab. —
3 Upon the death of Elimelech, her husband, Naomi was left
4 alone with her two sons. These two married Moabite girls, one
of whom was named Orpah, the other Ruth. After living there β[2]
5 for about ten years, Mahlon and Chilion died also. So Naomi
survived her two sons as well as her husband. —
6 When, along with her two daughters-in-law, Naomi arose
[from mourning,] she decided to return home from Moabite *a*
territory, for she had heard, while still in Moab, that the
Lord had been providing for His people by giving them food. —
7 Naomi left the place in which she lived, accompanied by
her two daughters-in-law. As they proceeded on the road
8 back to Judah, Naomi said to them: "Why don't you turn back, B
each to her mother's home? May God treat you as kindly as ⋮
9 you have treated me and the deceased. May God allow each
one of you to find security in a new marriage." As she
kissed them goodbye, they broke into loud weeping saying:
10 "We want only to return with you, to your people."

1 See "The Literary Genre of Ruth" in chapter 5 for an explanation of the symbols in the right-hand column.

11 But Naomi responded: "Turn back, my daughters, why go
with me? Are there still more sons in my womb to be your fu-
12 ture husbands? Turn back, my daughters, just go! I am indeed too old to conceive. Were I to maintain that there is
hope for me, that I could conceive this very night and bear
13 sons, would you patiently wait for them to become of age?
Would you, on their account, deny yourselves the pleasure
of marital embraces? Enough, my daughters, it has been far
more bitter for me than for you; indeed, the Lord's hand
has struck me."
14 They broke once more into loud weeping. But while
Orpah kissed her mother-in-law goodbye, Ruth clung to her.
15* Naomi said: "Well now, your sister-in-law has returned
16* to her people and her god, follow her example." To this
Ruth replied: "Do not press me to desert you, to resist
following you; for wherever you go, I too will go; whatever your shelter, I will share it; your people will become
17 mine, and your god will be my own. Wherever you die, I will
die, and be buried alongside. May the Lord strike me at
anytime with afflictions, if anything but death parts us."
18 When Naomi realized how determined she was to accompany her, she ceased arguing with her. Together, they went
19 on until they entered Bethlehem. As they entered Bethlehem,
the whole town hummed with excitement because of them.
20 "Could this be Naomi?" asked [the women]; to which she responded: "Do not call me Naomi, but Mara, for Shadday has
21 painfully embittered my life. I left [Bethlehem] full, but
the Lord brought me back empty. How could you call me
'Naomi,' then, when the Lord *has witnessed against me,* and
Shadday has brought me misfortune."
22 This, then, was how Naomi returned, with her daughter-
in-law, Ruth of Moab, accompanying her from Moabite territory. They reached Bethlehem at the beginning of the barley
harvest.

---

*See "Foreword to the Second Edition" for alternative rendering of starred (*) passages.

II
1 Now Naomi knew of an acquaintance of her husband, a
property holder who belonged to Elimelech's clan; his name
2 was Boaz. Ruth of Moab said to Naomi: "Should I go to the
fields and glean among the ears of grain, in the hope of [↑]
pleasing him?" "Go ahead, my daughter," answered Naomi.
3* She went her way, and gleaned in the field behind the reapers. It so happened that she found herself in the field —
belonging to Boaz, of Elimelech's clan. DONOR
4 Just then, Boaz arrived from Bethlehem and greeted the
reapers: "The Lord be with you." "The Lord bless you,"
5 they replied to him. Boaz asked his servant, in charge of
6 the reapers: "Whose girl is that?" "She is the young —
woman from Moab," replied the overseer, "who returned with
7 Naomi from Moabite territory. She requested permission to
glean, and to gather grain among the sheaves behind the §
reapers. She arrived and has been waiting from daybreak until now; thus, she must have spent little time at home."
8 Boaz said to Ruth: "Now listen, young lady, do not go —
to glean in another field. You should not leave this one,
9 but keep close to my girls. Keep your eyes on the field
that they are reaping, and glean behind them. The men have
been ordered not to interfere with you; so that, should you D^2
thirst, you are free to go to the jars and drink from the
water that the men have drawn."
10 She threw herself forward, touching the ground with her —
forehead, and asked: "Why is it that I pleased you enough
to notice me? I am but a foreigner!" E^2
11 "I have been fully told," Boaz replied, "all that you —
have done with your mother-in-law after your husband's death.
You forsook father, mother, and native land to join a people
12 you scarcely knew previously. May the Lord repay your good (D^2
deed. May your full reward come from the Lord, God of
Israel, under whose wings you seek shelter."
13* Ruth answered: "I must have pleased you, my lord, —
since you have comforted me and have spoken tenderly to E^2)
your maidservant. Yet, I am not even considered as one of
your maidservants." —

14 At mealtime, Boaz said to her: "Come over here and share
in the meal, dipping your morsel in the vinegar." As she sat
beside the reapers, [Boaz] handed her roasted grain. She ate
her fill, yet still had some left over.
15 When Ruth resumed her gleaning, Boaz ordered his men as
follows: "You are not only to permit her to glean among the F
16 sheaves without rebuke, but you must also pull some stalks
out of the bundles, dropping them for her to glean without
ever scolding her."
17 So Ruth gleaned in the field until dusk. When she beat G
18* out her gleanings, it amounted to an ephah of barley. This K^{4-6}
she carried, and proceeded to town. Her mother-in-law saw how
much she had gleaned when Ruth brought out the leftovers from †
19* her full meal in order to give them to her. "Where did you
glean today?" asked Naomi, "and how did you accomplish it?
Blessed be he who took notice of you." She revealed to her
mother-in-law that which she had accomplished with him, adding:
"The man with whom I dealt today is called Boaz."
20 Naomi said to her daughter-in-law: "Blessed be he to the
Lord, who has not withheld his kindness from the living or the
dead." "The man is kin to us," continued Naomi, "He is one of §
21 those in a position to redeem us." Ruth of Moab added: "He
even told me to remain close to his men until they finished
22 harvesting his fields." Naomi declared to Ruth, her daughter-
in-law: "It is best daughter, that you join his girls and not
be pressed into another field."
23 So she kept close to Boaz's girls, gleaning until the end
of the barley and wheat harvests. Meanwhile she lived with
her mother-in-law

III

1 [One day,] Ruth's mother-in-law, Naomi, said: "Daughter, A1'
2 you know that I seek for you a happy future. You also know
that Boaz, whose girls you joined, is our relative. Now, he
3* will be winnowing barley at the threshing-floor tonight. So B2'
bathe, put on perfume, and dress up before going down to the
threshing-floor. Your presence should not be known until after

4* he finishes eating and drinking; then, as he lies down, find
out the place in which he plans to sleep, approach him, bare
his 'legs,' and lie down. He will tell you what next to do."
5 "I will do as you say," answered Ruth. C'
6 She went down to the threshing-floor and did just as
7* her mother-in-law had charged. Boaz ate, drank, and felt
free of care. He then proceeded to lie down at the edge of †'
the grain pile. Approaching quietly, Ruth bared his "legs,"
and lay down.
8 Around midnight, the man was shaken by fright; he twisted
9 away--there was a woman lying close to him! "Who are you?" he D2'
exclaimed. "I am Ruth your handmaid," she replied, adding:
"spread your robe over your handmaid; you are indeed a re- E2'
10 deemer." "May you be blessed by the Lord, daughter;" said
Boaz. "You have acted in a worthier fashion in the last instance than in the first. There will henceforth be no need
11 to seek men whether poor or rich. Now, have no further worry,
daughter, for I will do in your behalf whatever you have suggested, inasmuch as your status as a wife of a notable is
12* public knowledge. Now, since there is a redeemer with rights
prior to mine, despite the fact that I myself am most cer- F9'
13* tainly a redeemer, spend the night here. In the morning, we
shall see; should he decide to redeem for you, well and good;
should he choose otherwise, I myself will do so. I swear it
by the Lord. Lie down until morning."
14 Ruth stayed by him until daybreak, but rose before a
person's features could be recognized, for Boaz had thought
it best that her arrival to the threshing-floor remain un-
15 noticed. "Bring over the shawl that you are wearing and hold >Y
it open," he said. As she held it, he placed six measures of
barley. He helped to raise it on her back, then proceeded to
town. G'
16 Ruth came back to her mother-in-law, who asked: "Who
are you [now], my daughter?" Ruth revealed to her all that
17 occurred with the man, adding: "He gave me these six measures §
of barley, telling me not to return empty-handed to my
mother-in-law."
18 "Stay put, daughter," responded Naomi, "until you find

out how the matter turns out. The man will certainly not rest
unless he resolves it by the end of the day."

IV

1 No sooner had Boaz gone up to the [town's] gate to wait O
there, that the redeemer, mentioned [earlier] by Boaz, chanced L
to pass by. [Boaz] hailed him: "Turn around, and sit over
2 here, Mr. So-and-So!" The man complied. Boaz chose ten
[leading] citizens among the [local] elders, and asked them to
3 sit by. They did. He then addressed the redeemer as follows:
"Naomi who returned from Moabite territory is selling the
4 field belonging to Elimelech, our "brother." For my part, I
am declaring: Let me publicly enjoin you to purchase the land
in the presence of the magistrates and the elders of my M
people. Should you choose to redeem it, well and good.

"But, should he decide not to redeem it [added Boaz as
he addressed the elders before turning back to the re-
deemer], tell me that I may understand. There is no one with
better right to redeem it than you; but I come next."

The man replied: "I shall redeem it." N

5 Boaz declared further: "Know that on that very day you
are purchasing the field from Naomi, I am acquiring Ruth of Q
Moab, wife of the deceased, in order to perpetuate the memory of the deceased upon his estate."

6 "In that case," replied the redeemer, "I cannot redeem
[the field] in my behalf, lest I damage the future of my own Ex
estate. Please go ahead, and act in my stead, for I am in no
position to redeem it."

7 --Now in Israel's past days, in order to validate any
legal act, be it of redemption or of exchange, it was the
practice for one man publicly to remove his sandal and to hand
it over to another. This was the form of attestation in §
Israel.--

8 So, as the redeemer was telling Boaz: "Purchase it for
yourself," he removed his sandal.

9 Boaz then addressed the elders and the rest of the people:
"You are witness today that I have indeed purchased from Naomi

10* all that belonged to Elimelech and to Chilion and Mahlon. As
to Ruth of Moab, wife of Mahlon, I have also purchased her, in
order to perpetuate the memory of the deceased over his estate; for, 'the memory of the deceased may not be obliterated
from among his kinfolk and his native village'. You are all
witnesses today."

11 The people, native to the town, and the elders responded: —
"We are witnesses. May the Lord make the wife entering your
home like Rachel and like Leah, the two who built up the House
of Israel, so that you may prosper in Ephrathah, and maintain
12 a reputation in Bethlehem. May your house be like that of T
Perez, whom Tamar bore Judah, through the offspring that the
Lord will give you by this young woman."

13 Subsequently, Boaz married Ruth. When she became his —
wife he had relations with her. The Lord allowed her to conceive; she bore a son.

14 Women said to Naomi: "Blessed be the Lord who, on this
15 very day, did not deny you a redeemer. May his name be proclaimed in Israel. He shall become a comforter for you, and W
is to sustain you in your old age; for he was born to a daughter-in-law who loves you and is dearer to you than seven
sons."

16 Naomi took the boy, setting him on her bosom; she thus —
became a foster mother to him.

17 Female neighbors established his reputation, saying: "A
son was born to Naomi!" So they called him Obed, he being the
father of Jesse, who was the father of David. X

18-19* This is the genealogy of Perez: Perez bore Hezron;
20-21 Hezron, Ram; Ram, Amminadab; Amminadab, Nahshon; Nahshon, [α]
21-22* Salmah; Salmon, Boaz; Boaz, Obed; Obed, Jesse; and Jesse bore
David.

—

2. THE BOOK OF *RUTH*

*The Text of Ruth**

The Hebrew text of *Ruth* contains relatively few difficulties (contra: Joüon, 1953: 18; Vincent, 1952; 144). Its reliability is indicated by the fact that the dozen examples considered by Joüon to be infractions of Hebrew grammar and lexical usage prove to be otherwise on closer inspection. Moreover, our annotations will show that of the fair number of scribal marginal notations intended either to improve the text or to indicate (mistaken) variants, *not one* of the very few that we shall adopt will be of consequence to the understanding of the narrative. To be more specific, the first of the *qerē* suggested by the Masorites (at 1:8; 2:1; 3:3, 4, 14; 4:4, 5) as preferable to the *ketîb* will alone be adopted. Furthermore, the three suggested insertions into the text (*qerē welô᾽ ketîb* at 2:11; 3:5, 17) and the one suggested deletion (*ketîb welō᾽ qerē* at 3:12) will not be accepted. We shall, however, adopt some of the thirteen grammatical and lexicographical emendations (at 1:10, 14, 20; 2:14; 3:13[2x], 14, 15; 4:1, 4, 6, 18, 22); but these are not crucial to the interpretation of the text. Indeed, we shall show that many of the scribal suggestions, especially the famous *qerē* of 4:5, are based on a misunderstanding of the tale's basic plot.

Our study will hardly ever find it profitable to adopt the readings of the non-Hebraic versions in preference to those in the text of Kittel's BH^3. This is not to say that these versions, which will be described below, slavishly reproduce the Hebrew; but that the differences such as do exist rarely improve our understanding of individual passages. In most cases, variations from the Hebrew of Kittel's BH^3, which will serve as our

*Bibliography in Rudolph, 1962: 34-35; twelfth-century fragment with Palestinian-Tiberian vocabulary in Van der Heide, 1974.

basic text in the following study, may be ascribed to the necessity of making a translation conform to the requirements of the respective languages. To illustrate our point one might choose a relatively uncomplicated paragraph from *Ruth* and compare the renderings of modern languages. Indeed, one would hardly be able to reproduce translations of the same paragraph in the *English* of modern American and British editions of the Bible without finding variation in meaning and nuance!

With the above in mind, we shall survey the various versions of *Ruth*. We shall refer to more complete treatments or specific topics whenever possible so as not to unnecessarily burden this survey.

A. *Qumran*.

1. Fragments of two exemplars from Cave 2 have been published by Baillet, Milik, and de Vaux, 1962: 71-75. The following are deviations from the Hebrew text which we have adopted:

First exemplar:	2:18	*b*śbʿh	(BH³: *m*śbʿh)
	2:21	ʾmr *ly*	(BH³: ʾmr ʾ*ly*)
	2:22	nʿrwtw	(BH³: nʿrwt*y*w)
	2:23	llw^q^ṭ	(BH³: llqṭ)
	3:3	[śml]tyk	(BH³: śmltk. Cf. *qerē*).
Second exemplar:	3:14	m[rg]lt*y*w	(BH³: mrgltw; cf. *qerē*)
	3:14	ky bʾh hgrn	(BH³: ky bʾh *hʾšh* hgrn)
	3:15	wymd *šm* šš....	(BH³: wymd šš śʿrm)
	3:16	[w]tʾmr m*h* ʾt	(BH³: wtʾmr m*y* ʾt)

2. Fragments of two unpublished exemplars from Cave 4 have been used in Campbell, 1975: 40-41.

B. *Greek* (referred to henceforth as LXX, for the sake of convenience).

Rahlfs's 1922 edition of the Greek of *Ruth* allowed him to place a large number of Greek manuscripts within four textual traditions. Thornhill (1953), tries to be more precise in establishing the bases of these traditions. Campbell (1975: 36-39) describes Rahlfs's finding in general terms, and champions Cross's reconstruction of their background; Cross's thesis, however, has met with some opposition (see IDBS, 878-79); Joüon (1953: 10-19) gives a list of the presumed additions and subtractions which distinguishes the Hebrew from Greek manuscripts *Vaticanus* (*B*) and *Alexandrinus* (*A*). He also gives a short list of eight moments in which LXX differs substantially from the Hebrew. De Waard (1973: 499-515), shows that most of these differences could be attributed to translational necessity. Both he and Rudolph (1962: 25) agree that LXX hews closely to the Hebrew. In Rudolph's opinion, in most cases in which variations exist between it and the Greek, the Hebrew gives better sense.

C. *Latin.*

1. *Old Latin* (OL). The ninth-century *Codex Complutensis* (Madrid) contains an incomplete translation of *Ruth*. Opinions on the origins and antecedents of this differ; a bibliography and short discussion appears in Rudolph (1962: 25-26).

2. *Vulgate.* Joüon (1953: 20) thinks that St. Jerome may have worked with a Hebrew original that differed sensibly from ours (e.g., in instances found at 2:7, 14; 3:15; 4:5). Obvious expansions that could not have depended on any known Hebrew text make it clear that St. Jerome's translation was not slavish.

D. *Peshitta (Syriac).* Joüon (1953: 20) characterizes the Syriac version of *Ruth* as "mediocre." Gerleman (1965: 3-4) recognizes the rather free rendering of this version. Yet he thinks it of enough value that he devotes some space to charting its sources.

The above-listed versions reproduce rather faithfully the available Hebrew texts. Other attempts tend to elaborate didactically on certain vocabulary and episodes. In this category, we might place Josephus's personal reading of *Ruth (Jewish Antiquities,* V, ix), datable to the first century A.D. Additionally, we list the following:

E. *Ruth Rabbah.* Often dated to the sixth through seventh century, this aggadic midrash is the product of the *amoraim* of Palestine. Essentially a close reading and exposition of *Ruth* in Mishnaic Hebrew and Galilean Aramaic, it is intended to further a pious interpretation of the tale; cf. Ginzberg, 1946: index *(Ruth)*; Hartmann, 1901; Lerner, 1971.

F. *The Targum.* A homiletic version of *Ruth,* this Aramaic translation seems to have much affinity to the *Peshitta.* Sperber's edition (1968) relies on a fifteenth-century manuscript in the British Museum (Or. 2375); it is not annotated. Levine (1973) used an earlier manuscript, *Cod. Vat. Urbinas. Ebr. 1.* His edition, although criticized by its reviewers, is a rich repository of information on Rabbinic as well as medieval interpretations of *Ruth.* Additionally, his lists of references, in these and other sources, are very useful. The Targum of *Ruth,* however, will remain of questionable value to understanding the difficulties in the Hebrew of *Ruth.*

G. Of uneven value for the purpose of this study are the commentaries of medieval Rabbis. We found to be most suggestive in specific cases those of Yaphet Ben-'Ali, Ibn-Ezra, and Rashi (cf. *Biblia Rabbinica* edition). Zlotowitz (1976) is a recent traditional commentary anthologizing Rabbinic sources. Beattie's recent volume (1977b) is certainly the most elaborate and scholarly treatment of this subject. Two examples of contemporary orthodox homiletics on *Ruth* are available in Y. Bachrach's *Mother of Royalty* (Jerusalem, 1973) and D. Barsotti, *Meditazione sul libro Ruth* (Brescia, 1973).

The Canonical Status of Ruth

Despite a scene that was, to abuse Auerbach's vocabulary, "fraught with eroticism," Ruth's canonicity and inspired nature were never seriously questioned (on the distinction in terminology see Leiman, 1976: 127-35). Rabbi Simeon b. Johai (ca. 125-170 A.D.) was quoted in *Megillah* 7a as saying: "*Ecclesiastes* is among the lenient decisions of the School of Shammai and among the stringent decisions of the School of Hillel; but [all agree that] *Ruth, Song of Songs,* and *Esther* 'defile the hands' [i.e., were canonical]." Leiman (1976: 133, 190 [n. 504]) discusses possible hesitations on the sacredness of *Ruth* as suggested by this quotation. But Ruth's connection with David and his ancestors, the beauty of Ruth's language, the nobility of its characters, the frequent mention of the divine name--all these were elements which doubtless played a role in securing the scroll a place within Scriptures. That Samuel was regarded as its author *(Baba Bathra,* 14b-15a*)* is testimony to Rabbinic recognition that *Ruth's* language was strongly reminiscent of that of *Samuel* and *Judges*.

On the *position* of *Ruth* within Scriptures, Wolfenson's iconoclastic article of 1924 is still the richest repository of information. Since *Ruth* never attained a sacredness of status equivalent to the Pentateuch, its position within the canon was never as decisively established as those of the *Five Books of Moses*. Neither the content of *Ruth* (contra, Campbell, 1975: 35-36) nor its purpose (however formulated) seems to have played a role in determining the order in which it was set. We meet most often with two arrangements:

A. *After Judges*. This position, obviously influenced by the opening verse of *Ruth* ("During the time of the Judges. . . ."), occurs in most of the non-Hebrew versions of the Old Testament (listing in Wolfenson, 1924:

152-53). Josephus (*Contra Apionem*, I, 8, 38-42) speaks of twenty-two books in the Old Testament, comprising five of Laws, thirteen of Prophets, and four of Hymns and Precepts. To account for two books missing from our present roster, it is often presumed that *Ruth* and Lamentations must have been considered as appendixes to Judges and Jeremiah. Wolfenson, however, maintains that the two omitted works were Canticles and Ecclesiastes.

B. *Among the Ketubim (Writings).* Of the differing arrangements of *Ruth* within the Writings, we mention the following:

1. *Preceding Psalms.* This arrangement is witnessed in Baba Bathra, 14b, and Berakhot, 57a, b. *Ruth* thus prefaced a work attributed to David. This arrangement is continued in some manuscripts mentioned by Wolfenson (1924: 160-61) in his valuable chart, "Order of Books of the Hagiographa."

2. *As Part of the Megillot (Festival Scrolls).* Relatively late--no earlier than the sixth century A.D.--*Ruth*, Ecclesiastes, Canticles, Esther, and Lamentations were collected into what came to be known as the five *megillôt* (scrolls). *Ruth's* place within this collection differed:

a. *Chronological Sequence.* *Ruth* (Judges period); Canticles (Solomon as a young man); Ecclesiastes (Solomon as an old man); Lamentations (Jeremiah); Esther (Persian period).

b. *Festival Sequence.*

(i) *With Nisan as the First Month of the Year*: Canticles (Pesah/Passover/Easter); *Ruth* (Shabuʿot/Weeks/Pentecost); Lamentations (Ninth of Ab); Ecclesiastes (Succoth/Tabernacle); Esther (Purim). This is the most commonly attested arrangement in the Hebrew Bible.

(ii) *With Tishri as the First Month of the Year* (rare arrangements): Ecclesiastes, Esther, Canticles, *Ruth*, Lamentations.

Liturgical Use of Ruth

The five scrolls were not introduced into the festival liturgy all at once. Esther's identification with Purim is at least Talmudic in origin. Some authorities think that Lamentations' link to the Ninth of Ab, traditionally the day in which both the first and second Temples were destroyed, is also as old as the Talmudic period. The post-Talmudic tractate *Soferim* (ca. eighth-century Palestine) (xiv: 3ff.) says that *Ruth* was read on the first day of Shabuʿot. Whether it was to be recited at home or in the synagogue is not clear.

Shabu‘ot is an agricultural festival that celebrates the end of the grain harvests. It falls seven weeks (hence "Weeks") or on the fiftieth day (hence "Pentecost") after the second day of Passover. At least as early as Rabbinic times (third and fourth centuries A.D.), this festival was identified with the "time of the giving of the Torah" (Kretschmar, 1955: 209-53). Shabu‘ot is a particularly joyful celebration that lasts two days in the month of Siwan. During those days, food is supposed to be plentiful, with particular emphasis on dairy products. Wine is copious.

The events told in the Book of *Ruth* span a period somewhat equivalent to that from Passover to Shabu‘ot. Ruth and Naomi are said to have entered Bethlehem at the beginning of the barley harvest; Ruth manages to persuade Boaz to do his duty at the end of the barley harvest. It is most natural, therefore, that the scroll should be read during Shabu‘ot. That the story ended in a most happy fashion, that Ruth became a model for future proselytes, that her acceptance of God symbolized Israel's acceptance of the Torah, that her loyalty to Naomi symbolized Israel's devotion to its vows, that David, it is said, died during Shabu‘ot--all these elements helped, no doubt, to consecrate *Ruth* to Shabu‘ot.

3. PHILOLOGICAL COMMENTARY

In Moab (1:1-6)

1 During the time of the Judges,[a] when a famine occurred in the
land,[b] a certain man from Bethlehem in Judah,[c] migrated[d] to Moabite
2 territory[e] together with his wife and two sons.[f] The man's name was
Elimelech,[g] his wife's Naomi,[h] and those of his two sons Mahlon and
Chilion.[i] They were members of the Ephrathite[j] clan, from Bethlehem
in Judah. They came to settle in Moab.
3 Upon the death of Elimelech, her husband, Naomi was left alone[k]
4 with her two sons. These two married Moabite girls,[l] one of whom was
named Orpah,[m] the other Ruth.[n] After living there for about ten
5 years,[o] Mahlon and Chilion died also. So Naomi survived her two sons[p]
as well as her husband.
6 When, along with her two daughters-in-law, Naomi arose [from
mourning], she decided to return home from Moabite territory, for she
had heard, while still in Moab, that the Lord had been providing for
His people by giving them food.[q]

1:1. In a masterly fashion, with no more than twenty Hebrew words, the author succeeds in establishing the period and the circumstances which saw a specific Hebrew family migrate to foreign territory.

(a) *wayehî bîmey šepōṭ haššōpeṭîm*. A number of Old Testament books begin with *wayehî*, literally: "and it was. . . ." Since it inaugurates the books of Joshua, Judges, Samuel, Ezekiel, Jonah, and Esther, all of which were considered by the Hebrews to have been "historical," we must presume that the *author* of Ruth did regard the events that are to unfold as belonging to his past. We have avoided translating with "once [upon a time]" or "long ago," lest it be assumed that an ancient audience perceived the opening as a mark of "fiction."

bîmey šep̄ōṭ haššōpeṭîm, "In the days of the judging of the Judges," would be a literal but too precise a translation. What is of interest is a lack of precision on the actual period in which the narrative of Ruth unfolds. But the author of Ruth does try to compensate. Boaz, according to the genealogy that closes the book, is reckoned as two generations removed from Moses and three ahead of David. If aware, either by tradition or actual sources, of the narratives in Judges, *Ruth's* author would have noted that, except for Eglon's brief reign, Moab was either ruled by Israel or fell within its sphere of influence (cf. van Zyl, 1960: 131-32). Thus, the period between Ehud and Jephtah might offer a likely period in which *Ruth* was set. Rabbinic commentators, in general, identified Boaz with Ibzan of Bethlehem (Judg. 12:8-10).

The grammatical construction of this phrase, containing a noun in masculine plural "constructed" to an infinitive that, itself, is dependent on the word following, is unusual. However, both Joüon (1953: 30) and Myers (1955: 21) offer examples of similar patterns.

(b) *wayehî rā῾āb bā᾽āreṣ*, "there was famine in the land." The last word, '*᾽āreṣ*', "land," implies a widespread famine not merely localized to the area of Bethlehem. The book of Judges does not record any famine as having occurred. But, during a period which lasted for generations the absence of such a catastrophe would have been most unusual.

(c) Bethlehem in Judah is to be distinguished from one found in Zebulon's territory (Josh. 19:15, Judg. 12:8[?]). The former lies five miles south of Jerusalem, some 2,350 feet above sea level. The region in which the town is found is very fertile, producing in abundance wheat, barley, olive, almond, and grapes. This richness may have been responsible for the town's name. At least as early as the Amarna period (second half of the second millennium B.C.) [folk]-etymology conferred upon the town's name the meaning "House of Bread/Food."

Ever since H. G. Tomkins (1885: 112) proposed it as a theory, however, it has often been suggested that Bethlehem stood for "House/Temple of (the god) Laḫ(a)mu." H. Lewy, who believes that the Assyrian god Assur was a West-Semitic deity, also understands Laḫ(a)mu as having originated in West-Semitic circles (1966: 40): "As West-Semitic Shemesh appears in Amorite as Samsun, Lekhem is bound to appear as Lakhmu. In other words, Ashur's father and creator is one of the deities worshiped in Bethlehem."

It could only be said that lack of evidence, indeed the paucity of profitable attestations for deities such as Lakhmu, render it most difficult to properly assess this theory. See also below.

The interconnection among Bethlehem, the god Lakhmu, and Goliath's brother Laḥmî, once widely discussed in "Pan-Babylonian" days, need not detain us here (cf. EB, II, 1264-65 ["Elhanan"]; IDB ["Elhanan, Lahmi]; unfortunate reiteration of this discussion by Sheehan, 1973: 41).

(d) *lāgûr*, "Migrated for the purpose of settling." Such a step could only have followed momentous disasters, for, to Near Eastern man, the prospect of living in another land was not to be welcomed. In the OT, those who left Israel to become *gērîm* invariably sought escape from hunger (Gen. 12:10; 26:3; 47:4; 2 Kings 8:1) or war (2 Sam. 4:3). Living in a foreign land, the *gēr*, "stranger, foreigner, immigrant," was cut off from clan and family and other ties that assured him some protection in moments of danger. Furthermore, a *gēr* was forced to rely upon the mercy of his hosts, who at the slightest occasion might turn against him (e.g. Gen. 19). On the legal status of the *gēr* in Hebraic laws and customs, a status that very likely obtained among the Moabites, see TWAT, 979-91; IDB, IV, *sub* "proselyte," "sojourner." In the Pentateuch the *gēr* is described as defenseless as the *yātôm* or *ʾalmānāh*, "orphan" or "widow."

Later traditions assumed Elimelech and his sons to have become royal officers at the Moabite court, and the innocuous word *ʾîš*, "man," was interpreted as "leader" (Levine, 1973: 45, 47).

(e) *biśdēy môʾāb*, "the fields of Moab." For obscure reasons (Myers, 1955: 9, on forms, 32), the MT uses two different forms for the first word: *śedēy* (masculine plural construct) in 1:2 (1:6a, 22; 2:6) and *śedēh* (masculine singular construct) in 1:6b and 4:3. It might be that, at the time *Ruth* was written, there was some scribal indecision concerning the proper vocalization of *lamed/he* words in the construct. In our translation, repetition of "Moabite territory" will sometimes be avoided for stylistic reasons.

"Moabite territory" for the literal "field(s) of Moab" is preferred in some of our renderings since *śādeh*, "field," does not necessarily describe regions that were fit for agriculture. Note, for example, the allusions in Gen. 36:35 (=1 Chron. 1:46): "When Husham died, he was succeeded by Hadad son of Bedad who defeated Midian in *Moabite territory*. . . ." See further 1 Chron. 8:8 and compare Num. 21:20 with Deut. 34:6.

(f) "Two sons." A didactic device frequently resorted to by Biblical writers is to limit the spectrum of choice to two alternatives, only one of which will prove to be correct. An obvious method of putting such a concept in effect is the creation of two brothers, only one of whom will ultimately fare well. In our narrative, Mahlon marries Ruth. As a consequence, his memory will forever be perpetuated (cf. 4:10). Other examples include Cain and Abel, Jacob and Esau, Ishmael and Isaac, and so forth.

1:2. The name of each member of the family that emigrated to Moab is now given. The clan and place of origin of each is specified.

(g) Elimelech means "[My] El is King" or "El is Milku." Both elements of this personal name, *ēl* and *melek*, should not be taken as the substantives "god" and "king," respectively, but as the divine names El and Milku (Noth, 1928: 33ff; note the remarks of Thompson, 1974: 22ff.).

Although there is nothing exceptional about its coinage as a personal name (examples of West Semitic equivalents are collected in Huffmon, 1965: 230-33; Gröndahl, 1967: 266-67, 344-45), Elimelech occurs only in *Ruth*. Gray (1896: 115-20, 163-69) claims that the personal names with *mlk* as one of the elements no longer appear in the postexilic period. This position is no longer tenable in the light of modern research.

The LXX reads the name as Abimelech, possibly because it is a better attested name, borne by a contemporary of Abraham and Isaac (Gen. 20-21; 26), a son of Gideon (Judg. 8:31ff.), and at least one more individual (IDB, I, 9-10). It is not possible to assess the genuineness of either the LXX or the MT traditions. One *would* favor that of the MT, precisely because of the uniqueness of the name.

(h) The root *nʿm*, "good, pleasant, lovely, winsome," is widely used in West Semitic appellatives (see Benz, 1972: 362). The vocable is known to have been used as an epithet for Canaanite heroes such as Keret and Aqhat (UT, 19: 1665), deities (CTA, 23[UT, 52]: 1ff; 5[UT, 67]: III: 15), and heroines (CTA, 14[Krt.]: III: 145ff.). The goddess Anat was deemed especially well endowed with *nʿm* (CTA, 10[UT, 76]: 2, 16; 3: 11; 14[Krt.]: III: 145).

In line with GKC, 9v(p. 50), we shall transliterate this personal name as *noʿomî*; that is, we shall undogmatically adopt the opinion that a *qameṣ* which occurs before a *ḥatep-qameṣ*, even when in an open syllable and with a *meteg*, shall be considered as a short *u*-vowel. But we shall, however, retain the form traditional in English "Naomi" in our discussions.

In the Biblical *no*^{c}*omî*, the *(hîrēq) yōd* at the end of the name is generally taken to represent the first person pronominal suffix; hence "Naomi" would have been conferred by a proud parent moved to exclaim: "my pleasant one!" However, it might be better to understand the final *yōd* as reflecting an element in a "hypocoristic" name. Such appellatives preserve fully only one of their elements, the other being given in a shortened form. In our case, the original ending might have been pronounced *-iya* or, better, *-aya* (see Gröndahl, 1967: 50, 211). As it is, Ugarit has given us a personal name *n*^{c}*my* (102 [UT, 323]: 5b: 6). *-iya* and *-aya* could also be rendered by "that/he/she of." In UT 8: 54, Gordon collects a number of female names which end in *-y*. Some of these were borne by goddesses, e.g. *pdry, ṭly,* and *rḥmy* (i.e. Asherah); others by heroines, e.g. *ḥry, dnty*. In all of these names, the *-y* could be rendered by "she of. . . ." In light of this, the name Naomi could mean "She of Pleasance, Loveliness," and so forth.

The hypothesis that Naomi's name is made up of two elements, the last of which should not be related to the first person pronominal suffix, is substantiated by the LXX's consistant reading of the name as Νωεμίν. It is likely that a form of the LXX name is attested in Ugarit. *N*^{c}*myn* (UT, 2016: 1:9) contains an expanded form of the hypocoristicon of which only the *-n* may still be reflected in LXX's *-ιν*. For further discussion of this element, see Benz, 1972: 241-43. On "Naomi" as a second-millennium personal name see Glanzman, 1959: 205-6. Note also Palmyrene [*n*]*ʿym, nʿm,* and *nʿmy*; cf. Stark, 1971: 99-100.

(i) The first thing to be noted about the names Mahlon and Chilion is that they rhyme. Such "rhyming" names are not uncommon to the OT: *ʿûṣ* and *Bûz* (Gen. 22:21), *Muppîm* and *Huppîm* (Gen. 46:21), *Ḥemdān* and *ʾEšbān,* and *Yitrān* and *Kerān* (Gen. 36:26). Such "rhyming," concoted very likely for mnemonic purposes, might indicate that Mahlon and Chilion were but marginal to the real aim of the narrator of *Ruth*.

A root **mḥl*, from which the name Mahlon seems to be derived, is not known to Biblical Hebrew except in personal names (BDB, 563). Recourse to another Semitic language, notably Arabic, has permitted scholars to relate it to *maḥala*, "to be sterile." Others relate it to the root **ḥlyʿ*, "to be weak, ill," and **ḥly* III, "adornment, crown" (BDB, 318), or **ḥwl*, "circle-dance"; Astour (1965: 279[n. 3]) thinks of a derivative of **ḥll* I, "to pierce, to bore," as in *meḥillāh*, "cave." In these examples, the *-ôn* would be considered as a suffix well-known to Semitic onomastica (Gröndahl,

1967: 51 [84]; Huffmon, 1965: 135; GKC, 85u-v[pp. 238-39]). On the possibility of a pun on *naḥalāh*, see below.

The name Chilion is usually related to the root **kly* (BDB, 563), "be at end, finished, spent." Attempts are made to translate this name in such a way as to complement "Mahlon." Thus a majority of opinions favors something like "Weakening and Pining" or, with midrashic commentators, "Blot out and Perish" for Mahlon and Chilion, respectively.

Ugaritic texts contain the personal name *klyn* (UT, 19: 1238). Gröndahl (1967: 204(3), 236) prefers to interpret, with less than overwhelming reasoning, this example as Hurrian in coinage. *Kly* as a personal name is also known from Phoenician and, despite Benz's protestations (1972: 330-31), is comparable to our Kilyon. Cf. Palmyrene *kylywn*, *kyly;* Stark, 1971: 92.

(j) *ʾeprātîm*. Succumbing to Tamar's hidden charms, Judah produced Perez. Perez fathered Hezron. In turn, the latter fathered Chelubai (1 Chron. 2:3-9). When the line is resumed, Chelubai's name (*klwby* in the consonantal text, with the *w* possibly secondary in origin) is replaced by Caleb (*klb*). The MT contains more than one tradition concerning the latter's origins. One considers him a Kenizzite, hence ultimately originally from Edom. The other, reflected mainly in Chronicles (but cf. Num. 13:6) sees him as a Judaite. See IDB, I, 482-83; Myers, 1965a: 15-16, 27-31.

Despite the lack of useful evidence, it has been claimed that the Calebite penetration into the region of Bethlehem developed over an extended period of time, and in a number of stages (Aharoni, 1967: 197-200; de Vaux, 1971: 496-97). Our sources have Caleb father descendents through a wife (1 Chron. 2:18) and two concubines. Traditions concerning one of these, Ephrat(ah), are complex. In 1 Chron. 2:19, Ephrat(ah) bore Hur, ancestor of the craftsman Bezalel. According to 1 Chron. 2:50; 4:3-4, Hur is the eponymous ancestor of those who lived in Bethlehem and nearby communities. For our purposes, we should note that the traditions concerning the founding of Bethlehem and Ephrat(ah) were, by the time of the Chroniclers, much intertwined (de Vaux, 1971: 501-10). Micah (5:1) presumes the merging of the two settlements. The parallelism Bethlehem/ Ephratah of *Ruth* 4:11 conveys a similar attitude (cf. Gen. 35:19; 48:7; 1 Sam. 10:2). See further Campbell, 1975: 54-55.

1:3. With the statements of verses 3-5, the stage is set for the return to Bethlehem. On later rabbinic elaborations about Elimelech's death, see Levine, 1973: 47-49. Elimelech, it was taught, was punished either because of extreme avarice or because he forsook the Holy Land; he should have stayed put to alleviate its difficulties in time of drought. As to the untimely deaths of Mahlon and Chilion, recounted in verse 5, it was clear to rabbis that these two were punished for marrying non-Jews. In addition, all three were eternally punished by being buried in Moab.

After the death of the male members of the family, neither Naomi nor her daughters-in-law for that matter were spoken of as ʾalmānāh, *"widow." The* targum *"corrects" this peculiarity.*

(k) *wattiššāʾēr hîʾ. niphʿal* of *šāʾar*, "to remain." In verse 5 the same form is constructed with *min*, "from." Examples of such a construction are found in Deut. 3:11 (=Josh. 13:12); Jer. 8:3; Neh. 1:3. Cf. Myers, 1955: 21. The root **šʾr* is carefully studied by Wildberger in THAT, II: 845-55.

(l) *wayyiś(ś)eʾû lāhem nāšîm mōʾabiyyôt.* Joüon, among a number of scholars, believes the idiom to come from the later period of the Hebrew language, occurring as it does in Chronicles, Ezra, and Nehemiah. Such occurrences do not necessarily "prove" a passage, if not a total segment of a narrative, to be "late" in origin. In Akkadian, a better and more broadly attested Semitic language, we often find vocabulary and expressions in Mari Old Babylonian (*ca.* 1800-1775 B.C.) which recur only in Late Babylonian at least twelve centuries later. Moreover, Ugaritic literature is well stocked with idioms and vocabulary which are paralleled in Ezekiel and 2 Isaiah.

Not cited by Joüon, but by Myers (1955: 29), is the occurrence of this expression in Judg. 21:23. Rabbinic literature pointed out that the marriage to heathens occurred after the death of Elimelech, who, it was felt, would certainly have opposed such unions (Ginzberg, 1961: 517).

(m) *ʿorpāh.* Etymologies for the name vary; some suggest derivation from *ʿorep*, "nape (of the neck)," in other words, the one who turned her back to her mother-in-law, or the one with a thick mane; others connect with *erpettu*, "cloud." Plausibly, one could also refer to Arabic *ʿarafa* (e.g., *ʿarf*, "scent, perfume, aroma"; *ʿurf*, "kindness, benevolence"). In view of the most likely derivation for *Ruth* (below), Arabic *ǵurfa*, "a handful of water," might be promoted as offering a fine balance.

(n) "Ruth." The traditional derivation from *reʿût*, "friendship," while edifying, could not satisfactorily explain the loss of the second consonant *ʿayin*. The root *rāwāh* (BDB, 924), "to be saturated, to drench, irrigate," may offer a better solution. Other speculations are given by Campbell (1975: 56). Bruppacher (1966: 12-18) understands the name symbolically: *Tränkung, Labung, Erquickung*. The etymologies offered by Mendenhall (1973: 197, 162) for Ruth (Luwian: Ruwanda/Ronda/Ruta) and Orpah (Hurrian: Hurpa) cannot be taken seriously.

Later traditions concerning Ruth and Orpah considered them sisters, daughters of Eglon, king of Moab (Levine, 1973: 486).

(o) *keʿeśer šānîm*. It is not clear whether Mahlon and Chilion lived in Moab altogether ten years, a view favored by Joüon, or that they were married for ten years before their death. The number of years may have been chosen as a round figure. On the other hand, it may have been consciously patterned after the narrative of Gen. 16. Having lived in Canaan for ten years without issue, Abra(ha)m cohabited with Hagar to produce Ishmael, a child who was considered as Sarah's own. Rabbinic laws later established that after ten years of sterile marriage, grounds for divorce existed (Epstein, 1927: 208). We do not know, however, how far into the past this custom could be followed. To drive an interpretation to its extreme, the point may be that, had Mahlon and Chilion been married longer than ten years, the fertility of Ruth and Orpah might have been questioned. Boaz might not have favored union with a young woman with such unimpressive credentials.

(p) *yelādeyhā*. As pointed out by Joüon (1953: 35), the use of *yeled*, "boy, young man," to refer to a married man is exceptional. According to Campbell (1975: 56), "it [the mention of *yeled*] forms a very effective inclusio with 4:16, where Naomi takes a new *yeled* to her bosom."

1:6. This verse properly concludes the introductory matters discussed above. The translation offered needs some remarks by way of explanation. The MT of verse 6 contains a difficulty. While Hebrew grammar allows wattāqom, *although third person feminine singular by form, to refer to Naomi and her two in-laws, the context of* wattāšob, *similar in form to* wattāqom, *could only be applied to Naomi. At this stage of the narrative, Naomi should not have expected her daughters-in-law to accompany her into foreign land. With due caution, we refer to Gen. 23:3: "when Abraham arose* [wayyāqom] *from mourning his dead, he addressed the*

Hittites [wayyedabbēr. . . lēʾmōr]. . . ."

(q) *lātēt lāhem lāḥem.* Myers (1965: 21) points out that the expression "to give food to X" is found mostly in the older literature. On *leḥem*, here rendered as "food," see BDB, 537 (2). In addition to the alliteration that is evident in the Hebrew text, the mention of *leḥem* might be a play on the name "Bethlehem."

The Parting (1:7-14)

7 Naomi left the place in which she lived, accompanied by her two
daughters-in-law. As they proceeded on the road back to Judah, Naomi
8 said to them: "Why don't you turn back, each to her mother's home?[a]
May God treat you as kindly[b] as you have treated me and the deceased.
9 May God allow each one of you to find[c] security[d] in a new marriage."[e]
As she kissed them goodbye, they broke into loud weeping saying: "We
10 want only to return with you, to your people."
11 But Naomi responded: "Turn back, my daughters, why go with me?
Are there still more sons in my womb[f] to be your future husbands?
12 Turn back, my daughters, just go! I am indeed too old to conceive.[g]
13 Were I to maintain that there is hope for me, that I could conceive
this very night and bear sons, would you patiently wait[h] for them[i]
to become of age? Would you, on their account, deny yourselves the
pleasure of marital embraces?[j] Enough,[k] my daughters, it has been
far more bitter for me than for you; indeed, the Lord's hand has
struck me."[l]
14 They broke once more into loud weeping.[m] But while Orpah kissed
her mother-in-law goodbye,[n] Ruth clung to her.[o]

Verse 7 has been considered by Joüon (1953: 35), among others, as redundant. It seems to me, however, that the author of *Ruth* sought to heighten the drama of verses 8-18 by sandwiching it between two verses, the first of which (7) speaks of *three* people about to leave Moab, while the second (19) speaks of only Ruth and Naomi. The contrast not only underscores Ruth's decision but also confers upon this scene fluidity and spontaneity.

1:8-9. Naomi bids adieu to her daughters-in-law, fully expecting them to begin a new life in their own homeland.

(a) *bēyt ʾimmāh*. More commonly, it is to the house of the father that a woman would return (Gen. 38:11; Lev. 22:13; Num. 30:17; Deut.22:21; Judg. 19:2, 3). This usage, however, is known from Gen. 24:28 (on which, see Skinner, 1930: 344; Cant. 3:4; 8:2).

(b) On the vocabulary of *yaʿaśeh YHWH ʿimmākem ḥesed*, see Myers, 1955: 21, 30; Joüon, 1953: 36. *Ḥesed* cannot be translated uniformly by the same English word. N. Glueck, who wrote the first substantial study on this vocable, showed that the term connoted a relationship either between a deity and humans or simply among individuals (Glueck, 1967: 35-42). In the case of *Ruth* 1:8, as well as the occurrences in 2:11 and 3:10, *ḥesed* defines the bonds of marriages and consanguinity which existed between Naomi and her daughters-in-law. Whatever happiness the marriage brought to the sons of Elimelech, whatever decent treatment Naomi received from her in-laws, a commensurate response was expected from Naomi. As she was leaving, therefore, Naomi was asking her own god, Yahweh, to fulfill such an obligation, at least until the girls find happiness in newer marriages. For targumic additions to this passage see Levine, 1973: 51, 90-92.

Humbert (1958:83-110) considers *ḥesed*, which he renders as *pietas* ("devotion"), as the "word on which is the key to the whole story" (P. 86).

On the (alleged) (mis)use of the pronominal suffixes in *Ruth*--usually masculine plural endings substituted for feminine plural--see Joüon, 1947: 149b (p. 457). GKC, 135o (p. 440), believes the phenomenon to be influenced by colloquial language. Myers (1955: 20) thinks it to be a "relatively early dialectical peculiarity." Much more interesting is F. I. Andersen's point as stated by Campbell (1975: 65): "There must have been an early Hebrew feminine dual suffix which ended in *-m* just as the masculine plural ending does but contrasted with the feminine plural *-n*."

(c) *yittēn YHWH lākem ûmeṣeʾnā (menûḥāh)*. Campbell (1975: 65-66) discusses the grammatical peculiarities of this verse, in which a jussive *(yittēn)* is followed by an imperative attached to a conjunction *(ûmeṣeʾnā)*, and supports the interpretation of GKC, 101i (p. 325) over that of Joüon (1947: 177h [p. 534]). He adopts, therefore, a solution that understands this phrase as composed essentially of two separate clauses. This in turn forces him to seek, somewhat elaborately, a noun that could properly be considered as the direct object of the verb *nātan*, "to give." Despite some difficulties, our rendition accepts Joüon's analysis and avoids searching for a "lost" word.

(d) On *menûḥah*, see Hulst, 1970: 62-78. Hoftijzer (1970: 440) renders it as "tranquility, relief." Campbell (1975: 60) has "security." Note the related term *manoaḥ*, in 3:1. Discussion of both terms can be found in Stolz, THAT, II, 45 (3,d). Brichto (1973: 12) thinks that the term refers to "repose in eternity," a goal denied Naomi, to her husband, and to her dead sons since no progeny is available to invoke the memory of the deceased.

(e) *ʾiššāh bēyt ʾîšāh* literally means: "each woman in the house of her husband."

1:10-13. Verse 10 sets the stage for Naomi's elaborate retort, which aims to discourage her daughter-in-law from accompanying her. Hers is a soliloquy containing a triple argument which, at times, is devastating in its mordant self-deprecation. At one point, it even borders on sarcasm, giving the reader the impression that Naomi was questioning her in-laws' motives in their decision to follow her into Hebrew territory.

(f) *meʿay*, a word which occurs only in the plural *mēʿîm*, refers to the bowels, intestines, i.e. the internal organs below the abdomen. It is a much more "picturesque" term than *beṭen*, "belly," or *reḥem, qereb*, "womb," and expresses emotions that were very deeply felt, e.g. Cant. 5:4 (sexual yearning); Isa. 16:11; Jer. 31:20 (pity). See further Dhorme, 1923: 134-36. On the poetic quality of this verse see Campbell, 1975: 6.

Since there is no question here of "levirate" marriage--such marriages depending, as they do, on issues from the same *father*, not *mother*--it may be that Naomi was a bit more biting than needed be, *possibly* even suggesting that, left on their own, her daughters-in-law might not relish the prospect of searching for new mates.

(g) *zāqantî miheyôt leʾîš*, literally: "I am too old to be(long) to a man." While "to be(long) to a man" doubtlessly means "to be married" (Lev. 22:12; Num. 30:7; Deut. 24:2; Jer. 3:1), it would be foolish to imply that a woman would not, because of her (advanced) age, be able to marry. Speculations on Naomi's age when she uttered these words are interesting but, ultimately, irrevelant (cf. Campbell, 1975: 76). To be preferred for this passage is the literal meaning of "belonging to a man" such as is found in Hos. 3:3 (and, possibly, Lev. 21:3), that is, "to have sexual intercourse." The point of Naomi in verse 12 is not that she is too old to be married, but, having passed menopause, too old to have sexual relations that would result in pregnancy. The *Targum* noted the difficulty and resolved it by adding "even if I were a young girl" and by rendering *heyôt leʾîš* by the unequivocal *mibbaʿlah*, "from mating" (Levine, 1973: 54-55).

(h) *tešabbērnāh*. This form of the verb *šābar* in the *piʿʿēl* has often been labeled "an Aramaism." Campbell (1975: 69) discusses the controversy and rightly rejects this contention.

(i) *halāhēn*. This form, a subject of age-old contention among scholars, has often been cited as an "Aramaism" (cf. Dan. 2:6, 9; 4:24) with the meaning "therefore." Campbell (1975: 68-69) details the controversy. With him, and partially with other commentators (Myers, 1955: 27; Joüon, 1953: 40; Levine, 1973: 21, 54), it is better to suppose an original *halāhem* composed of the interrogative *h*- prefixed to the preposition *lamed*.

(j) *tēʿāgēnāh*. The verb *ʿāgan* occurs only here in Biblical Hebrew. The form preserved here is a defectively vocalized and pointed *nipḥʿal*, which should have been **tēʿagannāh*. Campbell (1975: 69-70) somewhat circuitously rejects a derivation from the root *ʿgn* in favor of *ʿgw*, a root attested in the Ugaritic personal name *bn ʿgw*. His solution is highly debatable since the list in which this Ugaritic personal name occurs contains non-Semitic names. We also know nothing about such a root from cognate languages and, although the consonant *ʿayin* tends to be mostly restricted to Semitic personal names, we have no assurances that *ʿgw* was not a name borne by an Egyptian (Egyptian likewise has a *ʿayin* phoneme).

Be that as it may, we prefer, for the moment at least, to retain the view of most commentators who point out Syriac and Mishnaic cognates. We do, however, agree with Campbell that one ought to avoid using Mishnaic references for establishing a precise meaning for *Ruth* 1:13 since the former may have, ultimately, depended on the latter.

tēʿāgēnāh lebiltî heyôt leʾîš, literally: "You restrain [?] yourselves, so as not to be(long) to a man." In the previous (rhetorical) statement, Naomi had emphasized the length of time it would take for any son of hers to reach maturity. Now she makes it clear to the women that, were they to wait, they would lose much of the pleasures that marriage has to offer. It should be remembered that Naomi was addressing young ladies who were probably in their early twenties. That ancient Near

Eastern man--and this of course includes the Hebrews--realized women's healthy appreciation of sexual participation is clear from the Song of Songs (cf. also Gen. 3:16; Deut. 24:5; Joel 1:8; Prov. 7:6-23; 1 Cor. 7:1-11). Note also the remarks of Biggs (1967: 1-10). "Marital rights" *(ʿōnāh)* were guaranteed by Exod. 21:10 even for an *ʾāmāh*, "handmaiden." (But cf. Paul [1969: 48-53], who argues, on the basis of Near Eastern documents, another meaning for *ʿōnāh*).

(k) *ʾal*, negative particle which is normally followed by a jussive form. Campbell (1975: 70) gives examples of usage akin to ours. Here it "fits" the emotional context. On the "absolute" use of *ʾal* in "spoken" Hebrew, see MacDonald, 1975: 172-73.

(l) *kî-mar-lî meʾōd mikkem kî-yāṣeʾāh bî yad-YHWY.*

Translations and commentaries agree on the sense of the second colon, that is: God's hand struck Naomi. The OT is replete with examples in which a blow by the hand of God (Yahweh/Elohim) resulted in harsh consequences for the individuals involved. On the other hand, as pointed out by J. J. M. Roberts in an article on "The Hand of God," VT, 21 (1971), 244-51, there are many examples in which God's deed had beneficial consequences. At one point, Roberts states that the OT appends an adjective, "good, gracious," or the like, whenever beneficial results of such blows are indicated. This practice, however, is not uniformly followed since there are many instances that fall in this category yet are unaccompanied by "positive" qualifications (2 Chron. 30:12; Eccles. 2:24; Isa. 25:10).

What makes our passage in *Ruth* difficult to assess is the exceptional and unusual construction of this colon. There are over thirty examples of the verb *yāṣāʾ* constructed with the preposition *b-*. A few of these do indicate a martial situation (e.g. Num. 31:36; cf. Joüon, 1953: 41). Most, however, are embedded in much more innocuous contexts, with *b-* denoting: time (e.g. Exod. 13:4; Lev. 25:54), place (e.g. 1 Kings 20:39; Ps. 19:5), condition (e.g. Cant. 5:6; Ps. 44:10; Gen. 15:14), means (e.g. Exod. 14:8; Num. 33:3), and manner (Jer. 43:12; Dan. 11:44). Despite Myers (1955: 30) on Judg. 2:15, there are no examples of the "hand of God" as the subject of *yāṣāʾ b-*. We do have instances of the "hand of God" regulating the verb *hāyāh b-* to suggest unpleasant situations (1 Sam. 12:15; Exod. 9:3; Job 19:21, *nāgaʿ b-*), but this does not resolve our immediate problem. At this point an observation should be made: in all passages in which the "hand of God" brings evil to an individual, a community, or even a nation--be it by means of plagues, sickness, or war--it is the *offender* who directly bears its brunt. In the case of Naomi, this does not occur. On the contrary, she alone among her family was spared. Indeed, we must think Naomi doubly foolish to expect to escape God's wrath by returning into the land in which He is most powerful.

Despite the ambiguities arising from the above considerations, we might, nevertheless, adopt the commonly shared notion concerning the second colon. In view of the unfortunate events that had transpired while in Moab, it might well be that Naomi considered God to have been especially unkind to her, carrying, so to speak, a private *vendetta* against her.

The first colon, *kî-mar-lî me*ʾ*ōd mikkem*, has elicited a number of renderings which differ largely in their understanding of the preposition *min* prefixed to the pronoun *-kem*. Of the following possibilities that are tolerated by grammar, "For it grieveth me much for your sake" (e.g. KJV; cf. Bible de Jérusalem, JPS), "I am much too unhappy for you" (Joüon, 1953: 40-41; Rudolph, 1962: 41), "For it has been/is far more bitter for me than for you" (cf. AB, JPS^2), the last is deemed by this translation as more likely following the context. The translation of Brichto (1973: 12-13), "my bitter condition is too grave for you to share," seems to me unwarranted.

On *me*ʾ*ōd*, understood by Dahood (1970: xl) and others (Campbell, 1975: 71; Freedman, 1973: 268) as an epithet of God, see the criticism of Marcus (1974: 404, 407) and the remarks of Loretz (1974: 481-84).

1:14. "Nowhere is the quality of the Hebrew style (with its exclusion of all unnecessary comment) better exemplified than in this verse. Action, emotion, and contrasting character are expressed in six Hebrew words" (Smith, 1953: 836).

(m) On the absence of *ʾaleph* in *wattiśśenāh*, "they lifted [their voices]," see Myers, 1955: 9, 30; Campbell, 1975:771-72.

(n) The Hebrew does not state that Orpah began her journey home, only that she kissed her mother-in-law as a sign of accepting her judgement. On kissing as an act of farewell, see Campbell, 1975: 72.

In later traditions, Orpah, whose name was understood as "One who turned back," was considered as the ancestress of David's foe Goliath (Levine, 1973: 55[n.1]; Ginzberg, 1961: 518).

(o) *dābeqāh bāh*. The verb *dābaq* has been studied by Wallis (TWAT, II, 83-88). As applied to human relationships *dābaq*, "to cling, stick," expresses the ideal closeness experienced by a married couple. As such, it is most often paralleled by *ʾāhab*, "to love." In Prov. 18:24, *dābaq* describes a friendship that is more binding than brotherhood. The author of *Ruth* uses the verb almost as a leitmotif, repeating it four times in two chapters. In 1:14, its use is at once simple and moving. But when, in 2:8, 21, 23, Boaz employs the verb to advise Ruth to remain with his workers, one has the feeling that the narrator has unfolded playfulness a bit too daringly. For further material on *dābaq* see Campbell, 1975: 72 and THAT, I, 431.

The Pledge (1:15-19a)

15* Naomi said: "Well now, your sister-in-law[a] has returned to her
16* people and her god,[b] follow her example." To this Ruth replied: "Do
not press me to desert you, to resist following you; for wherever you
go, I too will go; whatever your shelter, I will share it;[c] your
17 people will become mine, and your god will be my own. Wherever you
die,[d] I will die, and be buried alongside. May the Lord strike me at
anytime with afflictions,[e] if anything but death parts us."[f]
18 When Naomi realized how determined she was to accompany her, she
19a ceased arguing with her. Together, they went on until they entered
Bethlehem.[g]

1:15-17. Naomi, successful in persuading Orpah to return homeward, asks Ruth to follow the latter's example. In this she succeeds only in eliciting from Ruth one of literature's most poignant declarations of affection and love. We await our comments to 4:5 to suggest the proper implication of Ruth's declaration.

(a) *yebimtēk*. The word **yābām*, (feminine **yebēmet*) does not occur in the absolute state. Aside from that of *Ruth* 1:15, all attestations of the substantive occur in Deut. 25:5-10, a passage which delineates levirate laws. A denominative verb, that is one developed from this noun, is invoked in Deut. 25:5, 7 and in Gen. 38, a chapter concerned with "levirate" complications between Tamar and Judah. Because of such contexts, the occurrence of **yebēmet* in 1:15 justified the search for leviratic practices in *Ruth* (see Campbell's discussion, 1975: 72-73). However, the connection of **yebēmet* with the custom of leviratic marriages, that is ones in which a widow is married to her deceased husband's brother, should not be presumed. For, as it should be pointed out, the Bible contains few occasions to invoke the kinship terms: sister-in-law or brother-in-law. Fortunately, the masculine form of this substantive has now been noted in a text that stems from West Semitic circles of the Middle Bronze Age (ca. 1775 B.C.). Because this attestation is, so far, unique in cuneiform literature the document in which it occurs will be translated below. The text is published by Page (1968: 93-94 [Dalley, 1976: 116-17]), and has been discussed by Batto (1974: 61-62):

Tell Iltani: Azzu. . . . says the following: Do not keep on writing to me about Belassunu. This woman does not want to live here with her husband, so let her proceed with her children to her own brother-in-law's house [*bīt ya-ba-mi-ša*]. You live nearby, while I am far away and cannot write to Mutuḫadki. This woman wants to go to Andariq. Furthermore, this Belassunu, her husband Abdušuri is constantly maltreating her, and I am constantly distressed by her wailing. This woman is (much too) close to me.

From this letter it is to be noted that Belassunu is not a widow. Furthermore, she is the mother of a number of children (contrast Deut. 25: 5). Thus it is obvious that whoever is Belassunu's *yabamum,* he is not so titled because he is legally bound to marry her. The word is simply a West Semitic term for brother-in-law. For this reason, we should understand *yebimtēk* as "your sister-in-law," and avoid overly elaborate theorizing on its usage in our Ruth passage (e.g. Campbell, 1975: 72-73). Incidentally, as seen from the evidence of the al-Rimah text, there should be no reason against retaining a similar translation for a Ugaritic epiteth, *ybmt limm* applied to ʿAnat (on this see Kapelrud, 1969: 31-33 but cf. Campbell, 1975: 73). We concede that *yabamum* is understood, circuitously enough, on the basis of Biblical references to its cognate.

(b) *ʾelōheyhā.* This usage suggests not only the act of worshiping, but also alludes to all the deeds and acts which cement a bond between individuals and their deities. The closest we come to a term would be "faith." Though *ʾelōheyhā* (literally: "her gods") is plural, it is translated above as a singular, for the same reasons that the Hebrews' *ʾelōhîm* is correctly rendered by "God." Chemosh, the deity worshiped by the Moabite Orpah, seem to have evolved and developed along lines that paralleled the Hebrews' YHWH; on this last point, see van Zyl, 1960: 193-202.

(c) *ba'ăšer tālînî 'ālîn.* Most translations understand as follows: "For wherever you go, I will go; Where you lodge, I will lodge (AB)." Campbell (1975: 73-74) comments: "Apparently we are to take 'Wherever you go, I will go; wherever you lodge, I will lodge' to refer to the current journey homeward, . . . and this verb [*lwn/lyn*] to have its usual sense of 'stay the night.' Our story-teller is up to his old trick of using a word twice at crucial points; see 3:13!" It seems to me, however, that the *area* in which Naomi will rest on her way homeward is not of interest here; but rather the emphasis is on the *type of dwelling* which will ultimately become her home. Ruth's statement concerns events, situations, and relationships which will permanently bind the two women. Whether Naomi's future home is in a palace or in a hut, Ruth is determined to share her mother-in-law's dwelling. Furthermore, by using the verb *lûn*, "to lodge," the narrator not only has selected a more poetic verb, but may also have implied that Ruth was willing to share with Naomi any unsettled future, so long as nothing parted them.

(d) *ba'ăšer tāmûtî 'āmût.* The preposition *b-* can also be understood as "by means of." In wishing to share Naomi's fate, Ruth expected to die from hunger, plague, war, or whatever should end Naomi's life. The *šam*, "there," of the next statement, however, favors the translation offered above.

(e) *kōh ya'ăśeh YHWH lî wekōh yōsîp*, literally this means: "Thus shall the Lord do to me, and thus shall he add." That this formula is an oath is recognized by all authorities. The "curse" section of such an oath, that is the portion that delineated the actual calamity awaiting the transgressor, is discretely replaced by *kōh. . . wekōh*, Thus . . . and thus." We imagine Ruth to have, either by gesture or words, described the evil events. Thus, Ruth finalizes her declaration by appealing to YHWH, Naomi's god and now her own, as a future witness and judge to all her subsequent activities. Upon hearing such an oath, Naomi is left with little choice but to accept Ruth's decision. On this formula of imprecation see Myers (1955: 30) and Campbell (1975: 74), who refer to other Biblical passages for similar constructions. On the grammar of this oath, see Joüon (1953: 42); IDB, *sub*, "oath, vow." On the causative *(hiph'îl)* of *yāsap*, "to add, multiply," used to extend an action expressed by another verb, see GKC, 120c (p. 385). In the oath formula the "governing" verb, here *yāsap*, occurs in second position and appears independently of the principal idea, here expressed by *ʿāśāh* (cf. Joel 2:2).

(f) We do not share Campbell's understanding of *kî hammāwet yaprîd beynî ʾûbeynēk*. He renders (1975: 74-75) it "(Thus may Yahweh do to me,/ And thus may he add,/). If even death will separate/ Me from you," and cites the practice of "second burial," an archaeologically attested burial custom in which the bones of an individual were gathered into a family ossuary, in order to support his contention that Ruth was adopting an Israelite funerary practice. On the grammatical side of his argument, Campbell's discussion of the function of *kî* in the concluding clause is admirable in everything but in its application, for it permits the contents of the oath, that is the pledges, to be on both sides of the oath formula. This would be most unusual. Furthermore, as has been made amply clear by Rahmani (1973: 121-26), it would be most premature to develop elaborate conclusions concerning "secondary burial" practices in Israel from the rather sparse evidence available to us. Brichto (1973: 13[n. 18]) offers a similar position without, however, reference to secondary burial.

On the meter of this very lyrical section, see Humbert, 1958: 87-88. On the targumic additions that stress the difficulties of conversion, see Levine, 1973: 56-62.

For verse 18 and its function, see the comments, above, sub *verse 7.*

(g) On the form *bōʾānāh*, see GKC, 91f (p. 256). The recourse to the rarely attested third person feminine plural pronominal suffix, *-ānāh*, might have promoted euphony with *wattēlaknāh*, "they proceeded."

Back to Bethlehem (1:19b-22)

19b As they entered Bethlehem, the whole town hummed[a] with excitement because of them. "Could this be Naomi?"[b] asked [the women];[c]
20 to which she responded: "Do not call me Naomi, But Mara,[d] for
21 Shadday has painfully embittered by life.[e] I left [Bethlehem] full,[f] but the Lord brought me back empty.[g] How could you call me 'Naomi,'[h] then, when the Lord has *witnessed against me*,[i] and Shadday has brought me misfortune."[j]
22 This, then, was how Naomi returned, with her daughter-in-law,

Ruth of Moab, accompanying her from Moabite territory.[k] They[l] reached Bethlehem at the beginning of the barley harvest.[m]

1:19b. Judiciously choosing his verb, the storyteller invites his listeners to decide on the nature of the welcome accorded to the returnees. To be sure, this segment is concerned with Naomi only. Depending on how the listener chooses to interpret the precise shading of the form wattēhōm, *he might think of the welcoming party either as buzzing with delightful excitement as it spies the approaching Naomi (c.f. the usage of the same verb in 1 Sam. 4:5; 1 Kings 1:45) or as hushedly expressing its shock as it sees a woman in abject condition. Our translation "hummed with excitement" seeks to be neutral on this point.*

(a) *wattēhōm* is parsed as a *niphʿal* of **hāmam* or, as most authorities have it, *hûm*. The verb was probably chosen because of its onomatopoeic qualities.

(b) *hazōʾt noʿomî* could also be rendered, "This, indeed, is Naomi." If a question, the statement is surely rhetorical. The prefixed *ha-* could either be interrogative (GKC, 150c [p. 473]) or exclamative (GKC, 150d [p. 474]). *zōʾt* is often used as an enclitic to emphasize either construction (GKC, 136c [p. 442], 148a-b [p. 471]).

(c) "Women" is not in the text, but the Hebrew verbal form *wattōʾmarnāh* is feminine plural. When Saul returns with the Goliath-slaying David (1 Sam. 18:6-7), it is a chorus of women who greets them with songs and cheers. Note also the function of the "women" below (4:14).

1:20-21 preserve Naomi's reply. Undoubtedly, there is more to Naomi's reply than is met at first glance. On the one level, there is a play on the names noʿomî/mārāʾ. *This is well represented in AB's translation: "Don't call me 'Sweet One,'/Call me 'Bitter one'." (As we shall soon see, however,* mārāʾ *could be considered as a "vestigial doublet.") Verse 21 contains Naomi's reason for questioning the aptness of her name. Her statement employs a vocabulary with legal nuances.*

(d) *mārāʾ.* Myers (1955: 10) notes that seventeen manuscripts read *mrh*, i.e. with final *-h* rather than *BH*[3]*'s ʾaleph*. Along with other commentators (GCK, 80h [p. 224] and Joüon, 1947: 89k [p. 215]) he considers this to be an Aramaism. Campbell (1975: 76) insists that technically this is not an Aramaism, but that it "may reflect only an orthographic change in the course of scribal transmission." Such a change, however, would be difficult to explain since no Aramaic root, **mrʾ*, seems appropriate as a given name for a female.

One could resort to West Semitic *mrʾ*, attested both in Hebrew and Ugaritic. In both languages, a *mrʾ* I conveys the meaning "to fatten," while, in Ugaritic only, a *mrʾ* II is known to mean "to command" (UT, 19, 1544). While plausible, we have no West Semitic personal name that is derived from that root. We are left with two other possibilities, both of which require us to understand the *ʾaleph* as an afformative hypocoristicon. This afformative *ʾaleph* is known in West Semitic onomastica from as early as the second millenium B.C. (On this, see the bibliography assembled in Benz, 1972: 240-41). In Mari, this ending appears as an *-a* appended in feminine names (Huffmon, 1965: 133-34). The first possibility would involve the root **m(?)r* that is found in Phoenician onomastica (Benz, 1972: 353-54). Of uncertain definition, this root may be explained, faute de mieux, as a divine name. Although hypocoristic particles could be appended to theophoric elements, it is best to avoid resorting to such explanations.

It might be better, therefore, to return to the root **mrr*, which despite recent denials (Pardee, forthcoming in UF) bears the multiple meaning "to bless, strengthen, be bitter" (cf. Dietrich, 1973: 119-22; Sasson, 1972: 249-51); Gordon (UT 19, 1556) has given examples in which the biblical **mrr* is best rendered "power" (e.g. Exod. 1:14; Judg. 18:25). *Maraʾ* could then be understood as a name influenced neither by Aramaic vocabulary nor orthography, but rather as a hypocoristicon, coined in West Semitic circles. It would be composed of the substantive *mar*, derived from the verb *mārar*, to which is appended an *ʾaleph*. For reasons to be explained, we opt for a meaning that underscores the biblical writer's ability to play on words. Thus, it is here suggested that *mārāʾ* be understood as recalling "fierceness, strength," and the like. The name of Levi's third son, Merari, can be similarly interpreted and is perhaps better rendered as "He of Strength"(on constructions with *-î*, see above). Now what makes Naomi's second name interesting is that, much like the root **nʿm* (see above), the root **mrr* is attested in Ugaritic, this time as a participle applied to Pughat, sister of Aqhat and daughter of Danel. In CTA, 19 [= UT: 1 Aqhat], iv: 195, Pughat asks her father: "Bless me so that I could go blessed/Strengthen (or beatify) me so that I could go strengthened (or beatified - *mrrt*)" (Cf. Ginsberg in ANET[3], 155). Another derivative of **mrr* (but cf. Margulis, 1970: 297) is *nmrr*. Occurring among other substantives such as "power, protection," it is used to describe the Rephaim, chthonic powers appearing in Ugaritic texts (*Ugaritica*, V, 2: rev. 8). The precise meaning of the geographical name *mrrt.tǵll.bnr* (CTA, 19] = UT: 1 Aqhat]: 156, 157-58) is still obscure. To be noted, however, is the mythological context in which this place name is preserved.

(e) *kî-hēmar šadday lî meʾōd*. It is obvious that this sentence is constructed on a pattern reminiscent of *kî-mar-lî meʾōd mikkem* of verse 13. Here, however, the verb is in the causative, and the subject is Šadday, "the Almighty." (Job 27:2 provides an interesting parallel in that Šadday, curiously enough balanced by El, is said to "embitter Job's life.")

However the narrator of *Ruth* (or its final redactor if one insists) wanted to understand *mar-(lî)* of verse 13, it is certain that he used it to anticipate, even to explain the mention of Naomi's "doublet" *mārāʾ*. In verse 20, however, he offered yet another explanation, one which depended on connecting the root *mrr* with the meaning that is most often met with in the MT: "to be bitter." By using the *hiphʿîl* of *mrr*, a form which is rarely found in the OT, he arrived at what must have appeared to him a satisfactory etymology for *mārāʾ*. Despite this, another poetically forged statement immediately follows, offering a third, more elaborate discussion of Naomi's "bitterness." To this we turn now.

Šadday. Following the LXX's παντοκράτωρ and the Vulgate's *omnipotens*, *Šadday* is usually rendered by "The Almighty" (but cf. Bertram, 1959: 502-13). With Pope (1965: 44) it is best to resist translating the name since no satisfactory explanation has, so far, been proposed. Suggestions as to etymology have ranged widely from "The Breast," "The Devastator," to "[The One of the] Field/Mountain." The place of origin of this deity, the configuration of his powers, even the period which saw him syncretized by the Hebrew theographers, are all obscure; hence, these issues are much discussed among Biblical scholars (cf. IDB, II, 412; Pope, 1965: 44; Joüon, 1953: 44; de Vaux, 1971: I, 263-65 [with good bibliography]). A most exhaustive discussion is given in Weippert, THAT, II, 873-81).

1:21. This verse is quite complex. It is divisible into two major parts, each of which carries a complete accounting of Naomi's unhappy state of affairs. The second part is itself divisible into three clauses, the last two paralleling each other. The first chides the townswomen for calling Naomi by that name. The second clause contains a "YHWH," while the third offers a "Šadday" explanation for Naomi's misfortune.

(f) *ʾanî melēʾāh hālaktî.* The independent pronoun *ʾanî*, "I," is placed at the head of this section since Naomi wants to emphasize that she is the only one left of Elimelech's family. It is to be noted that in verses 21-22 the verbs are singular, indicating that Naomi clearly perceives herself as alone, almost as if Ruth was not following her footsteps.

(g) *werēyqām hešîbanî YHWH.* The emphasis is on *rēyqām*, offering a strong contrast to *melēʾāh*, "full," of the preceding clause. Joüon (1953: 44-45) suggests reading **rēyqāh*, in order to "parallel" *melēʾāh*. He would change the adverb *rēyqām*, "empty-handed," to an adjective more suitable to the parallel and to the context. We may, however, be meeting with an example of those ubiquitous enclitic *mems*, which may have been appended to the root *ryq* both for poetic reasons and to allow long-range word play with *rēyqām* of 3:17. For enclitic *mem*, see Pope, 1965: 363; Dahood, 1970: 408-9; Gordon, UT, 11.4-11.8 (pp. 103-4).

Note that now that she has returned to a Hebraic milieu, Naomi naturally gives YHWH full responsibility for her unhappiness. On this, however, see Kaufmann, 1960: 130-31.

(h) *lāmmāh tiqreʾnāh lî noʿomî* is obviously related to *ʾal-tiqreʾnāh lî noʿomî* of verse 20. This, of course, permits the writer to furnish further materials to explain Naomi's sad lot.

(i) *waYHWH ʿānāh bî.* Much has been written on the verb of this clause. With many others, Myers (1955: 22) points out that while the *qāl* of *ʿānāh* is constructed with the preposition *b-* to mean "to testify against" (e.g. 2 Sam. 1:16; 1 Sam. 12:3; Isa. 3:9; Jer. 14:7; Mic. 6:3; Hos. 5:5; 7:10), there are no instances in which YHWH is regarded as the testifier. For this reason he, again with other commentators, follows the LXX and Vulgate and emends the Massoretic pointing to read *ʿinnāh*, "to oppress, humiliate" (the transitive *piʿʿel* of *ʿnh* II). *ʿinnāh* occurs in Deut. 8:2, 3, 16; 1 Kings 17:20; Isa. 64:11, but in none of these instances is it constructed with *b-*. Despite its lack of precedence, it might be best, therefore, to retain MT's reading and, along with recent students of *Ruth* (see Campbell, 1975: 77), to regard the statement as couched in and flavored by juridical terminology. Note the discussion of Labuschagne in THAT, II, 335-41, in particular 339 (3b).

We stated above that *kî-hēmar šadday lî me᾽ōd* of verse 20 seemed to have recalled a clause in Naomi's address to her daughters-in-law: *kî-mar-lî me᾽ōd mikkem* (verse 13). For this reason, we wonder if we cannot explain the peculiarities of *waYHWH ᶜānāh bî* by alluding to *yāṣe᾽āh-bî yad-YHWH*, also of verse 13. Both these phrases share in the mention of YHWH and in the unusual usage of the preposition *b-*. A further piece of speculation: just as in verse 20 an obvious pun explained the relationship between the name *mārā᾽* and the root *mrr*, so too the verb *ᶜānāh*, which shares with the name *noᶜomî* the consonant *nûn* and *ᶜayin*, may have been chosen for its ability to permit a parasonantic play on words and thus "explain" the name *noᶜomî*. On "parasonantic" puns, we quote from IDBS, p. 969: "Possibly the most widely attested type of wordplay, parasonancy involvès the use of verbal and nominal roots which differ in one of their three consonants. . . . A somewhat more sophisticated parasonant pun is the type in which consonants of one word are found in another word but in a differing order. . . ."

(j) Paralleling the preceding statement, *šadday hēraᶜlî* offers a "šadday" explanation for Naomi's difficulties. This statement may possibly have been fashioned and positioned here to integrate the "*mārā᾽*" account of verse 20. Campbell (1975: 77) recognizes a legal nuance to the usage of the verb *rāᶜaᶜ*, in the *hiph'îl*, followed by the preposition *b-*.

1:22. As pointed out by Joüon (1953: 46), this verse consists of two sections. While the first recalls, in capsule form, the preceding events, the second sets the stage for the ensuing narrative. By being specific about the time period in which Naomi and Ruth entered Bethlehem, the narrator succeeded in giving the tale one more touch of "historicity." Furthermore, he was able to proceed without unnecessary topical detours, to his main concern: the meeting of Boaz and Ruth. Finally, he will depict his heroine, Ruth, as singularly efficient in achieving her goal, since she will have only ninety days or so from the beginning of the harvesting to the end of the winnowing seasons in which to accomplish her purpose.

(k) *haššābāh miśśedēy mô᾽āb*. The penultimate accent on *haššābāh* reveals it to be a perfect with a prefixed article which, in this circumstance, acts as a demonstrative/relative pronoun (GKC, 138k]p. 447]; Joüon, 1947: 45e [p. 448]). Contrary to the opinion of these authorities, I do not believe that one could consider a text with such a feature as "late."

If this form is documentable in other passages of the OT, albeit uncommonly, its usage in *Ruth* is not easily understandable. We note first that this phrase, or its equivalent, is mentioned in 2:6 and 4:3, as well as in our passage. The verb *šûb*, "to turn back, return," is normally applied to persons who return to a place they once left. This is clearly the case of 4:3 in which this phrase is used in a legal context connected with Naomi. In 2:6, however, it is applied to Ruth. But a careful reading of that sentence reveals that this reference is only *tangentially* connected to Ruth, since the narrator is quick to add "with Naomi" after "the one who has returned"; it might thus be better to render *šûb ʿim* by "accompany." Our major difficulty in this usage of the verb *šûb*, therefore, is limited to our sentence where *haššābāh miśśedēy môʾāb* appears in apposition to Ruth. The solution to this difficulty could be approached from a number of avenues: (1) We first note, as did many scholars commenting on this verse (lastly Campbell, 1975: 79-80), the *leitmotif* quality of the verb *šûb*, particularly in the first chapter of *Ruth*. With much trepidation, we might consider the narrator to have unfolded his playfulness a bit too loosely in this context. (2) We could point out that the verb *šûb* is not necessarily limited to the meaning mentioned above; in particular, *šûb* could refer to activities that do not share the same point of origin and return. In this passage however, we might strain credibility were we to insist on this approach. (3) We might consider that our particular reference to *haššābāh miśśedēy môʾāb* actually harks back to *wattāšob noʿomî*; this suggestion would rely on understanding *werût hammôʾabiyyāh kallātāh ʿimmah* as a parenthetical statement. Such a "solution" would gravely offend the literary reputation of a narrator of genius; for it would have him authoring repetitious and inelegant formulations. (4) One might consider the *hē* in *ʿimmāh* as a product of dittography. If excised, we would have the following: "Naomi thus returned; with Ruth of Moab, her daughter-in-law with the one [i.e. Naomi] who returned from Moabite territory." (5) Ehrlich (1900: II, 395) cleverly reverses the sequence into *haššābāh ʿimmah,* thus suggesting; ". . . . and Ruth of Moab, her daughter-in-law, who returned with her. . . ." (reference courtesy Y. Gitay).

(1) *hemmāh.* Campbell (1975: 78) accepts D. N. Freedman's suggestion to regard this demonstrative adjective, incorrectly applied to females [correctly: *hennāh*], as representing the particle of emphasis *hm(t)*, allegedly attested in Ugaritic. He thus would translate this section as

follows: "Now *as it happened* [emphasis mine], they arrived in Bethlehem at the beginning of the barley harvest." See, however, de Moor's (1969: 201f) objections to this position.

(m) *qeṣîr śeʿōrîm*. According to the Gezer Calender, *yrḥ qṣr śʿrm*, "month of barley harvest," is the eighth month of the agricultural calendar, the first two months of which were equivalent to our September/October. The barley harvest, therefore, occurred in April/May. The wheat harvest took place a few weeks later, probably in May/June. On the Gezer Calendar, see Donner and Röllig, 1964: III, Tafel XII [text]; I, #182 (p. 34) [transcription]; II, #182 (pp. 182-83) [translation, notes, and bibliography]. See further, IDB, *sub* "calendar, Agriculture."

A Plan (2:1-7)

1 Now Naomi knew of an acquaintance of her husband,[a] a property
2 holder[b] who belonged to Elimelech's clan;[c] his name was Boaz.[d] Ruth
of Moab said to Naomi: "Should I go to the fields and glean among
3* the ears of grain, in the hope of pleasing him?"[e] "Go ahead, my
daughter," answered Naomi. She went her way, and gleaned in the
field behind the reapers. It so happened[f] that she found herself in
the field belonging to Boaz, of Elimelech's clan.
4 Just then, Boaz arrived[g] from Bethlehem and greeted the reapers:
5 "The Lord be with you." "The Lord bless you," they replied to him.[h]
6 Boaz asked his servant, in charge of the reapers: "Whose girl is
that?"[i] "She is the young woman from Moab," replied the overseer,
7 "who returned[j] with Naomi from Moabite territory. She requested
permission to glean, and to gather grain among the sheaves behind
the reapers.[k] She arrived and has been waiting from daybreak until
now;[l] thus, she must have spent little time at home."[m]

2:1 Boaz enters the scene. His relationship to all those involved is quickly established in three short statements. The first, which we loosely translate: "Now Naomi knew of an acquaintance of her husband," reveals his connection to Naomi and will thus explain her interest in him. The second, "a property holder," will make Ruth's interest in this man of means understandable. The third statement, "who belonged to Elimich's clan," will clarify the legal situation in which all concerned will presently be involved.

(a) *ûlnoᶜomî môdaᶜ [ketîb: mydᶜ] le)îšāh.* Literally, this sentence means, "To Naomi, [there was] a *môdaᶜ* to her husband" or RSV's "Now Naomi had a kinsman of her husband's. . . ." There is no reason to accept AB's "Naomi had a "covenant-brother" through her husband. . . ." However, in his commentary, Campbell (1975: 88-90) is surely correct in prefering the *ketîb* over the *qerē*, if simply because *meyuddāᶜ* is well attested elsewhere (at least six other examples are known where the term is synonymous with "intimate friend, companion", cf. BDB, 394). *môdaᶜ*, however, appears only in a passage (Prov. 7:4) whose highly poetic, if not artificial, language does not allow for precise rendering. This statement is made despite the fact that *môdaᶜ* is paralleled by *)aḥôt*, "sister." But Campbell's proposal to translate *mydᶜ* with "covenant-brother" ultimately rests upon applying a validly understood meaning for the verb *ydᶜ* ("to recognize"), legitimately drawn from the politico-theological context (Huffmon, 1966: 31-37; 1966b: 36-38), to a situation that clearly lacks such implications.

It is to be noted that in 2:20 Naomi uses a different vocabulary in describing Boaz: "the man is 'near' to us, *qārôb lānû hā)îš*." Now in Job. 19:14 *meyuddāᶜ* is paralleled by *qārôb*, while in Ps. 15:3 and 38:12 *qarôb* is paralleled, respectively, to *rēaᶜ*, "friend," and *)ōhēb rēaᶜ*, "beloved friend." It is also to be noted that in 3:2, whose vocabulary is strongly reminiscent of 2:20, *qārôb* could only awkwardly be associated with kinship terms. Thus, it may be best to retain the *ketîb, meyuddāᶜ*, and to translate this term by its most commonly attested meaning, "friend, acquaintance." On the *mōdaᶜtānû* of 3:2, see *sub* that verse. On the unusual vocalization of the *qerē, môdaᶜ*, in 2:1 with a *pataḥ* rather than a *qāmeṣ*, thus indicating it to be in construct, see Joüon, 1953: 46. If not a (scribal?) error, this may be yet one more example of the construct chain broken by an intervening preposition (cf. Ps. 9:10; 10:1).

(b) *)îš gibbôr ḥayil.* This term may have acquired a wide range of meaning as it evolved through the ages. A recent *mise-au-point* by Kosmala for the TWAT series, I, 909-11, shows that the term could be applied to a warrior ("powerful"), a functionary ("able"), a landowner ("rich"), and so forth. Boling's commentary on Judges (1975: 197), translates *gibbôr ḥayil*, in a military context, by means of "knight," and explains: "one trained in upper-class combat, and who furnished his own equipment as well as a squire and/or a unit of soldiers." In *Ruth*, the point which is made concerning Boaz is that he was not an ordinary, run-of-the-mill Israelite, but a man of substance. That he may have inherited his property from ancestors who belonged to military circles remains plausible. As sketched in our story, Boaz could best be described as a *pater familias*.

Later Jewish commentators understood *gibbôr ḥayil* of *Ruth* as qualifying a man especially versed in Hebraic and Torah lore, and as a transmitter of oral tradition handed down from the days of Moses. There was even a tendency to identify Boaz with the obscure Ibzan, tenth Judge of Israel (Judg. 12:8-10). The fact that both were connected with Bethlehem apparently played a major role in this identification. However, modern scholars are generally agreed that Ibzan's Bethlehem was rather a northern village in the heart of Zebulon (Levine, 1973: 66-67).

(c) *mimmišpaḥat ʾelîmelek*. Following Josh. 7:16-18, scholars generally divide Israel's social organization into the following units: [*benēy yiśrāʾēl*, "nation of Israel"], *šebeṭ* or *maṭṭēh*, "tribe," *mišpāḥāh*, "clan," and *bēyt-ʾab*, "extended family." This vocabulary was sometimes supplemented or even altered during the many periods of social change which Israel experienced through the years. For our purposes, there is no reason to disagree with the definition for *mišpāḥāh* offered by IDB, IV, 699 (*sub Tribe*) and supplemented by de Vaux, 1961: 8, 21:

A "clan". . . . was a group of households or an extended family. . . . Usually they claimed a common ancestry. . . . The clan was the link between the family and the larger unit, the tribe. . . . In the Priestly Code this Hebrew word [*mišpāḥāh*] is regularly and consistently used for a subdivision of the tribe. . . . [Members of the *mišpāḥāh*] usually lived in the same place, and . . . met for common religious feasts and sacrificial meals. . . . In particular, the clan assumed the responsibility for blood-vengeance. [The *mišpāḥāh*] concentrated in one area, occupying one or more villages according to its size, like the *mishpāḥāh* of the Danites at Soreah and Eshtaol [Judg. 18:11]; alternatively, several *mishpāḥôth* might live together within a city. . . . The clan had common interests and duties, and its members were conscious of the blood-bond which united them: they called each other "brothers" (1 Sam. 20:29) [and see below, *Ruth* 4:3].

(d) *Boʿaz*. A root **bʿz* does not occur in the OT. As a result, an etymology for this name is not readily apparent. A slightly attested

Arabic word, **baǵz*, as in *baǵiz*, "lively, spirited, jolly, vigorous," is cited by some scholars (Noth, 1928: 228; Rudolph, 1962: 48). Many explanations for the name *bōʿaz* proceed from the enigmatic names given to the pillars that faced Solomon's temple. Yakin and Boaz (1 Kings 7:21 = 2 Chron. 3:17). S. A. Cook (*apud*, EB II, 3205) believes *bōʿaz* to be a corruption of Baʿal since he considers *yākîn* ("he affirms") as the "Phonician equivalent of YHWH." Most scholars, however, understand the name "Bōʿaz" as composed of two elements. T. K. Cheyne, in discussing the name of the temple's left pillar, which he considers as antedating that of *Ruth*'s hero, offers *bʿ[l]z[bb]* (EB, II, 2304-05). Klostermann (*apud*, ibid.) proposes *b[ʿl]ʿz, baʿal ʿoz*, an etymology which, he feels, is supported by the Codex Vaticanus, which reads βαλαζ. This hypothesis, generally ignored when first proposed, was given a new lease on life as a result of the discoveries at Ras Shamra. Bauer (1932: 73) reintroduced the proposal on the basis of the occurrences of precisely such an exclamatory phrase, *(mtʿz) bʿlʿz*, (Môt is strong) Baal is strong," in UT, 49 [CTA, 6]: 6: 17-19. To be noted also is the occurrence of *ʿz bʿl* in *Ugaritica* V: 14: B: 13. On these points see also Astour, 1965: 279; de Fraine, 1955: 148.

R. B. Y. Scott (cf., conveniently, IDB, II, 780-81, followed by Albright (1968: 135), believes the names of the Solomonic columns to represent the first words of dynastic oracles. These words were, supposedly, inscribed on the columns themselves. In the case of *Boʿaz*, Scott offers the following elucidation: "in the strength of [*beʿōz*] of [*sic*] Yahweh shall the king rejoice." Note also the reverse hypothesis offered by Yeivin, 1959: 21-22. Scott's idea, minus its dynastic implication, has been suggested by a host of ancient and modern commentors who proceeded from the LXX of 2 Chron. 3:17, which renders *Boʿaz* as "ἰσχυς, "strength, might," and which thus connects *Boʿaz* with the root *ʿz(z)*, "to be strong." Folk etymology, as reflected in the LXX's Boόζ in *Ruth* 2:1, understood the name as *bôʿōz*, "in him [there is] strength." Finally we record P. Cassel's unlikely proposal (*apud*, Rudolph, 1962: 48) that *benʿoz*, "son of strength," be considered as the original form of the name of our protagonist.

The grammatical structure of the phrase, "and his name [was]," followed by a personal name, has been treated in Joüon, 1947: 158c (pp. 481-82); see also Joüon, 1953: 47. Some two dozen examples of this type of construction are given in Mandelkern's concordance *sub šēm* (p. 1193). Of these, the examples in Jer. 37:13, Zech. 14:9, and 2 Sam. 20:1 could be dismissed as not properly belonging to our type. A few instances contain

names of persons who play no further role in the ensuing narrative, e.g. Gen. 38:1, 2; 2 Sam. 17:25. Of the remainder, only three examples state an individual's name in an anticipatory fashion *without proceeding immediately* to recount his activities. These concern Doeg the Edomite (1 Sam. 21:8), Mephibosheth the Lame (2 Sam. 4:4), and Mica, Mephibosheth's son (2 Sam. 9:12). The rest, amounting to about two dozen instances, consistently introduce, *immediately* after the introduction of a character's name, materials of major import to the narrative. These statistics will be important when we discuss 2:2.

2:2. This verse has been translated by us quite differently from the attempts of others. Typical is RSV: "Let me go to the field, and glean among the ears of grain after him in whose sight I shall find favor." Since proper rendering for this verse is important to our thesis, we offer the following objections to translations examplified by RSV's:

1. According to the ancient custom of gleaning, as codified in Lev. 19:9; 23:22; Deut. 24:19, Ruth did not need to confine her activity to plots owned by friendly landowners. As a widow, and a resident alien, she had the right to gather grain anywhere she pleased.

2. Ruth might well have decided to glean because of Naomi's needs. To balance this, however, the evidence of 4:3 suggests that Naomi was in a position to sell her land and thus be in possession of a modest, albeit temporary, income. The RSV rendering, therefore, does not provide us with an immediate reason for Ruth's decision. Moreover we are, perhaps too critically, puzzled by Naomi's failure to participate in the gleanings if her situation was as dire as some commentators are wont to believe. Surely old age could not have been enough of a reason to prevent famished individuals from gleaning during the relatively cool months of spring.

3. Perhaps most crucial as an objection is that "after him in whose sight I shall find favor" does not adequately explain the peculiarities of the Hebrew ʾaḥar ʾašer ʾemṣāʾ-ḥēn beʿēnāyw. *It is on this phrase, therefore, that we shall dwell further.*

(e) *ʾaḥar ʾašer ʾemṣāʾ-ḥēn beʿēnāyw.*

1. The idiom *limeṣoʾ ḥēn beʿēnēy* [*X*], literally, "to find favor in the eyes of [X]; i.e. to find favor with [X]," is well represented in Hebrew literature, cf. Mandelkern's concordance, 411 (*sub ḥēn*). In *no case* involving the verb *māṣāʾ*, "to find," and possibly only once involving

the verb *nāśā᾿*, "to raise" (in Esther 2:15), is the one whose favor is sought left undetermined. Thus, the third person pronominal suffix *waw*, *ʿênāyw*, "his eyes," *must* refer to a definite individual. It would be somewhat circuitous, if not incorrect, therefore, to consider *ʾăšer*, the relative pronoun, as the antecedent of our *waw*. In the light of our findings, above, concerning *ûšemô* followed by a personal name, it would not be foolhardy to assume that our *waw* specifically recalls Boaz. It is noteworthy that in 2:10 as well as in 2:13 the same idiom is used by Ruth to refer to Boaz. Nor should we consider the change from indirect discourse in 2:1 to direct discourse in 2:2 as presenting insufferable difficulties to our thesis.

2. *ʾaḥar ʾăšer*, usually translated "after he who . . . ," deserves closer inspection. Ezek. 40:1 contains the only other Biblical example to use our compound. There, however, it is treated as a temporal conjunction, "after [that which] . . ." (cf. BDB, 29-30).

Examples of *ʾaḥarēy ʾăšer*, that is ones in which the preposition *ʾaḥar* is given in the plural construct form, are more plentiful (cf. BDB, 20-30). Three instances of this "compound" (Josh. 9:16; 23:1; 24:20) are rendered by an adverb of time, "when, after." The rest (Deut. 24:4; Josh. 7:8; Judg. 11:36; 19:23; 2 Sam. 19:31) could best be translated by "since, seeing that. . . ." In no case is either *ʾaḥar ʾăšer* or *ʾaḥărēy ʾăšer* plausibly translatable by means of the adverb of place "after, behind," as is commonly rendered in the *Ruth* passage under study. As a matter of fact, when preceded by most other prepositions (e.g. *mibbelî*, *ʿal debar*, *yaʿan*, *baʿabûr*, *lemaʿan*, *ʿal*, *kepî*, and so forth; cf., BDB, 83[8f]) *ʾăšer* forms a compound that almost always is better rendered by a conjunction.

3. It should be noted, moreover, that all the above-listed attestations of *ʾaḥar(ēy) ʾăšer* are followed by verbs in the perfect. *Ruth* 2:2, however, is constructed with the imperfect. A literal translation of the whole verse, therefore, would read as follows: "Let me go into the field in order to glean among the ears of grain since I shall find favor in his eyes. . . ." Since we have chosen to cast the first part of Ruth's statement in the form of a question, we have loosely translated *ʾaḥar(ēy) ʾăšer* by "in the hope of . . ." (i.e. "seeing that I shall").

On objections that might be raised to this interpretation, see below, *sub* 2:3 and 20. Ibn Ezra, it is interesting to note, knew a tradition which paralleled our rendering. In his commentary to *Ruth*, ad loc., he cites, but chooses to ignore, that tradition.

2:3. Ruth arrives at the fields and begins gleaning. Note that in agreement with the customs of the time, she requires no special permission to begin her task. The second half of this verse, however, will require special attention. The use of three verbs to suggest continuing action occurs a few times in Ruth. *Since, as we shall note, Ruth did not begin gleaning until the end of her interview with Boaz, it may be best to translate 2:3 as follows: "She proceeded to begin gleaning in the field behind the reapers* [wattēlek wattābô̂ʾ wattelaqqēṭ baśśādeh]. . . ."

(f) *wayyiqer miqrehā*. The Hebrew has an obvious play on the root *qārāh*, "to happen." Elsewhere, only in Eccles. 2:14, 15 do both verb and substantive, derived from the same root, occur in the same verse.

Much has been written on this phrase. In general, those who search for a "theology" in *Ruth*, specifically those who wish to promote the workings of God in the meeting between Boaz and Ruth, are generally puzzled by the absence of God's name. To quote from Hals, 1969: 11-12:

In 2:3*b* the narrator observes that Ruth "happened to come to the part of the field belonging to Boaz." In view of the story's stress on God's providential guiding of the lives of this family, it is surprising to find such a crucial item in the pattern of events which brought Ruth and Boaz together attributed to chance. Such a secular point of view is startling, to say the least. How can the same writer trace a chain of events whose beginning (1:6) and ending (4:13) are found in God's all-casuality, and then describe one of the links in the middle of that chain as accidental? The answer, of course, lies in the subtlety of the writer's style. Surprising as it may seem at first glance, the author's real meaning in 2:3*b* is actually the opposite of what he says. The labeling of Ruth's meeting with Boaz as "chance" is nothing more than the author's way of saying that no human intent was involved. For Ruth and Boaz it was an accident, but not for God. The tenor of the whole story makes it clear that the narrator sees God's hand throughout. In fact, the very secularism of his expression here is his way of stressing that conviction. It is a kind of underplaying for effect. By calling this meeting an accident, the writer enables himself subtly to point out that even the "accidental" is directed by God.

In his commentary on *Ruth*, Campbell takes a similar though more sophisticatedly argued position (1975: 112). Such sentiments as expressed by Hals, while uplifting and based on venerable homiletics (cf. Levine,

1973: 68), are surely much too clever. The author of *Ruth*, who invokes YHWH's name eighteen times, not to speak of the mention of Elohim and Shadday, could easily have inserted it *one more time* in this most crucial of passages. We should resist, I believe, doing it for him!

Yet we still must seek an explanation for *wayyiqer miqrehā*. We search for it in the manner in which allotment and ownership of land obtained in the ancient and, to a great extent, in the modern Near East as well. Arable land was subdivided among its owners by no artificial and clearly visible boundaries. To do so might lead to withholding valuable land from active cultivation. Thus, when land was either bought or sold, in addition to listing natural boundaries (rivers, ditches, canals, and so forth), contracts would specify the location of a field by registering the names of owners of adjacent plots. Examples are collected in Schorr, 1913: 139ff. (no. 92ff). CT, 47: 48 offers a representative text: "in the matter of a field of 6 *ikū* in the plain of Buni, beside the fiels of PN_1, and beside the field of PN_2, a *nadītum*-woman of Shamash; daughter of PN_1, brought it from PN_4, son of PN_2, with her ring money. . . ."

The purpose of verse 3, therefore is to emphasize Ruth's good fortune, not so much that Boaz turned out to be the owner of the field which she happened to reach, but that she located Boaz's plot *without wasting precious time searching for it*. It must be remembered at this point that the harvest did not stretch over a long span of time. Depending on the size of a field, the job could be accomplished in a matter of days. We shall soon note why Ruth felt it particularly urgent to meet Boaz at the earliest possible occasion. This sense of urgency is furthered, we note, by the writer who immediately introduces Boaz into the scene. Note also the use of the verb *qārāh* in Gen. 24:12. There, Abraham's servant asks God to "make it happen" *(haqrēh-nā)* that Isaac's future wife reveal herself to him by fulfilling a pre-described act. Thus, similar to our passage, the element of chance is not to be divorced from a pre-desired end (courtesy of D. Halperin).

2:4. As the gibbôr ḥayil, *Boaz comes to check on the progress of the harvest. There is no reason to imagine him tarrying for long were he to learn that nothing unusual was occurring that day. But, of course, something that required his immediate attention had happened!*

(g) For a useful discussion of *wehinnēh-bō‘az bā’*, see Campbell, 1975: 93. Campbell, however, thinks the lapse of time between Ruth's and Boaz's arrival at the field permitted "the overseer to have formed a positive impression of Ruth." We shall note that the overseer is but incidental to the narrative.

The use of *wehinnēh* may be an attempt on the part of the narrator to clock the arrivals of both Boaz and Ruth within seconds of each other. *Just as Ruth wasted precious little time in finding Boaz's field, neither did Boaz in noticing Ruth.*

(h) On greeting formulae, see T. K. Cheyne in EB, IV, 4255 (*sub* "Salutations, Greetings"). Smith (1953: 840) feels that "the form of the greeting gives immediate insight into the character of Boaz." On the grammar of greeting formulae, see Joüon, 1947: 163(b) (p. 501).

2:5. Boaz notices a young lady he had not encountered before. He asks the overseer a question that comes most naturally to those who lived in the ancient world.

(i) *lemî hanna‘arāh hazzō’t.* According to Myers (1955: 23), only Gen. 32:18 and 1 Sam. 30:13 contain a construction in which *lemî*, "for whom," is employed with a personal object. See also Joüon, 1953: 49. Most translators and authorities (e.g. already Ibn Ezra, *apud*, Levine, (1973: 69[n.1]) argue that Boaz is wondering about the person to whom Ruth belonged. Campbell understands Boaz's query as a deliberately vague formulation: "Boaz' question is more general than simply one of identification. It invites the answer which in fact it receives, namely information about Ruth which will move the story forward. A good paraphrase might be 'Where does this young woman fit in?' (p. 94)." It seems to us, however, that two points have to be resolved before such interpretations are accepted. First, if Ruth is gleaning already (verse 3), how does Boaz notice her so soon after he arrives on his land? Secondly, if Ruth went out to glean in a field whose owner is not known to her, she must have relied on the protection that immemorial custom had granted widows: the right to glean. Upon noticing a stranger, in the act of gleaning, Boaz would certainly have realized that she must have been either a widow or a *gērāh*, a "resident alien." If he thought her a widow, his question *lemî*, "to whom," would certainly not have referred to a "husband," since the latter would be presumed dead. We are left with the possibility that Boaz was asking of the overseer about Ruth's ancestry or, more immediately, about the clan to which she belonged. This might explain the overseer's immediate response to Boaz, "she is the young woman of Moab. . . ." It should be stated that the OT has no attestations of *lemî* with reference to "nations, tribes, clans," and so forth. We do, however, have examples of *mî* applied to such social units (Deut. 4:7; Mic. 1:5; Judg. 9:28).

2:6-7. The overseer's reply makes it clear why Boaz noticed this young woman from Moab at the outset of his visit to the fields. Verse 7 is most important for the development of the story. As we noted above, Ruth was a widow and a foreigner. Thus, the custom of the land would have guaranteed her the right to glean. Deliberately, however, she approached the overseer and requested of him permission to collect grains from among the sheaves. *Verse 15, however, will make it clear that this was a privilege granted only by the owner of the field. Was Ruth ignorant of the fact? We do not think so. Even if the custom of Moab were different than those of Bethlehem, she most certainly could have received proper counsel from Naomi. Our translation will support the thesis that Ruth was deliberately presenting the overseer with a request he was not in a position to grant. Unfortunately, it will also be noted that verse 7 contains a number of difficulties that do not allow unanimity in interpretation and rendering among scholars and commentators. Campbell (1975) has chosen to leave untranslated the last fourteen words of verse 7. Of interest to us is his long note (pp. 94-96) that details some of the problems encountered in the text of this verse. We shall take up some of these problems in the comments below.*

(j) The Masoretes accented *haššābāh* as a perfect here as in 1:22 (see above) with a definite article prefixed. There is no need to presume the loss of a definite article that would have been attached to *naʿarāh môʾabiyyāh*, as some scholars wish to do (e.g. Rudolph, 1962: 45, 46), following LXX and Old Latin. As is clear from verse 11, Ruth's saga had become the talk of the town.

(k) *wattōʾmer ʾalaqqoṭāh-nnāʾ weʾāsaptî bāʿomārîm ʾaḥarēy haqqôṣerîm*. Many scholars note that it is only after verse 15 that Ruth is given permission to glean among the sheaves. For this reason, *weʾāsaptî bāʿomārîm*,

"I shall gather grain among the sheaves," appears to be inconsistent with verse 15. Joüon (1953: 49) is followed by Rudolph (1962: 46) in revocalizing MT *ʿomārîm*, "sheaves," to read *ʿamîrîm*, "swath, row of fallen grain" (BDB, 771). Thus, the passage under discussion is translated by Rudolph: "I will gather blades (of grain) behind the reapers." Some scholars, among them Gressmann (*apud*, Rudolph, 1962: 46), delete "among the sheaves" entirely. In view of the discussion offered above, such ameliorations of the text are not only totally unnecessary but even miss a crucial moment in the development of the narrative. To repeat: *Ruth had come with a request that could not be fulfilled by a mere overseer. All that he could do was to ask her to step aside and wait until the "boss" arrived. In this way, Ruth was assured of meeting Boaz, since the latter could hardly fail to notice her as she stood by.*

(l) *wattābôʾ wattaʿamôd mēʾāz habbōqer weʿad-ʿattāh.* As noted by some authorities, translating *wattaʿamôd* with "standing on her feet" (i.e. "working without stop") stretches the meaning of the verb *ʿāmad* in a manner elsewhere unparalleled (cf. Campbell, 1975: 95). The text is sometimes emended to **wattaʿamôr*, "she gleaned" (Rudolph, 1962: 46). It should be noted, however, that our translation for this verb, "to wait for, to await," is supported by OT parallels (BDB, 764,3, a).

Despite apparent difficulties with rendering *mēʾāz* as "from (the time)" (see Campbell, 1975: 95), context and parallel occurrences (e.g. Exod. 4:10; Lachish letter 3:7; Ps. 76:8) might support the rendering offered above.

(m) Concerning the elusive search for an acceptable translation for *zeh šibtāh habbayit meʿaṭ*, see Lys, 1971: 496-501; Rudolph, 1962: 46-47; Campbell, 1975: 95. The above rendering is not entirely satisfactory; yet it ought, nevertheless, to resolve a few of our above difficulties. We understand *zeh* as an enclitic of time (GKC, 136d; BDB, P. 261, 41), thus permitting the overseer to add *his* comment on the matter at hand. The overseer tells Boaz that this young lady is the same woman who returned with Naomi from Bethlehem. Beattie (1973) unconvincingly views this phrase as a pre-LXX midrashic explanation.

Boaz and Ruth: The First Encounter (2:8-13)

8 Boaz said to Ruth: "Now listen, young lady,[a] do not go to glean

in another field. You should not leave this one,[b] **but keep close**[c]
9 to my girls. Keep your eyes on the field that they are reaping, and glean behind them. The men have been ordered not to interfere with you;[d] so that, should you thirst,[e] you are free to go to the jars and drink from the water that the men have drawn."

10 She threw herself forward, touching the ground with her forehead,[f] and asked: "Why is it that I pleased you[g] enough to notice me? I am but a foreigner!".[h]

11 "I have been fully told," Boaz replied, "all that you have done[i] with your mother-in-law after your husband's death. You forsook father, mother, and native land to join a people you scarcely knew
12 previously. May the Lord repay your good deed. May your full reward come from the Lord, God of Israel, under whose wings you seek shelter."

13* Ruth answered: "I must have pleased you, my lord,[j] since you have comforted me and have spoken tenderly to your maidservant.[k] Yet, I am not[l] even considered as one of your maidservants."

2:8-9. We could imagine Boaz addressing Ruth in a tone that was, if not stern, perhaps patriarchal. He was, after all, owner of the field upon whose munificence Ruth depended. We do note, however, a number of points of interest. In welcoming her to join "his girls" in gleaning, Boaz nevertheless is careful to instruct Ruth to work behind *them. By assuring her that his men have been instructed not to interfere with her, Boaz in reality is permitting little more than the customs of gleaning required of him. Boaz does, however, grant Ruth a privilege that might not have been expected: he allows her to share the water that his workers have drawn from the wells. But to repeat: Boaz's first speech to the Moabitess shows him exceeding the "correct" behavior expected of a* gibbôr ḥayil *by very little indeed.*

(a) *halôʾ šāmaʿat bittî.* For the interrogative sentence as a vehicle for expressing positive wishes and demands, see GKC, 150e (p. 474). Depending on the context, we have translated *bittî* literally ("[my] daughter") or with the extended meaning ("young lady").

(b) *lōʾ taʿabûrî mizzeh.* An alternate rendering could be: "Do not transgress this [command]." It should be stated that this usage of the verb *ʿābar* is normally confined to transgression of divine or royal commands and statutes (BDB, 717 [i,h]). Despite this, however, a rendering such as the one suggested here might free the text from an apparent redundancy, since *mizzeh* would no longer refer to the "field" (localis), but to "command," while the following *wekōh*, considered by some scholars as superfluous (Joüon, 1953: 52; but see Rudolph, 1962: 47 [8,1]; Campbell, 1975: 97), would retain its connection with the word "field." Thus, the whole section would read: "Is it understood, daughter, that you ought not to glean in another field? [Furthermore,] you are not to transgress this [command], but must keep close to my girls *here*!."

On the peculiarities of the form *taʿabûrî*, see Myers, 1955: 10, 17. Note that *lōʾ* could be used to render a command more emphatically (GKC, 190d [p. 322], 107 [p. 317]).

(c) The use of the verb *dābaq*, "to stick to, cleave, keep close to," as a *leitmotif* has been alluded to above (*sub* 1:14). Only in this example and in that of 2:21, however, is it constructed with the preposition *ʿîm*, "with." In 1:14 and 2:23, *dābaq* is found with the preposition *b-*, also meaning "with," a usage that is better attested to in the OT.

2:9. Boaz's generosity stops very much short of granting Ruth's request for permission to glean among the sheaves.

(d) *halōʾ ṣiwwîtî ʾet-hanneʿārîm lebiltî nogʿēk*. For this type of construction, an interrogative to be taken as an asseverative, see above on verse 8. The verb *nāgaʿ* hardly means "to molest" (RSV and others; AB: "to bother"), since it is unlikely that in the midst of the harvest, Ruth was to be pounced upon by crazed Bethlehemites. Even if one were to adopt the most innocuous meaning for the verb "to molest," it would certainly have been an infraction against the most elemental forms of courtesy and custom, should a widow be "molested" as she gleaned. Since this statement of Boaz prefaces one that exhorts his workers to permit Ruth access to communal water, it is not unlikely that Boaz was ordering his men not to shoo her away should she seek water from the communal jars.

(e) On *ṣāmît*, "should you thirst," see Myers, 1955: 53.

Referring to the verbal forms employed in Boaz's speech, Humbert (1958: 92) has this to say: "le narrateur [de Ruth] a soin de faire parler Boaz comme les gens âgés, car il lui fait employer des formes verbales archaïsantes et solemnelles qu'il mettra aussi dans la bouche de Naomi, mais qu'aucun autre interlocuteur n'emploie dans l'histoire de

Ruth. Il veut évidemment souligner par là la gravité de Boaz et prévient tacitement toute compromettante interprétation des prévenances de cet homme d'âge mûr." Campbell (1975:110) holds a similar position. We question, however, the notion that Boaz was aged at the time of his meeting with Ruth (see below).

2:10. With this verse, Ruth engaged Boaz into a conversation the import of which will become readily apparent. At this stage, we should note that Ruth is not satisfied merely to respond with words of thanks, but to elicit further statements from Boaz.

(f) *wattippōl ʿal-pāneyhā wattištaḥu ʾārṣāh.* For this idiom see Myers, 1955: 131, 18, 23. The root **ḥwy* apparently means "to strike" (UT, 19, 847). Thus, the meaning of the *S* (causative) *t* (reflexive) form is "to cause one's head to strike [the ground]." Emerton, 1977, unconvincingly tries to revive a derivation from the root *šāḥāh.* This is somewhat an exaggerated display of gratitude for the limited amount of privilege which Boaz granted to Ruth. The verb is usually reserved for usage in connection with deities, prophets, kings, and other potentates.

(g) On *māṣāʾtî ḥēn,* see above, *sub* 2:2.

(h) *lehakkîrēnî weʾānōkî nokriyyāh.* The play on words here is double: a metaphonic one which plays on the root **nkr: lehakkîr,* "to recognize" (in a friendly manner); and *nokriyyāh,* "a [female] foreigner"; and a parasonantic one that emphasizes the consonants *n* and *k.* On these terms, see IDBS, p. 969.

The term *nokriyyāh,* "foreigner," has been studied by Humbert (1958b). He points out that *nokrî,* and obviously its feminine counterpart, *nokriyyāh,* should not necessarily be restricted to the meaning "foreigner, stranger." On at least four occasions in the OT (Gen. 31:15; Exod. 21:8; Ps. 69:9; Job 19:15), to which I should like to add our reference in Ruth, the term may be better understood as someone who is not recognized as a member of a "family." Thus, when Ruth speaks of being "recognized, noticed," she may be implying more than Boaz would care to accept. With Humbert (1958: 93) we imagine Ruth broadly hinting acceptance into Boaz's clan, or perhaps better, into his "family." See also the discussion of Martin-Achard (THAT, II, 67-68 [3-4]). A. Bertholet, mentioned with approval by Loretz (1960: 393), thinks that Boaz's blessing will necessarily be fulfilled only when Ruth bears children. "The irony of the situation," adds Loretz "lies in the fact that Boaz, without realizing it, speaks of himself."

2:11-12. For reasons that were purposeful or otherwise, it is clear from Boaz's reply that he does not immediately respond to Ruth's overtures. Instead, he first offers a generous accolade to Ruth's deeds by way of explaining his orders to his men (verses 8-9). In the genuinely moving words of verse 12, he leaves any further recompense to God. This may be somewhat equivalent to the Arabic **ʾallah yaʿṭîk(î)**, *"May God give you," a formula automatically addressed to beggars and other seekers of help. For an Akkadian equivalent of the imagery in* **pāraś kenāpayim**, *note the inscription of Tiglath-Pileaser I,* ca. *1100* B.C., *which speaks of "[the god] Ashur, whose wings were spread like an eagle's over his land" (Grayson, 1976: 17 [§53]).*

As in verse 4 (see above), Boaz's speech as recorded in verse 11 may contain yet one more allusion to the patriarchal period. Specifically, it refers to Abraham forsaking his native land to journey toward Canaan (Gen. 12:1-9).

The construction of verse 12 and its archaic quality have been discussed by Campbell. I refer to his discussion (1975: 99-100) and wish to add only that this verse is divisible into four cola, the first two of which are framed by derivatives of the root, **šlm**, *thus creating what is called "metaphonic" paronomasia: 12a:* **yešallēm YHWH poʿolēk** *(eight syllables); 12b:* **ûtehî maśkurtēk šelēmāh** *(eight syllables).*

On the words **poʿolēk**, *"your deed,"* **maśkurtēk**, *"your full reward," and* **kenapāyw**, *"His wings," see Campbell, 1975: 99-100. On* **kānāp**, *"wing," as applied to a deity, see Joüon, 1953: 55. This poetic usage is elsewhere confined to Psalms, BDB, 489 (l,h). On Ruth's allusion to* **kānāp**, *see below,* sub *3:9. Basing himself on LXX's "καὶ ἰδοὺ ἐγὼ ἔσομαι ὡς μία τῶν παιδισκῶν σου," Driver (1973: 107-8) understands* **lōʾ** *as bearing either a negative or interrogative sense and therefore translates: "and shall I not [or,] and I shall indeed become like one of thy hand-maidens." This translation would presume, however, too much authority for Ruth in that she is given the power to change her own status.*

(i) Scribal addition, *qērē welōʾ ketîb: ʾet kol ʾašer*. This addition is preserved mostly in manuscripts of Eastern traditions.

2:13. Undaunted, Ruth tries once more to secure her desires. This time, however, she is less subtle in her approach.

(j) It is difficult to accept the common rendering that has *ʾemṣā* -

ḥēn beʿêneykā ʾadōnî as an optative (e.g. AB: "May I continue to find favor in your eyes, my lord"), since this sentence is linked to two verbs, both of which are in the perfect form (*niḥamtānî, dibbartā*). JPS (1969) has: "You are most kind, my lord, to comfort me . . . etc. . . ."; but this fails to communicate Ruth's role in eliciting acts of kindness from Boaz. What we are dealing with in this case is a causal clause introduced by an imperfect which is followed by perfects, with *kî* as a causal conjunction, GKC, 158 (p. 492).

(k) *wekî dibbartā ʿal-lēb šipḥāteka*. Wolff (1974: 42) thinks that the expression *ledabbēr ʿal-lēb* belongs to the language of courtship. Its appearance at this juncture of the narrative of *Ruth*, however, does not support this contention. It would simply be too presumptuous of Ruth to employ such a vocabulary so prematurely. Campbell (1975: 100-1) is correct in arguing for a meaning close to our own.

šipḥāh is translated, above, as "maidservant" and carefully distinguished from *ʾāmāh* of 3:9, "handmaid." These translations are but approximate, since English does not contain exact equivalents. As has been argued by some scholars, but often heatedly denied by others, the two terms cannot be synonymous, simply because no two words ever refer to the same condition or situation. Jepsen (1958: 293-97, 425) is quite convincing in refusing to ascribe *ʾāmāh* to *E* and *šipḥāh* to *J*. Campbell (1975: 101) thinks that *šipḥāh* is used in 2:13 because it is cognate to the word *mišpāḥāh*, "clan, subtribe." While this observation is quite right, it does not seem, at least to me, to resolve the distinction between the two terms. Nor is the occurrence, which he cites, of the term *ʾāmāh* in the eighth-to-seventh-century sepulcher of any help in the matter.

I share in the opinion that the terms were quite distinct, with *šipḥāh* originally applied to females belonging to the lowest rungs of the social ladder (Joüon, 1953: 57), while *ʾāmāh* probably represented women who could become wives or concubines of freemen. It could be said that a *šipḥāh* was a female who, given as gift to accompany a bride, was expected to perform menial labor. That, in moments of sterility, a married woman could present her husband a *šipḥāh* to bear a child does not change the latter's status. In the eyes of her master, the father of the child, she remained a *šipḥāh*. On certain occasions, however, a *šipḥāh* might be called a *ʾāmāh*, especially from the point of view of a third party (e.g. Gen. 21:10). In many episodes of the Bible, however, the two terms are freely interchanged, especially so in cases in which a woman needs to convey deference to whomever she addressed (e.g. the Abigail/David episode of 1 Sam. 25). In the context of *Ruth,* we should note that what is meant by *šipḥāh* is clearly outlined in verses 15-16, on which see below. In conclusion, what Ruth is saying to Boaz in verse 13 is as follows: "Were I one of your maidservants [*šipḥāh*], then all this kindness of yours would be understandable." Ruth, of course, had the last word in the first dialogue.

(1) We cannot accept Nötscher's suggestion (1953: 375; mentioned with approval by Dahood, 1965: 328) that *lōʾ* in 2:13 be taken as an emphatic, "certainly, truly." That, of course, would be to miss the point which pricked Boaz's conscience.

Boaz Responds (2:14-18a)

14 At mealtime, Boaz said to her: "Come over here[a] and share in
the meal,[b] dipping your morsel in the vinegar."[c] As she sat beside
the reapers,[d] [Boaz] handed[e] her roasted grain.[f] She ate her fill,
yet still had some left over.[g]
15 When Ruth resumed her gleaning, Boaz ordered his men[h] as follows: "You are not only to permit her to glean among the sheaves
16 without rebuke,[i] but you must also pull some stalks out[j] of the bundles, dropping them for her to glean, without ever scolding her."[k]
17 So Ruth gleaned in the field until dusk. When she beat out her
18a gleanings, it amounted to an ephah of barley. This she carried, and
proceeded to town.

2:14-18a. These verses report Boaz's actions after he pondered over Ruth's request. It is obvious that, this time, Boaz goes much further in securing privileges for Ruth. It would seem that these privileges might even be considered as more generous than rights accorded to a šipḥāh, *a woman who belonged to the lower stratum of society.*

(a) *wayyōʾmer lāh bōʿaz leʿēt hāʾōkel gōšî halōm. . . .* Despite LXX and Vulgate, most commentators rightly understand *leʿēt haʿōkel*, "at mealtime," to depend on the preceding "Boaz said to her" rather than on the succeeding *gōšî*, "come over here." An elaborate explanation for this position is given by Joüon, 1953: 35-36. See also Rudolph, 1962: 47;

Campbell, 1975: 102. Not only would a discourse about meal sharing seem inopportune were it immediately to follow Ruth's hints of verse 13, but it would seriously have marred the tension created by the lapse of time in which Boaz decided Ruth's future treatment. This, of course, will sharply be contrasted with another decision left up to Boaz, on which see 3:10-13.

The anomalous *gōšî*, rather than the expected **gešî*, has been explained by analogy to *bōʾî* (Joüon, 1953: 58; Myers, 1955: 18). It should be noted, however, that *gōšû*, also considered as "anomalous," occurs in Josh. 3:9 and 1 Sam. 14:38.

(b) *leḥem* might be taken in its widest sense, "food," rather than "bread."

(c) *ḥōmeṣ*, a liquid, was possibly a product of soured mash. We retain the traditional rendering "vinegar," but wish to refer the reader to Campbell's statements (1975: 102) that discuss the OT attestations of this term.

(d) *wattēšeb miṣṣad haqqōṣerîm*. It is to be noted that this act of sitting on the same side as the reapers must certainly have implied acceptance in the "familia." Beyond receiving water promised her in verse 9, she is now to share in the communal meal. Furthermore, Boaz himself introduces her in the circle of his family by presenting her with the first handfuls of roasted grain, *qālî*. It is not impossible that this act of Boaz was ceremonial, perhaps quasi-legal, in nature.

(e) *wayyiṣboṭ-lāh (qālî)*. The verb *ṣābaṭ* occurs nowhere else in the OT. The root is known in West Semitic as occurring in the Ugaritic word *mṣbṭm* (UT, 19: 2139), usually translated as "tongs, handles." Late Hebrew knows of a *bêyt haṣṣebiṭāh* (BDB, 840) with a meaning similar to the Ugaritic. The verb could be related to a very commonly used verb in Akkadian, *ṣabātu*, "to seize," especially so, when it is observed that Akkadian does not tolerate two emphatic consonants, in our case *ṣādē* and *ṭet*, in the same vocable. We might also state that *ṣebātîm*, which occurs in verse 16 and which is also a *hapax legomenon*, is nothing but another form of the same root; but one which has, apparently, preserved the form better attested in East Semitic. In this respect, it is worth noting that the Akkadian of Ugarit would, at times (e.g. PRU, 4: p. 110: 21), record the verb as *ṣabāṭu*, thus "bridging" the variance between the East and West Semitic forms. This position, that **ṣbṭ* and **ṣbt*, are but alternate spellings of the same root attested in Akkadian *ṣabātu*, could be bolstered by the LXX, which understands both as derived from the same form. Humbert (1949-50) thinks *ṣebātîm* of verse 16 should be rendered "handfuls."

(f) *qālî*, "roasted grain," played an important role in the diet of the lower classes. On the East Semitic equivalent, see CAD, *sub laptu* (B), AHw, *sub qalû(m)*. On the Hittite evidence, see Hoffner, 1974: 77. Note also 1 Sam. 17:17; 25:18; 2 Sam. 17:28. Grain used for this purpose could be roasted, thus cracking the kernels to make them easier to eat, or simply left to dry on the roofs of houses. On Dalman's supposition that it was wheat that the harvesters ate, see Campbell, 1975: 103.

(g) The series of three verbs, linked by three *waw* consecutives, which conclude verse 14 ("She *ate* her *fill*, yet still *had* some *left over* [*wattō*ʾ*kal wattiśba*ʿ *wattōtar*].") are meant to emphasize Boaz's generosity.

2:15-16. Verse 15 shows Boaz as taking further steps to establish Ruth's newly acquired position. Among these is the order permitting her to gather among the sheaves. As noted above, under 2:7, this was precisely what Ruth was seeking. Verse 16, on the other hand, indicates that Boaz was deeply affected by Ruth. Acting beyond the call of charity or courtesy, he commands his men to abandon in her path grain that has already been reaped.

(h) *ne*ʿ*ārāyw* is rendered above as "men." In view of 2:5, however, we might presume that "overseers" is meant here.

(i) *taklîmûhā*. The *hiph*ʿ*îl* of **klm* is usually rendered by "humiliate, shame, disgrace." This appears to be too strong. For this reason, Joüon (1953: 60) considers the verb **kl*ʾ, "to restrain," as the probable reading in the text of *Ruth* which Jerome translated. A probable translation, however, might be arrived at were we to consider our verb either as paralleling the verb *gā*ʿ*ar* of the following verse, or as representing a hostile act that is just a shade below *gā*ʿ*ar* in intensity. Since *gā*ʿ*ar* followed by the preposition *b* clearly means something like "to rebuke, to scold," we arrive at a meaning for the *hiph*ʿ*îl* of **klm* which, in our context, is satisfactory. Similar sentiments may have been expressed in the chapter 28 of the *Instructions of Amenemope*, an Egyptian wisdom text of the early first millennium B.C. Lichtheim's translation of XXVI: 9-10 (1976: 161) is quoted here: "Do not pounce [verb: *gm*ʾ*i*] on a widow when you find her (gleaning) in the fields/ And then fail to be patient [verb: *w3ḥ*] with her reply." For the verb *gm*ʾ*i*, others have translated, "expose, recognize, find," for it is clear that Lichtheim's "pounce" should be understood as an act of verbal rather than physical violence.

(j) *šōl-tāšollû* is a form that has presented difficulties to commentators. None of the responses has been satisfactory. See the notes in Joüon, 1953: 60-61; Rudolph, 1962: 47; Myers, 1955: 24; Campbell, 1975: 103-4). The meaning of the verb, however, is rather clear.

(k) On the theological aspect of the verb *gāʿar*, see McIntosh, 1969: 473-74.

2:17. The extent of Boaz's generosity is indicated by the fact that Ruth gathered as much as one ephah *of grain. Depending on the differing calculations of modern authorities, this would amount anywhere from twenty-nine to fifty pounds of grain (IDB, IV, 834-35; Campbell, 1975: 104). We agree with the latter's opinion that "The amount Ruth carried home was rather impressive for a gleaner, but we are not called upon to add to her list of virtues that she was as strong as an ox." Given the fact that at Mari of the Old Babylonian period, the ration of a* male *worker rarely exceeded one to two pounds per day, we are impressed by Ruth's ability to gather enough to last her and her mother-in-law a few weeks. On the Mari evidence, see Bottéro, 1958: 272 and note Gelb, 1965: 230-33. According to 1 Sam. 17:17, an* ephah *of grain satisifed a number of fighting men. See also Judg. 6:19.*

The Report (2:18b-23)

18b* Her mother-in-law saw[a] how much she had gleaned when Ruth brought
19* out the leftovers from her full meal[b] in order to give them to her.
"Where did you glean today?" asked Naomi, "and how did you accomplish
it?[c] Blessed be he who took notice of you."[d] She revealed to her
mother-in-law that which she accomplished with him, adding: "The man
with whom I dealt today is called Boaz."[e]

20 Naomi said to her daughter-in-law: "Blessed be he to the Lord,
who has not withheld his kindness from the living or the dead."[f]
"The man is kin to us,"[g] continued Naomi, "He is one of those in a
21 position to redeem us."[h] Ruth of Moab[i] added: "He even told me to

remain close to his men[j] until they finished harvesting his fields."
22 Naomi declared to Ruth, her daughter-in-law: "It is best daughter,
that you join his girls[k] and not be pressed into another field."[l]
23 So she kept close to Boaz's girls, gleaning until the end of the
barley and wheat harvests. Meanwhile she lived with her mother-in-law.

(a) No need to emend *wattērēʾ ḥamôtāh*, "her mother-in-law saw," into *wattarʾ (ʾet) ḥamôtāh*, "She [Ruth] showed her mother-in-law" just to harmonize the MT with some of the readings in the Vulgate (Rudolph, 1962: 50). A series of verbs need not be monotonously conjugated with the same person as subject.

(b) *hôtīrāh-min*. Joüon (1953: 62) is surely right in contrasting "she had a surplus from. . . ." with 1:5 in which Naomi is said to have "survived (her two sons and her husband)." Compare also *rēyqam* of 1:21, said of Naomi, to the same word as it is applied to Ruth in 3:17.

2:19. It is clear from the manner in which Ruth failed to mention the name of her benefactor until the end of her report that no one expected her, least of all Naomi, to succeed so quickly in achieving her goal. The storyteller must certainly be trying to convey the sense of triumph which Ruth felt, since by repeating, almost verbatim, *statements made in the same verse, he delays what must have been Ruth's crowning "punch line."*

(c) *ʾēypōh liqqaṭṭ hayyôm weʾānāh ʿāśît*. As has been generally maintained, Naomi must have been posing two different questions. Joüon (1953: 63) considers the text to be faulty. But Stinespring (1944: 101) offers the following for the second question: "To what purpose did you work?" The translation offered above is tentative, deriving its justification from the following considerations: (1) Naomi has already been presented with the results of Ruth's work; to wit, the large amount of barley which Ruth brought back from her gleanings. (2) The verb *ʿāśāh*, "to do [work]," albeit construed with the preposition *ʿim*, "[together] with," is repeated again in Ruth's reply, for which see below.

(d) *makkîrēk*. Based on the root **nkr*, this vocable reminds one of the play on words of 2:10, for which see above. Humbert (1958: 94[n.3]) correctly perceives the thrust of the writer in using this word: "Il y a ici, implicitement la même antithèse qa'à II, 10, car *makkīrēk* s'oppose naturellement à sa qualité de *nŏkriyyā*: 'Béni soit celui qui t'a reconnue pour la sienne!', alors que tu n'es qu'une étrangère que, par definition, on ne reconnaît précisément pas pour sienne. A noter au surplus le rythme (3 accents) de cette bénédiction."

(e) Ruth's reply to her mother-in-law's questions is contained in two sentences that balance each other in their vocabulary. Whereas most translations of Naomi's two inquiries (see above) reflect an awareness that they essentially differ, the renderings of Ruth's response are generally couched in identical language. Hence, these renderings promote a certain redundancy that may not be legitimate. The LXX, it should be noted at the outset, does preserve a reading for Ruth's reply which avoids any redundancy. That reading, however, cannot be harmonized with the Hebrew text which reads:

a. wattagēd laḥamôtāh ʾēt ʾăšer-ʿāśetāh ʿimmô

b. wattōʾmer šēm hāʾîš ʾăšer ʿāśîtî ʿimmô hayyôm bōʿaz

In both segments the personal pronoun attached to the preposition *ʿim* does not necessarily refer to a specific individual; for, at this stage of the narrative, Ruth is clearly keeping to the end of her account that piece of information which is most crucial to the plot.

The verbs that are used in these passages display nuances that may be of import to us. *lehaggid*, "to relate, reveal, inform," and so forth, presumes that an elaborate retelling of events was presented by Ruth upon her return home. Thus, the direct object of the verb, *ʾēt ʾăšer-ʿāśetāh ʿimmô*, "that which she accomplished with him," is but a phrase used to avoid repeating details of Ruth's interview with Boaz. The verb *ʾāmar*, "to say, to state," on the other hand, is much more precise, oftentimes demanding that a definite statement follow. The vocabulary of the two sentences attributed to Ruth warns us against considering them as redundant. By withholding from her mother-in-law until the very end of her report the name of her benefactor or, to be more precise, the name of the man under whose protection she had now come to be, Ruth's main purpose was to indicate how quickly she was realizing the objectives she had stated in 2:2. This explanation would account for the presence of *hayyôm*, "today," a word which would otherwise be superfluous. See, further, the comments of Campbell (1975: 106).

2:20. Upon learning of Ruth's remarkable success, Naomi reveals an important dimension of her own legal status vis-à-vis Boaz.

(f) The phrase *bārûk hû) laYHWH)ăšer lō)-(āzab ḥasdô)et-haḥayyîm we)et-hammētîm*, contains a crux that has received wide notice. Glueck's monograph on *Ḥesed in the Bible* (1967: 40-42) has influenced some commentators to regard Boaz as the antecedent of the relative pronoun *)ăšer*. Among his reasons are the following: (1) God's *ḥesed* is not attested as extending to the dead. (This argument's merits, however, are somewhat weakened if one considers "the living and the dead" as nothing but a *merismus* meaning "everyone.") (2) In 1:8, and again in 3:10, those who display *ḥesed* toward the dead are humans. (3) Glueck offers the narrative of 2 Sam. 2:5 as paralleling the blessing of our text. Other scholars are unconvinced by Glueck's arguments and prefer to relate *)ăšer* to YHWH. LXX is equally as ambiguous as the Hebrew text, and thus offers little succour in this respect. Campbell (1975: 106) alludes to Gen. 24:27 as offering a blessing similar in intent but one in which YHWH is clearly the benefactor. He notes, but dismisses perhaps a bit too hastily, the fact that the verbs in both examples differ only in their usage of prepositions.

In our translation we have followed Glueck's presentation; but we would like to make it clear that our endorsement is lukewarm. It may be that this vexing problem could be resolved, admittedly a bit too neatly, by regarding *)ăšer* as a conjunction with a causal force rather than as a relative pronoun. It is worth noting that BDB, 83 (8c), regards the passage alluded to by Glueck, 2 Sam. 2:5, as understandable whether *)ăšer* is taken as a conjunction or as a pronoun. Thus our passage in 2:20 would become "blessed be he to the Lord, *since* he has not withheld. . . ." In such a case, the actor could only be Yahweh. "The living and the dead" will have to be considered either as a *merismus*, as suggested above, or as a "proof-text" for His *ḥesed* to have extended to the dead. Porten (1976: 15) suggests that *(āzab* (root: *(zb*) may have been a pun on the name Boaz (root: *b(z*). In view of the context, this is very convincing.

On the "causative conjunction" *)ăšer*, followed by a verb in the perfect, in a spoken context, see MacDonald, 1975: 167-68.

(g) On *qārôb lānû hā)îš*, see comments *sub* 2:1.

(h) *miggō)alēnû hû)*. This statement introduces the figure of the *gō)ēl* and by extension, the concept of *ge)ullāh*. We shall have more to say on these topics later on. At this stage, let it be noted that the possibility of Boaz functioning as *gōʾēl* is first raised by Naomi, and not by Ruth. We make this clear at the outset since it shall be argued that the marriage of Ruth to Boaz is not necessarily to be connected with his role as a *gōʾēl*.

A number of manuscripts show *miggōʾalēnû* as written with a *yod* between the *lamed* and the *nûn*, but it is not clear whether or not our text is to be considered defectively written. See the comments in Joüon, 1953: 64; Rudolph, 1962: 51; Campbell, 1975: 107-8.

Staples (1938: 62-65) offers a contorted translation of our passage. Staples ultimately bases his translation, "The man is near unto us, [but] he is not our *gôʾel*," upon the hypothesis that a given family could have but one *gōʾēl*. Meek (1960:332-33) adopts a similar approach and renders: "The man is a relative of ours; he is next after our next-of-kin." While it may very well be that, ultimately, no more than a single individual ends up redeeming a striken family, it does not follow that the pool of potential redeemers was restricted at the outset to one person. Indeed, it would have been impossible for the scenario of chapter 4 to have been successfully staged had there been but one *gōʾēl* on the horizon for Ruth and Naomi. See also the criticism in Rudolph, 1962: 55, *sub* 3:2, and that in Rowley, 1965: 188[n.3].

2:21-22. Ruth reveals to her mother-in-law some of the steps taken by Boaz to confirm the Moabitess as a member of his clan. Far from displaying any annoyance at thus seeing her daughter-in-law under the immediate protection of another member of the clan, Naomi urges her to accept. However, as we shall note below, there is a crucial, albeit subtle, discrepancy in their vocabulary.

(i) *hammôʾabîyyāh*, "the Moabitess." Because there seems to be no particular reason for adding an ethnicon at this juncture of the narrative, many scholars (e.g. Joüon: 1953: 64-65; Rudolph, 1962: 51) prefer to replace it with LXX's "to her mother-in-law." However, as pointed out by Campbell (1975: 107), such a reading would also be superfluous. It seems to me that this mention of Ruth's background, as much as the reference to her relationship to Naomi in 2:22, may not have been accidental. The writer may be stressing that Ruth's connections with her native land and her mother-in-law will not be forgotten despite her newly forged links with Boaz and his *familia*. In view of the events that will occur in subsequent episodes, the storyteller may have felt it particularly important to underscore these points before proceeding further.

(j) *hanne⁽ārîm*, "[my] men." It is this concession of Boaz's which must have been most important to Ruth's new status and, of course, to the realization of the storyteller's plot. In our judgment, therefore, it would be mistaken to correct the text in order to read **na⁽arôtay*, "my girls," despite the fact that some LXX manuscripts try to harmonize this with Naomi's statement of verse 22.

(k) *na⁽arôtāyw*, "his girls." In view of Naomi's advice to Ruth as related in the following chapter, it is not surprising to note that Naomi's vision of Ruth's acceptance into Boaz's *familia* stresses advantages that differed from those expected by Ruth. An alternate translation which takes *kî* in its corroborative sense could be: "Good, my daughter! Do go out, indeed, with his girls so that some people may not urge you into another field."

(l) *welō᾽ yipge⁽û-bāk beśādeh ᾽aḥēr*. The verb *pāga⁽* basically means "to chance upon, to meet." Fortunate or adverse connotations in the employment of this verb largely depend on the context. In 1:16, *pāga⁽ be-* is usually translated as "to entreat [someone]." There is no overwhelming reason to believe that in this context Naomi's usage of this vocabulary differs radically from that of 1:16. Translations such as AB's "Then they will not *be rough with you* in another field," or JPS[2]'s ". . . and not *be annoyed* in some other field," (emphasis mine in both quotations), would allow the impression of uncouth Bethlehemite reapers about to attack a defenseless widow; in broad daylight and in the middle of a busy harvesting season at that! There is, I think, no need to accept the evidence of some Hebrew manuscripts and render: "she returned to [*wattāšob* ᾽*el*] her mother-in-law." As is correctly pointed out by Campbell (1975: 108-9), there is a need for a statement that would put a finishing touch at the end of each of the major scenes of *Ruth*. Rather than merely sharing his opinion and his translation ("Then she stayed (at home) with her mother-in-law") that this constitutes "a summarizing statement . . . which also points ahead," I imagine the storyteller is emphasizing, once more, that at this stage of his tale Ruth was not so completely taken into Boaz's *familia* that she no longer dwelled with Naomi. Until a *gō᾽ēl* is found for Naomi, it would certainly have been a cruel act on the part of Ruth, and all those concerned for that matter, to have left her to manage her old age all by herself. The plot, it will be seen, will become more complex, precisely to make proper provisions for everyone involved in the narrative.

We speculate on the mention of *qeṣîr haḥiṭṭîm*, "wheat harvest," below.

Naomi's Plan (3:1-5)

1 [One day,] Ruth's mother-in-law, Naomi, said: "Daughter, you
2 know that I seek for you a happy future.[a] You also know that Boaz,
whose girls you joined,[b] is our relative.[c] Now, he will be winnow-
3* ing barley at the threshing-floor tonight.[d] So bathe, put on perfume,
and dress up[e] before going down to the threshing-floor.[f] Your presence should not be known until after he finishes eating and drink-
4* ing;[g] then, as he lies down,[h] find out the place in which he plans
to sleep, approach him, bare his 'legs,' and lie down.[i] He will tell
you what next to do."[j]
5 "I will do as you say,"[k] answered Ruth.

3:1-2. The protagonist of this whole section is certainly Naomi. As she begins her monologue, Naomi devotes the first statements of verses 1-2 to presenting Ruth with reasons aimed at defeating any scruple and at quieting any anxiety which might, expectedly, have disturbed her daughter-in-law. Naomi asserts that her main concern is to provide Ruth with a welcome sense of security. She further reminds her of two matters worthy of consideration. First, that Boaz is one of their kinfolk; second, that he had already accepted Ruth as one of his girls, thus having welcomed her as a member of his familia. *Naomi may have understood that Ruth's protection was merely temporary, lasting only through the harvest season. Perhaps this is substantiated by 2:3 where Ruth is said to remain with Naomi although she was enjoying her newly found status. At any rate, in order to allay any doubts that may have lingered in Ruth's mind, Naomi finally assures her that it will be up to Boaz, and not up to a destitute widow, whether or not the relationship was to progress any further.*

(a) *mānôaḥ ʾăšer yîṭab-lāk:* *mānôaḥ* implies all the security and benefits which accrue to a woman as she enters married life; *ʾăšer yîṭab-lāk* could be rendered either as "which will please you," or "so that it will please you," depending on whether *ʾăšer* is taken as a relative pronoun or a conjunction. One cannot be as dogmatic as Rudolph (1962: 52) is on this point. Myers (1955: 25) finds this to be "apparently a Deuteronomic phrase."

(b) *ʾašer hāyît ʾet-naʿărôtāyw.* Because of 2:22, Joüon (1953: 67) thinks it better to read *neʿārāyw*, "his men." However, by emphasizing Ruth's relationship with Boaz's girls, Naomi is alluding not so much to Ruth's acceptance into the Boaz's clan, but to the sex of those in a position to be involved in the manner about to be described.

(c) *mōdaʿtānû*, a feminine (abstract?) form of the substantive *mydʿ*, which occurs in 2:11. There is no need to posit, as does Campbell (1975: 117), that a "separative *min* was lost from its prefixed position through haplography." On the grammatical peculiarity of the vocalization, see GKC, 256 (91f).

(d) *hinnēh-hûʾ zōreh ʾet-gōren haśśeʿōrîm hallāyelāh.* As pointed out by Hoftijzer (1965: 45), this sentence, which means literally: "He is the one who winnows the threshing floor of the barley," is quite unusual grammatically. With the possible exception of Lev. 15:33, it is unique in containing a transitive participle with *ʾet*, the last *not* functioning to indicate the direct object. On *hinnēh* as an element of "spoken" Hebrew, see MacDonald, 1975: 172. Contrast it with *wehinnēh* of 2:4.

Campbell (1975: 117-18) wonders about the correctness of the MT, which speaks of barley but not of wheat. Yet, according to 2:23, Ruth had gleaned in fields of barley, of an earlier crop, and of wheat. Campbell then questions Joüon's (1953: 67) understanding of the substantive "threshing-floor" as metonomic for the "product of the threshing-floor." Such an understanding would of course imply that the mention of barley, but not wheat, is but incidental. Campbell, therefore, proposes to read *šeʿārîm*, "gates," for the MT's *śeʿōrîm*, "barley." To bolster his point, Campbell alludes to 2 Kings 7:1-20, which contains a play on words on our vocables, whose consonants (*šʿr*) were not differentiated in the unpointed text. Despite Campbell's elaborate defense, his arguments are not totally convincing. The following reasons could be offered: (1) The word for "gate," *šaʿar*, occurs four times in *Ruth*, but only in the *singular*; while that for "barley," *śeʿorāh*, occurs six times, but only in the *plural*. (2) The threshing-floor mentioned in *Ruth* lay at some distance from the city gate. This conclusion could be drawn by contrasting the evidence of 4:1, which has Boaz *going up* to the gate of the city after leaving the threshing-floor, to that of 2:18 and 3:3, which has Ruth proceed from the city, *going down* to the threshing-floor. (3) By altering the word for "barley" into that for "gates," the *qāl* of the verb *zārāh* would be left without a direct object. This would be quite exceptional even if one takes into consideration the evidence of Exod. 32:20. We shall speculate on the mention of *śeʿōrîm* a bit further on: see *sub* 4:5.

Winnowing is a procedure that immediately followed threshing. In turn, winnowing is usually followed by sifting to make sure that only grains of barley or wheat are left behind. Any unbruised ear is thrown back, to be rethreshed. The winnowed and sifted grain is collected into heaps, shaped somewhat like a plump belly (Cant. 7:3). By means of a long fork, sometimes even a shorter shovel, the threshed grain is tossed up into the evening breeze, allowing the chaff to be carried some fifteen feet or more from the winnower. The straw falling at a shorter distance is picked up and used as fodder, while the chaff is collected and served to activate the fire. By sunset, the winnowing process normally ended, for the breeze blowing eastward from the sea would lose much of its strength. On this topic, see IDB, I, 59; IV, 852; EB, I, 84; de Moor, 1971: 210-15; Joüon, 1953: 67-68. It is difficult to accept the often stated proposal that *laylāh*, meaning "night," should be here interpreted as "evening" (Joüon, 1953: 67). Campbell (1975: 117), also resisting Joüon's proposal, points out that the author of *Ruth* could easily have used the word for "evening," *ʿereb*, as he did in 2:17.

One meets frequently with the explanation that Boaz's nocturnal activity was nothing but a vigil to protect his grain from thievery. Such an explanation however, cannot be taken too seriously. Boaz was far too important a man to keep watch through the night; he most certainly could have asked one of his many "men" to assume such a charge. Additionally, it would certainly have been strange for any man to prepare for an all-night vigil by copiously consuming food and drink. It cannot be avoided, therefore, that Boaz's activity at the threshing-floor must have satisfied different requirements. The fact that Naomi was aware of his intention to winnow grain, consume a meal, then spend the night in the open air of the threshing-floor, should evidently be interpreted to mean that this particular activity of Boaz was commonly known to anyone acquainted with Bethlehemite practices. Occurring as it does at the end of the harvest season, a period which saw many festivities, Boaz's act was possibly linked to ceremonial, if not cultic, preparations. We shall return to this subject with more detail later on.

3:3. Humbert, 1958: 98-99: "As to Ruth's preparation, its meaning is beyond doubt; it is a prelude to marriage (cf. Ezek 16:8; Est. 2:12; Judith 10:3). . . ." Humbert's reference to Ezek. 16 is worth highlighting by means of generous quotation from RSV since it contains elements that will be of interest to us:

When I [the Lord] passed by you [Jerusalem] again and looked upon you, behold, you were at the age of love; and I spread my skirt over you [wā᾿eprōs kenāpî ʿālayik], *and covered your nakedness; yea, I plighted my troth to you and entered into a covenant with you, says the Lord God, and you became mine. Then I bathed you with water* [wā᾿erḥāṣēk bammayim] *and washed off your blood from you, and annointed you with oil* [wā᾿asukēk baššamen]. *I clothed you also with embroidered cloth* [wā᾿albîšēk riqmāh] *and shod you with leather, I swathed you in fine linen and covered you with silk, And I decked you with ornaments, and put bracelets on your arms, and a chain on your neck. And I put a ring on your nose, and earrings in your ears, and a beautiful crown upon your head. . . . (verses 8-12).*

In contrast with Humbert's statement, echoed by other scholars, we might quote Joüon's (1953: 68) assessment of Ruth's toilette: *"Ruth was to bathe and anoint herself with aromatic oil (cf., Judith 10:3), not so much to please Boaz, but to show respect for a man whom she considers as much above her in status."*

These two quotations are fairly representative of two opposite viewpoints regarding the events that transpired at the threshing-floor. On the one hand, a number of scholars believe that Boaz and Ruth declared their troth; but nevertheless they differ on whether or not the marriage was consummated that very night. On the other hand, a number of commentators think the episode to have ended with nothing more than a commitment on the part of Boaz to resolve the difficulties experienced by Ruth and Naomi. Note for example, how a recent commentator (Campbell, 1975: 138) concluded his discussion of this episode: "It is not prudery which compels the conclusion that there was no sexual intercourse at the threshing-floor; it is the utter irrelevance of such a speculation. What the scene must end with is something far more fitting, the clear evidence of Boaz' determination to care for these two widows as custom and generosity dictate."

Our opinion on the matter will become clear shortly. At this stage, let it be said that a position such as Campbell's aside from being a bit too cavalier about an important point of discussion, cannot be maintained. It seems to us that a verse as crucial as 4:5 is to the resolution of the narrative would not be properly understood without positing the fact that Ruth and Boaz were betrothed that very night, at the conclusion of the barley harvest.

(e) *werāḥaṣt wāsakt weśamt *śmltk* [*MT: śimlōta(y)ik*] *ʿālayik.* Naomi's instructions are given in a series of verbs conjugated in the perfect form, with *waw conversives* attached as preformatives. Campbell (1975: 120) remarks on the unusual and arresting syntax. It is interesting to note the sequence of verbs in 2 Sam. 12:20 linked by the narrator to convey David's acceptance of the death of the child which Bathsheba bore him: "Then David arose from the earth, and washed and anointed himself, and changed his clothes [*wayyirḥaṣ wayyāsek wayyeḥalēp śimlōtāw*]. . . ."

We have cuneiform evidence that in Mesopotamian society bathing, anointing, and donning one's fineries were activities, possibly ritualistic if not ceremonial in nature, which engaged the bride as she prepared herself for marriage. On these ceremonies, see Greengus, 1966: 61ff. Evidence for these activities is often best preserved within a corpus of documents that have oftentimes been labeled as "hieros-gamos' texts." These documents recount the manner in which Inanna (Ishtar) and Dumuzi (Tammuz) were joined in holy marriage. Despite their religious, even theological, garb, it should not be doubted that such customs represented actual events that took place among mortals. I quote a segment relevant to us from Kramer (1963: 497-99 [= ANET[3], 639]): "Inanna, at the command of her mother,/ Bathed, anointed herself with goodly oil,/ Covered her body with noble *pala*-garment,/ Took. . ., her dowry,/ Arranged the lapis lazuli about (her) neck,/ Grasped (her) seal in her hand./ The lady directed her step,/ Opened the door for (?) Dumuzi,/ In (?) the house she came forth to him like the light of the moon,/ Gazed at him, rejoiced for him,/ Embraced him . . ." (11. 12-22; see also Falkenstein, 1950: 325-27).

The term *wesakt* is derived from the verb **swk* which, in some cases, takes *šemen*, "oil," as an accusative. Most noteworthy for our purpose is its occurrence in Ezek. 16:9, a text quoted above. In that passage, however, it is the speaker, i.e. the "bridegroom," who anoints his future spouse. It is unlikely, as proposed by Campbell (1975: 120), that the verb **nsk* , "to pour," was ever found in this context, since **nsk* is not attested in connection with human *toilette*.

The *ketîb* of **śmltk*, which suggests that Ruth was to don a single item of clothing, is preferred by most modern commentators over the *qĕrē*, which vocalizes the word in such a manner that only the plural enters the question. If the *ketîb* is accepted, however, a difficulty is encountered in 3:15 which mentions Ruth as having a *miṭpaḥat*. Thus, at issue is whether or not the terms *śimlāh* and *miṭpaḥat* are exact synonyms; that is whether or not Ruth wore only a single garment (thus, Campbell, 1975: 120). Unfortunately, the term *miṭpaḥat* is attested elsewhere only in Isa. 3:22, occurring in the following sequence: *maḥalāṣôt* ("festive garbs"), *maʿaṭāpôt* ("mantles"), *miṭpāḥôt*, and *ḥarîṭîm*. NEB translates this last term as "flounced skirt." But 2 Kings 5:23 indicates the *ḥarîṭ* to be an item in which precious metals are carried. It might therefore have been an item of clothing, possibly a (pocketed) apron, which was worn only in special circumstances. Since it would seem unlikely that Ruth, after loading her *miṭpaḥat* with grain, returned naked to her mother-in-law, it might be best to regard *miṭpaḥat* as a supplementary garment, worn possibly on special occasions. JPS[2]'s rendering, "shawl," for our term in *Ruth* as well as in Isaiah, would suit the context of 3:15 quite well. We would therefore regard *śimlāh* of 3:3 as the main item of clothing which Ruth wore. The "shawl" that is mentioned in 3:15 was an added garment that may have been used by Ruth to veil herself in order to avoid recognition. That it also served her to warm herself against the coolness of Bethlehem's nights is also possible. The "mythological" reconstructions of a veiled Ruth offered by A. Jeremias (1931) cannot be accepted.

On a source analysis of the attestations for *lāśîm (haś)śimlāh ʿal. . .*, "to don clothing," see Myers, 1955: 25.

(f) *weyāradt(y) haggōren*. The verbal form *weyaradt(y)* is preserved in a *ketîb* consonantal skeleton which suggests as subject of the verb either the first person singular (i.e. "I will go down") or the allegedly "archaic" second person feminine singular (i.e. "You will go down") (see GKC, 44th [p. 121]; Joüon, 1947: 42f. [p. 100]). It is worth noticing that these "archaic" forms are found in Jeremiah, Micah, and Ezekiel, some of which are authored relatively *late* (Myers, 1955: 11). The context of *Ruth*, with its series of conjugations in the perfect form with the second person feminine singular as subject, requires us to opt for the "archaic" sufformative. The case of *šakabt(y)* in 3:4 is to be similarly assessed.

The suggestion that the verb *yārad* be translated here by "go up" is firmly and convincingly rejected by Campbell (1975: 121). For bibliography on this issue, see Rudolph, 1962: 53[n. 3].

(g) *ʾal-tiwwādeʿî lāʾîš ʿad kallōtô leʾekōl welištôt*, "do not become known to the man until his finishing eating and drinking." It is not necessary to promote overdeveloped hypotheses concerning the "real" purpose of Naomi's request of Ruth to await the conclusion of Boaz's meal before presenting herself before him. Suffice it to say that the *niphʿal* of *yādaʿ* never conveys the meaning of carnal knowledge, as does frequently the *qāl* (cf. BDB, 394 [3]). It seems to me that verse 7 offers a valid explanation: Ruth was to wait until Boaz was filled with the proper spirit and thus brought to the proper frame of mind.

3:4 contains a statement that has become the object of great debate among rabbis of old and has continued to vex modern scholars: What did Naomi precisely advise Ruth when she bade her to "bare Boaz's 'legs'"?

(h) *wîhî bešokbô*. On the use of the jussive where an imperfect with a simple waw conjunction is expected, see Joüon, 1947: 119z (p. 335-36); GKC, 109k (p. 323).

(i) *wegillît margelôtāyw wešākābt(y)*. The substantive *margelôtāyw* occurs in a number of instances in this chapter (verses 4, 7, 8, and 14 [*ketîb: margelôtāw*]). Only one other attestation of this word occurs in the rest of the OT. In Dan. 10:6, this term is contrasted with "arms," and hence must certainly be rendered as "legs." In *Ruth*, the *margelôt* are constructed with finite verbal forms (*piʿʿel* of *gālāh*, "to expose, uncover, lay bare" [verses 4, 7]; *qāl* of *šākab*, "to lay [by]" [verse 14]), and with a participial form of the verb *šākab* (verse 8). There are no difficulties in identifying *margelôt* as a derivative of the word *regel*, "foot," to which is attached a preformative *ma-*. As is clear from other vocables such as *meraʾašôt* (BDB, 912), this preformative indicates the *place (localis)*, rather than the *means (instrumentalis)*, which affects the *regel*. The *-ôt* sufformative is not the feminine plural ending, but one which reinforces and slightly extends the purpose of the *ma-* preformative. GKC (124a-b [pp. 396-97]) calls this: the *ʾôt* of *"local extension,"* that is indicating a place or an area.

With these grammatical points in mind, the discussion surrounding our phrase *legallôt /liškab margelôt* revolves around the meaning of *regel*, and the precise connotation of the verbs associated with *margelôt*. As is well known, *regel*, "foot," is used in the OT frequently enough as a euphemism for the sexual organs (BDB, 920). Since, unlike the above-mentioned passage in Daniel, there are no vocables within the text of *Ruth* 3:4 which could be constrasted, paralleled, or compared to *margelôt*, we cannot conclude undisputedly whether or not *margelôt* promoted sexual overtones. We could point out that the *pi*ʿʿ*el* of *gālāh*, twice associated with our word, is often identified with the act of uncovering nakedness. Isa. 47:2 is instructive in this regard when the prophet speaks of a noble woman's degradation (in this case symbolic of Babylon) when her leg is bared, her nakedness is displayed, and her shame is exposed. (The word for "leg" is here *šôq* [not *regel*], a word which does not, however, bear euphemistic connotations). Nevertheless, there are enough exceptions to this usage of the *pi*ʿʿ*el* of *gālāh* to caution us against rashly accusing Naomi of urging Ruth on to such acts of boldness.

Dahood (lastly in 1972: 160-61 no. II: 142) thinks that the verb *gālāh* of our context is to be related to Ugaritic *gly*. Thus, he renders our passage as follows: ". . . and she came softly and she reached the place of his feet, and lay down. . . ." However, it should be noted that in Ugaritic, the verb "to reach" is regularly *mǵy*, not *gly*. For that verb, the usual meaning arrived at from contexts is "to leave, proceed [to penetrate?]." On the Ugaritic evidence, see Zobel, TWAT, 1, 1019. Westermann and Albertz (THAT, 1, 418-26) distinguish between a transitive ("to uncover") and an intransitive ("to remove, deport") form of the verb *gālāh*, and give exhaustive citations for each of these meanings.

The verb *šākab* is well attested as referring to sexual intercourse (BDB, 1012). For this meaning, however, *šākab* is most often constructed either indirectly by means of a preposition (ʿ*im*/ʾ*et*, "with") or directly by means of a cognate accusative. Our examples in *Ruth* 3:8, 14, fit neither category. Yet we cannot be totally certain that sexual involvement is to be rejected as a valid interpretation of *liškab margelôt*. While we shall try to show, in subsequent pages, that the narrative of chapter 4 could best be understood only if vows between Boaz and Ruth were exchanged that night at the threshing-floor, it may be prudent to avoid referring to *legallôt/liškab margelôt* as *the* proof-text for Boaz rising to the sexual challenge of Ruth. I am in full agreement with Campbell (1975: 121) who, along with other scholars, suggests that the "storyteller meant to be ambiguous and hence provocative."

Carmichael (1977: 333-34) believes that Ruth removes Boaz's sandal, by the act of *legallôt/liškab margelôt*, in order to place herself as his symbolic shoe. Thus, he has absolutely no doubts of the sexual import of the phrase. That nowhere is the word for sandal to be found in chapter 3 is seen as no problem: "even though no mention is made of a sandal or sandals in this context, it is clear [*sic*] that everyone knew that a sandal stood symbolically for a woman. In fact, this is why there is no explicit mention of the sandal in this part of the story--the readers were to be attentive in recognizing the hidden significance of the event." Such logic, it has to be admitted, is beyond dispute.

At this point, I recall the lines of comment (f) and note that the *ketîb* of *šakabt(y)* allows understanding the form as a perfect conjugated either in the first person singular or the "archaic" second person feminine singular. Again, we depend on the context for our translation.

(j) We immediately should note that Naomi's advice, "he will tell you what next to do," was not followed by Ruth; this despite her promise to this effect as recorded in verse 5.

(k) The Hebrew text has the vocalization, but not the consonants (*qērē welōʾ ketîb*), for the word *ʾelay*, "to me," sandwiched between *tōʾmerî* and *ʾeʿeśeh* (cf. also verse 17, below). The intent of the Masoretes is not clear, but it may be that they thus made it clear that Ruth was conscious of Naomi's charge and its implication (cf. Midrash: *Ruth*, verse 13). It may simply be a manuscript variant. The verb *ʾāmar*, "to say," is given in the imperfect. The debate over this usage is recorded in Campbell, 1975: 121. The practice, however, does not violate grammatical rules (see GKC, 107h [p. 316]).

Ruth and Boaz: The Second Encounter (3:6-15)

6 She went down to the threshing-floor and did just as[a] her mother-
7* in-law had charged.[b] Boaz ate, drank, and felt free of care.[c] He
then proceeded to lie down at the edge of the grain pile.[d] Approaching quietly,[e] Ruth bared his "legs," and lay down.
8 Around midnight,[f] the man was shaken by fright;[g] he twisted a-
9 way[h]--there was a woman lying close to him![i] "Who are you?"[j] he

exclaimed. "I am Ruth your handmaid,"[k] she replied, adding: "spread
10 your robe over your handmaid;[l] you are indeed a redeemer."[m] "May
you be blessed by the Lord, daughter;" said Boaz. "You have acted
in a worthier fashion in the last instance than in the first.[n] There
11 will henceforth be no need to seek men[o] whether poor or rich.[p] Now,[q]
have no further worry, daughter, for I will do in your behalf whatever you have suggested,[r] inasmuch as your status as a wife of a
12 notable is public knowledge.[s] Now, since there is a redeemer with
rights prior to mine,[u] despite the fact that I myself am most cer-
13 tainly a redeemer,[t] spend[v] the night[w] here. In the morning, we shall
see; should he decide to redeem for you,[x] well and good;[y] should he
choose otherwise, I myself will do so. I swear it by the Lord.[z] Lie
down until morning."
14 Ruth stayed by him[a'] until daybreak, but rose[b'] before[c'] a person's features could be recognized,[d'] for Boaz had thought it best
15 that her arrival to the threshing-floor remain unnoticed.[e'] "Bring
over the shawl that you are wearing[f'] and hold it open,"[g'] he said.
As she held it, he placed six measures of barley.[h'] He helped to
raise it on her back, then proceeded to town.[i']

3:6-7. Ruth proceeds to do as her mother-in-law had recommended. In these verses, a few details are added to the statement made in verses 3-4. Rashi was disturbed by the order of Ruth's activity as given in these verses. If taken literally, he felt, they would have Ruth failing to prepare herself physically for her encounter with Boaz.

(a) *wattaʿaś kekōl. . . .* Following a suggestion by D. N. Freedman, Campbell (1975: 121) proposes that the *kaph* in *kekōl* be taken as the *kaph veritatis*. Thus he would render: "she did everything exactly as her mother-in-law had commanded her." Such an understanding of the function of the *kaph*, however, has been commonly expressed in most translations (cf. Joüon, 1953: 70).

(b) *ṣiwwattāh*. This form, which does not explicitely reflect a third person feminine suffix (i.e. "to her"), has been explained in a number of ways by grammarians and by commentators: Joüon, 1947: 62 (p. 132); GKC, 58g (pp. 156-68), 59g (p. 160), and 91e (p. 256); Campbell, 1975: 114 (n. *e . . . . e*). It should be noted, however, that it would not be necessary for *ṣiwwāh* to reflect an accusative of person, even when a specific individual is the direct object of a command (cf., for example, 2 Kings 11:9 (= 2 Chron. 23:8) and, further on this topic, BDB, 846 (3).

(c) *wayyîṭab libbô*. Hebrew regularly combines anatomical features with verbs and adjectives to convey various shades of emotion. This feature, in general, is common to the Semitic languages. On this, see Dhorme, 1923: 115-17; McCurley, 1969: 125ff. To express happiness and joy, a number of idioms are attested, among which are *ṣahal/ṭōb panîm* (literally, "the face shines/is sweet") and *śāmaḥ/ṭōb lēb(āb)* (literally, "the heart is glad/sweet").

Drinking and eating were deemed major factors in fostering a sense of contentment and well-being. Whether one became to any degree inebriated (e.g. 1 Sam. 25:36; Esther 1:10); satisfied (1 Kings 8:66; Prov. 15:15; Eccles. 9:7), or at peace with the world (2 Sam. 13:28) is not usually distinguishable merely by the use of the idiom *ṭōb lēb*, but rather by the context of a narrative. It is therefore impossible to ascertain Boaz's condition at the end of the meal. In addition, since his dialogue with Ruth occurred just after midnight, a number of hours may have elapsed since the last drop of wine was taken. Nevertheless, it might be pointed out that in the Hittite tale of Appu, the protagonist is advised by the sun god to become totally drunk before attempting to cohabit with his wife. In his case, it is clear that a good dose of liquor was deemed the proper medicine to cure a possible sexual derangement (impotence?). Appu, we are told, was, subsequently, totally successful since he managed not only to achieve his desired end, but also to impregnate his wife with a male child. On this tale, see Friedrich, 1950: 242ff.

Although our translation does not reflect it adequately enough, the Masoretic punctuation of verse 7 indicates Boaz's activities in a series of four finite verbal forms. This pattern may have been consciously established in order to "balance" the series of four verbs contained in Naomi's advice to her daughter-in-law.

(d) *biqṣēh hāʿarēmāh*. "At the edge of the grain pile" may have been indicated in order to offer an adequate reason for the full privacy, from both vision and hearing, which Ruth and Boaz enjoyed in subsequent scenes. This statement may have, however, satisfied cultic requirements whose precise import has by now escaped us. Joüon's position (1953: 70-71), which would have Boaz lying at the edge of the pile of grain in order to more adequately protect the harvest, has been dealt with above.

(e) *ballāṭ*. Commentators have correctly referred to incidents recorded in Judg. 4:21 and 1 Sam. 24:4, in which approaches are made *ballā(ʾ)ṭ*, that is, "quietly," by persons determined to harm sleepers. In our case this point may have been made perhaps in order to stress that Ruth's approach was unheard by people other than Boaz. We shall have more to say on secrecy as an essential ingredient of this tale's dénouement.

On the etymological search for the root of *ballāṭ* [**lʾṭ* (?); **ʾṭ* (?)] see Joüon, 1953: 71; Myers, 1955: 28.

3:8. Boaz's sudden awakening is vividly sketched. Since the exact source and nature of Boaz's fright is not immediately apparent, a number of translations have been offered which, ultimately, attenuate the basic meaning of the vocabulary found in this verse.

(f) *way(y)ehî baḥaṣî hallaylāh*. Humbert's (1958: 101) poetic words are worth quoting as introduction to this scene: "Le choix de cette heure unique et mystérieuse, ce milieu de la nuit, doit marquer le point culminant l'heure de la péripétie. La richesse inventive de l'auteur a su, par ce moyen si simple mais si expressif, fixer même extérieurement la cime de l'action, le point à partir duquel on redescendra vers la conclusion. Ce minuit, s'est la faîte du livre, le sommet de l'édifice si harmonieusement composé, l'heure pathétique par excellence."

Midnight is the time of reckoning; God chose to strike the Egyptians first-born at that hour (Exod. 11:4; 12:29; cf. also Job. 34:20); Samson hoisted Gaza's gate at midnight (Judg. 16:3). For other significant activities that took place at that time, see 1 Kings 3:20, and the listing in Campbell, 1975: 119. It might be of interest for our forthcoming thesis to note at this point Matt. 25:1-13. In a curious parable, a wedding feast is said to have occurred slightly after midnight. While unusual circumstances delayed the enactment of this particular ceremony until that hour, we have Joachim Jeremias's testimony for the practice of midnight nuptials in Syro-Palestine (1963: 172ff).

(g) *wayyeḥerad hāʾîš̃*. The *qal* of *ḥārad* conveys a rather precise meaning: "to be terrified, to shudder from fear." Other OT attestations of this verb, with human beings as subjects, indicate that such anxieties were occasioned by frightful circumstances, sometimes even supernatural in nature; on this point, see Joüon, 1953: 71-72; BDB, 353. Since the text of *Ruth* tells us nothing about the occurrence of fearsome, or even unusual manifestations, we are left to wonder about the source of Boaz's fear. Rabbis of old debated whether or not Boaz's discomfort was but a response to sexual excitement (Levine, 1973: 89). Joüon disdainfully recalls suggestions by Cassel, Bertholet, and Ehrlich which would have Boaz recoiling from contact with Ruth's body. With most modern scholars who expressed their opinion on this matter, Joüon, however, thinks that Boaz was responding to the unexpected cold, a consequence of Ruth turning back the "covering at his feet." Driver (1967: 54-56) thinks that Hebrew *ḥārad* developed from three or four roots that differed in their original phonemes. He relates the *ḥārad* of our passage to Arabic *ḥariḍa* I, "was chaste," II, "was modest"; Akkadian *ḫarādu*, "to be alert"; Ugaritic *ḫrd*, "anxious, afraid." Yet Driver would translate our occurrence by "restless."

It might be appropriate to suggest an alternate way to resolve our difficulty, one which finds precedence in midrashic elaborations (Ginzberg, 1961: 519) and which, in addition, refrains from diluting the essential meaning of the verb *ḥārad*, "to fear, to shudder in fear." We would insist from the outset that the following long exercise should be regarded as no more than a hypothesis, a theory which, unfortunately, cannot be better substantiated even by further evidence. Our hypothesis, it might be said further, could gain in plausibility, were one to credit the storyteller with an earthy sense of humor.

We first reconstruct the following scene: Boaz had finished dining. Under the benevolent influence of the proper spirits, he had chosen a quiet corner in which to sleep away the night. If (as they may have been) his nocturnal activities were linkable to either ceremonial or cultic functions, they would have coincided with harvest celebrations of the type wellknown to us from the Semitic world. Now in Israel, as well as among its neighbors, festivities were most often timed to fall either at the new or the full moon. On this, see the convenient and extensive discussion in EB, III, 3196-97, 3401-4, and the references gathered in BDB *sub kesē*ʾ, "full moon," and *ḥōdeš*, "new moon." In general, it could also be said that Israel's religious festivals of agricultural origin fell on the full moon. This is true of Passover, after (?) it was merged with the Feast of Unleavened Bread (fifteenth of Nisan), of the Feast of Tabernacles/Sukkot (fifteenth of Tishri), and of the non-Biblical festival in honor of the newly sprouting fruit trees, *Ṭû-bišbāṭ* (fifteenth of

Shevat). According to some sectarian calendars, even Shabbuot/Pentecost/ Weeks, a harvest festival now celebrated on the sixth of Siwwan, once fell on the fifteenth of that month. On this last statement, see de Vaux, 1961: 494.

Boaz was rudely awakened by some presence that exposed his legs. We do not need to be certain of the precise nature of Ruth's act. In the light of the full moon, Boaz could easily make out that the human presence next to him *was that of a woman,* and not that of a man. We could be certain that this indeed was *his* perception, since his question "Who are you?" was addressed to a female, an address in which the "you" is rendered by the independent pronoun of the *feminine* singular, *ʾāt*. That he did not add *bittî*, "my daughter," at the end of his question, as he was wont to do when addressing Ruth, also makes it clear that he did not recognize her as being the female at his side. At this point, therefore, we might wonder about the nature of the situation that would lead a mature man to tremble in terror at the sight of an unknown woman.

Among ancient folk, and the Semites in particular, there was fear from the harm of ever-present demons. Cuneiform literature from the early second millennium B.C. knows of an elaborate assortment of demons, spirits, ghosts, shades, and the like. Some of these creatures were benevolent, but most were not. A brief survey on this topic is to be found in Leibovici, 1971: 87-112, but one should further consult Bottéro, 1975: 95ff., 132ff. Among those that were considered baleful, the Mesopotamians listed the *lamaštu*, a female demon, and a nocturnal trio composed of the male *lilû* and the female *lilītu/ardat lilî* ("Maiden *lilû*"). It is not possible to offer a precise account of the development and the categorization of these demons, since cuneiform sources, mostly stemming from the first millennium B.C., are not without discrepancies and inconsistencies when tackling these subjects. A recent writer, Lackenbacher (1971: 148-58), plausibly proposes that the above-mentioned creatures were thought to share one thing in common: an inability to achieve destinies commonly attributed to members of their respective sex. Thus, the *lamaštu*, a demon whose origin may be sought among the ranks of divine beings, was constantly frustrated in her ability to produce children. Enraged, this creature roamed far and wide, ready to attack and harm unsuspecting children and women in labor. The *lilû*, *lilītu/ardat lilî* may have originated from human ranks, representing individuals who were never able to consummate their marriages. Crazed with unquenched desires, these creatures sought to mate with humans of their opposite sex. Out of pure jealously, they were also ready to ruin marriages, and lure prospective mates into their own madness.

Viewed from modern perspective, the *lilītu/ardat lilî* myths may have provided explanations for a number of questions asked by ancient man. On the pathological side, the legend explained nocturnal emissions prompted by sexual dreams. Additionally, the activities of these demons may have been regarded as one factor in a man's loss of potency. An omen warns against allowing a female to be sexually aggressive: "If a female mounts a man, that female will take his virility for one month and he will have no god" (CT, 39: pl. 44:28 [#17]). *Lilītu*-demons, of course, were considered as being particularly aggressive. Additionally, sexual congress in the open air was considered injurious to health: "If someone has sexual relations with a woman on a roof--a demon will strike him" (Moren, 1977: 67 line 3). On the other hand psychopathic characteristics were easily attributable to man's possession either by a *lilītu* or by one of her cohorts or her equivalents (e.g. the *ḫallaḫiya*-demoness; cf. CAD, H, 46 [2]).

We do not know how far back to retroject the notion that held, in Syro-Palestine of Jesus' time, that malevolent *lilītu/ardat lilî* known in Hebrew as Lilith, sought out men unsuspectingly resting in secluded places, mated with them, and produced a breed of demonic offsprings who, oftentimes, came back to haunt and torment those who fathered them. Leaving aside the elaborate, even fantastic, development of the Lilith legend in later Jewish and Mediterranean lore (on which see IDB, I, 819; Yamauchi, 1965: 517-18; *E. Jud.*, XI, 244ff), we do note that the prophet Isaiah knew of her sinister character. In his description of a land (Edom) wasted on the day of God's vengence, Isaiah speaks of desolation in which: "Wild cats shall meet hyenas, / Goat-demons [*śāʿîr*] shall greet each other;/ There too the *lilith* [*lilît*] shall repose/ And find herself a resting place" (Isa. 34:14; JPS[2]). Many renderings of this passage avoid identifying Isaiah's *lilît* with a demoness by offering to translate with "screech-owl" (RSV) or with "night-jar" (NEB). But such interpretations, most recently defended by Caquot (1971: 117) and Driver (1959: 55ff.), are not likely to stand uncriticized. The Isaiah text, which some would date no earlier than the end of the sixth century B.C. (e.g. Eissfeldt, 1965: 327-28), is not alone in recording the Lilith's presence in the West Semitic world. In a seventh-century Phoenician magical plaque from Arslan

Tash, Upper-Syria, the following inscription was written on a description of a winged sphinx: "Oh flyer(s) into/from a dark room, pass over! Right this moment! Liliths [*llyn*--plural of *llt*]." In the latest treatment of this text, that of Cross and Saley (1970: 42-49), *llyn* was translated as "night-demon." In this Cross and Saley may have been influenced by the mention of "dark room" in the preceding line. To be pedantic about it, however, we have no way of knowing whether, at this state of the development of West Semitic demonology, folk etymology had already forged a link between Hebrew *laylāh*, a masculine noun meaning "night," and *lilît*, a word that ultimately owed its origin to Sumerian LÍL (= Akkadian *zaqīqu*, "ghost, spirit"). It may be, however, that such a linking was quite ancient, aided by assimilation in West Semitic milieu of *llt*, "lilith," with a deity *ll*, "night," known to us from Ugaritic sources (UT, 22:9; 23:7).

To sum up: upon awakening, Boaz discerns the figure of a woman. Fearing that it might be that of a Lilith, he shudders in fear. The storyteller's joke is that Ruth turns out to be equally as aggressive in her demands to be accepted as a mate. In this case, however, we shall shortly be reassured (if we do not know it already) that matters will turn out well for all concerned.

On the possible vestigial remainder in the OT of the *lilû*-demon, see Ps. 91:5-6 *(mippaḥad) lāyelāh*, and note the context that mentioned Deber ("Plague"), Qeteb ("Scourge"), and probably Reshep (*ḥēṣ*; cf. Psalms 76: 4; UT, 1001:3). On Rabbinic exegesis of *laylāh* as a demon in Job 3:3, see Jastrow, 1950: 707 (s.v.)

(h) *wayyillāpēt*. The verb *lāpat* occurs only three times in the OT. In the Samson story, the *qāl* is used to describe the manner in which the blinded hero grasps the columns of Dagon's temple (Judg. 16:29). The other two examples are *niphʿal* in forms and are found in Job 6:18 and in our passage. Of these citations, only the Samson passage provides a context that allows us to establish a precise meaning: "to grasp, touch." It happens that this meaning is equivalent to that of Akkadian *lapātu*, a verb that also shares the same consonant as Hebrew *lāpat*. Loretz (1964: 155) would like to understand the other OT attestations of our verb in the light of the Akkadian *lapātu*. He proposes that *yillāpetû ʾorḥôt* of Job 6:18 be considered as an idiom similar to the Akkadian. *ḫarrānam ṣabātu*, literally: "to seize the road," but figuratively understood as "a caravan making its way." Since *ṣabātu/lapātu* share and overlap in some of their semantic ranges, Loretz finds it probable that *yillāpetû* could be understood in the light of *lapātu*. It must be said, however, that there is no idiom in Akkadian in which *ḫarrānum*, "road, caravan," or even *urḫum*, a word that is a closer cognate to Hebrew *ʾōraḥ*, is constructed with *lapātu*, either in the G or in the N-stems. I therefore believe that Loretz's thesis, shared by Campbell (1975: 122), strains the possibilities of the Hebrew of Job. In the same vein, I would like to question his application of the same theory to the passage in *Ruth*.

According to the CAD, L, 93, the N-stem of *lapātu* means "to be touched, be affected, be written down." Were one to accept the Akkadian at face value, one would have to render *wayyilāpēt* by "[Boaz] was touched." This, however, will result in a series of actions that would obviously be out of sequence (i.e. "Boaz shuddered in fear and he was touched. . . ."). One cannot, therefore, share Loretz's (1964: 156) opinion that "das Verbum *LPT* bezeichnet hier wie in Ri 16, 29 eine Bewegung mit den Händen, die etwas anfassen, abtasten bzw. nach etwas greifen."

Joüon (1953: 72-73) adopts a meaning for *yillāpēt* which, he claims, is based upon Arabic *lafata*, "to look around." But such a meaning, it is clear, is but secondarily derived from "to twist, turn around." Additionally, in order to arrive at an understanding such as the one suggested by Joüon, Arabic often attaches *nazar*, "eyesight," to *lafata*.

Rudolph (1962: 55) somewhat uncomfortably offers "bend forward" as a translation of our verb. It must be admitted that other opinions on *yillāpēt* are to a large degree unsubstantiated. The rabbis, in general, adopted meanings that were not spoiled by philological accuracies. The Targum playfully associates *yillāpēt* with *lepet/liptaʾ*, "turnip," and translates: "his flesh was made as a turnip from fear" (Levine, 1973: 88; Jastrow, 1950: 71a). Rashi relies on *Tanh.Behar.*, 3 (cf. Jastrow, 1950: 715) and adopts *lāpap*, "to enfold," as a parasonantic "cognate." He thus has Ruth embracing Boaz in her arms.

The context of our narrative remains our best avenue for developing an acceptable solution to *yillāpēt*. If we are correct in our perception that the verb *ḥārad* paints a picture of a Boaz fearful of an evil night-spirit, we might then imagine him as anxious to escape its imminent attack. We could, therefore, adopt Arabic *lafata* in its most basic meaning, "to turn, twist away," and regard the *niphʿal* conjugation of its Hebrew cognate as promoting a reflexive dimension to the act (cf. the usage of *lāḥaṣ* [*niphʿal*] in Num. 22:25 in this regard). Thus, we could tentatively arrive at a rendering that would have Boaz reacting sharply to avoid the Lilith's clutches. (For a wonderful Hellenistic decorative relief which depicts a man in a rustic setting, enjoying [?] the favor of a winged demoness, see Vermeule, 1964: 334, pl. 104, fig. 24.)

(i) *wehinnēh ʾiššāh šōkebet margelōtāyw.* The use of a participial form in connection with the demonstrative particle *hinnēh,* usually rendered by "behold, lo," gives "there was a woman lying close to him" an explicative purpose (cf. Gen. 24:30; 37:15; Judg. 11:34; other attestations collected in BDB, 244 [4,c]). Thus, this sentence should not be considered as recording one more act in a series performed by Boaz (Joüon, 1953: 72); rather, it provides the audience with an explanation that accounts for Boaz's violent behavior. The storyteller's intent, therefore, is to sketch a scene in which the awakened Boaz trembles, twists away, and speaks (*wayyōʾmer* of verse 9) in a succession quick enough to appear simultaneous.

3:9. Responding to Boaz's question, Ruth introduces herself, then, unhesitatingly, proceeds to make a twofold demand upon him; requests that should, if granted, totally change her position as well as that of Naomi.

(j) *mî-ʾāt.* We have alluded above to the absence of *bittî,* "my daughter," a word invariably used by Boaz when addressing Ruth, at first patriarchally (2:8), then no doubt affectionately (3:9, 11). That some Hebrew manuscripts add this word at this point could certainly be influenced directly by the pattern of 3:16 (Rudolph, 1962: 55). Campbell (1975: 122-23) is quite perceptive in arguing that the addition of *bittî* would only shatter "the air of anonymity and shadowy movement which the storyteller has so effectively created."

(k) *ʾānōkî rût ʾamāteka̅.* There are some points of interest to us in this opening statement of Ruth. We first note the *absence* of the ethnicon: "of Moab." Indeed, except for the two occasions in which Ruth's origins are recalled for legalistic purposes, there will be no more mention of her place of origin. For all intents and purposes, Ruth was, by then, a Bethlehemite or, to be more precise, a member of Boaz's clan.

Ruth speaks of herself as an *ʾāmāh,* a "handmaiden." We tried above to suggest that a *šipḥāh* was a female belonging to the lowest rung of a *mišpaḥāh's* social ladder. When she first approached Boaz, Ruth, a foreigner with little privilege, was eager to find acceptance in his clan.

By now using the term *ʾāmāh*, Ruth imagines herself as ranking among those females who might be taken by a freeman either as a concubine or as a wife. It does not seem to me likely that the storyteller is using "synonymous words in parallel situations [*sic*] for rhetorical effect" (Campbell, 1975: 123).

(l) *ûpāraśtā kenāpeka ʿal-ʾamāteka*. Ruth's first request is blunt and explicit: she asks Boaz to take her into his immediate family. As has been often stated by commentators, Biblical texts containing similarly couched phrases are found in contexts in which marriage is definitely at stake (Deut. 23:1; cf. the Ezek. 16 passage quoted above). Moreover, parallel practices are known from other Near Eastern communities (Joüon, 1953: 73; Campbell, 1975: 123). It is noteworthy that the Targum, not willing to be misunderstood on this sensitive issue, substitute an unequivocal formulation based on Isa. 4:1 (Levine, 1973: 89). Brichto (1973: 14) is too imprecise when he translates: "Take me under your aegis."

The occurrence of *ʾāmāh* does not make it clear, however, whether Ruth expected herself to be taken as a bride or merely as a concubine. This issue must also have been of interest to the rabbis, for they chose to have Boaz's wife die most opportunely, at a moment precisely coinciding with Ruth's arrival from Moab. (*Bab. Bathra*, 91a). In a polygamous society, however, such a coincidence would not be necessary.

kenāpekā. Some of the Hebrew manuscripts record a plural form for *kānāp*, "wing" (BH[3], l.c.), no doubt to take full advantage of a play on Boaz's words of 2:12. If it be remembered that Boaz's lofty pronouncements in that verse were essentially unbeneficial to Ruth's fortunes, it might well be that her choice of words in 3:9 was a shade too ironic. Perhaps this might be considered as a humorous touch of the storyteller. On *kānāp* with the meaning "extremity [of a garment]," see BDB, 489 (2,a); v.d. Woude, THAT, 1, 835 (b).

(m) *kî gōʾēl ʾāttāh*. It is of interest to us to ascertain whether *kî* is necessarily to be taken as the conjunction, "because, since, when, that," etc. Most translations and commentaries understand it as such (e.g. AB: "Now spread you 'wing' over your maid-servant, for you are a redeemer"). Such an understanding would link Ruth's desire to be taken as wife, to Boaz's obligation as a redeemer. Yet such a presumption would result in a singular expansion of the role of the *gōʾēl*, concerning which see below. However, as it will be clear from the form of Boaz's response, the two statements should not be connected in such a manner. At this point, let it be simply stated that we understand this *kî* in its corroborative sense. On this form of *kî*, see GKC, 159 (p. 498); 148d (p. 471); Joüon, 1947: 164b (p. 503). For an elaborate survey see Dahood, 1970: 402-6.

3:10-13. Boaz's reply is patterned somewhat after Ruth's tripartite declaration. Verse 10 offers her an accolade on her behavior; verse 11 responds positively to her request for marriage. Verses 12-13 raise the matter of a gō⁾ēl *who has precedence in the matter or redemption.*

But if the question of precedence in the matter of redemption was obviously not forseen by Ruth, could it be possible that Naomi was equally unaware of an issue that most certainly was most crucial to her future welfare? Campbell (1975: 89, and more particularly 123) addresses himself to this issue:

In the NOTES on 2:1 . . . 2:20 . . . , and 3:2 . . . , I have argued that Naomi knew of the existence of a circle of redeemers or confederates. But did Naomi and Ruth know anything about the order in which these men would be expected to act; that is, who was the nearest relative? It is possible that they did know, and that Ruth asked Boaz to marry her without assurance that civil custom would in fact lead directly to that. Her approach would then be a ploy to force him to act, to start the wheels rolling toward marriage whether to another person or to himself. Support for this interpretation would come from the fact that Ruth calls Boaz "a redeemer," not "the redeemer" or "my/our redeemer." Also, notice that Boaz gives Ruth assurance that he will do all that she has asked before he mentions the existence of the nearer redeemer, which seems to suggest that her request could be answered by marriage to another as well as by marriage to Boaz.

Campbell's discussion, it seems to me, is marred by two assumptions that are worth disputing. We shall entertain the major one, which links marriage and redemption, further on. At this point, we should like to concentrate on Campbell's (1975: 90) opinion, central to his above-quoted cogitation: "We have nothing certain to indicate that a real semantic distinction existed between meyuddā⁽ *and* gō⁾ēl *at the time of the composition of the Ruth story." Campbell bases this startling statement on evidence that is slim indeed. Leaving aside a questionable attempt at finding a "convenantal" dimension in the use of* meyuddaʿ, *we find his equation of this last term with* gōʾēl *ultimately rests upon the acceptance of a Lucianic LXX reading of 2 Kings 10:11 which appears to have added* *gōʾālîm *at the head of a series of vocables concerned with important followers of Ahab. In that recension the verse reads: "And Jehu executed all those who were left in the house of Ahab in Jezreel, as well as his redeemers [Lucianic addition presuming a Hebrew* *gōʾalîm], *his close friends [MT's* meyuddāʿîm], *his nobles [MT's* gedōlîm], *and his priests [MT's* kōhanîm], *until he left him not one survivor." Even if one is to accept the Lucianic reading as having been based on a genuine Hebrew manuscript, a proposition that is far from certain, it would be quite daring to equate* gōʾalîm *with* meyuddāʿîm, *not on the basis of* parallelism *or* replacement *but solely on the basis of* proximity. *On the contrary, the point being made by this verse is that a large number of courtiers, made up of followers belonging to a* variety *of groupings, were eradicated by Jehu.*

Freed from the unnecessary equation between the terms discussed above, we return to our narrative and make the following observations. (1) When Naomi learns that Ruth succeeded in attracting Boaz's attention, she informs her that "he is one in a position to redeem us" (miggōʾalēnû hûʾ; *2:20). Naomi* does not, *it ought to be noted, apprise her of his position in the series of potential redeemers. Were we to take the text at face value, therefore, we could not presume that Ruth was aware of any other redeemer with prior rights in the matter. (2) In instructing her daughter-in-law to prepare herself for Boaz, Naomi shares not one word about the latter in his function of* gōʾēl. *Whether or not Naomi planned to confront that particular problem after Ruth's marriage to Boaz is a moot point. At this juncture of the narrative, all that we can be certain of is that Naomi was not concerned about resolving her own problem when she sent Ruth on her "sentimental" journey; her instructions to Ruth were motivated only by her desire to seek a happy future for one who risked all in her behalf. (3) The first two observations lead us to conclude that Ruth broached the subject of* geʾullāh, *"redemption," uninstructed by Naomi and, as it turns out, insufficiently informed about Boaz's precise position in the chain of possible redeemers.*

Be that as it may, it is clear that Ruth's requests in verse 9, and Boaz's response to these requests as stated in verse 10-13, are pivotal to the rest of the narrative; for it is at this juncture that the fates and futures of all three protagonists, Naomi, Ruth, and Boaz, interlock.

Meek (JBL, 79 [1960], 333-34) supports an oft-repeated contention, rash in our opinion, that this episode is indicative of "the wily ways of a woman to get her man."

(n) *hēyṭabt ḥasdēk hā'aḥarôn min-hāri'šôn.* In this sentence, it is of interest to find out what Boaz meant by *hā'aḥarôn* and *hāri'šôn*, "the last [deed]; the first [deed]." Most commentators who express their opinion on these terms identify Ruth's decision to accompany her mother-in-law as "the first [deed]," and promote as "the last [deed]" her interest in marrying Boaz in order to permit him to fulfill a leviratic responsibility to perpetuate Elimelech's seed (cf. Humbert, 1958: 101-3; de Fraine, 1955: 155; *Bible de Jér.*, 277b; Joüon, 1953: 74; Rudolph, 1962: 56).

It seems to me much more likely, however, that, rather than evoking events that transpired months in the past, Boaz was responding to Ruth's immediate statement of verse 9. By praising her "last [deed]," Boaz singled out her unselfish attempt at finding a *gō'ēl* to resolve her mother-in-law's difficulty as worthier than her self-serving hope to acquire a husband. We shall presently note that Boaz turns to issues raised by Ruth and offers a separate opinion on each one of them.

(o) *lebiltî-leket 'aḥarēy habbaḥûrîm.* There are some difficulties connected with this phrase. Foremost among them is that of evaluating and ascertaining its proper relevance to Boaz's pronouncements that have just been made. If we are correct in our assessment Boaz was praising Ruth above all for her interest in Naomi's plight. In other words, what may be implied here is that Ruth's identification of Boaz, her choice as husband, as a *gō'ēl* for her mother-in-law, was meant to resolve Naomi's search for a *gō'ēl*. If Ruth was at all anxious to retain bonds with Naomi, it must have occurred to her that the best way to achieve such an end was to have her prospective husband act as Naomi's *gō'ēl*. From the ensuing narrative, it is clear that Boaz could easily have been preceded in this obligation by Mr. So-and-So.

To such a reconstruction, it might be objected that, as verse 12 and the events of chapter 4 show, Naomi had neither control nor choice in the matter of redemption, since custom and common law clearly directed the nearest kinsman to fulfill that requirement. In response, however, we would wish to develop the theme that placing Boaz in that slot was *precisely the issue* in the final resolution of the story. Boaz clearly perceived the issue to be as such for, as it will be shown, he takes it upon himself to direct the events at the city gate aiming *solely* at achieving that end. His marriage to Ruth was to become the trump card in the game in which the future of *Naomi*, not Ruth, was at stake.

On the subject of *(la)leket ʾaḥarēy* . . . , the Targum unhesitatingly chose a commonly attested understanding of the idiom and translated "to whore [after young men]" (cf. Levine, 1973: 90). Campbell (1975: 124) rightly stresses that such a rendering is not necessitated by the Hebrew since *(la)leket ʾaḥarēy* . . . could bear a number of meanings (for a discussion, see TWAT, I, 220-24). However, he errs in our opinion on the fanciful side when, on the evidence of the verb in Gen. 24:5 and 1 Sam. 25:42, he offers the following: "Apparently Ruth had received marriage proposals. . . probably from the youths who harvested Boaz's crop." *Additionally, this proposal damages his own claims to regard the future union of our protagonists as fulfilling leviratic requirements. For no Bethlehemite would have approached a woman* required *to marry a next-of-kin.*

The term *baḥûr* is used to describe men in the prime of their lives, that is, those who are considered as neither *neʿarîm*, "adolescents, youths," nor *zeqenîm*, "old men." The vocalization of the plural of this noun, *baḥûrîm*, makes it clear that the singular must be derived from a *piʿʿel* construction that theoretically should be **baḥḥûr*. Since the verb *bāḥar*, the most likely candidate whence to derive an etymology, is not available in the *piʿʿel* (but cf. the *puʿʿal yebuḥar* [*ketîb*] in Eccles. 9:4), other candidates have been proposed; see the discussion in Seebass, TWAT, I, 593-94 (II). Despite the apparent difficulty, it might be best not to abandon too quickly a connection with *bāḥar*, "to chose." The *bāḥar* element apparently implied in *bāḥûr* might refer to the fact that those referred to in the OT as *baḥûrîm* belonged either to military groupings or to the more established strata of society. In this instance, note the interesting distinction reflected in 2 Chron. 13:3, concerning which see H. Wildberger, THAT, I, 275-76 (I. 1,2b); *baḥûr* might, on the basis of its connection with *bāḥar*, be thought of as a *qattûl* formative, akin to *ḥannûn*, *raḥûm*, *ʿammûd*, and so forth (cf. GKC, 84g [p. 234]).

The term *baḥûr* is hardly concerned with the physical attractiveness of men (Campbell, 1975: 124). Here it represents men (of means) who could either marry Ruth or fulfill the requirement of *geʾullāh*, "redemption." Boaz could certainly have fallen in either category; for the usual image of him as an old man is based on no internal evidence of the text (contra Campbell, 1975: 110). Such a notion might be abandoned without harming the wonderful conception of the story. Parenthetically, it might be stated that midrashic descriptions of Boaz as an old man, or, to be more precise, an octagenarian (*Ruth Rabba*, III:10) follow a *topos* which is constructed whenever puritanical interests are at stake (it would be much easier to accept the possibility that the threshing-floor involved no sexual activity, if the protagonist were sketched as a wise old man). Something of the sort also occurs in the apocryphal literature concerning Joseph, Jesus's father. In writings such as the *Protoevangelicum of James* (second century) and the *History of Joseph* (fourth century), he too was pictured as an octagenarian, a widower, and a father of many children before marrying the twelve-year-old Mary. In the case of Boaz, Rabbinic literature did not hesitate to see him dead the moment he fulfilled his function of fathering Obed (Ginzberg, 1961: 519; *Yalq. Shimʿoni*, 608). On Boaz as an old man, see Rowley, 1965: 192-93.

(p) *ʾim-dal weʾim-ʿāšîr*. Syriac manuscripts reverse the order. The words are somewhat anthitetical and might best be considered as constituting a *merismus* in which the whole idea is divided into its opposite parts. Thus "poor" and "rich," each of which is preceded by the particle *ʾim*, might better be translated "persons from all walks of life." For a bibliography of these terms, and an extensive treatment of the word *dal*, see TWAT, II, 221-44; THAT, II, 347-48 (g,1-2).

(q) *weʿattāh*. It should be noted that verse 11 and verse 12-13 each begin with *weʿattāh*. BDB (774 [2,b]) tells us that *weʿattāh* is used whenever a practical conclusion is drawn on the basis of stated arguments. *Sub* (1,3) BDB further points out that, on the occasions when it is followed by an imperative, *weʿattāh* gives a special urgency for the exhortation or the advice to be acted upon. In the case of verse 10, *weʿattāh* is followed by *ʾal-tîreʾî*, "do not fear," a negated jussive used in our passage since Hebrew does not tolerate a negated imperative. In verses 12-13 the imperative that follows *ʿattāh* is not to be found until verse 13, namely: *lînî*. Thus the occurrence of *weʿattāh* as a heading for two separate clauses may bolster the thesis presented above, one which holds that Ruth's address in verse 9 contained two separate entreaties and thus necessitated individual responses from Boaz. On this adverb, see Brongers, 1965.

LXX does not reflect the *weʿattāh* of verses 12-13. Many commentators, therefore, choose to delete it. Our discussion, we hope, will make it clear that this would be a grave mistake. If it is retained, however, it should be so because it fulfills the important function delineated above, and not because "Boaz' speaking style is purposely made redundant by the story-teller" (Campbell, 1975: 125).

(r) *kōl ʾašer-tōʾmerî ʾeʿeśeh-lāk.* BH[3] (l.c.) cites a number of manuscripts that have *ʾēlay* inserted after *tōʾmerî.* "I will do in your behalf whatever you suggest," is Boaz's response to Ruth's marriage overtures. Yet Boaz felt the need to give a reason for so readily agreeing to marry Ruth.

(s) *kî yôdeyaʿ kol-šaʿar ʿammî (kî ʾēšet ḥayil ʾāt),* literally: "for all the gate of my people knows." Myers (1955: 36) points out that the other two attestations of *šaʿar ʿammî* are found in poetic contexts. In Mic. 1:9, the phrase is rendered by some to parallel "Jerusalem." The context of Obad. 13 may reflect a similar situation. We do not know, therefore, of *šaʿar ʿammî* as the subject of *verba cordis,* such as *yadaʿ.* Nevertheless, the meaning of the whole sentence is clear, and could be arrived at satisfactorily whether one choses to translate literally ("car tout le monde à la porte de Bethleem sait . . . [*Bible de Jérusalem*]"; "All the gate of my people knew [JPS]") or one decides to paraphrase with varying degrees of attachment to the text of the MT.

As noted by Campbell (1975: 124), LXX understands *šaʿar* of this passage as (something like) "clan"; while in the instances of 4:1 and 4:10, it offers the usual meaning for *šaʿar,* "gate." Supported by this, Campbell opts for "assembly (of my people)" as a word that would communicate the notion of "legally responsible body of this town." Among other commentators, Joüon (1953: 74) and Rudolph (1962: 35) have arrived at renderings that are fairly similar to Campbell's. Note also JPS[2]'s translation, "the elders of my town," and De Waard (1973: 510[n.2]), who defends the Greek as a *synecdoche* of the Hebrew.

Never forgetting Boaz's presumed status of a "Judge," the Targum adds to *šaʿar* the words: "The great Sanhedrin (of my people)" (Levine, 1973: 92).

kî ʾēšet ḥayil ʾāt. That *ʾēšet ḥayil* recalls the description of Boaz as a *gibbôr ḥayil* (2:1), is noted by all commentators. Many scholars, however, add a note to suggest that "Here *ḥayl* says nothing about wealth or social status, but emphasizes the quality of Ruth's person" (Campbell, 1975: 125; similarly, Joüon, 1953: 74). Such a statement, however, may have missed the point at issue.

Whereas *ḥayil* is used as an attribute of masculine words such as

ʾîš/ʾanāšîm "man/men," *bēn/ bānîm*, "son(s)," as well as *gibbôr/gibbôrîm*, "notable(s)," it occurs as such in connection with only one feminine vocable, *ʾiššāh*, "woman," which is presented always in the construct, always in the singular. Thus, we never find *ḥayil* even succeeding the feminine equivalent of *gibbôr/ gibbôrîm*, which would have been **gebîrat/ geberet ḥayil*. This observation leads one to suspect that a lady's status as an *ʾēšet ḥayil* was determined by her marriage to an *ʾîš/ bēn/ gibbôr ḥayil*. It is in such a connection that the exquisite paean in praise of an *ʾešet ḥayil* is best understood (Prov. 31:10-31). The phrase *ʾešet ḥayil mî yimṣāʾ* is a rhetorical question that asks "who shall find an *ʾešet ḥayil?*", then proceeds to describe the merits of a particularly gifted wife of a notable. Gordon (1965: 241-42) has reminded us of the close parallels that could be drawn between the deeds of an *ʾešet ḥayil*, wife of a man important enough to sit at the "gate," i.e. "council," of his town, and those of Penelope, wife of Odysseus.

When Boaz tells Ruth that her status as an *ʾēšet ḥayil* is well known to any one in town who matters, he might therefore be saying that her marriage to Mahlon had conferred upon her credentials proper enough for her to (re)marry a *gibbôr ḥayil*. He, moreover, chooses to marry Ruth, when accepting her as a concubine would have been enough.

(t) *weʿattāh kî ʾomnām kî ʾim [MT: ʾm] gōʾēl ʾānōkî.* The Hebrew of verses 12-13 is difficult. Joüon (1953: 75) finds it too full of affirmative words. While the sense of verse 13 is rather clear, translations have differed in the degree of faithful attachment to the literal import of each word. Two renderings, however, should be noted for their major deviation from the commonly perceived issues. Staples's contorted conjectures, which would have Boaz denying that he was a *gōʾēl*, have been treated above; note also the criticisms in Campbell, 1975: 125 and Rudolph, 1962: 55. NEB also presented a translation that is difficult to match with the original; "Are you sure that I am next-of-kin?" is the statement attributed to Boaz.

The apparent surfeit of particles, adverbs, and the like in verse 12 has caused some problems. The Masoretes, for example, chose not to vocalize *ʾim*, thus encouraging the readers to ignore that particle *(ketîb welōʾ qerē)*. LXX's translation, it would appear, ignored *weʿattāh* of verse 12 and *kî ʾim*. Modern scholars delete this or that word (see Myers, 1955: 25; Rudolph, 1962: 55; Joüon, 1953: 74-75; Campbell, 1975: 125). Above, we have tried to show that *weʿattāh* of verse 12 should not be deleted since it is a crucial element in the pattern of Boaz's responses to Ruth. We have also stated that this *weʿattāh* should be linked to *lînî*, the imperative form that begins verse 13. If these proposals are deemed acceptable, then all the material of verse 12, sandwiched between *weʿattāh* and *lînî*, will have to be considered as parenthetical asides, spoken by Boaz in order to clarify his orders of verse 13. When the material is so understood, a better defense of the MT could be attempted.

From the root **ʾmn*, adverbs with the meaning "truly, verily" are formed, by affixing either *-āh (ʾomnāh)* or *-ām (ʾumnām; ʾomnām)*. While *ʾumnām* seems to be reserved for use in interrogative sentences, *ʾomnāh* is found in asseverative sentences (cf. BDB, 53-54). This *ʾomnām*, possibly because of its derivation from the root *ʾmn*, could be considered as the mildest of oaths; *ʾomnām* could either be preceded or succeeded by *kî* (e.g. Job 36:4; 12:2) without any apparent change in its effect on the sentence. It is very likely that, in these cases, *kî* should be dealt with as an emphatic rather than as a conjunctive particle.

With these observations in mind, we are left with at least three possible avenues of resolving our difficulties. (1) Were we to take *kî ʾomnām* as a compound asseverative adverb, we might be able to treat *kî ʾim* as conjoined particles, affecting the clause that immediately follows. (2) We could proceed with the idea that *ʾomnām kî* is to be treated as the compounded asseverative adverb. In this case, the first *kî* would then have to be treated either as the conjunction "when, since, because" or as an emphatic particle, "behold." The word *ʾim*, usually an (interrogative) conjunction, would be difficult to treat. It could be remembered, however, that *ʾim* was the Masoretes' candidate for deletion, no doubt since it may have been transposed from the verse below *(ʾim yigʾālēk)*. (3) Finally, we could treat the first *kî* as a conjunction, *ʾomnām* as the asseverative adverb, and *kîʾim* as the conjoined particles.

(1) and (3) appear to me to be the likeliest of possibilities. Without wishing to be dogmatic in any way, or to proclaim the following solution as exemplary, I opt for (3), primarily in order to be consistent in understanding the words of verse 12 as explanatory in nature (but cf. BDB, 475 [2c]).

(u) *wegam yēš gōʾēl*. . . . For examples, never too plentiful, of *gam* in its adversative sense, see BDB, 169 (5); Joüon, 1953: 75.

(v) *lînî*. Either the *lamed* or the *nun* are found in some manuscripts to be written with a larger script than is normal. Joüon (1953: 75) conjectures that if in this manner a scribe meant to attract attention, then it would be to point out the absence of a word, such as *pōh*, "here," or the like. Campbell (1975: 125) records Joüon's opinion but gives examples (Gen. 24:54; Judg. 19:6) where an accusative of place is lacking. It would be fair to say that we really cannot explain this scribal peculiarity.

The verb *lûn*, "to pass the night," is really more concerned with denoting the passage of time than in determining the manner in which this time is spent. Unlike *šākab*, "to sleep, lie down," *lûn* bears no sexual connotations. In our opinion, it is not accidental that the storyteller chose to use this unambiguous term in precisely that segment of Boaz's response which is concerned with Naomi's redemption. We shall note that the former will return to the more indefinite verb *šākab* at the end of his exhortations.

(w) The term *hallaylāh* is considered by some to be somewhat redundant, especially when placed after the verb *lûn*. From the perspective of a theory that tries to differentiate between Boaz's promise to marry Ruth (verse 11) and his resolve to become Naomi's redeemer (verse 12-13), the function of *hallaylāh* would be for Boaz to provide Ruth with some indication of his intention to settle the matter with dispatch. As a matter of fact, his next statement will be to assure her that he shall proceed with his plans on the next morning, *(bab)bōqer.*

(x) *ʾim yigʾālēk ṭôb yigʾāl.* The second person feminine pronominal suffix, attached to the verb *gāʾal*, occurs three times in verse 13 (also *legāʾolēk*, *ʾûgʾaltîk*). Taken at face value, these occurrences, which, we stress, all occur in one verse, could certainly damage the case we have tried to present in the preceding series of annotations, to wit: that in *Ruth* marriage and *geʾullāh* were two separate issues that concerned Naomi and Ruth, respectively. Nevertheless, we might pose the following query: What did Boaz mean when he told Ruth; "Should he [the *gōʾēl*] decide to redeem (for) you"? Joüon (1953: 65-75) is certain of the following: "Here *ʾim yigʾālēk* does not precisely mean *if he wants to act as a gōʾēl toward you* (for this idea we would expect an adverbial *hiphʿîl*) [by *hiphʿîl* Joüon means an infinitive absolute in an adverbial sense; see Joüon, 1947: 269 (102b). It ought to be noted, however, that *gāʾal* does not occur in the *hiphʿîl* -jms], but, much as 4:6 *if he wants to acquire you (qānāh,* 4:5*) as a gōʾēl*, i.e., to marry you in his function of a *gōʾēl*." As is clear, Joüon's understanding of *yigʾālēk* heavily depends upon accepting the *qerē* for **qnyty* of 4:5. Below we shall deal at length with this issue (s.v.), and shall try to uphold the integrity of the *ketîb*. Setting this issue apart, we shall examine the other attestations of *gō)ēl* and the verb *gā)al* in *Ruth* in order to determine whether or not there is any support for the notion that any other individual but Naomi stood to benefit from the process of redemption. See also the note on 4:13-17, below.

Perhaps the clearest indications that *ge)ullāh*, "redemption," is tied to Naomi's situation rather than that of Ruth, can be found in two passages, 4:3-4 and 4:15 (see below, s.v. for further remarks). In the second of these, the function of the *gō)ēl* is made explicit. When Ruth bears Obed, destined to perpetuate the memory of the deceased Mahlon over his *naḥălāh*, his "estate," the child is referred to as the *gō)ēl* of Naomi. Obed's future role as the redeemer of Naomi is to comfort Naomi and to sustain her in her old age. These duties, it is evident, Obed inherited from Boaz, the latter having acted as a *gō)ēl* by purchasing Elimelech's land when "Mr. So-and-So" gave up his right to undertake this transaction.

In 4:3-4, Boaz presents the essentials of the case before "Mr. So-and-So" and the assembled witnesses. It is to be noted that Boaz speaks only of Naomi, her parcel of land, and the duty of redemption. That the points presented by Boaz were common knowledge to anyone familiar with custom and procedure in the matter of redemption, is evident in the matter-of-fact response of "Mr. So-and-So." He was ready to intercede in behalf of Naomi by purchasing Elimelech's land. Evidently this step was all that was necessary for him to have fulfilled his obligation. Since the whole town knew about Naomi's return, which occurred a few months previously, and about the circumstances of a Moabite girl leaving her homeland to share the future of an old woman from Bethlehem, it would be unreasonable to think that "Mr. So-and-So" alone was ignorant of these events. It would, therefore, have been most singular of the latter to be ignorant of his duty toward Ruth *if marriage and* ge)ullāh *were issues that were inalterably linked by custom and law.* We must, again, conclude that these two institutions were deemed by everyone concerned as wholly unconnected. It is only when Boaz reveals a fact known to no one present at the gate (about which more anon) that "Mr. So-and-So" decided to forgo his privilege of purchasing Naomi's land.

If the evidence available to us from *Ruth* conforms to our thesis that marriage and *ge)ullāh* were independent issues, how then should we treat the information found in 3:13? Perhaps the best approach is to admit many difficulties in incorporating these data in the scheme of our tale. We might offer an explanation that, at best, should inspire modest confidence. It is observable that Boaz's exhortation of verse 13 occurs *after* he assures Ruth of his intent to marry her (verse 11). Since, as has been shown above, Ruth's requests of verse 9 were aimed not only to secure Boaz as husband, but also to retain Naomi under the care of the latter, it might have seemed most natural to Boaz to respond in terms that, ultimately, made Ruth the beneficiary of his subsequent activity. In this context, note that in 2:20 Naomi obviously considers Ruth to share her *gōʾēl*-less status when she speaks of Boaz as "one of *our* redeemers." Nevertheless, we shall speculate on this matter (see below *sub* 4:14).

(y) *ṭôb* could be taken either as an adverb ("should he redeem well, i.e. in an acceptable fashion, for you") or as a perfect. We follow most commentators and translations in regarding *ṭôb* as a finite verbal form with an indefinite subject.

Midrashic commentators (*TB Baba Batra*, 91a; *Ruth Rabbah*, IV:1; Ginzberg, 1961: 519)--but not the Targum (cf. Levine, 1973: 94)--think *ṭôb* to be the name of Elimelech's (some say Boaz's) brother. Lipiński's (1976) opinion is given below.

(z) *ḥay YHWH*. Our translation, "I swear it by the Lord," tries to convey the nature of the statements as an oath. A literal translation of *ḥay YHWH* is in dispute. The most commonly rendering, "As (surely as) Yahweh lives/is living," treats *ḥay* as a participle. Greenberg (1957), however, convincingly argues that a proper translation of this oath should be "By Yahweh's life." He thus understands *ḥay* as a noun in construct to YHWH (see further, Wolff, 1974: 89-90). On the occurrence of this formula in 'spoken' Hebrew, see MacDonald, 1975: 172. An analysis of the use of this formula is given by Gerleman, THAT, 1, 554-55 (4, a).

Of interest to us is the observation made by a few commentators (e.g. Campbell, 1975: 126) that *ḥay YHWH*, occurring over thirty times in the OT, is uniformly found to *precede* the segment of the oath which contains a promise. Only one exception, recorded in 1 Sam. 20:21, is known to this rule. Our passage in *Ruth* could be considered as a second attestation of this exception. If so, we would have to highlight other peculiarities in the use of the *ḥay YHWH* formula in connection with 3:11-13. We should note that *ḥay YHWH* controlled *two* promises of Boaz which were quite distinct in nature: a pledge to marry Ruth, and a promise to act as a *gōʾēl* should the opportunity arise. These promises, therefore, differed in matters of content (marriage versus *ge*ʾ*ullāh*), of time (immediate versus the next day), of beneficiary (Ruth versus Naomi), and of potential success (outcome depended on Boaz versus on "Mr. So-and-So").

It may be that *ḥay YHWH* of our passage should be considered as connected to the succeeding statement, in conformity with all but one other attestation of the oath formulary. In this case the promise, *šikbî* ʿ*ad-habbōqer*, would be a shortened version of verse 9, that is, Boaz would be invoking Yahweh as witness to his marriage to Ruth. In itself, such a declaration before Yahweh would be deemed sufficient for the consecration of a marriage. In addition, such a hypothesis would resolve an apparent redundancy in the text of verse 13 in which *lînî hallaylāh* and *šikbî* ʿ*ad-habbōqer* occur. Since the verb *šākab* bears a sexual undertone not available to the verb *lûn*, its connection with a promise of marriage would be most suitable.

This approach is not without its difficulties, however. Aside from having to presume an apocopated promise given in the imperative rather than the usual imperfect (but cf. GKC, 110c [p. 324]), our example would be without the particles, such as ʾ*im-(lōʾ), kî-(*ʾ*im)*, which normally connect *ḥay YHWH* to the content of the promise.

On the peculiarity of the LXX on this matter, see Sheppard, 1918: 277.

Verse 14 introduces a new element into the plot, the function of which becomes apparent in the narrative of chapter 4. Additionally, the storyteller unveils yet another facet of his literary style.

(a') *margelōtāw*. For unknown reasons, the *yôd* that should be found between the *taw* and *waw* has not been preserved. The use of this vocabulary, reminiscent of passages discussed above, suggests that Ruth was resuming whatever activity her mother-in-law recommended to her. Whatever its precise nature, it should be reminded that her activity was sufficiently physical to awaken a man deep in slumber.

Our previous discussion has made it clear that Boaz's response to Ruth's first request was positive; he not only agreed to become her spouse, but also invoked the name of Yahweh as witness to his marriage. If *liškab margelôtāyw* is ever to be taken as idiomatic for sexual congress, it would be best to refer to verse 14 as providing the locus whence such a rendering could be derived. But whether one believes the issue of sexual involvement for our protagonists is forced, irrelevant, or even untenable, one point is nevertheless clear: when dawn appeared over the threshing-floor, Ruth and Boaz were no longer bound merely by their common relationship to Naomi. Indeed, they planned to be husband and wife. For only with such supposition in mind could we properly understand the dénouement at the city gate.

(b') *wattāqom.* For reasons well detailed in Campbell (1975: 126-27), the MT's reading is preferable to Joüon's suggested emendation to **wayyāqom,* "he rose."

(c') *beṭereum.* MT's reading with a *waw* between *rēš* and *mēm* is difficult to explain. Most manuscripts have the expected *beṭerem.*

(d') *yaqqîr ʾîš ʾet-rēʿēhû.* This *hiphʿîl* of *nākar,* "to recognize," so important to the storyteller of *Ruth* (cf. 2:10, 19), is invoked once more here. We have translated this phrase somewhat loosely, rather than offering the literal meaning: ". . . before a man could recognize his companion." In French, *entre chien et loup* is a similar idiom used to describe that narrow span of time in which human shapes could be recognized while their individual features could not.

(e') *wayyōʾmer ʾal-yiwwādaʿ kî-bāʾāh hāʾiššāh haggōren,* literally: "it should not be known that the woman came to the threshing-floor." The MT does not make it clear to whom Boaz was addressing his remarks. While the Peshitta has Ruth warning Boaz not to reveal her visit, midrashic commentators think that the overseer of 2:5 was there to hear Boaz's statement, and not incidentally, to play "chaperon" for the pair. Other Rabbinic elaborations contain a prayer addressed to God in which Boaz proclaims the innocence of the occasion and the triumph of chastity. On all these, see Levine, 1973: 94-95. Shearman and Curtis (1969: 236-37) offer totally insensitive thoughts on this as well as other episodes in *Ruth.*

While morally uplifting, such interpolations are hardly necessary. The usage of the verb *ʾāmar* to refer to the thought process is well documented in Hebrew. At such moments, a noun such as *lēb/lebāb,* "heart," is often placed in proximity. We have, however, a number of examples in which even that substantive is deemed unnecessary (Gen. 20:11; 26:9); cf., BDB, 56 (2). Moreover, in opposition to the stance taken by most commentators, we do not think that Boaz was overly concerned with the opinion of others regarding the quality of his own morals: Biblical man displayed no evident scruples in contracting marriages in the manner arrived at by our protagonists.

For us, the only item at issue at this point is whether or not Boaz *told* Ruth to take extra precautions lest she be seen returning home. I do not believe we have indications to confirm any speculations on this score. It could be stated, however, that to load a young woman with a large quantity of barley is certainly no way to insure her discreet return home. Additionally, if one looks into the drama at the city gate, it would appear that it was written with Boaz as the sole hero. Since, as it may well be, 3:14 does nothing but set the stage for that section of the narrative, we might infer that Boaz's cogitations in that verse were his alone. As we shall see, his little secret was of no mean import to the ultimate resolutions of the legal arguments presented at the city gate.

*hā*ʾ*iššāh.* LXX indicates a reading in which the article was not preserved. Rudolph (1962: 56) wonders whether the *hē* betrays a scribal dittography. It seems to me, however, that one could defend the integrity of the MT reading. We should note that Boaz had, up to this point, spoken of Ruth either as a *na*ʿ*ărāh,* "young woman," or as a *bat,* "a daughter." The use of ʾ*iššāh* in 3:8 is peculiar to the circumstance of that episode, since, in that situation, Boaz could only discern a female presence near to him. Now that she was trothed to him, neither *na*ʿ*ărāh,* nor *bat* would have been suitable as terms which *Boaz himself* would have applied to Ruth. Therefore, ʾ*iššāh,* which bears the meaning of "wife" in addition to "female, woman," is well suited to the occasion. To add the article to ʾ*iššāh* would, then, have been most natural since a specific individual was in Boaz's mind.

3:15. The great nocturnal scene at the threshing-floor ends with a display of largess on the part of Boaz. It has been of interest to some commentators to assess the purpose and function of this gift. Was it meant for Ruth or for Naomi?

(f') *hābî hammiṭpaḥat* ʾ*ăšer*-ʿ*ālayik.* We have taken some liberties in translating *hābî,* imperative in form from *yāhab.* On the form, see Myers, 1955: 18; GKC, 69o (p. 190); Joüon, 1947: 75k (pp. 150-51). On Biblical usage, see Campbell, 1975: 127. *Yāhab,* attested only in the imperative (but cf. Ps. 55: 23), is not translatable by means of a uniform English equivalent.

On *miṭpaḥat,* see above, *sub* 3:3.

(g') *weʾeḥozî-bāh.* Campbell (1975: 127) thinks that *ʾḥz b-* is more frequently used in "early" passages than is *ʾḥz ʾt* (that is with an accusative particle), and has a stronger implication. This may well be so, but it is noteworthy that in Ugaritic, the verb *ʾḫd*, cognate to Hebrew *ʾḥz*, is constructed with or without *b-*, with no discernable difference in meaning.

On the grammatical peculiarity of the vocalization, see Joüon, 1947: 69b (p. 138), and GKC, 64c (p. 169). Many manuscripts have *ʾeḥezî-bāh*, (Rudolph, 1962: 56).

(h') *wayyāmod šēš-śeʿōrîm.* In Hebrew, it is not uncommon for the precise weight measure not to be explicitly stated. Thus, the search for the amount of barley Ruth carried back to her mother-in-law relies, to a large extent, on a plausible choice among alternatives. This approach is complicated by the fact that scholars are still not agreed on a uniform equivalence between the Hebrew and European systems of measurements. What follows is based on the chart, "Old Testament Measures with Modern Equivalence: B. Capacity," given on page 1323 of the *New Bible Dictionary:*

Measure	Capacity (liters)	Weight (kg) (1 = .6kg)	Boaz's gift
1. Homer	220	132	792 (1740 lbs)
2. ʾEphāh (cf. 2:17)	22	13.2	79.2 (174 lbs)
3. Seāh	7.3	4.38	26.3 (57.8 lbs)
4. ʿŌmer	3.66	2.20	13.2 (30 lbs)

Since one could not expect Ruth to have had superhuman strength, it is obvious that only measures 3 and 4 above, i.e. those involving the *seāh* and the *ʿōmer*, could be taken into considerations. It must be said, however, that I have often witnessed women in Lebanon carry an enormous amount of goods, which could not have weighed too much below six ephahs of grain (about 174 lbs). In these cases, however, the load was placed in a huge basket which was carried on the back, with ropes or belts strapped around the head and waist to provide added support. It would be unlikely, however, that Ruth could have matched such feats with only a *miṭpaḥat* to serve as a carrying instrument. Most commentators, having limited their choice to either the *seāh* or the *ʿomer*, opt for the former; this for at least two reasons: (1) *šēš*, "six," should be followed by a noun in the feminine; while *ʿōmer* is masculine, *seāh* is feminine. (2) Were the *ʿōmer* to be chosen as the weight measure recorded in our verse, Boaz's gift of barley would have amounted to about 30 lbs, just slightly more than the amount Ruth singlehandedly gleaned in just one day of work (2:17 - an *ephah* weighs about 29 lbs). Despite all these remarks, we should not forget that the narrator's emphasis is directed toward Boaz's generosity.

Campbell (1975: 128) would read **šeʿarîm*, in the place of MT's *seʿorîm*. He refers to Gen. 26:12 where this *hapax legomenon* occurs and concludes: "This must be a measure of some sort, unknown to us elsewhere unless it be the unit *we need* [italics mine] in Ruth 3:15. If Isaac raised one hundred such units (of what commodity?) in a season, then for Ruth 6 per cent of that amount could well be correct, and would be a generous gift." It should be said, however, that the context of Gen. 26:12 does not favor regarding *šeʿarîm* as a measure. As pointed out by the commentaries, *šaʿar* is better understood as a mathematical factor rather than as an "unknown" standard of measure. In Gen. 26:12 what is stressed is the fertility of Isaac's seeds, each of which produced a "hundredfold" when planted. Campbell's suggestion on this score might, therefore, better be avoided.

The precise purpose and destination of this gift of Boaz has been the subject of some discussion. Humbert (1958: 104) thinks that Boaz thereby gave Ruth an excuse to use should her nocturnal visit be discovered. It would have appeared to anyone who chanced to see her homeward bound, that she was about her business of gathering grain for her meals. This suggestion could hardly inspire confidence. A woman loaded with a generous amount of grain, returning home at dawn, *after* the harvest season's end, could not but arouse suspicion. Gunkel (1913: 78) somewhat jocosely considers the gift as symbolic of Boaz's earnestness in his dealings with Ruth. Rudolph (1962: 57) thinks that the gift was intended for Naomi, claiming that Boaz, informed of Naomi's role in precipitating the liaison between the protagonists, chose to repay her solicitude.

Staples (1937: 152) thinks it natural that a grain god--Boaz is viewed as such in Staples's scheme--would naturally offer barley "in the morning." May (1939) regards Boaz's present to Ruth in the same light as that of Judah to Tamar (cf. Hos. 9:1); that is, the gifts were given as payment for sexual favors. We need not refute these viewpoints based as they are on elaborate hypotheses which ought to be disputed *in toto*. For now, I would refer to Rowley (1965: 189-92) and to Campbell (1975: 6-7) as containing adequate disproof of the arguments of Staples and May.

Midrashic commentaries deduced from this passage that six *seāhs* of barley were the minimum amount required for a proper betrothal to take place (Levine, 1973: 95-96). Robertson (1949-50: 218-19) thinks that there may be substance to the betrothal idea but adds that Naomi should have been the ultimate recipient of Boaz's gift. While we share with Robertson the notion that links Boaz's largress with an act of betrothal, we do recognize that it is not without difficulties. In the first instance, it could be observed that Ruth speaks of this gift as addressed to Naomi (verse 17). We know of no case, custom, or regulation in which the in-laws of a widow benefited from her remarriage. Moreover, the amount of shekels equivalent to six *seāhs*--even six *ʾepāhs*--of barley must certainly have been too paltry a sum to be an adequate gift to the bride or to her family *(mōhar)*. At its maximum Boaz's gift would have been worth nine shekels; at its minimum, 3 (cf. 2 Kings 7:1, 16-18). In time of plenty, these measures were evidently worth much less. From texts such as Lev. 27:4-7 and Hos. 3:2 (on which see Wolff, 1974: 61), we surmise that a woman was "worth" thirty shekels of silver.

(i') *wayyābōʾ hāʿîr*. Many Hebrew manuscripts (BH^3, *ad locum*), the Peshitta and the Vulgate have or presuppose **wattābōʾ*, "and she proceeded. . . ." Joüon (1953: 78) approves of this last reading since "Boaz could not have left the threshing-floor before someone came to guard it (in his stead)." Such reasoning, however, depends on an explanation of Boaz's activity at the threshing-floor which we have disputed above.

We would retain the MT for reasons detailed by Campbell (1975: 128) and Rudolph (1962: 56). The latter points out that, were we to accept the proposed emendation, our text would display an obvious redundancy, since **wattābōʾ* would end verse 15 and begin verse 16. In agreeing with Rudolph's position, we should add that this duplication is unlikely in a text in which the elegant literary style of the writer is repeatedly attestable.

Campbell holds that a majority of LXX copies also support the MT's *wayyābōʾ*. Moreover, in order to avoid any ambiguity, the Targum explicitly places the name of Boaz in the text (Levine, 1973: 97).

We stated above that verse 14, containing the germ of Boaz's plan of future action, would be regarded as anticipatory of the legal discussion that unfolds in chapter 4. Just as the storyteller found it *thematically* useful to anticipate his hero's scheme of action, so too he found it *stylistically* important to promote a continuity in the narrative by ending one scene and opening another with verbs describing the movement of Boaz: *wayyābōʾ* in 3:15; *ʿālāh* in 4:1. As a final argument in favor of preserving the masculine form in verse 15, one should read a translation that has adopted the emendation (e.g. Joüon's, JPS[2], or NEB). Does not one thereby obtain the feeling of something left "hanging in the air"? Is Boaz not cut off so abruptly from the concluding portions of the narrative?

Nothing to Do But Wait (3:16-18)

16 Ruth came back to her mother-in-law,[a] who asked: "Who are you
[now], my daughter?"[b] Ruth revealed to her all that occurred with
17 the man,[c] adding: "He gave me these six measures of barley, telling
me[d] not to return empty-handed to my mother-in-law."[e]
18 "Stay put,[f] daughter," responded Naomi, "until you find out[g]
how the matter turns out.[h] The man will certainly not rest[i] unless[j]
he resolves it by the end of the day."

3:16-18 are vaguely reminiscent of 2:18b-23, verses in which Ruth is "debriefed" by Naomi upon her return from the first day of gleaning. We note the following pattern as shared by both:

(1) Ruth returns home (verb: bōʾ*), but refrains, initially, from adressing Naomi.*

(2) Naomi poses a question (verb: ʾāmar*) to Ruth.*

(3) Ruth replies by summarizing (verb: nāgad *in the* hiphʿîl*) in general terms the events that transpired (verb:* ʿāśāh*).*

(4) Ruth adds (verb: ʾāmar*) further information at the conclusion of which . . .*

(5) Naomi offers advice (verb: ʾāmar*) on Ruth's future activities. In 2:19-21, items (4) and (5) of our typology are given in a more elaborate form than in 3:17-18. In the former case, these items are actually expanded into a twofold set of statements and responses. The first consists of a discussion concerning the identity of Ruth's benefactor (2:19c-20); the second deals with Ruth's newly conferred*

status as a šiphāh in Boaz's clan (2:21-23). Furthermore, 3:17 and 2:21 are comparable in that both record Ruth attributing to Boaz words that are not elsewhere documented in the narrative.

(a) *wattabô' 'el-ḥamôtāh.* It is worth noting that, despite Ruth's obvious troth to Boaz, the narrator--as indeed Ruth herself does later (verse 17)--still speaks of Naomi as the mother-in-law of Ruth.

(b) *mî-'at bittî,* literally: "who are you, my daughter?" That Naomi's query is reminiscent of Boaz's frightened exclamation, *mî-'at* 3:9 has been noted by many commentators. We drew attention above to the absence of *bittî*, "my daughter," in 3:9, and have speculated on its significance. By adding *bittî* to her question of 3:16, Naomi clearly indicates that she recognizes the approaching figure as Ruth. In view of Naomi's interest in her daughter-in-law's welfare, we might even imagine Naomi as anxiously awaiting Ruth's return. Thus, in this instance, the surprise factor that obtains in 3:9 would not have come into play. For reasons such as the ones delineated above, commentators are generally agreed that *mî-'at* as posed by Naomi would be singularly unsuited to the occasion of 3:16 should it be taken literally. LXX apparently simply excised *mî-'at* from its text. The Peshitta on the other hand, has Ruth identifying herself in reply to Naomi. Joüon (1953: 78), followed by Rudolph (1962: 57), understand *mî* in light of Amos 7:2, 5 (cf. also Isa. 51:19), as an "accusative of condition." Campbell (1975: 116) loosely paraphrases accordingly with: "How do things stand with you, my daughter?"

Ugaritic usage of *my*, regarded by most scholars as the interrogative pronoun "what," has often been cited to buttress a translation such as: "What [about] you, my daughter?" (bibliography in de Moor, 1971: 194; van Zijl, 1972: 177-78; cf. GKC, 137c [p. 194]). Texts such as Gen. 33:6, Judg. 13:17; and Mic. 1:5 are similarly interpreted. Dahood (1968: 195) (on Ps. 73:25) puzzles me with his translation of our Ruth passages: "What ails you, my daughter?"

While finding the above-stated position most defensible and, indeed, very attractive, we might wonder, nevertheless, whether the commonly attested meaning of *mî*, namely "who," might not be retained as appropriate to the occasion. Naomi could simply be asking whether Ruth should still be considered as the widow of her son Mahlon or whether she has become the wife of Boaz. "Who are you?", perhaps better: "Whose [wife/woman] are you?", would be a natural question to pose to Ruth upon her return from the threshing-floor (for the "genitival" use of *mî*, usually preceded by a noun, see GKC, 137b, p. 443; for *mî* somewhat similarly used, see Num. 22:9 [reference courtesy Y. Gitay]). It should be made clear that our translation has added a word not in the MT: "now," in order to avoid a rendering that would otherwise give the impression that Naomi was merely requesting the identification of an apparent stranger rather than inquiring about Ruth's success.

(c) *wattaged-lāh ēt koe-ʾašer ʿāśāh-lāh hāʾîš*. See our remarks *sub* 2:19.

(d) *kî ʾāmar* [ʾ]*ē*[*l*]*ay*. The consonants for *ʾēlay* are not given in the Hebrew text *(qērē welōʾ ketîb)*. Joüon (1953: 79) thinks that haplography is at work here.

(e) *ʾal-tābôʾî rēyqām ʾel-ḥamôtēk*. This phrase invites some attention, if only because it contains the last words uttered by our heroine. It is easily recognizable that Boaz is not recorded as having made such remarks, despite the fact that Ruth attributes them to him. Campbell (1975: 129) believes that the storyteller is thus displaying a literary technique that "keeps the story free of repetition and gives each scene its own contribution to the developing dramatic effect." He further cites 2:7 as providing other examples of this technique. Indeed, it may be appropriate to have Ruth make her exit from our story with a quotation from Boaz as her last statement. Moreover, Boaz's words should depict him as a man most attentive to Naomi's needs and well-being: a most fitting image for a man who will later become Naomi's *gōʾēl*.

While Campbell's insight is praiseworthy, it seems to us, nevertheless, that there may be some merit in judging Ruth's statement as a product of her own mind. Seen from that perspective, Ruth would be revealed once more as actively engaged in promoting Boaz as a benefactor of Naomi. In this manner, she eases whatever anxiety Naomi may have had in risking the loss of her daughter-in-law. This would be yet another instance in which Ruth could be seen, not as a passive woman waiting for events to shape her fate, but as a woman actively engaged in planning its contours. We discussed above (*sub* 2:2; 3:9) at some length two other occasions in which she was similarly engaged.

But it is in assessing the use of *rēyqām*, "empty-[handed]," that we are emboldened to regard this sentence as Ruth's rather than Boaz's. As has been noted by most commentators (cf. Campbell, 1975: 129; Humbert, 1958: 104-5), *rēyqām* also occurs in 1:21, in which Naomi bitterly claims:

"I left Bethlehem full, but the Lord brought me back *empty*." How much more subtle and sensitive on the part of the narrator should he have assigned this use of *reyqām*, not to the wealthy Boaz who could have arrived at it only accidentally, but to a sympathetic Ruth who had heard it from the depth of Naomi's despair. This example of long-range word play, called *inclusio* by some, ends Ruth's message on a word of hope from Naomi.

(f) *šebî bittî*. Campbell (1975: 129) says: "As it was in 2:23, the story is brought to a stand-still, at least for a few moments, by a form of the root *yšb*."

(g) *ʿad ʾašer tēdeʿîn*. For the conjunction *ʿad ʾašer*, used to introduce temporal clauses, see GKC, 164d (p. 502); BDB, 724-25.

(h) *ʾēyk yippōl dābār*. Two peculiarities in this phrase are worth noting. The word *dābār*, "word, matter, event," is without the article *ha(n)*. While LXX Vaticanus also reflects the same situation, Lucianic LXX renders: "*the* matter will (be)come" (Campbell, 1975: 129). The latter second reading is very likely the beneficiary of an emendation to make sense out of an unusual reading in the MT. No doubt the fact that *haddābār* occurs in the same sentence might have influenced the Lucianic version. On the absence of the article in some interrogative sentences, see Joüon, 1947: 137p (427 and n. 2).

The idiom (?) *nāpal (had)dābār* occurs but rarely in other contexts (BDB, 657 [5]). The Targum seized the occasion of this exceptional usage of *nāpal*, "to fall," to speak of the "fall" from heaven of a divine decree to regulate Ruth's future life (Levine, 1973: 97-98).

(i) *yišqōṭ*. The root *šāqaṭ* properly means "to be quiet" when applied to persons, and "to be pacified" when said of the land.

(j) *kî-ʾim*. "*Exceptive* clauses, depending on another sentence, are introduced . . . (After negative sentences . . . by) *kî-ʾim* with the perfect (equivalent to *unless previously*) after imperfects which contain a declaration" (GKC, 163c2[p. 500]; BDB, 474[2]).

Legal discussions (4:1-12)

1 No sooner had Boaz gone up[a] to the [town's] gate[b] to wait there,[c] that the redeemer,[d] mentioned [earlier] by Boaz,[e] chanced to pass by. [Boaz] hailed him: "Turn around, and sit over here, Mr. So-

2 and-So!"[f] The man complied.[g] Boaz chose ten [leading] citizens
among the [local] elders,[h] and asked them to sit by. They did. He
3 then addressed the redeemer as follows: "Naomi who returned from
Moabite territory[k] is selling[j] the field belonging to Elimelech, our
4 'brother.'[i] For my part, I am declaring:[l] Let me publicly enjoin
you[m] to purchase the land in the presence of the magistrates and the
elders of my people.[n] Should you choose to redeem it, well and good.
"But, should he decide not to redeem it[o] [added Boaz as he addressed the elders before turning back to the redeemer], tell me
that I may understand.[p] There is no one with better right to redeem
it than you;[q] but I come next."
The man replied: "I shall redeem it."[r]
5 Boaz declared further:[s] "Know that on that very day you are
purchasing the field from Naomi, I am acquiring Ruth of Moab, wife
of the deceased, in order to perpetuate the memory of the deceased
upon his estate."[t]
6 "In that case," replied the redeemer, "I cannot redeem [the field]
in my behalf,[u] lest I damage the future of my own estate.[v] Please go
ahead, and act in my stead,[w] for I am in no position to redeem it."
7 --Now in Israel's past days,[x] in order to validate any legal
act,[z] be it of redemption or of exchange,[y] it was the practice for
one man publicly to remove his sandal and to hand it over to another.[a'] This was the form of attestation in Israel.--[b']
8 So, as the redeemer was telling[c'] Boaz: "Purchase it for yourself,"[d'] he removed his sandal.[e']
9 Boaz then addressed the elders and the rest of the people:[f']
"You are witnesses today[g'] that[h'] I have indeed purchased from Naomi
10* all that belonged to Elimelech[i'] and to Chilion and Mahlon.[j'] As to
Ruth of Moab, wife of Mahlon, I have also purchased her,[k'] in order
to perpetuate the memory of the deceased over his estate; for, 'the
memory of the deceased may not be obliterated from among his kinfolk
and his native village.'[l'] You are all witnesses today."
11 The people, native to the town, and the elders responded:[m']
"We are witnesses.[n'] May the Lord make the wife entering your home
like Rachel and like Leah,[o'] the two who built up the House of
Israel,[p'] so that you may prosper in Ephrathah, and maintain a repu-
12 tation in Bethlehem.[q'] May your house be like that of Perez, whom
Tamar bore Judah,[r'] through the offspring that the Lord will give
you by this young woman."[s']

4:1. With an economy of words, the narrator succeeds in establishing the scene that will occupy his attention for the better part of the chapter. It may be that the alliteration in the consonants beth *and* ʿayin, *shared by the last two words of 3:15* (wayyābōʾ hāʿîr) *and the first two of 4:1* (ûbōʿaz ʿālāh), *may have subtly allowed the storyteller to convey a continuity in the activity of Boaz. Note how this sentence begins with the subject, rather than the verb, giving the reader a sense of immediacy.*

(a) *ʿālāh*. In form, *ʿālāh* is in the perfect. As noted by commentators (e.g. Joüon, 1953: 79-80; Campbell, 1975: 140-41), the writer may have purposely avoided the use of the imperfect with a *waw* conversive in order to achieve a sense of vagueness about the sequence of activities assigned to Boaz as well as to Ruth after their parting at the threshing-floor. We have chosen to interpret this sequence to be somewhat simultaneous; that is, as Ruth was reaching her home and was beginning her *tête-à-tête* with Naomi, Boaz was arriving at the city gate and assembling his witnesses.

We had occasion to comment on *ʿālāh* when we discussed the use of *yārad* in 3:3. Here we quote from Shibayama's article on *yārad* and *ʿālāh* (1966: 360): "Therefore, the rule for the selection of *yārad* and *ʿālāh* to describe movements was depended upon 2 things: . . . [the] erstwhile standing place and the place to which they were going." Accepting Shibayama's postulates, we select Naomi's home, doubtless located in town, as the place in which to begin our discussion. From that position, the threshing-floor would be reached by going down *(yārad)* to the fertile plains below. In turn, Boaz went up from the fields and the threshing-floor *(ʿālāh)* to the city gate, which was likely to be found atop the *tell* on which Bethlehem's fortifications were built.

(b) *šaʿar*. As noted in BH^3, *ad loc.*, the Syro-Hexapla presumes **hāʿîr*, "[of] the city," after "the gate." Our translation follows its example without, however, suggesting that the MT necessarily read that way in its primary form. The Targum speaks of "the gate of the court of the Sanhedrin" (Levine, 1973: 98).

(c) *šām*. Syriac reads: "[and he sat] at the gate of the city." Targum somewhat prematurely adds: "and he sat there with the elders" (Levine, 1973: 98).

(d) *wehinnēh haggōʾēl (ʿōbēr)*. In this passage, as well as in 2:4 and 3:8 (see comments there), the use of *wehinnēh* when followed by a participle affords the narrative with the sense of an instantaneous action: just as Boaz reached the gate of the city and took his position there, the *gōʾēl* chanced to pass by. There seems to be some eagerness on the part of the storyteller not to allow too much time to pass before matters are resolved. We shall know why presently. At this stage, let it be said that, in view of Naomi's prediction of 3:18, the plot could not suffer the *gōʾēl* either to be ill or "out of town" at that particular time.

ʿābar. In view of the well-attested use of *ʿābar* to mean "to transgress," especially when terms such as "covenant, command," and so forth are placed as direct objects (cf. THAT, II, 203-4[4]), it might not be accidental that the storyteller applied this verse to the movements of a *gōʾēl* who will fail to accept his duties toward the widow Naomi. Note also our comments on *taʿabûri* of 2:8.

(e) *ʾašer dibber-bōʿaz*. Joüon, 1953: 80: "With *verba dicendi* the preposition giving the meaning *concerning whom (b, l, ʿal)* is regularly omitted after *ʾašer*" (cf. Joüon, 1947: 158i [p. 484]). Rudolph (1962: 59) adds that the relative pronoun *ʾašer* could be considered as the accusative of *dibbēr*.

(f) *pelōnî ʾalmōnî*. Discussions concerning the meaning and purpose of this appellative began in Talmudic times. The few occurrences of *pelōnî ʾalmōnî* (1 Sam. 21:3; 2 Kings 6:8) are applied to places. Ours--and possibly the "contracted" form *palmōni* that occurs in Dan. 8:13--is the only example that is applied to individuals. LXX versions have had difficulties in achieving a uniform rendering for all these instances. They opted for renderings that *interpreted* the possible meaning of *pelōnî ʾalmōnî* rather than for ones that communicated a consistent translation. For example, the instance in 1 Samuel (= 1 Kings 21:2) is rendered: ". . . and I have charged my servants to be in the place that is called, The Faithfulness of God, *phellani maemoni*" (cf. MT's ". . . and I have made an appointment with the young men [for *pelōnî ʾalmōnî*]--RSV.").

In our passage, some LXX mss have κρύφιε, "oh hidden one" others have κρυφῆ, "secretly," for *pelōnî ʾalmōnî*. This seems to be in line with an evidently old tradition that regarded our appellative as somehow bearing veiled connotations. Levine (1973: 98-99) thinks that these traditions regarded *pelōnî* as derived from *pālāʾ*, which in the *niphʿal* and the *hiphʿil*--its only occurrences in Hebrew--means "be surpassing, extraordinary." The term *ʾalmōnî* was impossibly related to the root *ʿlm* (with a *ʿayin!*), which might have meant either "to be hidden" or "to be permanent." Recently, Campbell (1975: 143) devoted a large amount of space to this problem and, for reasons unsatisfactorily detailed, chose to resurrect this idea. For unknown reasons, the Targum went its own way and chose to replace *pelōnî ʾalmōnî* with *gebir diṣeniʿin*, "modest man" (cf. **ṣnʿ* in Mic. 6:8; Prov. 11:2).

Better founded are, in our opinion, the equally long-standing interpretations that understood *pelōnî ʾalmōnî* merely as an indicator of an unknown place or personal name; thus, "such and such," "so-and-so" (in our renditions, the last is capitalized). This position is in harmony with an understanding held consistently in Talmudic times which related *pelōnî* etymologically with the Semitic root **f/pln* (modern scholars sometimes promote the less likely **f/ply*). On all these points, see Rudolph, 1962: 59; Campbell, 1975: 143; Gerleman, 1965: 35.

In the supplement to IDB (p. 969), *sub* "Wordplay," I discussed a type of word play labeled *farrago:*

Confused, often ungrammatical wording which gains meaning only because of the context (e.g. English "hodge-podge," "helter-skelter," etc.). One characteristic of farrago is that some of the elements involved often display a tendency to rhyme. *Mahēr šālāl ḥāš baz* (Isa. 8:1, 3) affords a good example. Each word is understandable, but when they are strung together the result is awkward grammatically; yet it is quite precise in conveying the intention of the speaker. . . .

Whatever the precise meaning of *pelōnî ʾalmōnî* is, it is obvious that the writer of *Ruth* did not wish to name the next-of-kin. Campbell (1975: 141-42) has listed a number of possible explanations and offered rebuttals to each. In the absence of further information on the matter from within the tale, we shall very likely never be fully satisfied with any single solution to the anonymous status of the *gōʾēl*. It seems to me that at least three explanations that Campbell has gathered either singly or overlappingly, to some degree could be plausible: (1) The writer was unaware of the actual name of the *gōʾēl*. (2) He felt it unimportant, if not unnecessary, to record it. (3) He might have purposely refused to reveal it lest he either promote speculations on what David's genealogical line might have looked like or (less plausible, in our opinion) invite criticism of the *gōʾēl* for having lost the opportunity to sire a royal house in Israel. To all these we should add, however, that one characteristic of a well-told short story is the avoidance of saturating the narrative with names that do not seem immediately relevant to the fortunes of the protagonists.

(g) The Hebrew has *wayyāsar wayyēšēb*, literally: "he turned aside and sat," using the same verbs as those employed by Boaz's order to "Mr. So-and-So."

4:2. This verse is concerned with making it quite clear that a duly constituted legal forum was to hear the case.

(h) *wayyiqqaḥ ʿaśārāh ʾanāšîm mizziqnēy hāʿîr*, literally: "he took ten men from among the elders of the city." In accordance with Hebrew judicial procedure, it was left up to the plaintiff to initiate legal action (cf. Deut. 25:7, 8; Job 13:18; Jer. 49:19). It would also appear that among the plaintiff's activities was the gathering of a group of elders to which were sometimes added *yōšebîm* (cf. verse 4), "councilmen/magistrates" (cf. Gen. 23:10, 18; Job 29:7; Prov. 24:7; 31:23). The role of the *zeqēnîm*, "elders," was most often that of arbitrators. In order to settle a dispute, the elders sat and listened to opponents detail their arguments by means of evidence and witnesses. However, it was understood that whenever necessary the elders had the power to impose a sentence and to see it carried out. On all these matters, see de Vaux, 1961: 152-57. On *zeqēnîm*, see Conrad, in TWAT, II, 644-50.

The plural of *ʾîš* is, for all intents and purposes, *anāšîm*, "men." It could at times refer to the important citizenry of a town; see Brichto on 1 Kings 21:11 (1963: 160). Note also the Akkadian usage of *awīlum* (CAD, A/2, 55-56).

4:3(-4). Boaz presents his argument before the seated assembly. This scene, as well as that which will immediately follow, is quite vividly described. As it unfolds, we should have the following picture in our mind: ten elders and magistrates are seated in the open court adjacent to the city gate. Curious onlookers abandon their stalls, in which fruits and vegetables are offered for sale or barter, in order to press within earshot of the proceedings. Before the assembled elders, Boaz and the goʾēl *take their stand. Boaz, as the plaintiff, opens with a short description of the issue at hand, and follows it with a proposal addressed to the next of kin. At one point (see below* sub yig`al*) he dramatically turns to the assembly for a short moment, before resuming with his plan of action.*

(i) *'āḥînû.* In almost all Semitic languages, the word *'āḥ*, "brother," is given an extended meaning: to wit, "relative, kinsman, clansman," and so forth (see BDB, 26 (2); Ringgren, TWAT, I, 207-8; Jenni, THAT, I, 99-100 [3, a-b]). We had occasion above to comment on Campbell's needless presumption of "covenantal relationships" as obtaining in *Ruth*. We likewise take a similar position concerning his exposition of *'āḥ* in our verse (Campbell, 1975: 143).

Some Rabbinic literature took literally the term *'āḥînû* and elaborated an undocumentable, indeed improbable, position that had Boaz, Mr. So-and-So, and Elimelech as brothers (TB, *Baba Batra*, 91a; cf. bibliography in Levine, 1973: 118-19 *sub* family of Boaz/Elimelech/Kinsman). Recently, Lipiński (1976: 126-27) proposed to understand *'āḥ* in a similar vein. His primary consideration was to clarify the issue of Levirate marriage. Since we shall deal at length with this topic, we might just state at this point that Lipiński's position is not tenable.

(j) *mākerāh no'omî.* Parsing the verb in this phrase offers no difficulties. The root is clearly *mākar*, "to sell"; the stem is *qal*; it is a perfect conjugated in the third person feminine singular, with Naomi as the subject. But because difficulties abound in interpreting the context in which *mākerāh* is found, this form has not yielded to a broadly acceptable translation. The immediate problem is at least twofold. If one understands *mākerāh*, "she sold," as an act that took place in a distant past, it would become unclear what Boaz is asking the *gō'ēl* to do. Furthermore, if Naomi had returned from Moab at least a couple of months previously, why did this plot of land which belonged to her husband not become an issue until this very moment? LXX (codex B) confronts this problem and decides gingerly to sidestep it. It has ἣ δέδοται Νωεμίν. . . , "[the portion of land] which was given to Naomi [upon her return from Moab]. . . ." This reading could not possibly have been based on the MT, but must have been thought an adequate substitute *cum* explanation for *mākerāh:* Naomi was given land as a gift upon her return; but, unable to work it, she decided to sell it. Rudolph (1962: 59) thinks a scribal error led to this reading of the LXX.

One of the few scholars who tries to keep the MT unchanged, and at the same time retain the primary meaning of the verb *mākar*, is Ap-Thomas

(1967-68: 372): "Consequently the statement *mākĕrâ noʿŏmî* (4^{3}) should have the tense, not as in 'Naomi selleth' (R.V.), or 'is selling' (R.S.V.), but 'Naomi sold'; and the reason Boaz brings the matter up at this juncture is to remind the nearer kinsman of his right and duty to bring it back (Lev 25^{25}), apparently for the benefit of the hereditary owner (cf. Lev 25^{47-49})." However, Ap-Thomas is quick to offer a major objection to this thesis: "But however attractive this interpretation might be, it seems to be ruled out by two specific statements by Boaz, in the present form of the text, that the land is bought 'from the hand of Naomi' ($4^{5,9}$). Had the text told us that the property was to be redeemed *for*, and not *from* Naomi, the transaction would be much more easily understood." While apparently unaware of Ap-Thomas's paper, similar resolutions are nevertheless offered by both Westbrook (1971) and Gordis (1974). They find no objections, however, in Boaz's words of verses 5 and 9.

We shall analyze a sampling of the scholarly opinion on this crucial issue by successively discussing proposals: A. to emend the vocalization of the Hebrew text; B. to establish a meaning for *mākar* which would be more appropriate to what the text might have represented; C. to explain the somewhat sudden appearance of "Elimelech's land" as an issue presented before legal authorities.

A. Commentators are at a loss to explain how Naomi could have sold (*mākerāh: qal* perfect) a plot of land sometime *before* the legal discussion presented at the city gate (verse 3), yet still be described as *about to* sell it on that very same day (verse 5). Two solutions are offered:

1. A solution that has attracted an impressive array of backers--a list is given in Rudolph, 1962: 59--is one that emends the vocalization of *mākerāh* into *mōkerāh*; that is, one that alters the form of *mākar* from the perfect to that of a feminine participle. To be sure, the only attestation of this form occurs as *mōkeret* (Nah. 3:4). Nevertheless, it is argued that since **mōkerāh* is a perfectly acceptable (albeit unattested) form, and since it requires emendation only in the vocalization of the MT (a *ḥōlem* replaces a *qāmeṣ* after the *mem*), "clarity" in the development of the narrative would be attained by reducing speculations concerning Naomi and the land.

2. Other scholars, including Joüon (1953: 81) and Campbell (1975: 143-44) (with previous bibliography), think that the perfect form of *mākerāh* in this passage could easily be understood once its legal context is realized. It is pointed out that in formal, legal acts (as well as in

prophetic utterances for that matter), the perfect does not necessarily bind the action to any time factor. Rather, it is perfectly acceptable for the action to be seen as stretching even into the future, as long as that action *has not been completed or accomplished* at the time of writing (cf. 4:9; Joüon, 1947: 112f,g [pp. 298-99]; GKC, 106 i, m [p. 311-12]). Brichto (1973: 15) considers the form as "past and passive." I presume that he thus regards the subject not to be Naomi, but rather "the land." It is, however, not clear to me how the full sentence is to be rendered. Nor are his examples for *qal* passive (Gen. 29:34; 31:48) convincing.

B. A few scholars believe that the difficulty in 3:3 could be reduced significantly if one were to understand the verb *mākar* in a manner noticeably different from the usual "to sell."

1. Lipiński (1976: 126) for example, thinks that the primary meaning of *mākar* is "to deliver, to hand over." He suggests the following references, among others, as bearing this primary meaning of the root: Deut. 15:12; Jer. 34:14; Judg. 3:8. Objecting to the notion that a woman could sell land belonging to her husband, Lipiński thinks that Naomi was merely "delivering" her husband's land to the *gō'ēl*, permitting the latter to benefit from its cultivation until such time as a descendent of Elimelech reclaims it on behalf of his family. Only the refusal of the *gō'ēl* to fulfill his leviratic duties denied him the possession of land that would have been added to his holding without the outlay of a shekel. Lipiński's position seems to us inseparable from the issue of levirate marriage, an issue that we shall try presently to deal with.

2. Gordis (1974: 252-59) offers an explanation that, apparently, was developed independently from that of Ap-Thomas (see above). Gordis approaches the problem from the perspective that Naomi returned home totally destitute. Otherwise, he thinks it ludicrous to witness her sending her daughter-in-law to do the work of paupers. Nevertheless, land which belonged to Elimelech (4:3, 9) before he emigrated was due to be redeemed at the next jubilee (cf. Lev. 25:28); an event that could have occurred no sooner than thirty years hence. Naomi could redeem that land herself, following the laws of Lev. 25:26-27, or could seek a kinsman to do so on her behalf (Lev. 25:25). In Gordis's opinion, Naomi could not await the next jubilee; nor did she have the proper resources to do it herself. "What Naomi is disposing of," states Gordis in connection with the *mākerāh* of 4:3, "is the obligation-rights to redeem the land which originally had belonged to her husband and her sons [p. 255]. . . . In our context [4:3]

mākhar means 'to transfer the obligation-right of redemption' and *qānāh* [4: 4ff.] 'to accept, acquire the obligation-right of redemption [p. 258].'" Gordis, however, admits that such special usage of the verbs *mākar* and *qānāh* are not documentable from the OT. We shall have more to say on Gordis's thesis below. Brichto (1973: 14-15) promotes a similar position in which Elimelech's land was sold to him *before* the latter's voyage to Moab. What is at stake in *Ruth* 4 is that the *gōʾēl* is to acquire *(qnh)* from Naomi the right to redeem *(gʾl)* the land from its present incumbents.

3. An approach that somewhat parallels Gordis's, but is not quite as developed, has been advanced by Westbrook (1971: 374): "The transaction which is recorded is not a sale, but a cession of rights from one redeemer to the next in line." McKane (1961-62: 36-40) similarly thinks it essential that the financial distress of Naomi is of utmost importance to the narrative's development: "Unless the poverty of Naomi is assumed, the entire portrayal becomes unreal and incredible. What must be meant by the statement that Naomi has 'sold' the field of Elimelech is that it has passed or is passing out of the possession of Elimelech's house because of debt (mortgage) which cannot be repaid [p. 36]." He too alludes to Lev. 25:25, where *mākar* occurs in a "parallel" context.

C. To some students of *Ruth*, whether Naomi "has sold" (perfect of *mākar*) or "is selling" ("legal" perfect/participle) a plot of land, whether *mākar* should be translated by its usual meaning "to sell" or by a more elaborated rendering, are but secondary problems. In some opinions, the main difficulty with 4:3 is the emergence of the "strip of land belonging to Elimelech" as an object of contention between Boaz and the *gōʾēl*. The problem is often stated by means of the following questions: (1) How could Naomi claim possession of land if she returned from Moab after at least ten years of absence? (2) Did widows in Israel have rights of family property? (3) Why was the plot of land not mentioned earlier in the narrative? To issues such as these, responses have not been lacking.

1. Some scholars think that we have no choice but to accept the statements of 4:3, 9 as indicating than an *émigré* such as Elimelech was still capable of retaining ownership of land despite his decision to leave his homeland. Whether he chose to "sell" his land to a redeemer as a last act before he left to Moab in full expectation that he would repurchase it on his return (Lev. 25:25), or simply decided to leave it in the care of friends (Burrows, 1940: 447), Elimelech could have been fairly secure in thinking that his portions of land in Bethlehem awaited his return from

Moab. At this point, many commentators, lastly Campbell (1975: 157-58), refer to 2 Kings 8:1-6 as furnishing an instance in which a woman (widow?; cf. 2 Kings 4:14) regains her husband's property even after a seven-year sojourn among the Philistines. In their opinion, therefore, this situation, offering as it does an imperfect parallel, is nevertheless helpful to explain Naomi's retention of land after her return home.

2. Unlike the legislation and apparent customs of its neighbors, Israel's laws, as preserved in Num. 27:8-11, make it clear that widows were bypassed in favor of male relatives. Whether or not local custom was in reality less harsh than the written codifications on the fate of the widow (Rowley, 1965: 184[n. 2]; Neufeld, 1944: 240-41; Beattie, 1974: 251-67) cannot be ascertained. It remains plausible, however, that written laws may have exaggerated the superior position of agnates in the matter of inheritance, probably to insure that property could not be disposed of unwisely by unprotected widows.

Faced with the dearth of Biblical testimony on the subject, commentators have been limited to speculate on the manner in which the widow Naomi could have retained control over her husband's estate. The possibilities have been explored by the tenth-century Qaraite Salmon ben Yeroham (as quoted by Beattie, 1974: 254-55): a. Naomi's property did not become hers as a result of her husband's death, but rather because her sons died childless in a foreign country. b. Elimelech's property had really been part of Naomi's dowry; when he died, it was natural that it should return to her (cf. also Jepsen, 1937-38: 419; Caspari, 1908: 115ff; contra Burrows, 1940: 448). c. Naomi (and Ruth) were entrusted with Elimelech's property, until a proper heir was born to Ruth (cf. also Neufeld, 1944: 240). Rowley (1965: 184[n. 2]) invokes the evidence of Nuzi texts to suggest that Elimelech may have expressly willed Naomi a share in his estate. But this approach would rely on Near Eastern legal procedures that, as far as we know, may not have obtained in Israel. As a matter of fact, absolutely no problems would confront us in 4:3 if we could somehow presume that Near Eastern law had precedence over Israel's own codifications. But we obviously cannot, even should not, presume it.

3. As to some of the reasons that caused Naomi to be silent on the parcel of land, we are only offered speculations: totally destitute, Naomi was merely waiting for Ruth to have a (prospective) husband before she could act, claiming the first male issue of this union as a future *gōʾēl* (Neufeld [1944], see above). Campbell (1975: 158), following Rowley

(1965: 184), opines that Naomi was either ignorant of the existence of such a property or needed the help of someone (Boaz) who knew the law concerning abandoned property. The first of this two-part opinion is hardly likely: that a destitute woman should be ignorant of the single material advantage she possessed is a plainly unreasonable assumption.

We should come to some conclusion at the close of this lengthy annotation. To do so, we gather together what seems to us most plausible from among the arguments offered by various scholars, and add a few observations of our own. We shall be under no illusion that our proposal will advance the cause of the discussion on 4:3 beyond reproach.

Elimelech and his family left Bethlehem at the time of great famine. We might surmise that his plot of land was either abandoned or left to the care of family or friend. His family's sojourn in Moab lasted over ten years, but this is no reason to believe that Elimelech intended to find permanent shelter in a foreign land. As a matter of fact, it is a *topos* in Hebraic narratives to have short-term visits into foreign territory turn into long-term sojourns (e.g. Eisodus into Egypt; Jacob in Haran; Moses in the wilderness, etc.; cf. IDB, IV, 397-99). If this is the case, then we might stress the fact that Elimelech's land was certainly not sold as he left his homeland, since he would have expected to return as soon as "the Lord provides for his people by giving them food" (1:6).

Naomi and Ruth made their way homeward at the harvest season. In view of this time period, it is reasonable to assume that their land was being harvested either by family or neighbor. Thus, it would have been simply pointless for a masterly narrator to allude to Elimelech's plot of land during harvest time, when Naomi or Ruth could not be expected to enter into negotiations with anyone, as long as the land was in the hands of others. When that segment of agricultural life came to an end, however, attention could legitimately be focused on Elimelech's property. What is remarkable, in my opinion, is that this attention was centered *not* on Naomi, but on Ruth. For this point, we must backtrack a bit.

That it was Boaz who decided to act on the matter without any apparent urging on Naomi's part has puzzled a few commentators (e.g. Campbell, 1975: 158). It would be beyond plausibility, however, to suppose, as does Rowley (1965: 183), that Naomi did not know of her husband's land and thus had to depend on Boaz's memory to achieve a measure of prosperity. Nor could we accept the possibility that the *gōʾēl* was likewise ignorant of the status of Elimelech's land. Certainly, in a town as small as Bethlehem everyone was aware of his neighbor's business. In the absence of OT information, we might assume that the standing of women in the legal forum of Rabbinic times obtained in earlier periods. These laws were quite clear in that the rights of women during judicial proceedings, especially in matters of property transfer, were severely restricted (see Josephus, *Antiq.*, IV:viii:15; BDB, IV, 874. (But cf. the unusual statement in TB, *Shabuʿot*, 30a.) Thus, it would be very doubtful that Naomi, on her own, could have gathered a group of elders in order to initiate proceedings concerning her husband's land. For this, she needed a sponsor. That sponsor turned out to be Boaz. But it should be noted that the *initial impulse* to take up the cause of Naomi came from Ruth. On that fateful night when Boaz awakened in terror, Ruth brought forth the issues that concerned her in the following manner: (1) "protect me," (2) "become a *gōʾēl*" (3:9). We should also remember that, according to our exegesis of that verse and the one following it, Boaz praised Ruth more for her second request, that of his becoming Naomi's *gōʾēl*, than for the first, that of his becoming Ruth's husband. It is thus entirely possible that Naomi not only did not approach Boaz concerning her land, but that she became aware of his sponsorship of her cause only after Ruth came back home after her *tête-à-tête* with Boaz at the threshing-floor.

With Boaz initiating the confrontation at the city gate after the barley harvest had come to an end, it became legally and practically possible for the issue of Elimelech's land to be resolved. Never sold, Elimelech's land--and we would insist on calling it thus, rather than Naomi's land--could now be placed on the market. It is at this point that the *geʾullāh* of Naomi (or better, the *geʾullāh* of Elimelech's land in behalf of his widow, Naomi) became an object of discussion. Either because a widow may not (legally) or could not (physically) own arable property, that land was to be sold to a *gōʾēl* with the proceeds going to Naomi. We side, therefore, with those who understand *mākerāh* as a perfect form that, in view of its juridical setting, is best translated by "she is selling." The money would certainly have been hers to enjoy, since, as far as we know, no laws or customs prevented a widow from using the proceeds of such a transaction. Should Naomi ever become blessed with a male descendent, he would have had the right to repossess Elimelech's land, in accordance with the laws of Lev. 25:25.

To the mind of the next of kin, approached by Boaz, the matter was clear-cut. He must certainly have known of Naomi's plight, as did everyone in Bethlehem. If he was surprised at all when he heard Boaz's initial statement before the legally constituted assembly (verse 4) it could only be on account of its timing since the discussion occurs at the end of the barley harvest rather than at the end of the wheat harvest (see below). Nevertheless, when he responded "I shall certainly redeem it," he envisaged no way in which Elimelech's land could ever be returned; Naomi was an elderly widow whose chances of producing a future redeemer to the house of Elimelech were practically nil. He could not but gain from the transaction!

(k) *haššābāh miśdēh mô'āb*. The accent on the *penultima* indicates that the conjugation is in the perfect (cf. also *sub* 1:22). Here the reference to Naomi as the one who "has returned from Moab" is doubtless made for the purpose of identification in a legal forum.

4:4. At this point Boaz will play his trump card!

(l) *wa'anî 'āmartî*. Many commentators take this phrase as reflecting a thought process on the part of Boaz, not unlike the reference to the same verb in 3:14. Thus Joüon (1953: 81) comments: *"I told (myself), I thought,* here, in view of the activity, *'I have decided'"* (cf. 1 Sam. 30:6; likewise *dibbēr,* 1 Kings 22:23; 2 Kings 14:27). His proposal is accepted by Campbell (1975: 144), who nevertheless observes that the syntax in our passage is clearly different from the sentences invoked by Joüon. In particular, we think it quite odd that an imperfect cohortative such as *'egleh ('oznekā)* is used in a sentence that recalls a decision made in the past.

Campbell uses this understanding of *wa'anî 'āmartî* to further a proposal made previously by him: "It is as though Boaz were quoting a promise actually made earlier, so that we cannot entirely dismiss the possibility of a conversation between Boaz and Naomi, presumably falling between the events at the end of chapter 3 and those at the beginning of chapter 4." Our discussion above on *mākerāh* should have made it clear why Campbell's hypothesis is needless.

I understand *wa'anî 'āmartî* differently from the above-mentioned authorities. I think it to be another example of the perfect used in a legal context to speak of an act that is unraveling in the present. Although *dibbēr* is the verbal form most commonly used in legal situations, we do have some examples in which the verb *ʾāmar,* in the *qal,* with the meaning "to declare," is employed within juridical contexts (e.g., 1 Kings 3:22; cf. Schmidt, TWAT, II, 104-7, II, 2-3). For an equivalent usage in Akkadian, compare the various meanings of the verb *dabābu,* which range from "to tell, relate, speak," to "to plead in court, litigate" (CAD, D, 4-9).

(m) *ʾegleh ʾozneka lēʾmōr*, literally, "let me/I will uncover your ear, in saying [as follows]." The idiom "to uncover the ear" seems to be derived from the realm of symbolic gesturing that accompanied legal transactions. That the Ancient Near East knew of a wide variety of such gestures, is a topic which has recently been discussed by Kilmer (1974: 177-83; note in particular the list given on 182-83 [n. 24]), which associates a wide assortment of symbolic gestures with the corresponding legal interpretations. Not found in that list is an Akkadian idiom that parallels ours in meaning, *uznam puttû/šuptû* (verb: *pētu,* "to open"; Von Soden, AHw, 860-61 [*D*-stem, 11; *Š*-stem, 4]. For attestation of the *exact* Akkadian idiom albeit with the *qal* of *pātaḥ*, in the OT, note the *YHWH pātaḥ-lî ʾōzen* and *ʾoznēy ḥērš̂îm tippātaḥnāh*, expressions unique to 1 and 2 Isaiah [50:5; 35:5]).

Our idiom, *liglôt ʾōzen,* understood as a symbolic gesture that may have been defunct at the time Boaz addressed the next of kin, vividly sketches a quaint scene in which a plaintiff approaches his opponent to uncover his ears by either parting his hair or his *kaffiyeh* and then publicly speaks his complaint (Joüon, 1953: 81-82). For other attestations of this idiom, see BDB, 162 (1.); Zobel in TWAT, I, 1022-1023.

Whether the writer of *Ruth* chose this expression as a playful reminder of his *legallôt margelôt* of 3:4, 7, or as a parasonantic pun on the consonants *gimel* and *lāmed* which are shared with the derivatives of the roots **glh* and **gʾl (gōʾēl, geʾullāh* and various forms of the verb *gāʾal),* cannot be ascertained with any confidence.

The term *lēʾmōr* introduces the content of Boaz's proposal, which he is about to state before the legal authorities.

(n) *qenēh neged hayyōšebîm weneged ziqnēy ʿammî.* The meaning of *qānāh* is quite clear: "to buy." Since Naomi was selling a piece of land (verb: *mākar),* it is evident that the *gōʾēl* was being asked to purchase it. Campbell (1975: 145) has a good discussion in which he ably defends a translation that uses *qānāh* in its primary and most commonly attested meaning. It remains for us to reject Gordis's (1974: 258) conjecture that this verb carried a nuance available from no other text but *Ruth*: "to accept, to acquire the obligation-right of redemption" (see our discussion above). Gordis supposes the following to have obtained:

Naomi inherited no land from her husband and sons--only the right to redeem the family property that her husband had sold. Because she is unable to exercise this right, in view of her poverty, she transfers *(mkrh)* this obligation-right to her nearest kinsman. When he declines, Boaz, a somewhat more distant relative, accepts *(qnyty)* this obligation-right, which brings him Ruth as wife. His subsequent redemption of the land from the original purchaser from Elimelech, is not described in the book, because it is Ruth who is the focus of interest.

To this reconstruction, we offer the following objections:

A. It would be wrong to think that chapter 4 focuses exclusively on Ruth. As is clear, however, it is Naomi who is given a larger role to play in every subsequent scene within that chapter.

B. Gordis's thesis *assumes* that a woman had a right to redeem, or even to transfer the right of redemption, in cases in which property had been sold by a male.

C. Since Gordis's study also rejects the notion that levirate marriage was in effect in *Ruth* (pp. 246-52), it is curious that he links purchasing the right of redemption with acquiring Ruth as wife.

D. Most fatal to Gordis's thesis are verses 5 and 9 of chapter 4 (see above). There, it is made clear that the land was purchased "from Naomi." If it were only a matter of purchasing "obligation-right of redemption," Naomi would have hardly been involved. Rather, the original buyer of Elimelech's land whose existence Gordis presumes would have been mentioned as the one from whom Boaz purchased this "right of redemption." One more objection in this context: if Elimelech sold his land before leaving for Moab--as Gordis assumes--would he be so ignorant of Israel's laws and customs that he would have chosen as a buyer a person who is not a relative? Elimelech and his descendents would thus lose until jubilee time the opportunity to regain control of the property.

yōšebîm. For our translation of this term, see Brichto, 1963: 160-61. That *yōšebîm* is likely to refer merely to "onlookers" is implied by Rudolph,(1962: 59) but disputed by Campbell (1975: 145). However, we do not, in turn, agree with the latter's position that *yōšebîm* refers to a body of unselected elders. Joüon (1953: 82), translates with *"des assistants,"* despite the fact that his annotation on *yōšebîm* equates the term with "elders." The Targum distinguishes between "those who sit in the gate of the court of the Sanhedrin" and "the elders of my people."

(o) *we᾿im-lo᾿ yig᾿al.* Most commentators emend *yig᾿al,* "he shall/will redeem" (imperfect, third person masculine singular) into **tig᾿al,* "you shall/will redeem" (imperfect, second masculine singular), a reading preserved by many Hebrew manuscripts (BH^3, *ad loc.).* This proposed emendation, while it makes eminent sense, might rob the scene unfolding at the city gate of its opportunity to impart a powerfully vivid impression. As noted above, we think that *yig᾿al* is purposely used in order to attribute to Boaz a series of realistic movements, as he briefly turns to address the assembled elders in between harangues aimed at the next of kin.

We should also add, that Rudolph's (1962: 59) comments notwithstanding, it would be difficult to explain *yig᾿al* as a scribal error for **tig᾿al.*

(p) *we᾿ēdeʿā. qerē* gives the energic form **we᾿ēdeʿāh.* The consonantal text of the *ketîb,* however, implies *wā᾿ēdaʿ,* a form that occurs in Jer. 32:8 and shares with our passage a "redemption of the land" context. The verb *yādaʿ,* "to know," is used here in its legal sense; i.e. "I shall know for the purpose of taking [or abandoning] legal action." W. Schottroff (THAT, I, 692 [IV:1,a]) gives a bibliography of studies that understand *yādaʿ* as a term found in treaties and convenants (thus, not precisely applicable to our usage).

(q) *᾿ēyn zûlāteka lig᾿ôl.* Having formulated a theory that regarded the *gō᾿ēl* as drawn from a "circle of redeemers or confederates," Campbell (1975: 145-46) is hard pressed to explain Boaz's usage of *zûlāh.* This preposition, always found in construct with a personal pronoun, designates the only exception to that person represented by the suffixed pronoun. In other words, Boaz clearly feels himself as the only redeemer available as alternative to Mr. So-and-So. As noted above, Campbell's conjectures are not tenable.

(r) *wayyō᾿mer ᾿ānōkî ᾿eg᾿āl.* With this reply, the *gō᾿ēl* agrees to purchase Elimemech's land. As he considered his response, it must have occurred to him that he would be risking nothing by agreeing to purchase that land. Naomi had neither children nor grandchildren. The land could not, therefore, be redeemed from him. Furthermore, even the release of land to its original owner, which is a feature of the jubilee (if applicable to Ruth), would not have affected him. He could not lose!

4:5. This verse is pivotal to the remaining narrative. In its importance to the development of the complete tale, it equals 1:16-17, 2:13, and 3:9. It reveals Boaz's "trump card," his atout, *with which he hopes to dissuade the next of kin from purchasing Elimelech's land. This is agreed upon by the majority of commentators. The nature of this "trump-card," and the legal ramifications which it implies, however, have produced what must certainly be the lion's share of the* Ruth *bibliography. In the comments below, we shall allude to the main currents within that literature, but we note at the outset that we cannot hope completely to cover the topic at hand because of the wealth of arguments and counter-arguments. We refer here to the bibliographies assembled in Rudolph, 1962: 60-61; Rowley, 1965: 178-79; Levine, 1973: 100-1.*

(s) *wayyōʾmer bōʿaz*. See above for the usage of *ʾāmar* in juridical contexts.

(t) *beyôm-qenôtekā haśśādeh miyyad noʿomî ûmēʾēt rût hammôʾabiyyāh ʾēšet-hammēt qnyty* [*qerē: qānîtā; ketib: qānîtî*] *lehāqîm šēm-hammēt ʿal-naḥalātô*. Because of the peculiar difficulties associated with this verse, it is best to scrutinize, under a single annotation, its remaining segment.

The noun *yôm*, literally: "day," occurs some sixty times in the OT prefixed by a *be-* and followed by a verb in the infinite construct. Much less frequently, the prepositions *min, ʿad, ke-, l-* and perfect and imperfect forms are involved. For the relevant statistics, see E. Jenni, THAT, I, 711 (3, c). In constructions such as ours, it is advisable to weaken the precise meaning of *yôm*, and to replace it with the general "at the moment [that/of]," "at the time [that/of]," or simply with "when" (Joüon, 1947: 129 [2] [p. 392]). We have retained the word "day" in our translation purposely, in order to highlight the fact that Boaz may have intended a certain amount of vagueness to hover over the sequence of activities that are described in verse 5. We shall presently see what may be the actual consequence of this vagueness. At this point, we should only wish to state that, according to some Hebrew reckoning, the "day" was conceived to have lasted from one evening to another. Thus, Boaz would be technically correct in considering his troth to Ruth, which occurred the previous night, to date on the same day as his deliberations before the elders of Bethlehem. But we are anticipating! (On the controversy over the duration of the *yôm*, "morning-night" versus "evening-evening," see E. Jenni, THAT, I, 710; Skinner, 1930: 20, n. on 1:5; contra de Vaux, 1961: 180-81.)

*miyyad no*ʿ*omî ûmē*ʾ*ēt rût.* That the field is to be bought from Naomi is clear. The ʾ*atnāḥ*, a disjunctive accent that is used as the main divider within a verse, is placed under *no*ʿ*omî*. *miyyad*, literally: "from the hand of. . . ," is often found in conjunction with *qānāh*, "to buy." Beginning from this point, however, the text presents us with a number of difficulties the solutions of which are, unfortunately, crucial to the entire *Ruth* narrative. The first of these requires us to decide the proper syntactical position of *ûmē*ʾ*ēt*.

There is absolutely no reason why the verb *qānāh* cannot be associated with the compound preposition *mē*ʾ*ēt*, literally: 'from proximity with . . .' (cf. Gen. 25:10; Lev. 25:15; 27:24). As a matter of fact, Jer. 32:9, which is also concerned with redemption of land, has *wā*ʾ*eqneh* ʾ*et-haśśādeh mē*ʾ*ēt PN*. Further, there are no unsurmountable grammatical difficulties in having the *gō*ʾ*ēl* purchase the field simultaneously from Naomi and Ruth; this, despite the fact that the text has different compound prepositions, *miyyad* and *mē*ʾ*ēt*, preceding the personal names of our heroines. Although in no way offering a clear grammatical parallel, Lev. 25:14-15 could be alluded to as providing us with examples in which these prepositions are used without apparent discriminatory intents (*qānōh miyyad* ʿ*amîtekā* [verse 14] versus *tiqneh mē*ʾ*ēt* ʿ*amîtekā* [verse 15]). A problem confronts us, however, when we are to decide how much of the sentence in verse 5 is actually controlled by *(beyôm) qenôtekā*. It is conceivable, for example, to translate a healthy chunk of our verse as follows: "Know that on the day you purchase the field from Naomi and from Ruth the Moabitess, wife of the deceased. . . ." But if we do this, we shall be at a loss to frame a proper context for the remaining *qnyty lehāqîm šēm-hammēt* ʿ*al-naḥalātô*, since it would be unclear what the object (that is the item purchased) of **qnty* would be. Below, we survey some proposals that have in common a desire to retain unemended *ûmē*ʾ*ēt (rût)*. Such a desire is often legitimized by reference to the LXX, which clearly considers both Naomi and Ruth as selling land to the *gō*ʾ*ēl*. But it should be noted that the LXX resolves the ensuing difficulty we have just mentioned by *adding* "her," that is "Ruth," as the object of *qnyty*. We divide our choices into three categories: one that retains the *qerē*, *qanîtā*; another that resorts to the *ketîb*, *qanîtî*; a third that reinterprets *qnyty*. We note here, but refer to Rudolph (1962: 67) for appropriate criticism, L. Köhler's resolution of the problem by simply eliminating *ûmē*ʾ*ēt rût hammô*ʾ*abîyyāh*.

A. Were one to accept the *qerē* of *qnyty*, that is *qanîtā*, one would have the following: "Know that on the day you purchase the field from Naomi and from Ruth, the Moabitess, wife of the deceased, you would have purchased/are purchasing to perpetuate the memory of the deceased upon his estate." The rendering would be fairly regular Hebrew, but we would be left wondering about the *gōʾēl*'s volte-face in refusing his obligation to purchase the land.

B. If one accepts the *ketîb* of *qnyty*, that is *qanîtî*, we would have a rendering in which Boaz pledges to purchase an unknown item: "Know that . . . wife of the deceased, I am purchasing (?) to perpetuate the memory . . . ." In a letter to me dated May 28, 1976, C. H. Gordon offers a possible way to understand the text, though he is clear in saying that he does not favor that approach: "By shifting the *ʾatnāḥ* accent from "Naomi" to "Ruth" the passage would read: 'On whatever day you acquire the field from Naomi and Ruth, I will (nonetheless) have acquired the Moabitess, wife of the deceased, . . .' "

C. Vriezen (1948: 81) vocalized *qnyty* as *qinnētî* (for *qinnēʾtî*, root: **qnʾ*) and renders: ". . . I maintain with regard [*ûmēʾēt* understood as such by him] to Ruth the Moabitess, the wife of the dead, the right to raise up the name of the dead upon his inheritance." This interpretation has met with a practically unanimous scholarly rejection. But we chose to reject Vriezen's hypothesis not so much because, as some scholars maintain, it would result in divorcing the issues of *geʾullāh* and marriage (e.g. Campbell, 1975: 146, with bibliography), but because it would invoke the verb **qnʾ* in a most singular usage and spelling.

Lipiński recently revived a suggestion of Keil and Delitzsch (1876: 488) which upholds the integrity of the MT of verse 5 in every respect but in *qnyty*. The last is emended into *qnytw* in order to obtain the following: "On the day in which you will have acquired the field from the hand of Naomi and of Ruth . . . you would have acquired *it* [i.e. the field] in order to perpetuate the name of the dead upon his inheritance." This position would rob us of a reason for the *gōʾēl*'s subsequent behavior. Furthermore, I am not sure that a form such as *qnytw*, while eminently plausible, is in reality available in Hebrew. By that I mean to question the probability of having a *qāl lamed-he* verb conjugated in the second person masculine singular perfect construed with a third person masculine singular suffix. Such forms have a tendency to attach the pronominal suffix to the particle *ʾet*. Finally, in the case of Lipiński, his espousal of this proposal is inconsistent with his own explanation as to why the *gō'ēl* changed his mind (1976: 127).

It is clear from the above, therefore, that to retain *ûmē'ēt* might be too high a price to pay; for, it would inhibit congency within verse 5 and consistency within the rest of the narrative. In light of Boaz's declaration in 4:10, *wegam 'et-rût hammō'abîyyāh . . . qānîtî*, a number of proposed emendations have been advanced which would remove the *ûmē'ēt* as a source of difficulty. We shall mention but a few, all of which have in common a division of verse 5 into two main segments: the first ending with *no'omî*, the second beginning with an amended form of *ûmē'ēt*.

1. One could retain the *m* in *ûmē'ēt* but regard it as an "enclitic *mem*." Thus, for all practical purposes, the *m* would be ignored. Campbell (1975: 146) favors this approach but recognizes its eccentricity.

2. Gray (1967: q.v.) simply deletes the *m*, leaving the text to read *we'et*. . . . This approach is also favored by C. H. Gordon, (letter to me of May 28, 1976). The latter adds, "I prefer to regard the *m* of *m't* as a scribal addition inserted to fit the *qrē* and make the story less racy."

3. One could read *gam 'et-rût*. . . , thus proposing to regard the *waw* as an error for the *gimel*.

4. One could read *wegam 'et rût*. . . , thus harmonizing it with the reading of 4:10 and regarding the *gimel* as having been lost in the transmission of the text of *Ruth*. Bibliography on the last two proposals is available in Beattie, 1971: 493(n.2); 1974: 263(n.1).

In the absence of any overwhelming reason to prefer one proposal over the other--with the exception of the first, which seems most unlikely to me--I should prefer the fourth, followed by the second proposal.

With *ûmē'ēt* in its emended form connected with that segment of the verse which follows it, we now turn to further difficulties in connection with *qnyty*. First, we will discuss the unusual usage of the verb *qānāh*, "to buy, purchase," when used in connection with women/wives. We must then choose between the *qerē (qānîtā*, "you buy"*)* and the *ketîb (qānîtî*, "I purchase"*)*. When this is done, we should decide whether the chosen form of *qnyty* is to be translated by means of the past tense or that of the present. It shall be quickly evident that whereas the solution for *ûmē'ēt* was sought in researching the syntax of the sentence, that of *qnyty* will depend upon the particular understanding of what precisely occurred at the city gate.

Much has been written on the use of *qānāh*, "to purchase, acquire, buy," in connection with 4:5. While there are ample attestations in the OT for this verb in connection with the purchase of male and female slaves (Humbert, 1958: 168), we have scarcely any evidence to suggest that "marriage by purchase" was known to Biblical societies. The two attestations that are most often cited to suggest the existence of this institution, Gen. 31:14-16 and Hos. 3:2, cannot be used with assurance. Not only is *qānāh not* the verb employed in these contexts, but the literary function of the verbs that are used--*mākar*, "to sell," in Gen. 31, and *kārāh*, "to barter," in Hos. 3--cannot be ignored; for in these cases, the authors aimed at conveying deep sarcasm and total disrespect. Further on this topic, see Burrows, 1938: 28-29.

Burrows thinks that *qānāh* in 4:5 "indicate[s] acquisition in general, not necessarily by purchase." Weiss (1964: 244-48) adduces evidence from the Mishnah to support the thesis that *qānāh*, in passages where more than one specific item is commercially transacted, could be applied to "acquiring a wife." His thesis is adopted by Campbell (1975: 146-47). We object to Weiss's approach on the ground that the examples cited to further his opinion seem inspired by the usage of *Ruth*, that is, they concern problems of a childless widow and the duty of her levir towards her. Furthermore, the position of women during the Hellenistic period seems to have deteriorated markedly from that of Biblical times (cf. TB, *Kidd*, 18b, *Bar*, and the discussion of Jeremias, 1969: 364-65). Finally, we shall have occasion to point out that, according to 4:9-10, Boaz saw his purchase of Ruth and Elimelech's land as two separate transactions. We should not therefore accuse him of lumping together these separate, albeit sequential, acts.

We might approach a resolution of this problem by initially focusing not on the verb *qānāh* and its usage, but on the status of Ruth at the time she was being "acquired." What follows will be a speculative, but by no means implausible, assessment of events.

a. It is clear that once widowed and bereft of children and father-in-law, both Ruth and Orpah were free to follow their own desires. In this respect, Law 33 of the *Assyrian Code* (cf. ANET[3], 182), is of interest: "If a [woman's] husband and her father-in-law are both dead and she has no son, she becomes a widow *(almattu)*; she may go wherever she wishes." Note also that in Hebrew *ʾalmānāh* likewise refers to a woman without any means of support, not merely a "husbandless" woman. See Cohen, 1973:76-77.

b. While Orpah chose to return to the security and protection of her own parents, Ruth did not. She attached herself willingly to another widow who, as long as she remained in Moab, would also be ranked among *ʾalmānôt*. Naomi needed to return to her own homeland if she ever expected any help from her kinsmen.

c. When Ruth made her glowing moving address to Naomi, she was not merely declaring her love and affection for her former mother-in-law, but was in essence submitting herself to the will of Naomi. In other words, Ruth was giving up her freedom of movement and choice in exchange for permanent attachment to Naomi until such time as she finds--or more accurately, until such time as Naomi finds for her--a husband.

Our hypothesis, that Ruth submitted herself to Naomi's will, makes it clearer why Ruth alone is to go to the fields in order to glean for herself as well as for her mother-in-law; why Ruth easily received Naomi's permission to attach herself to the clan of Boaz, a man who was well known, perhaps even related to Naomi; and why, despite her newly acquired status as a member of Boaz's clan, Ruth nevertheless stayed in Naomi's home. Finally, this hypothesis may explain why Ruth accepted, seemingly blindly, Naomi's advice for her to visit Boaz at the threshing-floor. It would not be just because Naomi's urgings were wiser, stemming as they do from an older woman, but precisely because Ruth, despite any scruples which she may have had, had little choice in the matter.

d. One item of import to our thesis which has not received adequate attention in the literature on *Ruth* is the completely different vocabulary employed in verse 13 to speak of Boaz's marriage to Ruth. There, the commonly attested idiom *laqaḥat leʾiššāh*, "to take as wife," is used. Moreover, another well-known idiom, *lihyôt (lô) leʾiššāh*, is added after the verb *lāqaḥ*, as if to emphasize that the marriage of our protagonists did not occur until this juncture of the narrative. This pattern in the terminology could hardly have been accidental. We must therefore assume that our narrator was not coining a new phrase when he spoke, in verse 5, of the "purchase" of Ruth. We should conclude, therefore, that *qānāh* was neither accidental to the sequence of transactions occurring in 4:4-5, and again in 9-10, nor an oversight in the choice of vocabulary.

e. If Ruth gave up her freedom to return to her parents' home in Moab in favor of attachment to a Bethlehemite widow, it would follow that to obtain Ruth's release from the bonds that tied her to Naomi, Boaz may have had to buy her outright or at least to compensate Naomi for the loss of a valuable helper. This purchase price is in no way to be considered as a bride price since the appropriate receivers of such gifts were presumably still in Moab. It is simply the amount paid *to Naomi* to obtain Ruth's release from her promise and from her (unwritten) contract with Naomi. That Naomi benefits monetarily from this last transaction would clearly not be resented by an audience whose sympathy doubtless extended to widows in search of security and redeemers.

The *qerē, qānîtā*. "You purchase" is obviously based on an old interpretation of the text. LXX and Peshitta do not doubt that it was the *gọ̄ʾēl* who was charged with "buying" Ruth. This, in itself, is most puzzling, for we have no evidence that these versions were concerned with levirate marriage as an issue in *Ruth* (see below and Levine, 1973: 100-1; Gordis, 1974: 246-52). Furthermore, we have already noted that the LXX resolved somewhat differently the difficulty associated with our verse.

At least as early as the Targum, however, the issue of levirate marriage was associated with the text of *Ruth* 4 in order to solve the difficulty raised by the MT's *qnyty*. In particular, it was seen that if *qnyty* was translated as the verbal form required it, that is "I purchase," a "sexual" interpretation for the preceding scene at the threshing-floor could not be avoided. Thus, Boaz would be confirming that he and Ruth had spoken their vows after an event that might naturally have occurred whenever a fair maiden meets a young man under a starry sky. In Rabbinic times, with its severe restriction of the freedom of women, this was clearly not an acceptable choice. Reference to levirate laws, therefore, had a double purpose. It underscored the chastity of the preceding events by reasoning that Boaz could not have permitted Ruth to marry the *gōʾēl* had she become his betrothed; or, more important, it revealed the protagonists as concerned with fulfilling an obligation as legislated in Deut. 25.

The relevant section of the Deuteronomic laws reads as follows: "When brothers dwell together [i.e. (?) while their father had not divided his estate among them] and one of them dies and leaves no son, the wife of the deceased shall not be married to a stranger, outside of the family. Her husband's brother shall unite with her and take her as his wife, performing the levir's duty. The first son that she bears shall be accounted to the dead brother [*yāqûm ʿal-šēm ʾāḥîyw hammēt*], that his name may not be blotted out in Israel" (Deut. 25:5-6). In case the levir refuses to carry out his obligation, verse 9 specifies that "his brother's widow shall go up to him in the presence of elders, pull the sandal off [*ḥāleṣāh naʿalô*] his foot, spit in his face, and make this declaration: Thus shall be done to the man who will not build up his brother's house."

These laws and *Ruth* 4 share a legal vocabulary including: *ʾaḥ*, "brother"; derivatives of the verb *qûm*, "to arise," associated with the noun *šem*, "name" (cf. Gen. 38:8, *hēqîm zeraʿ*); *šaʿar (hāʿîr)*, "gate" of the city; *zeqenîm*, "elders," *naʿal*,"sandal." Because of such parallelism in vocabulary, medieval Rabbis and the majority of Biblical scholars have been encouraged to consider the *gōʾēl*'s duty as essentially that of a levir. This, despite the fact that, on the one hand, the issues of *geʾullāh* and the levirate would be merged in a manner unattested elsewhere in the OT (on this, more below) while, on the other, crucial vocabulary of Deut. 25 does not reoccur in *Ruth* 4 (e.g., derivatives of the roots *ybm*, *ḥlṣ*, *yrq*). The fact that 4:12 will allude to Tamar and Judah of Gen. 38, with its echoes of levirate principles at work, clinches the arguments, for many, in favor of the *qerē*, *qānîtā*, in 4:5 (cf. Rowley, 1965: 174-75). Accordingly, these scholars offer this understanding of the passage: Boaz tells the next of kin of the availability of Naomi's land. The last agrees to purchase it. But when he is told that he *must* marry Ruth as part of the total package, he refuses, lest he damage the future of his estate. As Rowley (1965: 187) puts it: "To beget children by Ruth without marring his estate the kinsman could have considered; to buy Naomi's land without taking Ruth he could also have considered. It was the bringing of these two things into relation with one another that made both impossible for him. And it was here that Boaz's resource became apparent."

Nevertheless, even those who understand our passage in light of "levirate" obligations recognize the divergences among the incidents recorded in *Ruth* 4, the requirements of Deut. 25, and the reconstructions of Gen. 38. Gordis (1974) has recently denied the existence of the levirate as a factor in the *Ruth* narrative. Curiously enough, Gordis nowhere proposes to reject the *qerē* in favor of the *ketîb*, thus leaving the purpose of his disagreement somewhat unclear. Nevertheless, Gordis's (1974: 246-52) article does contrast details in *Ruth*, Deuteronomy, and Gen. 38 in order to highlight the weaknesses of proposals made by advocates of "levirate" solutions in *Ruth* (pp. 246-252).

(1) Deuteronomy emphasizes the ideal of perpetuating the "name of the dead man in Israel" as the main purpose behind levirate practices,

however cloudy and unclear their origins. In *Ruth* the redemption of the land of Elimelech is primary in importance. Those who deny the primacy of this transaction have the plain meaning of the narrative with which to contend. (2) Deuteronomy emphasizes the stigma that attaches to a recalcitrant brother. In *Ruth*, however, the honor of the *gō᾿ēl* is in no way besmirched, even after his refusal to redeem the land. (3) *Ruth's* "pulling off of the sandal" is a totally different act, both in its nature and its consequence, from that of Deuteronomy (see below for our partial disagreement with the idea). (4) It is clear from 3:10 that Ruth was in a position to choose another mate; this situation would clearly indicate that she did not feel herself restrained by leviratic obligations; that is, she did not see herself restricted to marry the *gō᾿ēl*. To these points of Gordis, we add the observation of Gordon (letter to me of May 5, 1976): "Levirate marriage is automatic. A woman is considered 'married' without any formality to the deceased's brother unless in a thoroughly humiliating and ugly ceremony, she makes her appearance and obtains a 'divorce.'" There would therefore have been no need for the *gō᾿ēl* to "purchase" Ruth nor, for that matter, for Boaz to do so once the *gō᾿ēl* ceded him his right. The blessings that accompanied Boaz's successful negotiation of land and dame would therefore have been totally out of context.

These and other points have not been ignored by supporters of the levirate as an issue in *Ruth*. In general, we might say that three defenses were offered. The first reconstructed stages in the development of levirate marriages which harmonized, as best as possible, the incongruous and incompatible information found in Gen. 38, Deut. 25, and, to some degree, Lev. 18:16; 20:21. The sequence which is usually, but by no means unanimously, followed consists of *Ruth*-Deuteronomy-Gen. 38-Lev. 18-Lev. 20 (see Rudolph, 1962: 61-63; Bewer, 1902-3: 144; Neufeld, 1944: 37-39). Rowley (1965: 176-82, 190-91) includes a discussion of this position. The second defense of the levirate as an issue in *Ruth* is exemplified by Rowley, 1965: 192. Based on Neufeld's formulations, Rowley thinks that "Levirate marriage was not in early times limited to a brother-in-law; it neither required nor excluded full marriage; it neither required nor excluded the unmarried condition of the levirate partner." In urging a more flexible understanding of levirate laws, Rowley blames the lack of harmony in the Biblical information concerning the levirate on the disparate relationships between widows and next of kins (cf. Rowley, 1965: 174-75; 181-82). We must, however, consider Rowley's argumentation as classically circular; for one cannot simply amalgamate literarily diverse elements into a composite, then use such a reconstruction as a norm by which to judge these same diverse elements. Brichto (1973: 12[n. 16]) exemplifies the third approach. He (re-)defines "levirate" as "any union in which a boy sired on a widow by a kinsman of her dead husband is accounted as the latter's posterity."

Gordis's broadside against levirate marriage as a factor in *Ruth* is a challenge that distills the arguments of other scholars who, likewise, find it difficult to harmonize the social practices preserved in *Ruth*, Deuteronomy, Gen. 38, and Leviticus. I should like to marshall evidence from *within* the tale of *Ruth* to bolster such a stand.

1. It has been observed by McKane (1961-62: 38-39) and repeated by Beattie (lastly, 1974: 263) that one cannot presume the *gōʾēl* to be alone in his ignorance of either the affairs of Naomi or of levirate laws. That he turned down his right of purchasing the land--in itself an act which had no connections with levirate requirements--cannot, therefore, have resulted from sudden discovery of these facts, which, it must be assumed for the sake of the story's integrity, were commonly known by any Bethlehemite. Nor could one agree with Bertholet and Bewer, cited by McKane (1961-62), who consider the *gōʾēl*'s role as an artificial creation to balance that of Orpah. For to do so would render the last chapter of *Ruth* a flabby narrative.

2. If levirate duty was tied to purchase of land, and if Boaz wanted to marry Ruth and be in a position to accomplish both, he should have asked the *gōʾēl* to *release Ruth* rather than to merely desist from purchasing her. In doing so, the *gōʾēl*'s act might, no doubt, have required some form of the verb *ḥālaṣ*. Only then could Boaz have been in a position to become Ruth's *yābām*.

3. Moreover, if the matter was one of levirate marriage, we should have expected Ruth to have automatically entered the household of the next of kin, as soon as she crossed into Bethlehem. Above all, she would certainly not have been in a position, as Boaz puts it (3:10): "to seek out men of any sort."

4. It is clear that the initiative to obtain "release" from levirate obligations rested on the aggrieved women (cf. Deut. 25). Were our episode to fall in this category, Ruth should have been present during the proceedings which occurred at the city gate. The MT knows nothing of such an event.

5. Once released by the *gō'ēl*, Ruth would *automatically* have become Boaz's *yebēmet*-wife. The protagonists needed no marriage blessings. Note in this context the vocabulary used in Gen. 38. In that passage, there is absolutely no word that could be construed as suggesting any interruption in Tamar's marriages to the first two sons of Judah. Only Shelah's tender age prevented yet a third automatic marriage for Tamar.

6. Although it occurs in a highly rhetorical passage, we might, nevertheless, allude to the content of 1:11 as offering one more piece of evidence that even Naomi did not see the future marriages of her daughters-in-law as leviratic in character (contra David, 1942: 56; Thompson and Thompson, 1968: 96-97).

It must be obvious, by now, that this writer finds little satisfaction in the arguments advanced by those who would retain the *qerē* of *qnyty*. Methodologically speaking, however, it should be quite unacceptable to prefer the *ketîb*, *qānîtî*, solely on the basis of negative discussions of the *qerē*. We would, therefore, like to offer a few points in favor of the written text of the MT. Some of these have been alluded to above; others have been advanced by Beattie in the two articles published in VT. Beattie's arguments have been dismissed *ex cathedra*, and certainly too hastily in our opinion, by Campbell (1975: 146).

a. While one could always blame a scribe for his error in transmitting a text, it must be said that the addition of *yôd* to *qnyt* could not easily be explained. Above, we rejected the theory of Keil and Delitzsch which posited an original *qnytw*. Rudolph (1962: 59) assumes that this error in the text of 4:5 was influenced by *qānîtî* of 4:9. With Beattie (1971: 491[n. 5]), we are puzzled by this suggestion, especially since it would have been much simpler to posit a Masoretic "purification" of 4:5 by *removing* an existing *yôd*, thus ending with *qānîtā*. Beattie (1971: 494) has offered his own suggestion to explain the *qerē*'s vocalization:

The qere has arisen through a misunderstanding. Since, when he buys the land, Boaz also takes Ruth as his wife (vv 9, 10), it was assumed that the two things belonged together and that the redeemer of the land should take Ruth in marriage as a condition of his redemption, and so *qanîṯî* was taken to be second person. The emendation in pointing was, no doubt, assisted by the fact that twice already, at least, in the book, a verb, which in the consonantal text is apparently first person singular perfect qal, has been emended by a qere to read second person singular.

While the second segment of Beattie's proposal has some merits, we believe that the first unnecessarily presumes ignorance of the intricate details in *Ruth* on the part of the scribes who preceded the period of the LXX. We referred above to C. H. Gordon's opinion on the matter.

b. We proceed from McKane's observations, alluded to above, that Boaz's statement before the elders must have contained an element of surprise which, it should be noted, could not be based on the assumption that the *gōʾēl* was ignorant of customs of the land. We think that if Boaz's scheme was to please an audience, if the denouement at the city gate was to be appreciated for its realism by listeners who were, after all, aware of custom and tradition, the narrator of *Ruth* would not have dared sketch a portrait of the *gōʾēl* as an ignorant simpleton. As mentioned above, if we were to fault the kinsmen at all, it would be for allowing Boaz to precede him in calling an assembly for the purpose of witnessing the redemption of Elimelech's land. Even in this, the *gōʾēl* could not be blamed too harshly; after all, Boaz's act occurred rather unexpectedly. In order to elaborate on this point, we take this opportunity to introduce a much delayed speculation concerning 2:23 and 3:2.

We wondered above about the unusual mention of both barley and wheat harvests in 2:23, while in the subsequent narrative of 3:2 only that of barley occurs. By this apparent chronological lapse, it seems to us fairly possible that the narrator of *Ruth* means to give further evidence of Boaz's--and for that matter Ruth's and Naomi's--cleverness in achieving a successful transfer of Elimelech's land. Rather than await the end of the wheat harvest, which would have occurred anywhere from a couple of weeks to a little more than a month *after* that of barley, Boaz called an assembly and presented his case. Had he delayed until after the wheat harvest, Boaz might easily have found the *gōʾēl* in the process of accomplishing the transfer of Elimelech's land into his own estate, and thus may never have had the chance to outwit the *gōʾēl*. Since the last could not but gain from purchasing that piece of land, we could be fairly certain that he would not have delayed legalizing this transaction much beyond harvest's end. In addition, Boaz himself was under great pressure to put his plan into action at the earliest possible moment; for, as we shall see below, his whole scheme would be totally lost were the news of his meeting with Ruth at the threshing floor broadcast before he had had the chance to present his arguments in a legal setting. We might stress, however, that this presentation will gain credibility if one assumes that the particular plot of land belonging to Elimelech was sown with barley rather than with wheat.

What about 2:23 and its mention of the "wheat harvest" in addition to that of the "barley harvest?" We would like to suggest that these references be taken as the time span in which unfolded the full narrative of *Ruth*--minus of course the birth of Obed. That is, the few weeks' difference between harvests spanned the moment Ruth was advised to join Boaz on the threshing-floor through the moment she entered Boaz's household as an *ʾēšet ḥayil*. That the actual marriage of Ruth may not have occurred at the conclusion of the discussion at the city gate, but that it may have followed it by a few weeks, may seem a radical proposal. But in view of the differing vocabulary cited above to describe the two steps by which Boaz purchased *(qānāh)* Ruth, then married her *(lāqaḥ)* and in view of the fact that it would not be abnormal for the marriage ceremony to occur a few weeks after the betrothal (Jeremias, 1969: 368), such a hypothesis may not be without some supporting evidence.

We return to our discussion of 4:5 and the problem of the *ketîb*, *qānîtî*. Of all the events that overtook Ruth and Naomi, the *only* piece of information that was known only to our protagonists is precisely the fact that Boaz had, at the least, vowed to marry Ruth. If this is the only datum that is clearly unavailable to the *gōʾēl*, then we should seriously consider this piece of information as the "trump card" with which Boaz hoped to change the *gōʾēl*'s mind about purchasing Elimelech's land. But in order to understand precisely how the activity at the threshing-floor will be translated by Boaz into information that will cause the *gōʾēl* to give up his claims over Elimelech's land, we need to take, once more, leave from our *ketîb* and begin discussing the crucial *lehāqîm šēm-hammēt ʿal-naḥalātô* (verse 5). We shall presently return to tie the loose ends of this annotation.

The words *lehāqîm šēm-hammēt ʿal-naḥalātô* form another crucial phrase that has received scholarly attention (see lastly Thompson and Thompson, 1968: 84-88; Loretz, 1960: 391-99). Since there is little support nowadays for wholesale excision of phrases suspected of being additions to a given text, we shall not entertain the theories of Wolfenson (1911: 299) and Bewer (1903/4: 205) which considered our sentence as a Deuteronomic addition to the text in order to harmonize it with Deut. 25. On the individual words in this sentence, we refer to the surveys in THAT, II, by S. Amsler (*qûm*, pp. 640-41; not very satisfactory), A. S. v.d. Woude (*šēm* especially in its extended meaning, "reputation, memory," 947[3,h]), and G. Wanke (*naḥalāh*, 55-59).

Although we have tried to deny that levirate marriage was an issue in the story of *Ruth*, we do not want to give the impression that *one* of the two major *goals* of this institution--that of producing a male child who will continue the 'name' of the deceased--was not at stake in *Ruth*. What we dispute is the tendency in Biblical scholarship to regard Ruth as obligated to marry in fulfillment of levirate obligations. In my opinion, even Deut. 25 could be considered as preserving what are essentially two separate social institutions that, in due time, merged into one, conveniently labeled the "levirate." We should, however, distinguish between an institution devised to care for a "husbandless" woman (that is, a woman who has lost her husband but could still depend on his father and his brother[s]) and one that aimed not merely to produce an heir for the deceased but to insure that woman with a future provider. That such a "widow"--a term that imperfectly corresponds to the situation described above--was kept within her in-law's household in order to retain some material advantage brought in by her when she became a bride (discussion in Rowley, 1965: 177[n. 3]), is a plausible but by no means a better suggestion for the origin of this institution than one based upon humanitarian considerations. We believe that the reason why a "widow" in such circumstances is not returned to her own parents' home is related to the crucial *kî-yēšebû ʾaḥîm yaḥdāw* (Deut. 25:5), "when[ever] brothers dwell together. . . ." Such a situation implies that the brothers had not yet divided the estate of their father and begun separate households because he was still alive. The widow of a deceased under these circumstances was strictly speaking, not an *ʾalmānāh*, since she would not have been considered as such until no longer supported by her father-in-law. Were such a case to develop, as it indeed did for Ruth and Orpah, then the *ʾalmānāh* would be free, if not urged, to return to her own parents' home. The account in Gen. 38 is of interest in this regard. At the death of Er and of Onan, Tamar was ordered to her father's home as an *ʾalmānāh*. Yet, from verse 24, it is clear that she was still in Judah's care. As an *ʾalmānāh* with no freedom of movement, she was, therefore, doubly aggrieved. Fearing that she would not be able to produce a progeny for her first husband nor, for that matter, provide herself with means of support in her old age after the death of her father-in-law, she decided to resolve the matter in the manner described in Gen. 38. That sexual relations between the "widow" and the levir were only one element in what we call the "levirate" is suggested by the fact that when Judah had Tamar returned to his household, he ceased to have any sexual relations with her. See the remarks of Driver (1951: 284-85).

Before we proceed to describe what we believe to be the second social institution incorporated into the "levirate," it might be à propos to suggest that the incest law of Lev. 18:16 (= 20:21), "You may not uncover the nakedness of your brother's wife. . . ," may not be applicable to "levirate" formulations. First, we would be dealing, in the last case, with a situation in which the husband is dead; second, with one in which the woman is technically speaking a *betûlāh*, "a virgin," since her womb was opened neither by birth nor by miscarriage.

Now if a man dies, and his wife has not borne a son into a household in which her father-in-law still lives, a peculiar condition occurs. As long as the latter is still alive, she is to be provided for, whether or not she still has a family of her own; for, to repeat, strictly speaking she is not a *ʾalmānāh*, a "widow," but merely a "husbandless woman." When the time came to divide the estate, most likely after the death of her father-in-law, this woman could find herself with no one to care for her. Furthermore, the possibility that her deceased husband will never be remembered either as an individual or as a possessor of his own line was unacceptable to a community that feared the obliteration of the "name," *šēm*, above all eventualities. (On this see v.d. Woude, THAT, II, *sub šēm*.) It was therefore most logical to merge the social institutions that provided for "husbandless women," with another institution that attempted to continue the name of the deceased. In this way, the woman was given in "marriage" to her brother-in-law. With luck, a son would be born by means of this union, providing an heir for the household of the deceased. Any property that would have gone to the deceased would be kept in trust by the levir as long as the child was a minor. We should not be surprised therefore that, in practice, this union was one of convenience, one that theoretically could be terminated as soon as a male heir was provided for by the levir, or, more plausibly, as soon as the male heir was old enough to work the land of his father.

With this view of the development of levirate practices, we mean to deny that anyone but a brother of a deceased person, still under the protection of a living father, could ever be considered as under obligation to mate with his brother's wife in order to provide an heir for the deceased. This is one more reason why we reject the possibility that the levirate was at issue in *Ruth*. Boaz and "Mr. So-and-So" were neither brothers, nor sons of Naomi; for that matter, they were certainly not living under the same roof.

As we return to the story of *Ruth*, we should repeat our position that our heroine was under no obligation to marry anyone but her own choice (or perhaps better: Naomi's choice), since both her husband's brother and her father-in-law were dead. Nevertheless, it must have occurred to her that by selecting Boaz as her potential husband, she was not only choosing a man who was financially in a position to redeem Elimelech's land once the next of kin was dissuaded from taking advantage of his right, but that she might be able to retain her attachment to Naomi through her future husband. But such a bond could be kept only if Boaz declared, *before a legally constituted assembly*, that the first male child produced in his union with Ruth would be considered as Mahlon's son. That child, whom we shall all know fairly soon as Obed, will be able to accept the return of Elimelech's land from the redeemer, in this case, Boaz. We shall presently detail why "Mr. So-and-So" considered it to be ruinous for his estate to purchase the land *after* learning of Boaz's decision with regard to Ruth.

In order to confirm our hypothesis that the single most important trump card in the hand of Boaz was precisely his resolve to consider the first son born to him and Ruth as Mahlon's heir, we turn to verse 10. There, it is stated that Boaz made the following declaration before the assembly of elders: "I am acquiring for myself as wife Ruth of Moab, wife of Mahlon, in order to perpetuate the memory of the deceased over his estate." Boaz then continued with a statement that, at first glance, appears to be redundant; indeed, it is often treated as such by scholars: *welōʾ-yikkārēt šēm-hammēt mēʿim ʾeḥāyw ûmiššaʿar meqômô*, "The name of the deceased may not be obliterated from among his kinfolk and his native village."

The syntax of this sentence is that of a negative final clause (GKC, 109g [p. 323]; 165a [pp. 503-4]). This should not prevent it, however, from acquiring the quality of prohibition so often associated with the adverb *lōʾ* when followed by an indicative imperfect, even when the subject is inanimate and in the third person singular. We might, therefore, consider this statement of Boaz as a *quotation* from an existing body of written law, or based on oral formulations that were preserved by custom.

That it parallels so closely the law of Deut. 25:6--*welō᾿-yimmāḥēh šemô miyyiśrā᾿ēl*--in its usage of *welō᾿*, followed by a *niphʿal* indicative imperfect, third person masculine singular, should give us some confidence that we are proceeding correctly.

With all this information, we are now ready to fulfill our obligation and link together the various suggestions offered in our long annotation on verse 5. We have tried to show that "levirate marriage," as it is classically described in Deut. 25, does not fully obtain in the story of *Ruth*, if only because Ruth was never under obligation to enter the next of kin's household. Following Naomi's advice, Ruth succeeded in having Boaz vow a future marriage to her. Whether or not the two whiled away the night at the threshing-floor in tender embrace is doubtless of psychological significance. Yet, *juridically* speaking, this point becomes important only if the tryst is not discovered before the proper moment. Boaz must have quickly realized that if he were to convince the next of kin not to purchase Elimelech's land, the latter had to be persuaded that there would be no profit for him in the transaction. *This is successfully achieved when, in a totally unexpected fashion, Boaz announced before a duly organized legislative body his intention to pledge the first born son of Ruth as Mahlon's heir, the future owner of Elimelech's land.* Boaz could not have afforded to await the end of both harvests, wheat as well as barley, before making public his decision. To have done so, he would have risked being preceded in the purchase of the land by the *gō᾿ēl*. Furthermore, he might also have forever lost the opportunity legally to declare his intentions concerning Mahlon's inheritor if news of his meeting, however innocent, with Ruth at the threshing-floor had circulated in Bethlehem. For, as is obvious from verse 13, it was crucial that the conception of this child, an "opener of the womb," occur *after* the public presentation of the pledge. Thus, the possibility of raising a redeemer for Naomi would forever be jeopardized. In this context, we might add that Boaz would certainly seem an opportunist were he to make his pledge *after* the sale of the land to the next of kin.

Two inquiries related to this thesis might be made. The first, to be treated in future pages, is raised by our failure so far to explain precisely why the next of kin could not afford to purchase Elimelech's property once Boaz had stated his plans with regard to Mahlon's heir. The second inquiry is not one which yields satisfactory answers. It asks of us to explain why Boaz, or for that matter the *gō᾿ēl*, was so certain that a *son* would be born to Ruth, hence a redeemer to Naomi? I am not sure, however, that this is a query that a Hebrew audience, marveling over the ancestry of David, its glorious and beloved king, would ever insist on posing.

C. As to whether *qānîtî* should be translated by either a past tense ("I had purchased"; i.e., "the night before") or the "legal present" ("I am purchasing"), we opt for the latter. Since we are taking literally the meaning "to purchase, to buy," for *qānāh*, we cannot imagine Boaz purchasing an "indentured" Ruth without the proper array of witnesses and elders. It is to be observed that by this "sale" Naomi could publicly count on added proceeds to give security to her old age.

4:6. Faced with the certainty of Boaz's decision first to purchase, then then to marry Ruth with the publicly proclaimed purpose of producing an heir to Elimelech, the gōʾēl *changed his mind. An explanation for this decision will occupy most of the annotation for verse 6.*

(u) *lōʾ ʾûkal lgʾwl-lî.* *Ruth* contains the only examples in the OT of the *qal* infinitive construct of *gāʾal*. The three occasions on which this form is in the absolute, that is, without any pronominal suffixes, are each spelled differently according to BH[3]. The vocalization of our example, with a *qāmeṣ-ḥāṭûp* after the *ʾaleph*, indicates that the Massoretes believed the accent to have shifted to *lî*. However, the consonantal text, which may have been influenced by the instance in 4:4, is given in a *plene* form.

To be noted is the manner in which *lōʾ ʾûkal ligʾol (-lî)* begins and ends the *gōʾēl*'s statement in 4:6. Whereas the segment that succeeds the first mention of this phrase contains the *gōʾēl*'s explanation for his changed mind, that which precedes the last mention of this phrase records the decision publicly uttered by the *gōʾēl*.

(v) *pen-ʾašḥît ʾet-naḥalātî.* The verb *šāḥat*, not attested in the *qal* in the OT, has been studied by D. Vetter, THAT, II, 891-94. Carefully listing the verbs that are used either synonymously, in parallel, or in apposition to *šāḥat*, Vetter confirms the usual opinion on the meaning of this verb, "to ruin, bring to ruin, to damage." To Joüon (1953: 84), however, the *gōʾēl* is exaggerating the condition in which he will find himself. Even in adopting a translation that is derived from Jer. 49:9 "nuire, porter prejudice à," Joüon feels that the *gōʾēl* is protesting too strongly: "His [the *gōʾēl*'s] marriage with Ruth would not result in positive damage to his estate; his children would not in any way be injured. The field, it is true, would belong to the first-born [cf. Deut. 25:6, *habbekôr*] whom he will produce by Ruth; but until this child becomes the actual owner (of the field), the *gōʾēl* would be benefitting from it."

Rowley (1965: 186) puts it this way: "if [the *gōʾēl*] bought the land and also made Ruth a mother, he would be impoverished. For the land would revert to Ruth's child, as the heir of Elimelech, and he would be left with nothing in return for the outlay on Naomi's land." Note also Rowley's remark on page 187: "[The *gōʾēl*] would have to use part of what ought to become his own children's inheritance to buy Naomi's property, and then restore that property to Ruth's child." Brichto (1973: 15-16), who believes that the Hebrew considered the welfare of the dead to depend on a progeny that retained ancestral property, thinks that "Mr. So-and-So" was refusing to sire and support a child who would guarantee the after-life of Mahlon.

Similar opinions are commonly encountered in the scholarly literature concerning this passage. Some studies detail more elaborately *how* the *gōʾēl*'s estate might have been marred were he to purchase the land and then agree to produce an heir for Mahlon through Ruth (see Gerleman, 1965: 37). Opinions as to *why* the *gōʾēl* refuses Ruth--a matter which might be considered separately from the question of the land purchase--have been expressed ever since Rabbinic times. The Targum has the following: "I cannot redeem it [the land] for myself. Since I have a wife, I have no right to take another in addition to her, lest there be dissension in my house, and I [thereby] destroy my own estate." This opinion, of course, does not inspire confidence since polygamy was not prohibited, albeit not encouraged, until Europe of the Middle Ages. Yet this explanation is persistent even in contemporary scholarship (cf. Rowley, 1965: 186-87). Midrashic opinions varied on this matter: some suggesting that the *gōʾēl* wrongly understood the Deuteronomic prohibitions against trafficking with Moabites as applicable to intermarriage with their women (Deut. 23: 4-5); others thinking that he feared the fate of Onan, a fear that was prevalent in Israel for quite a while (cf. Matt. 22:23-38; Mark 12:18-23; Luke 20: 27-33; Tobit 3:7-9). On these matters, see Levine, 1973: 102; Rowley, 1965: 187 (with bibliography).

Our above-stated espousal of the *ketîb*, *qānîtî* in 4:5, with its rejection of the position that Ruth was ever obliged to marry the next of kin, relieves us of the duty to argue the *gō᾿ēl*'s case for refusing to marry Ruth. But we are obligated, however, to explain his decision not to purchase the land once Boaz's declaration in behalf of Elimelech's estate was publicly made. Beattie (1974: 262), who also rejects the levirate as an issue in *Ruth*, sidesteps the problem too neatly: "It is the belief of the present writer that no deeper meaning than 'I cannot afford it' should be sought in the phrase 'lest I destroy my inheritance'." Although we shall ultimately be in some agreement with this position, we should not fail to note that Beattie does not set out the reasons for coming to such a conclusion. We therefore offer the following details as a *plausible* explanation for the *gō᾿ēl*'s change of heart.

It would not be an overstatement to say that the redemption of a kinsman's property, when the vagaries of fate have conspired to force the sale of an inalienable piece of land, was designed to protect the poorer landowning classes from either sinking into unwelcome tenancy or losing their independent livelihood. In effect, the institution of *ge᾿ullāh* promoted permanent landholdings, secured economic stability, discouraged mass movement of landless populations, and prevented the amassing of land in the hands of few (cf. Mic. 2:2; Isa. 5:8; Daube, 1947: 43-45). The law concerning the release of land to its original owner at the end of a fifty-year jubilee cycle was probably a "second line of defense," protecting a landowner in cases when the laws of Lev. 25 were abused, ignored, or, in absence of a *gō᾿ēl*, inoperative. That the institution of *ge᾿ullāh* may or may not have fully functioned even at the time in which its features were codified, is not immediately of import to us.

From this perspective, we presume that the *ge᾿ullāh* land legislations were neither unsubtle in their function nor simplistic in their application. That much flexibility was built into the stipulations of this institution is clearly observable when the legislation in Lev. 25 is compared with an actual case study reported in Jer. 32:8-15. Despite the fact that the last has an allegorical setting, its features offer marked divergences from the conditions set in Lev. 25. On redemption of land in Ugarit see Heltzer, 1976: 89-95.

Limiting our inquiry to problems concerning the situation sketched in *Ruth*, we mention first the circumstances that make our example different from those in Lev. 25 and Jer. 32. First of all, the stipulations in Lev. 25: 26-28 apply to an impoverished landowner with no *gō᾿ēl* available to him. Since this was not the case in *Ruth*, we might concentrate on the other features available in Lev. 25:25 and Jer. 32. Lev. 25:25 reads: "if your kinsman becomes impoverished so that he had to sell [some] of his property, the *gō'ēl* nearest to him must come and redeem that which his kinsman sold." Jer. 32 assumes that an impoverished landowner might simply ask his *gō'ēl* to purchase the property he is selling. In this manner, it is presumed that the unfortunate landowner not only could hope to receive a better price for his parcel of land, but could expect to keep it within the holdings of his clan. That he might obtain better treatment whenever the jubilee comes around, might be another reason for him to approach a *gō'ēl*.

Now, in *Ruth*, it is obvious that the land was not being sold by an impoverished landowner, but by a widow who could not care for it and, because she had no surviving sons, could not expect to keep it as an inheritance in their behalf. Thus, neither the law of Lev. 25:25 nor to a lesser extent the prototype found in Jer. 32 could precisely control this situation. Therefore, the obligation of "Mr. So-and-So," which would have him repurchase the property from a nonmember of the clan (if not from a resident alien) in order to *release it back* to his impoverished kin, would certainly not obtain. As far as "Mr. So-and-So" was concerned, his "redemption" of Elimelech's land was similar to the situation of Jeremiah. In view of Naomi's circumstances, however, "Mr. So-and-So" would never have to part with the land for which he paid Naomi hard-earned shekels.

Enters Boaz, who pledges the first male child of Ruth as Mahlon's heir. "Mr. So-and-So" could have, nevertheless, gone ahead and purchased the land from Naomi, gambling that Ruth's first born would not be a son. In that case, he might certainly have won his gamble . . . and the land! On the other hand, in the few moments available to him before his reply, he had to think seriously about the other possibility. Were he to agree to purchase Elimelech's parcel and then, in a year's time, find Naomi, through Ruth and Boaz, with an offspring, he might have to return the land to her in her capacity as trustee of this offspring. This, of course, would not be all. Naomi and her infant "son" would now be regarded as impoverished kinfolk, able to survive only by selling the land once more. At that point, that is, a year after he purchased the land from Naomi, "Mr. So-and-So" would have found himself called upon to act once more as a *gō'ēl*. If he then chooses the avenue set forth in Jer. 32, he must repurchase the land, and thus expend more cash in a venture that could not be very welcome. For, in such a case, he would practically have had to guarantee Naomi and her infant "son" continuous financial support in lieu of economic security until that child grows to maturity. Elimelech's land may not have been worth all that expense! If he, on the other hand, chooses the avenue set forth in Lev. 25, the prospect of Naomi, acting in behalf of the child continually selling the land to other clansmen or possibly even to resident aliens must certainly loom as a nightmare. For not only might he repeatedly be paying to release the property of Elimelech's heir, but he would not even profit by its use. Either way, "Mr. So-and-So" must have been reluctant to gamble his "estate," that is, his fortune, on such a risky proposition.

One afterthought posed as a double question: why did Boaz choose to do all this for Naomi? How did his assumption of the *geʾullāh* on her behalf allow him to escape the very same problem which "Mr. So-and-So" decided to avoid? In reply to the first query, we might not only consider Boaz as generous and decent toward the wife of a deceased friend, Elimelech, but we should also not overlook his desire to please his future wife who, at the outset, made clear her wishes to retain some bonds with her erstwhile mother-in-law. The second question is more difficult to answer. As soon as Boaz declared on behalf of Mahlon's progeny, he would experience the same dilemma and face the same alternative as sketched above in connection with "Mr. So-and-So." But whereas there appeared to the *gōʾēl* nothing but bleak financial prospects were he to purchase Naomi's land, Boaz could do so with the knowledge that the first-born son pledged to Mahlon would nevertheless be a product of his own flesh and blood, born not to a strange woman who came from Moab, but to a wife whom he married for no other reason but love.

(w) *geʾal-lekā ʾattāh ʾet-geʾullātî.* This phrase, which precedes the second mention of *lōʾ-ûkal ligʾōl*, is the public declaration that Boaz was hoping to elicit from the *gōʾēl*. It is not surprising, therefore, that two derivatives of the crucial verb *gāʾal* are cited: an imperative, *geʾal (lekā)*, which is followed by a cognate accusative, a noun in the abstract, *geʾullāh* (cf. Joüon, 1953: 84-85). On the last as a technical word in legal terminology, see Horst, 1961: 153.

4:7. In an aside addressed directly to his audience, the narrator of Ruth *explains an element of folk-activity that either no longer obtained in his own days or was considered too arcane for him to miss giving a full description. It is interesting that he does so* before *he reveals the picturesque vignette that, no doubt, was drawn from the realm of symbolic gesturing that accompanied transactions. The vocabulary within that verse contains three abstract nouns with a tendency to rhyme; one of these,* teʿûdāh, *is fairly rare in Hebrew.*

(x) *wezōʾt lepānîm beyiśrāʾēl.* Campbell (1975: 147-48) has studied the usage of *lepānîm:*

These words underscore the similarity of 4:7 to I Sam 9:9, where two former and outmoded features are explained--the procedure for consulting deity and the term "seer" now supplanted by "prophet." The Hebrew *lepānîm,* "formerly," can indicate a previous time of close proximity or of hoary, even mythic, antiquity. The time span is a generation or less in Job 42: 11; Judg 3:2; Neh 13:5; and possibly Josh 11:10, and it is lengthy (seven hundred years!) in I Chron 9:20 and mythic (in effect, back to the beginning of time) in Ps 102:26. In other instances (see Deut 2:10, 12, 20; I Chron 4:40; Judg 1:10, 11, 23; Josh 14:15, 15:15) the time separation is difficult to judge. Much more to the point is to note that the passages cited tend to pertain to before and after a radical change in circumstances, whether of land possession, of city name (and perhaps therefore of population), or of social order, matters resulting from invasions, change of government, and the like. Altered circumstances require some altered modes--together with explanation and instruction. . . . The time need not be long.

The word *zōʾt,* feminine demonstrative pronoun, is often used in a neuter sense when it concerns events, announcements, and the like (BDB, 260 [1]). Some versions, e.g. LXX and Vulgate, parphrase the Hebrew more fully, obtaining "This is the *custom/regulation. . . ,"* presuming, as has been suggested in light of Jer. 32: 7-8, the word *mîšpaṭ.*

(y) *ʿal haggeʾûllāh weʿal-hattemûrāh.* On *ʿal* in the uncommonly attested sense of "concerning, with regard to," see BDB, 754 (1.f[h]).

The term *temûrāh* is an abstract derivative of the verb **mwr,* "to change," with a prefixed *tāw* (GKC, 85 (r), p. 238). It occurs three times in Job (15:31, a discussion of which is in Pope, 1965: 119; 20:18; 28:17) and in Lev. 27:10, 33. In all these passages, the notion is apparently of "substitute, barter, exchange, purchase" (Gordis, 1970: 102); that is, of a commercial transaction in which monetary values are ultimately at stake. While *geʾullāh,* "redemption," might also involve monetary exchange, its primary application was to social, rather than commercial, transactions. Since *temûrāh* and *geʾullāh* seem to evolve from different institutional spheres, it may be that the storyteller was creating another *merismus* (cf. comments *sub* 3:10, *dal . . . ʿāšîr*). Thus, the narrator would be informing his audience that, in Israel's past, the transfer of the shoe was used in all forms of transactions, whether social or commercial. This may be confirmed by the use of the substantive *kol*, preceding the word *dābār* on which we offer a quote from BDB, 82 (1, e): "Heb[rew] idiom in certain cases, affirms, or denies, of an *entire* class, where Eng[lish] idiom affirms, or denies, of an *individual* of the class; thus in a compar[ative] or hypoth[etical] sentence *kl* is = any, and with a neg[ative] = none." Brichto (1973: 18-19) believes that the two terms involved constitute a hendiadys equal to transfer (*temûrāh*) of the right of redemption (*geʾullāh*).

(z) *leqayyēm kol-dābār*. The *zāqēp qāṭôn* on the ultima of *dābār* suggests that this phrase was understood to control the preceding, rather than the succeeding, statements. This should provide us with one more confirmation that *kol* is best considered as qualifying a *merismus*. Most of the scholarly attention, however, has been devoted to whether or not the verbal form *leqayyēm* is an "Aramaism" (see Joüon, 1953: 85). Myers (1955: 19) points out that "several middle weak forms are found in the *Piel* as early documents. Then there is the *Hithpael* of *ṣîr* in Josh 9:4." As to the possibility of dating *Ruth* to a later period because of such a form, Myers adds the following: "Since it is an explanatory insertion, an Aramaic borrowing would not affect the question of dating the original, but only that of its final prose edition." On Myers's position, Campbell (1975: 148) remarks: "There is a large number of examples of *Piel* forms of *qwm* in the OT . . . with a variety of nuances, which at least suggests a rather early adoption of this Aramaism, if Aramaism it be. . . . In the final analysis, the possibility that this is a form from an old Hebrew dialect should be kept open." We shall discuss the problem of Aramaism in *Ruth* later.

(a') *šālap ʾîš naʿalô wenātan lerēʿēhû*. Campbell (1975: 148) collects instances of *ʾîš . . . (le)rēʿēhû* placed in contexts in which either reciprocal or unilateral actions are at stake: "we cannot tell from the Hebrew whether both parties gave and received shoes, or only one gave a shoe to the other." As is clear from verse 8, however, only *one* person transferred *one* sandal to the other.

We are nevertheless hindered in seeking an explanation for *šālap* *ʾîš naʿalô* by some ambiguities and difficulties in the Hebrew text. It is not clear, for example, whose shoe is bandied about during this ceremony; nor do we know who receives it or takes it upon himself to remove it from the foot. Since *šālap* is used in connection with "shoes" or "sandals" only in this passage, its precise connotation is still to be sought. Furthermore, in a passage that would require a "frequentive" or "habitual" form of the verb, the vocalization of *šālap*, a perfect, has elicited suggestions for emendations. We do take comfort, however, in the fact that there is very little at stake in an exact or proper explanation of all these points which would be crucial to the understanding and the development of the subsequent narrative. That the form of the verb *šālap* is perfect third person masculine singular has elicited a suggestion for revocalization into an "all-purpose" infinite absolute (*šālōp*). This would easily give *šālap* an iterative connotation (Rudolph, 1962: 60); BH[3] proposes *wayyišlōp*, i.e. an imperfect with *wāw* conversive; but this would hardly resolve the problem. Most commentators either prefix a *wāw* conversive to the perfect (thus: *wešālap*) or simply emend to the imperfect *yišlōp* (Joüon, 1953: 85). It is to be noted, however, that the text that most closely "parallels" (grammatically speaking) our context also has a verb conjugated in the perfect. There, too, a frequentive meaning would best fit the text (1 Sam. 9:9: "Formerly in Israel, someone would suggest [*kōh-ʾāmar hāʾîš*] going to inquire from God, in the following manner: 'Let's get going to a seer'. . . ."). Therefore, however inelegant this form appears to us, we might yet retain it, in view of the fact that two OT passages felt quite comfortable in using a perfect to communicate an interative mood.

The symbolic gesture of "drawing off the sandal/shoe" has caused interpretive disagreements among scholars and commentators. Campbell (1975: 149-50), who includes an account of scholarly debate on this issue, quotes from the *Midrash Rabbah* (VII:11): "Whose shoe? Rab and Lev disagreed. One said the shoe of Boaz, while the other said the shoe of the kinsman. It is more probable that he who says the shoe of Boaz is correct, for it is usual for the purchaser to give the pledge." Yet the Vulgate, and some LXX manuscripts assume a point of view opposite to the sentiments expressed in the Midrash. By critical additions to the Hebrew text, it is made clear that it was the kinsman's shoe that was the object of attention. The Targum, possibly mindful that *ḥālaṣ*, rather than *šālap*, is more commonly used in connection with the removal of footwear, neatly resolve the problem by replacing "shoe" with "glove." This change is strengthened by the insistence that it was the glove of the right hand that was at stake (cf. Levine, 1973: 103-4). Even more curious, albeit understandable as a conflation with Deut. 25, is Josephus's account in *Antiq.* (v:9-4): "So Boaz called the senate to witness, and bid the woman to loose his shoe, and spit in his face, according to the law. . . ."

Thompson and Thompson (1968: 90-93) recall some of the recent discussions concerned with elucidating the origin and purpose of this custom. The Thompsons rightly reject Speiser's contention (1940: 15-20 [= *Oriental and Biblical Studies*, 151-56]), that Boaz was purchasing, with the shoe as "price," the right to act as a next of kin. A priori, it would be quite unconvincing to think that a burden, such as the *geʾullāh* was meant to be, should be a marketable commodity, however symbolic the payment involved. Whether or not Lacheman's proposal, mentioned with approval by the Thompsons, elucidates our passage is still debatable. Lacheman's thesis (1937: 53-56) is based upon Nuzu parallels that, in our opinion, speak of a totally different symbolic gesture: that of planting the foot on newly purchased land in order to indicate transfer of power. Brichto's (1973: 18-20) opinion on this issue is that the transfer of shoes was symbolic of the transfer of redemption rights. See also Hurvitz (1975: 45-49). Deroy (1961: 374-76) rather (too) easily finds parallels for our "shoe" episode in the lore of the Greeks. Carmichael (1977: 335-36) is certain that "Mr. So-and-So" confers to Boaz the right over Ruth, who is *symbolized (sic)* by the shoe.

Campbell offers the suggestion than an exchange of shoes validated a commercial transaction while the handing over of a shoe to a new redeemer affected the transfer of redemption rights. Before proceeding further, we might take one more look at Deut. 25:5-10. We suggested above that "levirate" marriage was a composite of two distinct institutions: one cared for the "husbandless" wife (hereafter: "widow") of a deceased whose in-laws were still alive; the other provided an heir for the deceased through his brother's seed. Deut. 25:8 makes it clear that, at the complaint of a "widow," the elders put some pressure upon the potential levir to comply with the provisions of this (composite) institution. Were he to demur in a public pronouncement, his sister-in-law "shall go up to him in the presence of the elders, pull the sandal off his foot [*weḥāleṣāh naʿalô mēʿal raglô*], spit in his face [*weyāreqāh bep̄ānāyw*], declaring in reply: 'So will it be done to one who refuses to establish his brother's household.'"

From this point on, we offer speculative observations on these symbolic gestures, ones that keep in mind our hypothesis that two distinct issues were at stake in "levirate marriage." It seems impossible to us that the levir might have agreed to raise an heir for his brother without offering care and shelter to his "widow." The opposite, however, is potentially likely. The levir might have refused to impregnate his sister-in-law, while at the same time agreeing to care for her. If a levir chooses this last option, a "widow's" security would be assured, at least until the death of her brother-in-law. From then on, we presume, her fate would not be enviable. Unable to bear children, lacking any sons to protect her in old age, the "widow" would either return to her own family (brothers, if her parents had died in the meanwhile) or would rely upon the munificence and charity of her nephews. It is no wonder that, faced with the apparent refusal of her father-in-law either to completely release her when Onan died, or to marry her to Shelah when he came of age, Tamar of Gen. 38 took the drastic measure of pretending to be a harlot. With the birth of her twin sons, at least, Tamar could count on her own children to protect her in her old age.

In the case of Deut. 25, we presume that the levir is refusing not only to "establish his brother's household," but to care for his "widow." If he decides to withhold his protection from his brother's "widow" he would avoid future responsibility toward her and, it should be noted, he would have acted in a very humane manner toward a woman with a extremely bleak future. Releasing her from his own family's orbit might have involved him in a very humiliating ceremony, one that would forever have placed a sobriquet upon him and his family (verse 10). Nevertheless, releasing the "widow" from his immediate household would certainly have shown him to be courageous and kind. His sister-in-law would never have had to emulate the unfortunate and degrading example of Tamar.

The "widow," then, becomes involved in a twofold gesture rich in legal symbolism. By spitting on her brother-in-law, we venture to say, she publicly chastises and humiliates him for ignoring his obligation toward his deceased brother. On the other hand, by forcefully removing the sandal off his foot, the "widow" obtains her personal release from him, thus enabling her to return to her parents in the hopes of beginning a new life. If this interpretation is at all likely, we would like to propose that the shoe symbolism, an act that could theoretically validate any legal pronouncement, may be thought to indicate, in Deut. 25 as well as in *Ruth* 4, a release from social obligations (*geʾullāh*) rather than the purchase or transfer of property (*temûrāh*). In Deut. 25, this release is obtained from someone unwilling (at least officially) to give up protective custody of a "widow"; hence, she herself forcefully removes it (verb: *ḥālaṣ*)--in the symbolic form of a shoe or sandal--from him. In *Ruth*'s case, however, the next of kin was not involved in protecting or supporting a "widow." For reasons discussed above, he was quite willing to give up his *geʾullāh* obligations. Thus, he personally removed (verb: *šālap*) his own shoe and handed it over to Boaz.

(b') *wezōʾt hatteʿûdāh beyiśrāʾēl*. Outside of our own context, *teʿûdāh* occurs only in Isa. 8:16, 20. For Qumran evidence, see, conveniently, C. van Leeuwen, THAT, II, 220-21 (5,a). Because in the Isaiah passages this seems to parallel *tôrāh*, most renderings approximate a meaning such as "message, testimony, injunction." As this rendering is clearly inappropriate for our phrase, it is commonly proposed that *teʿûdāh* of *Ruth* 4:7 be understood in terms that differ from the ones in Isaiah. The dictionaries are agreed in assigning *teʿûdāh* to the root **ʿwd*, "to bear witness." Dombrowṣki (1971: 567-72) etymologizes from the root **yʿd*, "to appoint, assign, designate" (in the *qal*!). He points to other similarly constructed abstract nouns that share a weakness in their first consonant: e.g., *tešûʿāh* (from **yšʿ*), *tequpāh* (from **nqp*). He thus proposes the following meaning for *teʿûdāh* in *Ruth*, "offer, propoṣal, presentation." While we do not object to Dombrowski's etymology, we are at a loss to understand how any of these meanings clarify our context.

One of Dombrowski's objections to the commonly accepted derivation of *teʿûdāh* from the root **ʿwd*, however, clearly merits attention: "the actual witness to the legal acts involved in *Ruth* 4, 8ff is provided by ZQNYM ['elders'] and ʿM ['people'], but not the alleged exchange of shoes" (p. 568). This objection is echoed by Tucker (1966: 44):

Contrary to the usual interpretation, the narrator at this point is describing not one, but *two* archaic practices, "confirming" and "attesting." Only the former refers to the ceremonial act of handing over a shoe. . . . *hatteʿûdâ* refers to the means of validating . . . that the transactions--including the final act of transfer--had in fact taken place. Therefore, *hatteʿûdâ*, as its etymology suggests [Tucker derives from **ʿwd*] but the

order of sentences in the passage obscures, refers to the use of the witnessing formulae in the oral contract.

If I understand Tucker's argument, he would have our phrase better positioned, either to precede Boaz's declaration or to follow the elders' acceptance of their role as witnesses. A glance at Mandelkern's *Concordance* reveals that there are six attestations in the OT of *wezō᾿t* initiating an editorial comment. In four of these instances (Gen. 49:28; Deut. 4:44; 6:1; Isa. 14:26) the phrase *wezō᾿t* [. . .] was placed at the *conclusion* of remarks detailing the practice that required such an editorial addition. In one case, however, that comment *preceded* the discussion of the practice. But since this unique attestation occurs precisely in *Ruth* 4:7 (*wezō᾿t lepānîm beyiśrā᾿ēl*), it might seem that Tucker's suggestion could be accepted without one's necessarily thinking that the Hebrew text was in disarray.

4:8. With the statement of the gō᾿ēl *which is contained within this verse, all rights to purchase Elimelech's estate are passed on to Boaz. Once Boaz is left in a position to buy that field, "Mr. So-and-So"'s involvement with Naomi, either as a* gō᾿ēl *or merely as a supporter, would have come to an end. This verse, therefore, is not, as is generally assumed (e.g., Campbell, 1975: 149), a succinct recapitulation of 4:6.*

(c') *wayyō᾿mer haggō᾿ēl.* Until he publicly utters "purchase [the field] for yourself," "Mr. So-and-So" was still a *gō᾿ēl*, and would still be considered as such by the storyteller. We do not, therefore, agree with Campbell's assertion (1975: 149) that "There is a delicious touch of irony that the near redeemer is still designated the *gō᾿ēl* after having resigned his responsibility."

(d') *qenēh-lāk.* The LXX's τὴν ἀγχιστείαν μου, "[purchase] my redemption-obligation," is not in the MT, and must certainly be an interpretation: one which, moreover, would be exceptional in its presumption of a Hebrew text in which *ge᾿ullāh* would have stood as a direct object of the verb *qānāh*. Jer. 32:7, sometimes invoked as a precedent, is certainly not guilty of such a presumption. This text reads as follows: "Buy for yourself [Jeremiah] my [Hanamel's] field in Anatoth, for yours is the obligation to act as a *gō᾿ēl* in purchasing it [*kî lekā mišpaṭ hagge᾿ullāh liqnôt*]." It is clear that in this passage, Jeremiah is asked to purchase the field and *not* the *ge᾿ullāh*. We think Joüon (1953: 87-88) to be incorrect in assuming that "what the *gō᾿ēl* disposes of, when he disposes of his sandals, and what he transfers, in handing them over to him, is his right as *gō᾿ēl*, but neither the field nor Ruth, which he did not own."

Myers (1955: 26) points out that only in this passage and in 4:4's *qenēh neged hayyōšebîm* is the verb *qānāh not* followed by a direct object. His suggestion to read *qenēhā*, i.e., to regard the *hē* as bearing the third person feminine singular pronominal suffix ("purchase it"), is generally not followed. Despite its unusual nature the Masoretic vocalization may be retained.

(e') *wayyišlōp naʿalô*. The LXX (followed by the Vulgate) ends this verse with καί ἔδωκεν αὐτῷ, "and gave it to him." Joüon (1953: 88) is one of many commentators who believe that the Hebrew equivalent to this clause, **wayyitten-lô*, was original to the MT. Campbell (1975: 149) follows Rudolph (1962: 60) in suggesting a possible explanation for this scribal lapse. The former, however, rightly gives primacy to the MT. The Targum, once more, goes its own way: "And Boaz removed the glove from his right hand, and acquired [it] from him" (cf. Levine, 1973: 104).

4:9-10. Boaz presents publicly his intention first to purchase Elimelech's land, then Naomi's daughter-in-law. In view of the juridical setting, his formulations carefully and explicitly name the parties involved in both transactions. It is to be noted that Boaz viewed his purchases as two separate actions, *each of which would be complete in itself and independent of the other. This approach is quite consistent with Boaz's positions taken in the preceding narrative. In 3:10-13 and in 4:3-4, Boaz's declarations* never *confuse the purchase of the land with his purchase, and subsequent espousal, of Ruth. We stand in admiration of the artistry of the storyteller for the manner in which the constancy of Boaz's character is indicated. Here, as well as in his gentle admonition to Ruth (3:10), Boaz's sense of priority seems just right:* ge᾿ullāh *for Naomi precedes marriage to Ruth.*

(f') *lazzeqēnîm wekol-hāʿām*. We agree with Rudolph (1962: 60) and with Campbell (1975: 150-51) that it is unnecessary to insert the preposition *le-* between the *wāw* and the *kol*, as was proposed by Joüon (1953: 88) [cf., BH^3, ad loc.)

(g') *ʿēdîm ᾿attem hayyôm*. This phrase, repeated again at the end of verse 10, frames legal declarations. It contains two items of technical import to Israel's legal processes. Tucker (1966: 42-45) discusses references in the OT to *ʿēd*, "witness," and to *(hay)yôm*, "today," considering them as stereotyped expressions aimed at insuring the authentification of transactions contracted orally. In connection with the "witness" formula *ʿēdîm ʾattem*, to which a response is recorded in verse 11, a most impressive parallel example is available in the covenant ceremony recorded in Josh. 24:22. As to *hayyôm*, "this day," Tucker notes its lack of precision as a "date formula," that is, its unconcern with establishing the exact moment in time in which Boaz's declarations were made. We should interject, however, that the narrator, by speaking of the threshing of barley as occurring on the eve of the legal deliberations, might have provided his text with some temporal anchorings. Tucker may be right, in comparing *hayyôm* with the Akkadian formula *ištu ūmi annîm*. . . , "from this day [on]. . . ," and consequently in suggesting that whatever *hayyôm* lacked in conveying a specific moment in time it replaced it with the expectation that the transaction would last forever. See on this topic, C. van Leeuwen, THAT, II, 211-12 (3a), 214-16 (4b).

(h') *kî* introduces the stipulations of Boaz's agreements with Naomi, with regard to present and future settlement of her husband's estate.

(i') *qānîtî ʾet-kol-ʾašer leʾelîmelek.* As far as we know, only the field of Elimelech was at issue in the transaction. Nevertheless, the use of *ʾet-kol-ʾašer*, "all that which. . . ," releases the narrator from cluttering his tale with a tedious exposition of each and every item of movable and immovable property which formed part of the purchase. Additionally, the use of this phrase relieved the storyteller from detailing the dimension and location of that property. That such concerns were real, even when couched in the language of narrative, is clear from the example available in Gen. 23 (especially verses 17-20). Here, however, such an approach could not but weigh down the story with particulars that might not have been appreciated by an audience eager to reach a satisfying denouement.

(j') *weʾēt kol-ʾašer lekilyôn ûmaḥlôn.* A minor point of interest is the order in which the sons of Elimelech are listed. In 1:2 and 5, the order is the reverse. Some think that the manner in which Orpah precedes Ruth in 1:4 should have suggested the pairing of Orpah with Mahlon, and of Ruth with Chilion. That such was not the case is clear from the following verse in which Ruth is called "wife of Mahlon." Some manuscripts, Syriac and LXX [but *not* the Targum despite Levine, 1973: 36; 105], actually followed the order in chapter 1. Rudolph (1962: 60) cautiously wonders whether an alphabetic order, i.e., *kilyôn (K) ûmaḥlôn (M)*, is required in juridical formulations. This would be unlike any legal pattern known to us from the ancient world. Campbell (1975: 151) thinks that a chiastic principle may be at work which requires that a pair of words be presented in reverse order on their second appearance. We might suggest, however, that the principle followed by the storyteller is to place in *second* position the individual of most immediate importance to the subsequent narrative. Thus in 1:4 and in 1:14, Ruth's name is given last, since she will be the focus of attention for the rest of the tale. In 4:9, therefore, Mahlon's name is accorded the second position because his son, born to Boaz and Ruth, will interest the audience in the remaining portions of chapter 4. We shall note that this principle may also obtain in verse 11.

(k') *wegam ʾet-rût hammōʾabiyyāh ʾēšet maḥlôn qānîtî lî leʾiššāh.* It is of interest that Boaz's legal utterance pertaining to Ruth contains not one, but two appellatives: "the Moabitess" and "the wife of Mahlon." Either one might have been sufficient to identify Ruth in a legal discussion. In view of the appellative used in 4:3 in connection with Naomi, "the one who has just returned from Moabite territory," and, perhaps more à propos in view of the repeated references to Ruth as the "Moabitess" (1:22ff.), *hammōʾabiyyāh* would certainly have been expected. The phrase *ʾešet maḥlôn*, therefore, might have been placed here to satisfy the curiosity of an audience concerned with the deceased's identity. It is not impossible that a pun may have been fostered by the consonants *mḥln* and *nḥl*. As it is, Mahlon's name is never invoked again, even to the point that his son, a product of the union of Boaz and Ruth, will be considered as either Naomi's (and Elimelech's) in 4:14-17, or Boaz's in 4:21.

We do not see the necessity, as does Campbell (1975: 151), to overstate the function of *wegam* by translating it as: "And, more important." Why should Boaz place a higher value on one of his activities than the other? Such an approach would ill fit a legal setting.

qānîtî lî leʾiššāh. We would like to recall our opinion, stated above, that with this declaration Boaz was not actually *marrying* Ruth, but was merely purchasing her with that intent in mind. He could certainly do no less, if he were publicly to proclaim his first son as Mahlon's heir. It will not be until verse 13 that Boaz marries our heroine.

(l') *welōʾ-yikkarēt šēm-hammēt mēʿîm ʾeḥāyw ûmiššaʿar meqômô.* We refer to our discussion of this sentence above. There, we suggested that this clause is best understood as an extract from either an oral (i.e. customary) or a written body of laws. At this point, we make but a few random remarks. (1) On the *niphʿal* of *kārat* with a meaning similar to ours, see Isa. 48:19; 56:5. Note that in Deut. 25:6 the *niphʿal* of *māḥāh* is found. On this verb, see S. R. Driver, 1951: 283. (2) Bertholet's often challenged suggestion to vocalize *mēʿîm* into *mēʿam* never had merit (cf. Joüon, 1953: 88); Rudolph, 1962:60: "The '*people* [*ʿam*] of his people' would not be a meaningful expression." (3) The phrase *miššaʿar meqômô* has provoked some hesitance on the part of the versions. In general, 3:11's "assembly of [his] people" was preferred over "gate of his place/town" (cf. BH^3, ad loc.) Campbell (1975: 151-52) has a fine recapitulation of the differing opinions of the versions. He judiciously adds: "The connotation of 'from the assembly of his town' is more than simply membership in the legal body. Consistent with 'his inheritance' in the first clause of the long purpose expression of this verse, it connotes his legal rights as protected by the assembly, of which he would have been a member."

4:11-12. These verses contain a laconic response to Boaz's declaration, followed by a blessing, which in comparison with ones recorded in Gen. 48:20 and Ps. 45:17 is unusually and elaborately developed. It has generally been noted that this blessing, appearing almost as an appendix to the legal disputations, is divisible into three segments, sequentially addressing the future bride, the groom, and their posterity. Each of these three segments might stand for a blessing complete, on its own. The first and third segments are distinguished by verbs in the jussive form. The second, addressed to Boaz, seems central to the series of blessings. It is given in a classically poetic form in which two cola parallel each other by means of verbs given in the imperative, and by means of place names that had become quasi-synonymous when this segment of the blessing was authored. The first of these cola extols the personal prowess of the bridegroom as he unites with his bride. Thus, it harks back to the blessing accorded the bride. The second colon of this central blessing urges Boaz to establish a worthy family in Bethlehem. It will, therefore, dovetail neatly into the third segment of the threefold blessing with its concern over the house of Judah.

It has been suggested that this triple blessing may have incorporated individual expressions of good wishes which were drawn together expressly for inclusion in Ruth. Gray (1967: 405), for example, thinks of materials gathered from the Bethlehem area. Eissfeldt (1965: 65) and Würthwein (HAT, 18, p. 23) claim that individual sections may have been uttered during betrothal festivities. In view of the brilliantly worked out scheme into which these blessings were forged together, such approaches may not be overly instructive.

Recently, Parker (1976: 23-30) wrote a stimulating article comparing the blessings in Ruth *and those pronounced by the gods at the marriage of King Keret to Lady Hurriya, daughter of the King of Udm. We quote the relevant segment of this Ugaritic text from the translation most easily available in ANET*[3]*, p. 146 (Krt, B [= CTA, 15/UT, 128], ii:11-29. See further the treatment of Cross, 1973: 179):*

[The]n came the companies of the gods.
        And Puissant Baal spake up:
"[Now] come, O Kindly One [El Be]nign!
Wilt thou not bless [Keret] the Noble,
        Not beatify the Beloved, Lad of El?"--
A cup [El] takes [in] (his) hand,
        A flagon in (his) right hand.
        Indeed he blesses [*his servant*].
El blesses Keret,
        [Beatifi]es the Beloved, lad of El:
"The [woman thou ta]k'st, O Keret,
        The woman thou tak'st into thy house,
        The maid thou bring'st into thy court,
Shall bear seven sons unto thee;
        Yea, eight she'll produce for thee.
She shall bear Yassib (*yṣb*) the Lad,
        Who shall draw the milk of A[she]rah,
Suck the breasts of the maiden Anath,
        The two wet nurs[es *of the gods*].

Parker's article contains a careful list of comparisons between the Hebrew and Ugaritic series of blessings. Regarding similarities *(Parker, 1976: 28-29): both blessings (1) occur between the contracting and the consummation of the marriage; (2) follow a form in which the groom is addressed, after an initial paean to the bride (ii:21-23); (3) center their concern on the ability of the protagonist to produce progeny; and (4) take pride in comparing the bridegroom to his legendary ancestors (cf. Parker's treatment of the unquoted passage, iii:2-4). As for* dissimilarities, *Parker speaks of (1) the poetic (*Keret*) versus prose (*Ruth*) style of the accounts of their settings and (2) the mythic-epic framework of* Keret versus *the "historical," "real-life" setting of* Ruth. *Hence the benedictors in* Keret *are drawn from divine circles, whereas those of* Ruth *are mortals, drawn from Bethlehem's city gate. Concerning the first of these points of dissimilarity, we might note that the blessings in* Ruth *are, at least partially, couched in poetic form. As to the second, we shall entertain its implications in our Interpretation section below. At this juncture, suffice it to add one more observation drawn from Parker's article: blessings in* Keret *and* Ruth *are addressed to a reigning monarch and to the great-grandfather of a future King of Israel, respectively.*

(m') *wayyō'merû kol-hā'ām 'ăšer-baššaʿar wehazzeqēnîm.* Some translations (e.g. Joüon, 1953: 89; BH^3; *Bible de Jerusalem*), would follow LXX, which has "all the people who were in the gate said: 'we are witnesses'; and the elders said. . . ." Rudolph (1962: 60) points out that in 4:4, 9, 11, the activities of the elders and the "people" are not differentiated; hence he would retain the MT. Syriac recalls the pattern of 4:9, thus reversing the order of the MT, i.e., "the elders. . . ." In this, it is followed by NEB. The Targum once more speaks of the "gate of the Sanhedrin" (Levine, 1973: 105).

(n') *ʿēdîm.* "The affirmative answer is generally expressed. . . by repeating the emphatic word in question. . . ." (GKC, 150n [p. 476]). In such cases, the subject is often elided (Joüon, 1947: 146h [p. 452]).

(o') *yittēn YHWH 'et-hā'iššāh habbā'āh 'el-bēyteka kerāḥēl ûkelē'āh.* For the idiom *nātan* plus accusative plus *ke* . . . , see BDB, 681 (3,c).

Should *hā'iššāh* be rendered the "woman" or the "wife"? On the one hand, it may be too premature to call Ruth a "wife," as does the LXX. On the other hand, the blessing would be meaningless if it were directed to anyone but a future wife of Boaz. Nevertheless, note the use of *naʿarāh*, "young lady," in verse 12. The words *yittēn YHWH 'et-ha'iššāh* are strongly reminiscent of the last clause of this blessing series: . . . *'ăšer yittēn YHWH lekā min-hannaʿarāh hazzō't.* The similarity is shown only in the choice of vocabulary, but not in the usage of that vocabulary.

kerāḥēl ûkelēʾāh. Jacob's wives are the first to be invoked from among other ancestors, male as well as female. These ancestors, found only in the first and third blessing, include Jacob (Israel), Judah, Perez, and the latter's mother, Tamar. Vesco (1967: 235-47) thinks these names are recalled to confer a patriarchal texture upon the tale of *Ruth*. Hals (1969: 105) proposes that the narrator was equating Ruth's virtues with those of worthy ancestors. Humbert (1958: 107-8) thinks that these hyperboles were meant to extol David's ancestors. Parker's view is given above.

As to the order in which these marriages are listed, Rudolph (1962: 69) raises a number of minor questions: Is Rachel placed first because she was Jacob's favorite? Was this order affected by the tradition that Rachel was buried in Bethlehem (Gen. 35:19)? Was Rachel's barrenness comparable to Ruth's first ten years of sterility? Campbell (1975: 152) echoes these queries and adds an observation that is difficult to assess.

Above, we noted that there is a tendency in Hebrew narrative style to leave any person (or place for that matter) accorded special attention to the last position in a series of names. Since Leah was the mother of Judah, hence ultimately the progenitress of Boaz and David, it might be that she was accorded the second slot precisely because the remaining portion of the blessings are concerned with Leah's descendants and not those of Rachel.

(p') *ʾašer bānû šetēyhem ʾet-bēyt yiśrāʾēl.* For the pronominal suffix, see above *sub* 1:9. On *libnôt bayit*, "to establish a household," see the attestations, mostly "pre-exilic," which are gathered in Campbell, 1975: 152-53. Brichto (1973: 22-23, n.33) thinks the mention of *šetēyhem* is a clue that two lines were to be born to Boaz as well as to Jacob. The first son of Ruth, unnamed in our tale, would have become Mahlon's heir. The second child, later known as Obed, would be Boaz's son and heir. Thus, Brichto would account for the mention of Boaz as the ancestor of David.

yiśrāʾēl. In view of the mention of household associated with Judah and Perez (verse 12), it may be that *yiśrāʾēl* is also to be taken as the covenantal name of Jacob, rather than that of a nation. That the Targum understood it as such is clear from its addition, "our father," after the mention of this name (Levine, 1973: 105-6).

(q') *waʿaśēh-ḥayil beʾeprātāh ûqrāʾ-šēm bebēyt lāḥem.* This bicolon is cast in a classically poetic form. The verbs in each one of the cola are imperatives of third -weak *('lamed-he')* roots given in the *qal* stem, prefixed by the copulative *waw*. Syntactically the imperatives follow the jussive of the first sentence (*yittēn*), thus suggesting that these cola were to convey the result of an action (GKC, 110i [p. 325], 165a [pp. 503-4]). Such observations, in themselves, might be considered as bearing sufficient warning against too hastily emending *ûqrāʾ-šēm* into either *weniqrāʾ (niphʿal*, perfect with *waw conversive)* or *weyiqqārēʾ (niphʿal*, imperfect with copulative *waw)*.

This bicolon has been studied by Labuschagne (1967: 364-67), and Campbell (1975: 153-54) contains a good summary of the former's views. While we are aware of Witzenrath's (1975: 54-55[n. 29]) objections to Labuschagne's thesis, we nevertheless adopt its conclusions with respect to the first half of this blessing. In a context that praises the procreative qualities of the bride, Labuschagne thinks it reasonable that the groom should be similarly extolled. For this reason, he would render *ḥayil* as "procreative power," citing Job 21:7-8; Joel 2:22; Prov. 31:3 as contexts in which such a meaning is defensible. Thus, rather than the commonly offered renditions for the first colon, such as RSV's "may you prosper in Ephrathah," Labuschagne suggests: "engender procreative power in Ephrathah." However, it should be added that to some extent he has been anticipated by Humbert. Humbert (1958: 108) translates the first colon: "Montre-toi vaillant époux à Ephrata," adding the following charming comment: "Aucune hésitation ne peut plus subsister: nous n'assistons ici ni à des amours séniles, ni aux roucoulements d'une idylle de Gessner, le but de cette union est souligné sans fausse pudeur: ici la fécondité de Ruth doit être examplaire. . . ." Following Humbert, we take this opportunity, however, to object to Labuschagne's (and Campbell's) opinion that the blessing is revealed by its content to be addressed to an elderly person: it is one of the *topoi* in Ancient Near Eastern literature that heroes--but not always heroines--eventually always rise to the occasion when a male heir is expected to continue a line, regardless of the hero's age. On Boaz's age, see our remarks above.

The second segment of this bicolon, central to the blessings of verses 11-12, looks forward to the third and final blessing. That last blessing, we shall note, will be concerned with the foundation of a line worthy of Boaz's ancestors: Perez and Judah. Labuschagne, whom we have followed in the first half of this couplet, is not very convincing in his discussion of its second half. We believe that this is so because he overemphasizes the *content* of the bicolon, with its synonymous parallelism, at the expense of the *function* of the two cola as media by which to bridge and bind the first and third blessings. Labuschagne is certainly correct in avoiding the renderings of ancient versions: "and there shall be a name" (LXX-BA; other LXX manuscripts: "call a name"), "Call its name Bethlehem" (Syriac), as well as of some of the modern translations: "And be renowned in Bethlehem" (RSV--note NEB's "keep a name alive in Bethlehem" and JPS[2]'s "perpetuate your name in Bethlehem"). Labuschagne, however, agrees with Smith (1953: 850) that the blessing in the second half of the bicolon is as concerned with procreation and descendents as that of the first half. So he proposes: "and so act as name-giver in Bethlehem." In our opinion, however, the emphasis in the second half is no longer on the ability of Boaz to gather his strength in order to impregnate his wife with a male child, but on the hope that the forthcoming son will ultimately become ancestor of a ruling dynasty. As has often been stated (see BDB, 1028 [2,b]; Loretz, 1960: 394-95), *šēm*, "name," is to be taken in its meaning of "reputation," a term sometimes applied to royal lines, dynasties, or simply to meritorious groupings. With this in mind, it may not be incidental that *šēm*, "reputation," a term so important to the future of David's kingdom, is repeated precisely fourteen (2 x 7) times in *Ruth*. Brichto (1973: 21-22) would translate *šēm* as "family line, dynasty." Indeed, the formula *liqrōʾ šēm* is equated by him with the *lehāqîm šēm-hammēt* of 4:5 and the *wehāqēm zeraʿ* of Gen. 38:8. We shall have a longer discussion of the use of *qārāʾ šēm* in *Ruth* below, *sub* 4:14.

Joüon's (1953: 90-91) proposed emendation from *ûqrāʾ-šēm* to **ûqnēh-šēm* would not only be difficult to conceive orthographically, but would coin an idiom unknown to Hebrew. It has rightly been rejected by commentators.

(r') *wîhî bêytēka kebêyt pereṣ ʾašer-yāledāh tāmār lîhûdāh.* The narrator's focus on Perez has been noted by a number of commentators, most of whom consider it as providing the inspiration for the genealogy in 4: 18-22. At this point, we should only like to point out that, like Ruth, Tamar was also deemed a foreigner.

Parker (1976: 30) makes the following shrewd observation:

---

the suggestion that 4:11b-12 might be a royal marriage-blessing would entail an association with the genealogy of vss. 17b-22. The probably secondary character of vss. 11b-12 was argued above. What this association would mean is that *the genealogy would not have been influenced by the mention of Perez in vs. 12, as is sometimes supposed, but that the blessing would be based on the genealogy* [italics mine], and the linkage of the royal genealogy with the Ruth story (through the identification of the Boaz of Ruth with the Boaz of I Chronicles 2) would have prompted the incorporation into the book of the royal marriage-blessing as well.

We shall return to Parker's pregnant suggestion on two other occasions. In one of these, we shall adduce other evidence to support Parker's opinion which, if accepted, would regard the mention of Perez in the genealogy as influencing its recall in verse 12. On the other occasion, reserved for our Interpretation chapter, we shall speculate on the use and purpose of a royal blessing in the book of Ruth.

(s') *naʿarāh.* I do not think that the word *naʿarāh,* "young lady," is used here "as a further reminder of the discrepancy of age between Boaz and Ruth" Campbell (1975: 154); rather, I think that the context is of import in the choice of vocabulary. The storyteller uses *ʾiššāh,* "woman, wife," when he compares Ruth to the wives of Jacob/Yiśrāʾēl, but switches to *naʿarāh* when he invokes the memory of the "husbandless" and neglected Tamar. At any rate, marriages with even the severest of generation gaps do not seem to have attracted the attention of Ancient Near Eastern man. When they are alluded to, such as in the case of David and Abishag the Shunammite [1 Kings 1:1-4], the purpose is only to underscore the impotence of an aged dynast, and to prepare the reader for the consequent palace intrigues. This could hardly be the case in *Ruth.*

Birth of Obed (4:13-17)

13 Subsequently, Boaz married Ruth.[a] When she became his wife[b]
he had relations with her.[c] The Lord allowed her to conceive;[d] she
bore a son.[e]
14 Women said to Naomi: "Blessed be the Lord who,[f] on this very
day, did not deny you a redeemer.[g] May his name be proclaimed in
15 Israel.[h] He shall become a comforter for you,[i] and is to sustain
you in your old age;[j] for he was born to a daughter-in-law who
loves you[k] and is dearer to you than seven sons."[l]
16 Naomi took the boy,[m] setting him on her bosom;[n] she thus became
a foster mother to him.[o]

17 Female neighbors established his reputation, saying: "A son was born to Naomi!"[p] So they called him Obed,[q] he being the father of Jesse, who was the father of David.[r]

This episode, which we conveniently label "Birth of Obed," contains a number of unusual features. For this reason, we think it best to preface our annotations with a statement which will receive, in parts, further treatment in our Interpretation section.

1. It is important to reflect upon the past activities of each of the protagonists, and to summarize the position that each occupied at the end of the city gate scene.

a. Naomi had acquired Boaz as a *gō'ēl*. This relationship will become permanent unless a son is born to Boaz and to Ruth, for that child was pledged to Naomi as Mahlon's--and therefore Elimelech's--heir.

b. Ruth will be married to Boaz. Her connections with Naomi will be retained by virtue of the fact that her future husband had become Naomi's *gō'ēl*. Ironically enough, the birth of a son to her and to Boaz would, legalistically speaking, terminate this special relationship with her former mother-in-law; for that son will become Mahlon's (and Naomi's), while Ruth will remain Boaz's wife.

c. Boaz will become Ruth's husband and Naomi's *gō'ēl*. His first child, if male, is pledged to become Mahlon's heir. In that event, his activity in behalf of Naomi should come to an end. For that son would, in effect, end Naomi's reliance upon any *gō'ēl*.

To all this we have an added feature to consider: the blessings pronounced by the elders. Parker has convincingly shown that they are to be regarded as royal marriage blessings. Furthermore, he suggests that the inclusion of Perez in verse 12 be considered as evidence that the genealogical tree of verses 18-22 was known to the narrator of the blessings. Below, we shall present corroborative evidence for such a hypothesis. If this position is substantiated, it will mean that the sequence Boaz-Obed-Jesse-David was at the disposal of the storyteller when he penned the "Birth of Obed" episode, and that, in effect, he used that episode to tie the loose ends of his narrative together. We shall come back to all this presently.

2. In his book on etiological narrative in the Old Testament (1968), Long (1968) follows Fichtner's (1956: 372-96) analysis in isolating two

basic formulae that report and explore the naming of either a person or a place. "Form I" appears mostly in the giving of personal names. Displaying little apparent connection with the preceding narrative, Form I reports a name by means of the imperfect of *qārā᾿* with a *waw*-conversive and gives a paronomastic etymology for that name. "Form II," on the other hand, is introduced by *ʿal kēn*, "therefore." The act of naming is not narrated but is inferred, from either a speech or a reported event, with a word play providing the link between the speech and the name in question. Form II tends to be associated with place, rather than personal, names.

Long knows of (too?) many examples, labeled "mixed type," in which the narrative background available to Form II is combined with the etymological derivaties of names which is a feature of Form I. Long gives examples of cases that range from "slight mixing," in which incompletely worked out patterns of Form I are combined with differing segments particular to Form II, to "advance mixing," in which the distinctions between the two patterns have practically disappeared. It is unfortunate that Long, limiting his work to materials drawn from Genesis through 2 Kings, did not study our passage in *Ruth*.

With the above by way of introduction, we suggest that the "Birth of Obed" be regarded as comprising *two*--not *one*--separate birth episodes, each of which displays "mixing" of patterns found in Forms I and II. We shall label the first as the *"Gō᾿ēl"* episode; the second as the "Son" episode.

1. "Gō᾿ēl" episode.

   a. Setting: Boaz *lāqaḥ* Ruth; she bears a son (verse 13).

   b. Report of birth:

   i. Announcement by *nāšîm* of the *gō᾿ēl*'s birth [verse 14a-b].

   ii (Form I). Naming (?)-*niqrā᾿* element-. No name; no explanation (cf. notes to verse 14).

   iii. Role of the *gō᾿ēl* vis-à-vis Naomi (verse 15a-b).

   iv. Connection of the *gō᾿ēl* vis-à-vis Ruth restated (verse 15c-d).

In the *"Gō᾿ēl"* episode, Form I is given in a very rudimentary fashion. The *qārā᾿ šēm* element is in the *niphʿal*; the name of the child is not given. If an etymon to this missing name is to be sought at all, it may be that the verb *gā᾿al* offers the most likely prospect. As it is, the name *yig᾿āl* is known from the OT (Num. 13:7--a spy from the tribe of Issachar; 2 Sam. 23:36--a follower of David; 1 Chron. 3:22--a descendent of Zerubbabel).

It may be that Boaz's reply to Ruth in 3:13 *(ṭôb yigʾāl)*, which presented interpretive difficulties above, anticipated this name, now lost from the text.

2. "Son" episode.

a. Setting: Naomi *lāqaḥ* the child- formal adoption or legitimation (?) (verse 16).

b. Report of birth:

i. *šōkenôt*, "establish his reputation" (verse 17a; see annotations ad loc.).

ii (Form I). naming:

(1) explanation of name (verse 17b).

(2) naming (verse 17c).

iii. Appendix: dynastic information (verse 17d).

In the "Son" episode, Form I consists of section *b*. *ii* (1 and 2). We shall assess, below whether the information given as "explanation" for the name "Obed" is to be considered as part of Form I, or as a dislocated portion from Form II.

Each of these episodes has a special function. The "*Gōʾēl*" narrative permits the (unnamed) child of Ruth and Boaz to *remain theirs*, despite the pledge made by Boaz before the elders of Bethlehem. For, it is clear that the child could not be Naomi's and still retain his *geʾullāh* functions. In the "Son" episode, however, the child, definitely given a personal name (Obed), is Naomi's son and heir. The pledge made by Boaz--whose name is noticeably missing from this segment--is, in this manner, fulfilled. Thus, by means of this twofold birth narrative, the storyteller responded to a difficulty so obvious that it remains a subject of contention among modern scholars (cf. Rowley, 1965: 192-93, 193[n. 1]), to wit: how to successfully integrate an ending in which Ruth's child will be considered as the son both of her deceased husband Mahlon and of her second husband Boaz. We noted above that Brichto [1973: 22-23 (n. 33)] posits that Ruth bore *two* sons to Boaz. It should be obvious that the narrator could not hope to do the tale justice without providing it with a conclusion that would (1) permit Naomi to acquire a permanent *gōʾēl*, (2) allow Naomi to maintain a good relationship with a woman who abandoned all in order to follow her to Bethlehem, and (3) fulfill the pledge of Boaz to consider the first born of Ruth as Mahlon's son. Yet the narrator could not afford to ignore a genealogical tradition that claimed Boaz as the father of Obed, hence ultimately the progenitor of David the King.

As we shall see, these difficulties will not be resolved until the "Genealogical Tree" of verses 18-22.

4:13-15. These verses contain the birth narrative that we have labeled "Gō'ēl." *Literarily speaking, this account is much more successful than the succeeding one, which we call "Son." The writer manages, in the compass of three verses, to invoke the name of every one of his protagonists. Furthermore, he succeeds in providing his story with a nice twist that recalls many of the themes and leitmotives so fundamental to his tale: love and redemption; daughter-in-law and sons.*

In contrast to a story that has heretofore devoted some seventy verses (1:6-4:12) to cover a period of a few weeks--from the time of harvest to that of threshing--verse 13 describes the events of at least nine months in fifteen words. Of these fifteen words, fully one-third are verbs, grouped into two sequences, which consecutively treat human, then divine activities: (1) marriage (Boaz marries Ruth; she becomes his wife) and (2) birth (God allows Ruth to conceive and to bear a son). These two sequences are linked in the middle by the act of procreation (Boaz has intercourse with Ruth). As we have noted above, it is only with verse 13, and not earlier, that Boaz's marriage to Ruth is finally recorded.

(a) *wayyiqqaḥ bōʿaz ʾet-rût.* As is clear from other OT attestations (e.g. Exod. 2:1; 21:10; 34:16), the verb *lāqaḥ,* with the accusative of person, is sufficient to express the notion of marriage. This, of course, raises the question concerning the need for the next clause: literally, "And she became a wife to him." As a matter of fact, some LXX manuscripts (see Campbell, 1975: 162[n. a-a]) excise the next two clauses, obviously misunderstanding their function.

(b) *wattehî-lô leʾiššāh.* The emphasis here is on *ʾiššāh,* "wife." In this manner, it is made quite clear that Ruth, despite her past status as a *nokriyyāh* which later turned into that of a *šipḥāh,* despite her unenviable record of ten years of sterility when she was wedded to Mahlon, despite the fact that she was "purchased" by Boaz--despite all that--she still was worthy enough to marry a *gibbôr ḥayil* of Boaz's stature, becoming his *wife* and not merely a concubine or a handmaiden.

(c) *wayyābōʾ ʾēleyhā.* It may have been important for the narrator not to mince words at this juncture of the tale. If his audience ever wondered about the potency of a man who had not pressed his advantage that night on the threshing-floor, under an open sky, *wayyābō' 'ēleyhā* would certainly remove any such doubts. If, on the other hand, his listeners were not those who believed in the innocence of that evening's tête-à-tête, then *wayyābō' 'ēleyhā* would have other implications. Together with the following clauses, this statement would make it clear that Obed's conception occurred *after* Boaz's public avowals on behalf of Elimelech's estate. For, if it were otherwise--if Obed was conceived *before* Boaz's declarations--then Obed's connection to Naomi would certainly have been questioned.

(d) *wayyittēn YHWH lāh hērāyôn.* In addition to contributing to the above confirmation of the fact that Obed's conception occurred after the legal formalities that unfolded at the city gate, this clause has one more function. It explains why Mahlon, living as he did in Moab with Chemosh as its deity, was not successful in impregnating Ruth even after ten years or so of cohabitation. Mahlon does succeed, finally, in producing a son; but Obed will, of course, end by calling Boaz his father.

On the form of *hērāyôn*, see Joüon, 1953: 92.

(e) *wattēled ben.* The story of *Ruth* would be purposeless if it ended on this note (contra, to some degree, Rudolph, 1962: 70).

4:14-15. As it has been noted by many commentators, those women who heard Naomi's bitter lament as she entered Bethlehem (1:20-21) are now commissioned with the happy task of announcing the birth of the child. In the Interpretation section, we shall have much more to say about the possible role played by the "women" who so obtrusively are given prominence in the closing verse of Ruth. *Minc's article (1967: 71-76) contributes little to our understanding of their function.*

(f) *bārûk YHWH ('ašer).* On this rather common formula, see C. A. Keller, THAT, I, pp. 357-58 (1, c). Usages that are closest to ours are found in Gen. 24:27; Ps. 31:22; 66:20 (Elohim).

(g) *'ašer lō' hišbît lāk gō'ēl hayyôm.* The *hiph'il* of *šābat*, "to cease, desist," is often constructed with YHWH as its subject (cf. F. Stolz, THAT, II, 864-65 [3,c]). In contexts that are mostly prophetic, YHWH is said to "end" Israel's moments of festivities, happiness, and joyful celebrations. It is significant, I think, that of twenty-five such occurrences, only in our example--a non-prophetic context--is *hišbît* negated (by means of *lō*ʾ). (The example in Lev. 2:13, which also has this verb similarly negated, is so different in usage and style, that it does not affect the uniqueness of our occurrence). This might suggest, therefore, that a definite emphasis is on the fact that the women were glorifying God not so much for his *positive act* in which a *gōʾēl* is created to care for Naomi's needs, but for his *intervention to* prevent *the end of Elimelech's line*. This subtle difference may in fact have been purposely promoted to recall another patriarchal motif: the birth of Isaac. There, too, God's intervention was quite direct, bringing fertility to a woman ordinarily too old to conceive.

The mention of *gōʾēl* in verse 14 raises an interesting point: is this *gōʾēl* to be identified with the newly born child or with his natural father Boaz? Most of those who have an opinion on the matter think of the child as the redeemer of Naomi. Thus, it is proposed, that after the birth of this son, Boaz would no longer act as a *gōʾēl*, with the responsibility technically falling upon the former. That, effectively speaking, this responsibility is not shouldered until the child matures into manhood is not thought to effect his de jure position as a *gōʾēl*. In the meantime, Boaz would probably continue to care for Naomi's needs. Bewer (1903-4: 202-6), however, thinks that *Boaz* is the *gōʾēl* who is so welcomed by the women of Bethlehem. Among his arguments is the fact that the past narrative had consistently spoken of Boaz as the desired *gōʾēl* (e.g. 2:20; 3:3, 9, 12, 13; 4:10ff.). It should be quite unusual, thinks Bewer, that a mere child would suddenly be saddled with a duty ably shouldered by the honorable Boaz. In order to press his advantage, however, Bewer is forced to deal with a serious difficulty: on the basis of the occurrence of *gōʾēl after* the birth of the child--an occurrence whose sequence in time is accentuated by means of the quasi-juridicial *hayyôm*, "on this day"--it would seem that the identification of the *gōʾēl* with the child is strongly implied. Moreover, he who "becomes Naomi's comforter," and "sustains her old age" (verse 15)--clearly the *gōʾēl*--is said to be born to Ruth *(yelādattû)*.

Bewer's response to this difficulty is to reshuffle the text of 4:14-17 in order to give prominence to the "women of Bethlehem" equivalent to that of the elders of the city gate. Rudolph (1962: 70), who knows of Bewer's opinion, offers the weak response that *gōʾēl* in 4:14-15 should be taken as the generalized "protector" rather than as the legalistic "redeemer." This, of course, would be out of place in *Ruth*. Moreover, we do not know the term *gō'ēl* to apply to *sons* of individuals in unfortunate situations. The *gō'ēl*, who is called upon to protect an impoverished family, is drawn from the circle of relatives, and *not* of sons and husbands. Because Obed was pledged as a son to Mahlon (verse 10) and because he was to become Naomi's son, it would be quite singular were he to be labeled as *gō'ēl*.

While we acknowledge, therefore, the merits of some of Bewer's arguments in favor of regarding Boaz as the *gō'ēl* of 4:14-15, his resolution of the difficulties discussed above is drastic enough to be deemed unconvincing. Moreover, the fortunes of Bewer's thesis are bound to an even more extreme approach, which would delete from *Ruth* those passages that claim Mahlon as the (legal) father of the child. See, further, Witzenrath, 1975: 278(n. 139).

Our proposal to distinguish separate etiological accounts for the birth of the child might resolve this difficulty. For, as we tried to show above, the "*Gō'ēl*" episode may have been intended to promote the newly born son as the future "*Gō'ēl*" of Naomi. This episode considers the unnamed child as a son of Ruth and Boaz, thus ignoring the latter's pledge to regard him as Mahlon's son. Retaining his filial relationship with Boaz, this child could, therefore, properly be regarded as the future *gō'ēl* of Naomi, inheriting this responsibility from Boaz, his natural father.

Joüon's proposed emendation of *lāk* to *lammēt*, "to the dead," is based upon a (false) insistence on harmonizing the suffixed pronoun *lāk* (second person feminine singular) with that of *šemô* (third person masculine singular) of the following clause; see further, the criticism of Rudolph, 1962: 69; Witzenrath, 1975: 55(n. 30).

On *hayyôm*, "this day," and its legal implications, see above.

(h) *weyiqqārē' šemô beyiśrā'ēl*. Above, *sub* 4:11, we had indicated our belief that *šēm*, "name," should be understood in its meaning of "reputation" or even "dynasty." We had too cavalierly disagreed with Labuschagne's suggestion that *qārā' šēm* of 4:11 be rendered with "to give [somebody] a name." At this point, it seems opportune to discuss the four occasions in *Ruth* 4 in which the verb *qārā'*, "to call," is constructed with *šēm*, "name." To do this, however, we shall have to anticipate remarks and situations which will find elaboration and confirmation later on in our annotations. The occurrences within *Ruth* are as follows:

a. 4:11 *ûqrā᾿-šēm (bebēyt lāḥem)*

b. 4:14 *weyiqqārē᾿ šemô beyiśrā᾿ēl*

c. 4:17a *wattiqre᾿nāh lô haššekēnôt šēm (lē᾿mōr)*

d. 4:17c *wattiqre᾿nāh šemô ῾ôbēd*

Now in Biblical Hebrew, two patterns are regularly followed to express the notion of "to give a name, to name": (1) *qārā᾿ šēm* plus pronominal suffix/named object; (2) *qārā᾿ šēm* plus *le/᾿el* (cf. Labuschagne, THAT, II, 671 [3,c]). See further Witzenrath, 1975: 21-23. It has been my observation, based on a careful but not exhaustive survey of OT attestations, that the first pattern is regularly followed by the actual name given to the person or place that is the object of attention. The second pattern, on the other hand, appears not to specify a given personal name, i.e. no personal name is expected or found. Thus, of the occurrences in *Ruth* 4, only *d*, appearing in 4:17c, *seems to be truly a name-bestowing formula.* Thus, it should not be surprising that this example alone is followed by a personal name. *c*, occurring in 4:17a, was set in a pattern that *does not* specify a name. We should, therefore, not expect one to follow. The import of this observation will be readily apparent as we annotate that verse.

The case of *b*, the subject of this note, is more complex. The *niph῾al* of *qārā᾿*, with *šēm* as its subject, is fairly frequent in Hebrew. The idiom *niqrā᾿ šēm ῾al*, connoting (divine) ownership, need not concern us (see v.d. Woude, THAT, II, 957 [4,f]). Aside from our example, there are three others in which *niqrā᾿ šēm* is found with the preposition *be-*. Two of these provide us with examples of this preposition functioning differently from our usage in *Ruth* 4:14. The first of these, Gen. 48:16, contains, curiously enough, a reference to the verb *gā᾿al*. Jacob says as he lay ill: "The angel who delivered me from all harm bless the boys [Ephraim and Menasseh] and may my name be recalled in them and the name of my ancestors Abraham and Isaac [*weyiqqārē᾿ bāhem šemî wešēm ᾿abōtay ᾿abrāhām weyiṣḥāq*]." It has to be admitted, however, that the precise meaning of this verse is somewhat obscure. The second example, Jer. 44: 26, is equally difficult to assess. We refer to Bright's (1965: 262) treatment of this passage.

The third example offers our passage its best grammatical parallel. Deut. 25:10, which lies within a context of levirate legislation, speaks of a sobriquet that is to be applied to one who refuses to continue his deceased brother's line: "And he shall go in Israel by the name of: 'the family of the unsandaled one' [*weniqrā᾽ šemô beyiśrā᾽ēl bēyt ḥalûṣ hannā῾-al*]." It is worthy of note that a name, albeit for a whole family, is attached to the idiom *niqrā᾽ šēm* plus suffix. This would be quite in line with all the remaining attestations of this formula (that are not followed by the preposition *be-*), with the possible exception of its occurrence in Eccles. 6:10, which uses a circumlocution in the place of a proper name. Thus, each of the following passages, Gen. 17:5; 35:10; Ezra 20:29; Dan. 10:1; 1 Chron. 13:6, records this formula as preceeding a proper name.

This observation, in our view, would tend to confirm our opinion, expressed above, that the *"Gō᾽ēl"* birth etiology may have originally included the personal name of the child who was to become Naomi's *gō᾽ēl*, but who, at the same time, was to retain his filial relationship with Boaz. That child, it might further be speculated, may have been named with an appellative derived from the root *gā᾽al* (e.g. *Yig᾽āl*).

We now return to example *a* of the formulae attested in *Ruth* 4. A translation for this example at 4:11 is not easily obtainable; for 4:11 contains the only instance in the OT in which *qārā᾽ šēm* is given in its absolute form, that is, followed neither by a pronominal suffix nor a personal name. This anomaly allows us neither to follow Labuschagne's rendering, nor to emend the text in order to conform to example *b* of 4:14 (as suggested by Rudolph). We shall discuss Campbell's proposal in our annotations for verse 17.

(i) *wehāyāh lāk lemēšîb nepeš*. The few examples of *mēšîb nepeš* recorded in the OT brings us close to a general meaning of the idiom without, however, permitting us a precise definition. The beneficial and desirable state of mind called "restoration of the *nepeš*," is said to be derived from divine (Ps. 19:8--"*tôrāh*"; cf. 23:3--"God"), human (Lam. 1:16--"comforter"; Prov. 25:13--"messenger"), and material (Lam. 1:11, 19--"food") intercessions; cf. the discussion of Westermann, THAT, II, 79 (*nepeš*, 3, b). Since the *gō᾽ēl* of 4:14-15 will shortly be praised for sustaining (with food) Naomi in her old age, it may not be too bold to suggest that, as a *mēšîb nepeš*, his duties would consist of comforting and consoling an elderly widow (cf. Lam. 1:16); note also the remarks in Joüon, 1953: 93.

According to Campbell (1975: 164), "Most noteworthy here is that the story-teller picks up the dominant key word of the first chapter, *šwb*, 'to return,' especially as it was used in 1:21: 'empty Yahweh has brought me back' (or, 'caused me to return'). The signal is given: Naomi's complaint, dormant since 1:20-21, is here resolved."

(j) *ûlkalkēl ʾet-śēybātēk.* Rudolph (1962: 69) alludes to Jer. 44:19 as also preserving a participle that is followed by an infinitive construct prefixed by a conjunction. Although the syntax of each is not perfectly matched, their presence in the OT should warn us against an overhasty emendation of the infinitive to a participle (i.e. **ûmekalkēl;* cf. Mal. 3:2) merely to balance *mēšîb (nepeš).* Joüon (1953: 93) notes that the *lamed* of *lekalkēl* is related to the preceding *hāyāh.* We follow this clue by noting, with GKC, 114 (p. 348), that a combination of *hāyāh* with an infinitive construct does confer upon the action in question the notion of "definite purpose," of an urgency that is compelling.

Influenced by a misreading of the Greek τῆν πολιάν σου ("your old age"), Syriac and Armenian versions based their translations, "your city," apparently upon Greek πόλιν (cf. Rudolph, 1962: 69; Campbell, 1975: 162).

(k) *kî kallātēk ʾašer-ʾahēbatek yelādattû.* This sentence is of some importance to the thesis that a twofold etiological narrative is contained in the "Birth of Obed" episode. Its insistence on identifying the newborn as Ruth's child (*yelādattû,* "she bore him") cannot easily be reconciled with the exclamation, "a son is born to Naomi" (verse 17). Were one to assign verses 15 and 17 to a "Gōʾēl" and a "Son" birth narrative respectively, not only would this particular problem be alleviated, but a logical end would have been provided to one of *Ruth*'s main lessons: how Ruth, a foreigner, succeeded in providing her former mother-in-law, a Bethlehemite widow, with a perfect *gōʾēl,* a scion of Ephrathah's most prominent family.

It may be that *lekalkēl* was used, a few words previously, to play on the consonants it shared with *kallāh,* "daughter-in-law."

On the (mis)vocalization of *ʾahēbatek (for *ʾahēbātek),* see Rudolph, 1962; Joüon, 1953: 94; BH[3], ad loc.

On *yeladattû,* a contracted form of **yeladathû,* see GKC, 59g (p. 160). Joüon's supposition (1953: 94) that a *lāk,* "for you," should be placed after *yeladattû*--thus yielding a translation: "who has born him for you [Naomi] (in order to become your son)"--completely misses the points at issue in these episodes.

(l) *ʾašer-hîʾ ṭôbāh lāk miššibʿāh bānîm.* As is often pointed out, the number "seven" is here but conventional. In the eyes of Naomi, therefore, Ruth is not regarded as any less worthy than was Hannah who was said to be dearer to Elakanah "than ten sons" (1 Sam. 1:8). See also 1 Sam. 2:5, and the comments of Joüon, 1953: 94; Campbell, 1975: 164.

*4:16-17. We regard these two verses as reporting another birth episode. We label this one "Son," and distinguish it from the preceding one, which we have called "Gō*ʾ*ēl." We note the following as worthy of comparison: A. This episode also begins with the verb* **lāqaḥ**, *in this case with Naomi as its subject rather than Boaz (verse 13). B. In contradistinction to the previous episode, a major role is given to women who are called* **šekēnôt**, *rather than verse 14's* **nāšîm**. *C. In the "Son" narrative the women are explicitly announcing the birth of a son to Naomi, rather than that of a* **gō**ʾ**ēl**. *D. Boaz and Ruth are neither mentioned nor alluded to in this episode. Boaz's name is conspicuously missing from the fragment of the genealogy which ends verse 17. E. The name of Yahweh is not invoked in this segment. In verse 14, however, it is to be noticed that the child was placed under the protection of Yahweh ("blessed be he to Yahweh").*

Two problems confront us as we annotate 4:16-17. The first has been the object of a long-standing debate among commentators. To resolve it, one must come to some conclusion about Naomi's activity as she gathers the child to her bosom: is she displaying tenderness toward him, or is she adopting him as her own child?

The second problem is one that has rarely been posed. Below, we shall merely skirt it, reserving until our Interpretation section the discussion of its manifold implications.

As Ruth *unfolded, we followed the tale as it moved two women, Naomi and Ruth, from Moabite territory to Bethlehem. Their relationship, based on bonds formed by Ruth's marriage to Naomi's son, was ironically enough threatened by the former's remarriage to a prominent Bethlehemite. We have seen that, in an effort to maintain these bonds, Ruth asked Boaz to become Naomi's* gōʾēl. *We have also noted how Boaz managed to outwit "Mr. So-and-So," by promising that his* first born from his marriage to Ruth, if a male, will become Mahlon's *(and, therefore, Naomi's) heir. As far as either reader or audience of this tale could gather, the* sole reason for the storyteller even to consider speaking of the newborn as Naomi's (verse 17) *(rather than as Ruth's and Boaz's, verse 13)* is to fulfill the promise made by Boaz, at the city gate, when he effectively urged the next of kin to withdraw his candidacy as Naomi's gōʾēl. *But, in attempting to achieve this goal, the storyteller did pay a (literary) price; consider the following:*

1. By making the child Naomi's, the narrator was forced to end his tale with a birth account that was doubtlessly less satisfying than the previous one. Thus, in contrast to our so-called "Gō'ēl" episode of verses 13-15 which masterfully gathered for a final bow, so to speak, all the protagonists and had once more recalled Ruth's major themes, the "Son" episode focuses solely on Naomi and Obed: Ruth and Boaz are purposely forgotten.

2. By making the child Naomi's, the narrator missed the opportunity to reward properly a heroine who risked all to accompany her mother-in-law to Bethlehem. Such a failure to grant Ruth her own son might not only appear to a sensitive audience as a callous act, but might also rob the storyteller of the opportunity to invoke a pattern that was well established in Hebrew traditions: that the eponymous ancestors of the House of Israel and Judah produced their royal lines by marrying (or impregnating) foreign women. In the case of Joseph, it was Egyptian Asenath, daughter of the priest of On, who bore him Ephraim, the ancestor of Israel's dynasty; in that of Judah, it was Canaanite, Tamar, who bore him Perez, the ancestor of David. (Note also that Judah's wife, Bathshua was also a Canaanite; on these matters, see M. D. Johnson, 1969: 159-62; 165-70. On the clans of Judah as evolved from a fusion with Canaanites, see De Vaux, 1971: 507-10.) Two further remarks are in order at this point.

a. As is obvious from the blessings of verse 12, the narrator was not unaware of the parallels that might be established between the conclusion of his story and that of Judah and Tamar (Gen. 38). The fact that the "Son" birth narrative, by regarding Obed as Naomi's son rather than Ruth's, effectively destroyed the pattern discussed above was not likely missed by the storyteller. Nevertheless, he consciously proceeded with that approach! We shall learn why in our Interpretation section.

b. Despite the fact that, on crucial occasions, Hebrew traditions acknowledged that foreign blood flowed in the veins of its kings, almost all modern commentators chose to marvel at the integrity of a tradition which provided David with a Moabite ancestress. We, on the other hand, are impressed by precisely the opposite condition. We understand full well why the writer of Ruth did not hesitate to declare Ruth of Moab as the progenitrix of David. He could do no less for David's ancestors than to follow a pattern set for Joseph, and Judah. We might even invoke the NT as further evidence of the tenacity of the tradition; Salmon (married to Rahab of Jericho--Matt. 1:5), and David himself (married to Bathseba, the "Hittite" by marriage cf. the Bath-shua of 1 Chron. 3:5), were also *considered to have infused Israel's royal line with more foreign blood. What we do find as worthy of attention however, is that the narrator of Ruth chose to* break away *from that pattern precisely when he has us consider Obed as the son of the Bethlehemite Naomi, rather than the Moabite Ruth. Leach (1969: 61) uses structuralist methods to prove the opposite.*

3. By making the child Naomi's and hence ultimately Mahlon's and Elimelech's, the narrator was contradicting the genealogy of 4:18-22, which insists on regarding David as a descendent of Perez through Boaz. Even if one were to consider this genealogy as an "appendix," it would still be difficult to explain an editor's failure to eliminate or resolve this contradiction.

Nevertheless, our narrator did dare to speak of Obed as Naomi's son! Why he did so despite the above-stated difficulties will be entertained in the Interpretation segment of our study.

(m) *yeled*. Campbell (1975: 164) has this to say: "The close of the most poignant and lovely inclusio used by the story-teller, a framing device reaching from 1:5, where Naomi is bereft of her two lads, to this new lad, son of Ruth."

(n) *wattešitēhû beḥēyqāh*. Hebrew is rich in vocabulary for the word "breast, bosom": *dad, zīz, ḥōb, ḥēyq, ḥōšen,* and *šad*. The terms *ḥōb* and *ḥōšen,* rarely attested, are not exclusively applied to human organs; *zīz* (Isa. 66:11) and *šad* are employed exclusively to denote the female breast. Male and female, however, are provided with a *ḥēyq* (on these terms, cf. McCurley, 1969: 40).

Our passage offers the only attestation in which the verb *šît,* "to place," is joined, by means of the preposition *be-*, to the substantive *ḥēyq*. The placing of a child upon the *ḥēyq* could denote an act of tenderness and love (e.g. 1 Kings 3:20). To give the notion of suckling, however, Hebrew consistently uses *šad* (once *zīz* in Isa. 66:11) as a term for "breast." In such a case the verb *yānaq*, "to suckle," is employed (once, in Isa. 66:11, *māṣaṣ*, "to suck").

As mentioned above, the precise nature of Naomi's act is a subject of debates: is it one of love or one bearing legal implications? One school of thought thinks this to be symbolic either of adoption or legitimation (full bibliography in Witzenrath, 1975: 280-81[n. 142]). De Vaux (1961: 42) makes no distinction between Naomi's act and others that speak of a child as placed on the genitals *(birkayim,* literally: "knees") of a would-be bearer (cf. Gen. 30:3-8; 48:5-12; 50:23): "we are almost bound to see in all these cases one and the same rite expressing adoption." In fact, however, the Genesis passages cited by de Vaux speak neither of adoption nor of legitimation (the last is a term used by Fohrer, 1969: 344-45). The children born "on the knees" of a matriarch are considered as *her natural issue;* there is, therefore, absolutely no need to adopt them. This point was noted long ago by Köhler (1909: 312-14). Nevertheless, Köhler chose to confirm the adoptive nature of Naomi's deed, by referring to comparative ethnology. Köhler's approach, as well as that of de Vaux, was criticized by Rudolph (1962: 70-71) and by Campbell (1975: 165). Hoffner (1968: 201[n. 27]) gathered some Hittite material that might have brought Köhler's gleanings for parallels closer to Israel's borders. These documents indicate that, at least in literary texts, the placing of a child on the knee was tantamount to conferring upon him official recognition and legitimization (cf. also Onians, 1954: 174ff.). Noting that in Hittite texts constructions with the word "knee" sometimes alternate with ones containing the Sumerian ÚR, Hoffner adds: "Since Summerian ÚR has a similar range of meaning to Hebrew *ḥêq*, it is possible to add Ruth 4:16 to the group of Old Testament passages in which placing the child on one's knee symbolizes recognition as legitimate child heir. . . ."

Despite these statements, however, we subscribe to Joüon's opinion that Naomi needed neither to adopt (nor to legitimize) a child that was declared as Mahlon's, even before his conception. Furthermore, we wonder whether an Israelite woman was ever in a legal position to adopt a child. The one example in the OT, in which a woman does adopt a child, involves an *Egyptian* princess acting in a foreign setting (Exod. 2:10). Additionally, it would be most unusual for an act of adoption (verse 17) to be linked to that of name giving (cf. Long, 1968: 57). Again, the only exception to this last observation is available only in Exod. 2:10, a passage whose setting is foreign to Israel. Gerleman, (1965: 18, 37) speaks of a "special type of adoption in which the newborn is given a mother who is truly Jewish." This proposal strikes us as too modern in its rationale. Gerleman's suggestion is inconsistent with other Hebraic traditions that welcome the infusion of "foreign" blood into royal veins (see above).

Is Naomi, then, merely bestowing her love upon the newly-born? This is the contention of Rudolph and Campbell. Perhaps! Yet, it has to be admitted that such an understanding would ill-fit the denouement of a well-told story. We find it hardly acceptable that, but a few words before the genealogical cadences of verses 17c–22, the narrator should engage in flabby and purposeless sentimentalities.

We do have an opinion on this clause, one that considers 4:16–17a-b as a vestige of a motif that had currency among Israel's neighbors. We shall however, await our Interpretation section to elaborate on this position. At this point, we ask it to be remembered that the combination of *ḥēyq*, "bosom," with the verb *šît*, "to set," promotes a (deliberately?) vague context, one in which Naomi's activity escapes a precise definition. It seems to connote neither adoption nor legitimation; neither breast feeding nor affection.

(o) *wattehî-lô leʾōmenet*. At issue here is the precise meaning of *ʾōmenet*. This term is derived from the root **ʾmn*, "to confirm, affirm, be firm," which, in the *qal*-stem, is reserved for participial formations. Because of the peculiarity of its meaning, some authorities assign these participial derivatives to a root labelled **ʾmn II* (cf. KBL, 60b; HAL, 62b). The attestations within our range of meaning are divisible among masculine (Num. 11:12; 2 Kings 10:1, 5; Esther 2:7; Isa. 49:23) and feminine (2 Sam. 4:4; *Ruth* 4:16) participles. Only two of these citations occur in proximity with the verb *yānaq*, "to suckle"; both of these, however, refer to the masculine form, and are, therefore, to be regarded figuratively (Isa. 49:23; Num. 11:12). In the remaining attestations, including our own from *Ruth*, we cannot come closer than a general rendering such as "guardian, nanny [i.e. governess], foster parent." Although a child might be suckled until the age of three (2 Macc. 7:27; ANET[3], 420–21), it is most unlikely that an *ʾōmenet* would still be breast feeding the five-year-old Mephiboshet (2 Sam. 4:4). Nor is it likely that the aged Naomi served a similar function. Moreover, it is to be noted that Hebrew has a special term for women acting in that capacity: *mēyneqet* (derived from the root **ynq*). See further, Wildberger, THAT, I, 178–79; Jepsen, TWAT, I, 315–16; IDB, III, 572 ("nurse").

In view of the above, are we totally dismissing the possibility that *ʾōmenet* might mean "wet-nurse"? In our Interpretation section, we shall once more pick up the discussion.

(p) *wattiqreʾnāh lô haššekēnôt šēm lēʾmōr yullad-bēn lenoʾomî*. We should first note that the females involved in this particular passage are *šekēnôt* "neighborhood women," rather than the *nāšîm* of verse 14. With regard to the term *šekēnôt*, two matters are to be assessed: 1. Why are "female neighbors" given such attention in our text? Why are they given the honor to name the ancestor of David? 2. If it is clear that *wattiqreʾ-nāh ʾet šemô ʿôbed* (17c) is indeed a "naming" formula, what is the purpose of *wattiqreʾnāh lô . . . šēm* (19a)?

The word *šekēnôt* is a feminine plural participle (absolute) of the verb *šākan*, "to settle [down], dwell." We have no other OT examples in which females are recorded present at a naming ceremony. Below, we collect instances in which persons other than the immediate parents of a newborn are recorded as present during the birth and the naming of a child (see, further, Witzenrath, 1975: 23-26, and the bibliography assembled in those pages).

Text	Parent(s)	Child	Attendants	Purpose	Namer
a. Gen. 35:17	Rachel/Jacob	Benjamin	*meyalledet*	--Difficult birth	Rachel
b. Gen. 38:28	Tamar/Judah	Perez/ Zerah	*meyalledet*	--Sequence of birth	Judah
c. [Exod. 1: 15-22	Israelites		Shiphra/ Puah	--Fertility of Hebrews --Explain *battîm* (21)	No]
d. 1 Sam. 4: 20	?/ Phinehas	Ichabod	*niṣṣabôt* (attendants)	--Difficult birth --News of male child	The mother
e. 2 Sam. 12: 25	Bathsheba/ David	Solomon	No	--No	YHWH (Nathan)
f. [Jer. 20:15	?/Hilkiyah	Jeremiah	"A man"	--gives news of birth	No]
g. Luke 1:57-66	Elizabeth/ Zechariah	John (the Baptist)	Neighbors	--Give the "wrong name" --Divine involvement	Angel
h. Ruth 4:17	Naomi ?/?	Obed	*šekēnôt*	--Announce birth	*šekēnôt*

Cases *c* (Exod. 1) and *f* (Jer. 20) do not fit our pattern. We have given them for the sake of completeness, but have also bracketed them to indicate their unusual nature. Examples *a* (Gen. 35) and *d* (1 Sam. 4) record statements by midwives called upon to assist in difficult births. These statements in no way affect the naming of the newborns. There remain three cases in which those present were in some way involved in giving a child a name. In Luke 1 (example *g*) the neighbors suggest that Elizabeth's son be named after his own father, Zechariah. Signs and wonders, however, made it clear that the naming of this particular child was to be left up to heaven. It might further be noted that the naming of John the Baptist occurred at the time of his circumcision and not birth (cf. also Luke 2:21). Example *c* (2 Sam. 12:25) also records an instance of Divine involvement in name giving.

Not surprisingly, the two instances that indicate that non-members of the immediate family of the newly born played a role in establishing his name, are both concerned with Davidic ancestry. Again, it is not astonishing that of the two name-givings recorded in Gen. 38 (example *b*) that of Perez is alone accorded a truly etiological explanation (see, further, Long, 1968: 38-39). The MT insists that it was Judah who named his children *(wayyiqrāʾ šemô pāreṣ/zāraḥ)*. Most commentators emend the text so that Tamar names the child (cf. BH^3, ad loc.). Others prefer not to change the consonantal structure; hence **wyqrʾ* is vocalized as the passive form, **wayyiqqārēʾ*, "And his name was called Perez/Zerah." Though tempted by the last suggestion, we see no reason why Judah could not have named his own children. Such a practice is not abnormal in the Semitic world. Were we to retain the MT, as is suggested here, we are left with only *Ruth* 4:17 as an OT example in which the naming of a child is left in the hands of people other than the immediate parents. In order to find a pattern in birth giving that is equivalent to ours, we shall have to search the literature of Israel's neighbors. Fortunately, the very recent volume of D. Irvin on the comparison of tales of the Old Testament and the Ancient Near East will alleviate our task. Dr. Irvin gathers episodes, mythological and epic in style and content, from Mesopotamia, Egypt, Anatolia, Ugarit, and Israel. "Traditional Episode Table: Sheet I" breaks a number of birth narratives into plot-motifs that may include the following: "Childlessness; Promise of Conception; Month-Counting; Birth; Father Told; Father's Reaction; Naming and Reason; Prediction." Our focus will be on elements in the Ancient Near Eastern tales that best parallel those of *Ruth* 4:16-17. But since the search for such parallels will affect our understanding of the *purpose of Ruth* more than it will clarify particularly the episode contained in *Ruth* 4:16-17, we shall resist further discussion until our Interpretation section.

4:17. To many scholars, this verse preserves two mutually exclusive variants of the same name-giving formula. Eissfeldt (1965: 479-80) is one of many commentators who point out that if wattiqreʾnāh lô haššekēnôt šēm lēʾmōr *(17a) is to be considered as the name-giving formula, and if it is to* precede *the explanation recorded for that name* (yullad-bēn lenoʿomî*--17b), 17a should have contained a personal name, preferably in the place of* šēm. *Eissfeldt follows Peters (1914: 449) in suggesting the substitution of a name such as "Ben-noʿam" for the word* šēm. *Eissfeldt conjectures that a name such as "Ben-noʿam" may have been excised in favor of "Obed," a name traditionally assigned to David's ancestor. "In other words," suggests Eissfeldt (1965: 480), "the Ruth narrative had originally nothing at all to do with David, but has only secondarily been made into a narrative concerning David's ancestors." Ap-Thomas (1967-68: 870-71), however, protests as follows: "I cannot find in the Old Testament any example of a name explicitly given to commemorate another person, whether father or mother or grandmother." For his part, he suggests E/Obednoam as a plausible reconstruction of the original name. In this manner, he appends to the name, Obed, of 17c, an element derived from 17b and locates the whole in 17a. Gunkel (1913: 84 [n. 1] cautiously proposes for 17a a name such as Yibleʿam, since it would contain some of the consonants found in 17b* (y[ld]b[n]l[n]ʿm). *Gerleman (1965: 34) offers no suggestion of his own, but thinks that the name original to 17a may have sounded too "Moabitic," and hence was replaced with Obed. Cooke (1918: 18) conjectures that Obed may have been a shortened form of Obadiah. Schulz (1926: 128) thinks of Obed-naʿaman (with naʿaman = Adonis). Further discussion is to be found in Witzenrath, 1975: 281-82.*

Campbell (1975: 166) quite sensibly criticizes hypotheses such as the ones offered above:

How did the word šēm *instead of a proper name [such as the posited Ben-noʿam, Yibleʿam, E/Obednoʿam, etc.] get into the first clause [verse 17a]? If at a later stage of the transmission of the story there was a reason for getting the name Obed prominently into the picture, common sense seems to dictate that a better job of splicing would have been done. Meanwhile, we have noticed how much the story-teller seems to be making of this verbal combination of* qrʾ šm, *"call a name." If our reading in 4:14 is correct, that the wish is that the new-born sons's [sic] name be celebrated in Israel, then by far the simplest meaning for the beginning of verse 17 is that the celebrating has begun.*

Campbell's "simple" explanation for verse 17a depends, in reality, on a tortuous explanation given when he annotated verse 14 (1975: 163-64). For that sentence, Campbell toys with the idea that Yahweh's name may have been subject of the verbal form wayyiqārēʾ. *Furthermore, he postulated that* qārāʾ (be)šem *might have meant "to celebrate," in the sense of "rejoicing over." We object to Campbell's suggestion on a number of grounds. First, the translations in which he would prefer the meaning "to rejoice" for our idiom over the traditional "to invoke" (Deut. 32:3; Ps. 99:6; Jer. 44:26; etc.) are in no way improved thereby. Secondly, the three examples of* niqrāʾ bešem *which occur in the OT (Isa. 43:7; 48:1; Esther 2:14) cannot bear a translation such as Campbell's "to be celebrated." Thirdly, as Campbell (1975: 164) himself notes, "In view of the flow into verse 15, the new-born [rather than Yahweh] is the more likely antecedent of 'his name.'" Thus, a meaning for our idiom, initially developed expressly to fit Yahweh as its subject, cannot be maintained once this purpose is jeopardized. Since, as Campbell (1975: 166) himself admits, his translation of 17a ("And the neighborhood women rejoiced over him") depends heavily on acceptance of his thesis presented with regard to verse 14, we shall refrain from further discussion of the matter.*

We noted above that the grammatical construction of the clause wattiqreʾnāh. . . šēm *follows a pattern that is not associated with name giving. In other words, unlike 17c's unimpeachable credentials as a name-giving formula, 17a is not, indeed may never have been, intended to promote the name of Naomi's child. (We say this rather categorically despite a temptation to pursue a suggestion made by Witzenrath [1975: 24] that originally verse 17 may have contained two names--a personal [cf. Yedidyah] and a "throne" name [cf. Solomon]--of which only one survived.) For this reason, we believe that proposals that substitute a personal name in the place of 17a's* šēm *(e.g. Eissfeldt, Gunkel, Schulz, Ap-Thomas, etc.) are not only unnecessary but may well be misguided. This, despite the occurrence of* lēʾmōr *in 17a. (On this topic, see Eissfeldt, 1965: 479). We believe that 17a is vestigial of pronouncements made by the* šekēnôt *on the occasion of establishing the "fate" of Obed's royal line. This point will be defended in our Interpretation section.*

yullad-bēn lenoʿomî. As pointed out by F. I. Anderson, *apud,*

Campbell (1975: 166-67), this instance is unique in the OT; for a child is said to be born to a female. The syntax, also exceptional, doubtless is to emphasize the *birth* of a child to Naomi. By this means, the text sought to be *unequivocal* in considering this child as Naomi's. As far as I can tell, no one sought to remove the difficulty by revocalizing *yālad-bēn leno-ʿomî*, "[He, i.e. Boaz] begot a son for Naomi," invoking Isa. 49: 21 as a grammatical witness. Note the parallelism of *yeled/bēn* in a context whose vocabulary also includes the *puʿʿal* of *yālad* (Isa. 9:5).

(q) *wattiqreʾnāh šemô ʿôbēd.* Why we should resist emending our verbal form in order to read either **wattiqrāʾ*(!) (i.e. subject: Naomi) or **wayyiqrāʾ* (i.e. subject: Boaz) will be made clear in our Interpretation chapter. This form, third person feminine plural, may or may not include Naomi as the subject.

It is obvious that the name Obed is not derived from the vocabulary which either succeeds or precedes its appearance. Indeed, the root *ʿ*bd* does not ever occur in *Ruth* in any other form. As an element in personal names, *ʿ*bd*, "to serve," is extremely common in the Semitic world (for East Semitic, the substantive is *wardum* [Sumerian, ÌR]). For listings and bibliography see, conveniently, Benz, 1972: 369-72. In Israel, the root *ʿ*bd* is attested, in usage for personal names, in relatively few formations (for listings, see BDB, 714-15). The word *ʿebed*, a derivative of this root, does not merely mean "a servant, slave," but it could refer to persons of high standing in society. In such a case, the relationship between an individual (or a deity) and his *ʿebed* depends on their (formalized) status as unequals in power or authority. From God's perspective, for example, David (thirty-three times) and Moses (thirty-six times) are *ʿabādîm* (see IDB, IV, 292 [i.]; Benz [1972: 369-72] gives a bibliography of *ʿebed* used as a designation for royalties and their officials).

The word *ʿôbēd* is a participle of the active verb *ʿābad*, "to serve, to work." In this form, its usage is rather circumscribed to (1) "tiller of the soil" (seven times); (2) "corvée worker (six times); (3) "cultic worker, worshiper" (of YHWH, four times; of Baalim, etc., nine times). Two attestations could also be accounted to "corvée workers" (Mal. 3:17; 1 Kings 5: 1). In each of these categories, the references are not particularly bound to a specific period of Hebrew literature. From these possibilities, we think that the name "Obed," if its vocalization is based upon ancient traditions, may have meant either "The Laborer" (cf. Adam) or "The Worshipper" (cf. Obadiah). Josephus, V:4, thinks that this name was applied to David's ancestor for: "he was brought up in order to be subservient to [Naomi] in her old age." This opinion is often encountered in older commentaries on *Ruth* (see Witzenrath, 1975: 23-24[n. 22]). More modern interpreters, however, regard it as a shortened form of Obadiah (*ʿōbadyāh*), that is, "Follower of Yahweh."

(r) *hûʾ ʾabî-yišay ʾabî dāwid.* This genealogical fragment attaches Obed to Naomi, and hence to Elimelech and Mahlon. It is a matter of discussion among scholars whether this statement is to be reckoned as a "preface" to an (appended) genealogy or as a genuine segment of the original narrative. The issue shall be better focused once we annotate 4:18-22. At this point, I might say that I find Witzenrath's comments upon this clause to be very convincing. She points out (1975: 24) that other OT attestations of the formula *hûʾ ʾabî* [*x*], "he is/being the father of. . . ," immediately follow a personal name that *is explicitely recorded* (Gen. 19:37-38; 1 Chron. 4:11; 7:31 (cf. 2:42); somewhat different formulae in Gen. 4:20-21; 36:43). Thus, separating 17d from the preceding segment would go counter to Hebraic genealogical practices. Regard for the integrity of this pattern, furthermore, prevents us from considering 17b, which ends with *lenoʿomî* "to Naomi," as immediately preceding 17d, since *lenoʿomî* could not possibly be considered as a personal name upon which *hûʾ ʾabî* [*x*] depended. Witzenrath's overall approach to this section, however, has been criticized by Loretz (1977).

The Ancestry of David (4:18-22)

18-19* This is the genealogy of Perez: Perez[a] bore Hezron; Hezron,[b]
19-21 Ram; Ram,[c] Amminadab; Amminadab,[d] Nahshon; Nahshon,[e] Salmah;[f] Salmon,
21-22* Boaz; Boaz, Obed; Obed, Jesse;[g] and Jesse bore David.[h]

In his book, *The Purpose of the Biblical Genealogies* (1969: 77-82), M. D. Johnson, highlighted the functional diversity of Biblical genealogical lists. Johnson suggested that a proper assessment of any lineage in the OT must be derived both from an analysis of its individual and particular structure, as well as a study of the literary context in which it is placed. Johnson underscores the "apologetic" (I would say "didactic") nature of genealogical forms in which nationalistic and theological dogmas are advanced. "As such," adds Johnson, "a kind of Midrashic exegesis could be utilized to construct genealogies that communicated the convictions of the author" (p. 81).

We believe that Johnson's observations are of particular significance for the study of *Ruth* 4:18-22. No longer can the genealogical tree of David, contained within these lines, be dismissed as an "appendix" merely because it follows the *tôledôt* form (literally: "begettings"), usually associated with the "Priestly" redactors. At the outset, we might observe that the entire notion of genealogical "appendices" seem to be foreign to the OT. Thus, while a modern point of view might find it unexceptional that a genealogy should be reserved to the end of a tale whose denouement is precisely concerned with the birth of a major link in the sequence of ancestors, it nevertheless remains a fact that no other Biblical lineage is ever given at the end of a narrative. Summaries, such as those found in Gen. 2:4a and 37:2a as well as Exod. 6:19 and 1 Chron. 8:28 and 9:34, might be labeled *tôledôt*, yet they cannot be considered as "true" genealogies since no list of ancestors follows them. On this point, see Campbell, 1975: 172.

In tackling the problems which confront us, we might wish to entertain the following agenda concerning *Ruth* 4:18-22:

A. Its relationship to the preceding narrative

B. Its function as a royal genealogy

C. Its relationship to 1 Chron. 2

A. *The relationship of the genealogy to the tale of* Ruth.

It would be fair to say that the majority of modern commentators, of which only a sampling will be represented below, consider *Ruth* 4:18-22 not to be original to the tale itself (bibliography in Rowley, 1965: 173[n. 5]). Smith (1953: 851) succinctly states the two reasons that recur most often in scholarly publications: "The genealogy was added at a later time, since in the story the child of Ruth is reckoned as the son of Mahlon, not of Boaz. The introductory *now these are the generations of* is characteristic of P, and the regular repetition of *begat* is also P." As to why a genealogical list was appended to *Ruth*, many commentators agree with the following words of Smith (1953: 851): "The verses were probably added by someone who considered the book important only because it concerned David, and who felt that David's Judean descent needed fuller emphasis." Eissfeldt (1965: 479-80), however, would want to make it quite clear that the tale of *Ruth*, in its earliest form, had nothing to do with David or his ancestry.

He thinks that at least two factors played a role in assigning *Ruth* to Davidic lore: (1) The mention of Perez in 4:12 may have been one reason for appending a genealogy concerned with the descendents of Judah and his son Perez. (2) "The fact that the story actually dealt with people of Bethlehem made this assumption [that the figures of *Ruth* narrative were grafted as David's ancestors] easy, and since the narrative took place in the days of the judges, Boaz and Ruth could readily be understood as the great-grandparents of David" (Eissfeldt, 1965: 480).

Strong objections to a position such as Eissfeldt's have been voiced. Ap-Thomas (1967-68: 370), for example, protests that "As a folk-tale, if you disassociate [the tale of *Ruth*] from the family of David, you cut away its only root" (see, further, the bibliography assembled by Witzenrath, 1975: 352-54[n. 17]). It must be admitted however, that Eissfeldt's contention is but a logical extension, even if starkly expressed, of any hypothesis that regards Obed's filial relationship to Mahlon (i.e., to Naomi) as of primary importance to the integrity and development of the tale. Thus, if untouched by a later hand, the story would never have had to speak of David, since an Obed *who was merely a son of Mahlon* would obviously not recall a genealogy that claimed him as *a son of Boaz*. Therefore, it seems to us that any attempt at regarding the tale of *Ruth* as a prelude to the history of David, must consider the genealogy of 4:18-22 as immemorially linked to the preceding narrative. To do otherwise would be to espouse a contention such as Eissfeldt's: *Ruth* was originally unrelated to David's ancestry. *Conversely, were one to show that the genealogy of 4:18-22 could not be an "appendix" to the tale, one would confirm its status as an integral and original segment of Ruth.* Since scholarly means at our disposal do not permit an irrefutable proof of the first position--i.e. that *Ruth* prefaced the history of David's dynasty--we might undertake to demonstrate the second one: to wit, *that the genealogy of 4:18-22 was tailor made for inclusion as an ending to Ruth.* We first refer to the opinions of other scholars (1-2 below), before offering our own (3-5 below).

1. Rowley (1965: 193-94) criticized the "appendix" hypothesis on three levels. "If the appendix is really in conflict with the story," he first states, "it is surprising that the writer who added it was not aware of it" (p. 193). Secondly, presuming that Boaz was childless, Rowley suggests that Obed, as Mahlon's (legal) heir and Boaz's (natural) son, could conceivably inherit the fortunes of Boaz as well as those of Elimelech. Thirdly, Rowley points to the blessings of 4:11-12, addressed to Boaz,

which clearly consider him as the ancestor of a future royal household.

Despite these points, Rowley's arguments are not presented in a tone of total certitude. He feels it necessary to add: "That the genealogy was appended by another hand is likely enough, but not on [the ground that Obed is known as a son of both Mahlon and Boaz]" (p. 193[n. 2]). Rowley does not elaborate further on "likely enough."

2. By comparing the blessings in *Ruth* with those of Ugarit's *Keret*, Parker (1976: 23-30) convincingly demonstrates that both belonged to a genre that one might label royal marriage blessings. Among the elements they share is a reference to dynastic ancestors. Hence, Parker concludes, the mention of Perez in 4:12 must have depended on foreknowledge of a specific genealogy that claimed Perez as the founder of David's royal line. This is clearly the case in *Ruth* 4:18-22. Note that the other genealogy of David, preserved in 1 Chron. 2 (see below), does not give Tamar's son any special attention. We quoted above Parker's relevant statement on this matter. At this point, let it be noted that, as a result of Parker's insight, the genealogy at the conclusion of *Ruth* could be considered as an "appendix" only if one regards the blessings of 4:11-12 as interpolated at the same time as the addition of the "appended" genealogy.

3. We begin our own contribution to the discussion by explaining how the genealogy of *Ruth* 4:18-22 might have satisfied literary sensibilities. *a*. It permitted the tale to have additional moorings in a historical past by setting Boaz within three generations from David. *b*. It permitted the narrator to offer a fine contrast (some might say inclusio) within a tale that began in the drought of the Judges' period and ended in the promise of the Davidic kingdom. *c*. It permitted the audience to find pleasure in hearing the familiar names of ancestors as, in measured cadences, they tumbled from the lips of the storyteller.

4. In ZAW (90 [1978]: 171-85) (and in IDB, *Supplement*, pp. 354-56) we have discussed a genealogical procedure that obtained among Hebrew chronographers. Simply stated, our arguments proposed that in some cases minimal alterations were made in inherited lists of ancestors in order to place individuals deemed worthy of attention in the seventh position of a genealogical tree. (Among the lists that were examined in those articles were Gen. 4:17-24; 5:3-31; 11:10-26; 36; 46; Num. 26:5-51; 13:4-15; 1 Sam. 9-12; Matt. 1:2-16; Luke 3:23-38.) Since in *Ruth*'s genealogy Boaz is reckoned as seventh from Perez, it is very likely that David's line was arranged in order to focus attention on *Ruth*'s protagonist. Such an observation would

urge us to consider 4:18-22 (whatever its primordial shape; whenever its creation) as conceived specifically for inclusion at the end of *Ruth*, as early as the hero of this tale was given the name "Boaz." The alternatives, either that Boaz was not originally a hero of *Ruth* or that David's lineage was tailored to fit a tale with a nebulous purpose (cf. Eissfeldt's opinions), seem to us far fetched. A tangential, yet significant, insight that arises from our application of this "seventh-generation" hypothesis would lead us to postulate that a version of *Ruth*, tolerably close to our own recension in its major themes and development, was established whenever speculations about David and his ancestry were finalized by temple genealogists and royal panegyrists. This version, in its earliest shape, had already *linked its hero Boaz with the genealogy that was to be placed at the tale's end.*

5. We noted above that the narrative of *Ruth* contained two birth etiologies, each of which provided a satisfying denouement of the major themes pursued in *Ruth*. The first, contained in 4:13-15, described the birth of a son to Ruth and Boaz, a future *gōʾēl* for Naomi. The second, recorded in 4:16-17, fulfilled Boaz's pledge to provide Mahlon with an heir (cf. 4:10). Precisely because our storyteller was conscious of his obligations to his audience, he created a problem for himself which--we are quick to add--cannot be resolved in the manner suggested by Rowley: to wit, by regarding Obed as both son to Boaz and heir to Mahlon. As far as we could ascertain from Near Eastern documentation, a situation in which an adopted child retained his claim on the estate of the natural father would be most unusual.

With this difficulty confronting him, the narrator of *Ruth* turned to the genealogy of 4:18-22 as a medium in which to solve his problem. We propose to explain the process by which this solution was effected in a number of steps. But we would like to make it perfectly clear that this elaboration is highly speculative.

a. David's pedigree, trimmed at the top to allow Boaz a seventh position (see also below), was placed at the end of the tale. As observed above, this genealogy did not function, strictly speaking, as a true *tôledôt*. (Were it meant to do so, it would have been placed at the beginning of the tale.)

b. Our discussion of the *"Gōʾēl"* birth narrative indicated that the personal name of the child born to Ruth and Boaz was likely to have occurred in the clause *wayyiqqārēʾ šemô* [*x*] *beyiśrāʾēl* (4:14c). This name may have been nothing more than Obed's "personal," i.e. "non-dynastic" name. Thus, if paronomasia played a role in the formation of that appelative, **yigʾāl* might well have been the Obed's "personal" name. However, in view of the fact that Boaz promised his newborn to Naomi/Mahlon as a ploy to force "Mr. So-and-So" to relinquish his right of purchasing the "plot of land belonging to Elimelech," it remains plausible that "Obed," "The Laborer, Farmer," may have been perfectly suited as original even to 4:14c.

If the narrator of *Ruth* wished to take his risks in retaining a portion of his narrative imperfectly resolved, he might well have kept the name "Obed" in 14c (or changed **yigʾāl* into Obed), ended his narrative at 4:16, and concluded with the genealogy of David. A consummate artist, our narrator chose not to keep any loose ends untied. He therefore reserved the mention of Obed until the end of the "Son" narrative, using it as a punch line for the entire story of *Ruth*

c. The name Obed (or **Yigʾāl*), excised from its 4:14 position, was attached to 17c. It may be that, as others have pointed out, it replaced a name with the element **nʿm* as part of its etymon (cf. Gröndahl, 1967: 163; Benz, 1972: 362). The skeletal genealogy, possibly extracted from the more developed lineage which will succeed (v. 22), was appended as 4:16d. It served a useful purpose since it confirmed that the Obed who was a child of Naomi, was also the son of Boaz and was to become David's ancestor. While this shift of Obed's name from its previous position in 14c, did not, ultimately, solve the quandary in which the narrator found himself, it had the virtue of postponing the problem to a moment in which the audience's attention was riveted upon the roster of Israel's past heroes.

With these steps taken the tale of *Ruth* was then complete.

B. *The function of 4:18-22 as a dynastic genealogy.*

The genealogy of 4:18-22 consists of ten members, beginning with Perez, and ending with King David. Malamat (1968: 170-73) compares this line, ten members deep, to "Amorite" lists compiled in Babylon ("Genealogy of Hammurapi's dynasty") and Assyria ("Assyrian King List"). Malamat concludes, "David's table of ancestors is largely an artificial construction formed on an ideal, traditional model as befitting a royal lineage" (p. 171).

We need not retain Malamat's construction that carry this line of David to Shem, son of Noah. We may even agree with Wilson's (1975: 169-89, especially 188) criticism of Malamat's analysis of the Mesopotamian and Biblical sources. Nevertheless, in view of the predeliction of the Hebrew chronographers for organizing important blocks of time into lines of ten generations (e.g. Adam-Noah; Shem-Abraham), there is no overwhelming reason to reject Malamat's insistence that the royal genealogy of David was artificially restricted to ten members. As has been pointed out by many scholars, this listing of David's pedigree is divisible into two equal segments: the first of which covers the period between the Eisodus and the Exodus (Perez-Nahshon); the second of which witnesses the settlement and the early days of Israel's nationhood. Such an observation further underscores the artificiality of this lineage.

With our acceptance of Malamat's hypothesis, we find the author of *Ruth* to be controlled by two "conventions": one that expected him to place David in the tenth slot of genealogical tree; the other that had him place Boaz in the seventh (see above). For these requirements to avoid any complication, one minor adjustment was made to the inherited line of David's ancestry.

That Perez, and not Judah or even Jacob, headed the list of 4:18-22 has puzzled not a few commentators. In general, one meets most often with the explanation that the mention of Perez in the blessings of 4:12 influenced the selection of Perez as the ancestor with whom to begin the dynastic line. That this is an unsatisfactory explanation is easily perceived when it is pointed out that Judah's name also occurs in 4:12. We referred above to Parker's insight (based on his comparative analysis of the "royal marriage blessings" in *Ruth* and Ugarit) that the mention of Perez in verse 12 is secondary; that, contrary to the commonly held opinion, Perez's prominent position as the founder of David's line inspired the writer of *Ruth* to anticipate him in the blessings extended to Boaz. Our study of the genealogy of David corroborate Parker's opinion. Because he wished to place Boaz in the seventh slot, because he wished to place David in the tenth, and, possibly because he wished to retroject the beginnings of David's line into the Eisodus, the narrator of *Ruth* found it convenient to begin his royal lineage with Judah's son, rather than with the latter's father or grandfather.

C. *The relationship between 4:18-22 and 1 Chron. 2:5-15.*

Ruth 4:	1 Chron. 2 (1-3. yisrāʾēl- yehudāh):
18. pereṣ.	4. pereṣ
ḥeṣrôn	5. ḥeṣrôn
19. rām	9. rām
ʿammînādāb	10. ʿammînādāb
20. naḥšôn	naḥšôn

śalmāh (21. śalmôn)	11. śalmāʾ
21. bōʿaz	bōʿaz
ʿôbēd	12. ʿôbēd
22. yišay	yišay (13. ʾîšay)
dāwid	15. dāwid

Three positions are possible concerning the interdependence between the genealogy of David as preserved in *Ruth* and in 1 Chron.: that the first depended on the second (position *a*); that the second depended on the first (position *b*); and that both depended on commonly shared (temple) records (position *c*). A bibliography on this theme is available in Witzenrath, 1975: 28-38. The exposition of any of these positions, however, is to a large extent affected by the expositor's own conception of the purpose of *Ruth*, and by his own opinion on the dating of this text. Until recently, the majority opinion was that *Ruth* was a postexilic diatribe against too narrow a concept of ethnic identity. The Chronicler's obvious attachment to David and his family contributed to the predeliction of many of these scholars to regard the genealogy in *Ruth* as culled out from 1 Chron. 2; thus, it came to form an "appendix" to the tale of Boaz and Ruth. Wellhausen, in his remarkable dissertation of 1870, *De Gentibus et Familiis Judaeis*, 13-19 (cf. his *Prolegomena*, 1885: 217-18), is quite precise on the various stages taken by postexilic, if not post-Chronicles, chronographers to connect David the King, of Moabite ancestry, through Rām (i.e. "The High One"), to the princely line of Judah. The third position (*c*) is taken by scholars who note several variations between the lists in *Ruth* and 1 Chron. Campbell (1975: 173) sums up the observations of many when he points to the divergence in the writing of the name "Salma/Salmon" and to the difference in the use of genealogical forms. (Below, we shall investigate these variations.) Because of such complications, it is suggested that both lists may have been independently derived from "temple" sources, which were available to the narrator of *Ruth* and to the Chronicler. Position *b* has the merit of permitting wider latitude in dating the tale of *Ruth* and its "appendix." Thus, to return to Campbell (1975) as one scholar who would date the tale to "2nd quarter of the ninth century B.C.E." (p. 28), we find him able to state: "We are certainly not compelled to conclude that the later hand which added the Ruth appendix only did so after the era of Chronicler (around 400 B.C.E.)" (p. 173).

In order to claim that the Chronicler's list depended on *Ruth* (position *b*), one would have to maintain that both the story and its genealogy pre-dated his work. Smith sidesteps this problem by considering 1 Chron. 2:4-13 as a secondary intrusion within the genealogy of Judah (a suggestion defended as early as Wellhausen's dissertation; see below) brought about by a "Maccabean" editor who extracted it from *Ruth* (a suggestion which has little merit, especially since Maccabean authors were partial to the tribe of Levi [not Judah] and looked toward an "eschatological" resolution of Israel's kingship).

Then, too, the sources that are used by the Chronicler are not unknown to us. While scholars may disagree in individual cases, *Ruth* is not usually considered as one of his references. The fact that the Chronicler extends his lineage to David back to Israel/Jacob (in addition to suppl menting it both vertically and horizontally) is regarded by some commentators as evidence enough that the Chronicler was independently working from records, dissimilar but possibly related to those accessible to the writer of *Ruth* (cf. Myers [1965a: 13-14], who refers with approval to Goettsberger's opinion on the matter). It must be repeated however (see above), that *Ruth*'s author was under constraints that were not imposed on the Chronicler: the former had to place Boaz and David in the seventh and tenth slot in the genealogical tree. Freed from such requirements, Chronicles was able to trace the genealogy of David further back in time without, however, significantly altering the lineage that he commonly shared with *Ruth*.

We have tried to demonstrate, in previous pages, that both *Ruth* and its genealogy were composed contemporaneously. In our annotations for "Ram," we shall refer to further evidence that might indicate that the Chronicler's genealogy of David may have been dependant on *Ruth*'s. Nevertheless, we are reluctant to embrace position *b*, not so much because we know of additional data or of valid objections to this thesis, but simply because we think it unlikely that, as late as the Chronicler's time, only a single source--*Ruth*--was available whence to extract the genealogy of David! If any figure in Israel's royal past was constantly and consistently venerated, it must certainly have been David's. To suppose, therefore, that his lineage was not common knowledge any time after his death seems to me to be unreasonable.

To sum up: We regard position *a*, which would have the author of *Ruth* as poaching on the work of the Chronicler, to be indefensible. While we find many elements to attract us to position *b*, we nevertheless shall avoid it, if only because *Ruth* would be alone to remember David's ancestry.

Until further data become available, we opt for position *c*. But we should be quick to add that, if both *Ruth* and Chronicles referred to temple records from which to construct their lists, *the author of Ruth got to them first.*

4:18-22. These lines give the names of David's ancestors. It is not our purpose, in the following annotations, to exhaust the scholarly discussion surrounding each one of the names given below. We refer to the commentaries of Rudolph and Campbell, to the critical apparatus of BH[3], *and to the various biblical dictionaries and encyclopedias, for further elaborations.*

(a) *pereṣ*. The name is derived from a root **prṣ* common to Semitic languages (except for Ethiopic). Although a number of possible meanings could be assigned to the root, there is no reason to suspect that the (folk) etymology in Gen. 38: 29 is too far off the mark. For this name as it appears in Ugarit, see Gröndahl, 1967: 175.

(b) *ḥeṣrôn*. Some manuscripts assume a reading **ḥeṣrôm* (cf. EB, II, 2061). The exchange between *-ān/ōn* and *-ām/ōm* is known to occur in other Hebrew personal names, e.g. Gershon/m, Zeytan/m (cf. Campbell, 1975: 171; Noth, 1928: 38).

The root **ḥṣr* is used in Hebrew to coin personal as well as place names. While it is likely that the latter category etymologized from a cognate to Arabic *ḥaṣara*, "to encompass," or *ḥaḍara*, "to be present," the personal names may have been derived from an equivalent to Arabic *ḫaḍira*, "to be green" (cf., in this respect, the Koranic name al-Khidr, "the Green One," and the Judao-Arabic "Khduri," often given to boys whose Hebrew name would be Eliyahu).

On the role played by Hezron in the early Judah traditions, see IDB, q.v.

(c) *rām*. This name is based on a root, **rwm*, attested in most Semitic languages (except for Akkadian); see the bibliography assembled in Benz, 1972: 408-9. Apart from the Hebrew text, no other version of *Ruth* conserves this name as *rām*. Moreover, non-Hebrew versions of 1 Chron. 2 are slightly less unanimous in their preference for names such as Aram and Ar(r)an (on these points, see Campbell, 1975: 171).

The mention of *rām* in the MT of both *Ruth* and 1 Chron. provides us with our strongest *internal* evidence for the use of *Ruth*'s genealogy by the Chronicler. We first quote from Curtis (1952: 87) in order to gather the opinions generally expressed on the construction of the Chronicler's line, then proceed with an observation of our own:

As a second son of Hezron [(the name) Ram] is suspicious because (1) the Old Testament elsewhere knows of no Judean clan *Ram* co-ordinate with Caleb and Jeraḥmeel [cf. 1 Chron. 2:10], (2) the descendents of *Ram*, which follow vv[10-12], are given not in families and cities as in the case of those of Jerahmeel and Caleb, vv [25-33,42-44,46-48], but simply in the pedigree of David. *Ram is plainly introduced as a son of Hezron by the Chronicler from Ruth 4*[19] [italics ours!]. . . .

With other scholars, Curtis proposes that the names Amminadab, Nahshon, and Salma/Salmon were culled from OT sources by a genealogist who, in sandwhiching them between the well-known sequences Perez-Hezron and Boaz-Obed-Jesse, artifically produced the line of David's worthy ancestors. Curtis continues: "Two facts probably led to the selection of Ram: (1) in genealogical lore, the ancient Ram was the son of Jeraḥmeel 1 Ch. 2[25], but David plainly was not a Jeraḥmeelite, hence the father's name could not be used in his pedigree, and we have not Hezron, Jeraḥmeel, Ram, but simply Hezron. Ram; and (2) the appropriate meaning of the word 'lofty,'. . . ."

What is of interest to us in Curtis's opinions, partially shared by other scholars of Chronicles (cf. Rudolph, 1962: 71-72; 1955: 16-17, with previous bibliography), is the probability that 1 Chron. 2:10-17 may have been inserted to supplement information on David. Note that precisely in verses 12-13a, which duplicates--minus the gloss "Prince of Judah" culled out from Num. 1:7 and the names of David's brothers--*Ruth* 4:19b-22, the Chronicler consistently uses (seven times!) the form *hôlîd*, "he fathered," to link father to son. In the large number of passages that record genealogical trees, *hôlîd*, as well as other forms and conjugations of the verb *yālad*, are mixed with no apparent consistency. In fact, this unusual pattern is duplicated in both books of Chronicles only rarely: *a*. in 2:36-46 (twelve times [six *hôlîd*/ six *hōlîd*], descendents of Attai, son of an Egyptian slave, tenth generation from Perez [*sic*] until Elishama); *b*. in 5:30-36 (thirteen times [twelve *hôlîd*/ 1 *hōlîd*] linking fourteen [!] generations from Eleazar the High Priest in Solomon's temple to Azariah); and *c*. in 5:37-40 (seven times [!] linking Azariah's son, Amaryah, to Yehozadak, the exile to Babylon, father of Jeshua, the High Priest).

Therefore, both because of the unusual pattern (for the Chronicler) of linking the descendents of Ram, and the peculiarities surrounding the spelling of this name, we think that a direct connection between *Ruth* and 1 Chron. 2 is made more plausible.

These observations provide the strongest proof that position *b* might be viable as a solution to the interdependence between the lists found in *Ruth* and Chronicles.

(d) *ʿammînādāb*. Usually connected with Aaron's father-in-law (cf. IDB, I, 107-8). The elements in the name *ʿammu*, "uncle, kinsman," and *nādab*, "to be generous, noble, munificient," occur either independently or in combination with other elements in Hebrew personal names (Noth, 1928: 76-79; 193; bibliography for each of these elements is available in Benz, 1972: 359, 379). A speculation: is the mysterious reference in Cant. 6: 12 to the "chariots of ʿammīnādib" to be associated with David's illustrious ancestor? The mention of *bat nādib* in 7:2 may (or may not) be similarly inspired. But see the commentaries, ad loc. On Amminadab, King of Ammon, see Veenhof, 1973: 300.

(e) *naḥšôn* is usually identified with the "Prince of Judah" who asisted Moses in taking the census of Israel (IDB, III, 498). Although the word *nāḥāš*, "serpent," is now known to occur in Ugarit, recourse to its root for use in personal names is, so far, attested to only in the OT (see Noth, 1928: 230). But we should note that according to a number of references (BDB, 638), the King of Ammon was named Nahash.

While it is possible to seek an etymology from other meanings for the root **nḥš* (e.g. "bronze"; "to practice divination (only in *piʿʿel*)": "to be full, healthy"--if related to Akkadian *naḫāšum*-), it might be best to retain a derivation from "serpent." Other Hebrew personal, not to say place and mythic names are similarly related to "snakes," e.g. "Levi" and "Saraph."

(f) *śalmāh/śalmôn*. In 1 Chron. 2:10-11, the name is given as *śalmāʾ*. Non-Hebrew versions are unsettled on a common spelling for this ancestor of Bethlehem (verses 51, 54). The debate among scholars concerning the "original" version of the name in *Ruth*--whether Salmāh or Salmon--is half-hearted. Predictably, some would sponsor "Salmah" (e.g. Rudolph, 1962: 71), others would (unenthusiastically) opt for "Salmon" (e.g. Campbell, 1975: 171-72). We believe that all three of these spellings--to which we could also add that of *š/śalmay*, Neh. 7:48--are "original" in that all were but variants of the same name, which appends to the root **ślm* different hypocoristic affirmatives: -ʾ(Aleph), -*āh* (= *ātu*), -*ōn* (= -*ānu*), and

-y(odh). We should also like to make it clear that these differing constructions may well have been contemporaneous in usage. We note the same phenomenon as it occurs in 1 Chron. 2:12-13. There, the father of David is known both as *yišay* and *ʾîšay* (on the use of a prothetic *ʾaleph* as preformative in personal names, see Benz, 1972: 202). By recording, side by side, the variants of a well-known name, a genealogist is thus not necessarily quoting differing documents. Rather, he is merely indicating to his audience that his subject's name was not uniform at any given time. We might also add that the element *-āh* is not necessarily to be considered as a feminine ending; on its "caritative" sense, see Huffmon, 1965: 133 [n. 12].

As to the meaning of the root *ślm*, a connection with Hebrew *śalmāh/śimlāh*, is often perceived to be unconvincing; this despite the apparent equation between some mss. *śalmay* (Neh. 7:48) and the *ketîb śmly* in Ezra 2:46. Recourse to cognates has not been especially edifying in this respect.

Matt. 1:5 considers Rahab, apparently the harlot of Jericho (but note the unusual spelling with a *chi-*), as wife of Salma; hence, the mother of Boaz. Rabbinic literature of the first centuries generally considered her as the wife of Joshua. Johnson (1969: 162-65) makes a brave attempt at explaining Matthew's unique opinion.

(g) *yišay*. We are still unable to offer a plausible etymology for Jesse's name. It is far from clear whether one is to relate to the particle *yeš*, "being, existence," or to the roots **yšh* (cf. *tušiyyāh*, "wisdom") and *šy/wh*, "to resemble, be equal to." The search for useful cognates is hindered by the "weaknesses" in the roots and by the uncertainty regarding the *šin*'s "proto-Semitic" equivalent. At any rate, the form *ʾîšay*, recorded in 2 Chron. 2:13, is but an expansion of the name by means of a "prothetic" *ʾaleph* (see above). We should, therefore, not seek to explain the name as *ʾîš y(ahweh)*, "man of God." It could be said, however, that by offering this variant, the Chronicler may not have been unaware of its potential interpretation.

(h) *dāwid*. Non-Hebrew versions (e.g. LXX^A, Syriac, OL; cf. Matt. 1:6) add "the king," "the king of Israel," or "the king; and David bore Solomon." See Rudolph, 1962: 71; Campbell, 1975: 170; BH^3, ad loc.

4. AN INTERPRETIVE SYNOPSIS

The purpose of this Interpretive Synopsis is to integrate the Commentary's conclusions concerning the purpose of each episode within a retelling of the tale. In order to allow easy access to those portions of the Commentary where these findings are proposed and defended, the division into fourteen sections, which was featured there, will be observed.

I. The story, set during the Judge's period, opens on an Ephrathite family that had fled a drought-stricken Bethlehem in Judah. Elimelech, his wife Naomi, and their two sons, Mahlon and Chilion, had come to settle in neighboring Moab. After Elimelech's death, the two sons married Moabite girls, Orphah and Ruth. The young men, however, died within ten years, forcing Naomi to seek protection among her own kin. Since Judah was experiencing plenty, Naomi was resolved to return homeward to Bethlehem.

II. Naomi urges her two daughters-in-law to remain in Moab, where it would be easier for them to find happiness in new marriages. When Orphah and Ruth refuse to accept her initial argument, Naomi reminds them that she cannot be expected to produce the sons needed to protect foreigners in Judean territory. Orphah is convinced by this point, and proceeds to her own family.

III. Ruth, however, resists yet one more urging on the part of Naomi, countering with a moving insistence on attaching her own fate to the fortunes of Naomi. She ends her plea with a powerful oath, thus leaving Naomi with little choice but to accept her companionship.

IV. As Naomi and Ruth enter Bethlehem, Naomi bitterly bemoans her condition, finding God to be responsible for her sad fate. But the prospect of a harvest season--starkly contrasting the circumstances of a decade ago--ends the first chapter on a hopeful note.

V. Boaz, a wealthy landowner and a relative of Naomi, is introduced by the narrator. Ruth tells Naomi that she intends to glean in the fields, hoping to catch his attention. With Naomi's blessings, Ruth departs and finds Boaz's parcel of land without much waste of time. Seconds later, Boaz arrives at his field, greets his workers, and turns to the business at hand. For, standing next to the supervisor is a young lady who is not known to him. The supervisor informs him that she is the Moabite woman who had come back with Naomi. Ever since her arrival she had been waiting for permission not only to glean but also to gather grain among the sheaves.

VI. Boaz is extremely gentle with Ruth, urging her to continue gleaning in his fields behind his girls. He permits her a share of the waters drawn from the communal wells. He does not, however, respond to her initial request. With curtsies, perhaps too elaborate for the circumstances, Ruth presses further, referring to her own status as a *nokriyyāh*, an unprotected foreigner. Once more, Boaz eloquently praises Ruth's virtues and selflessness, but he does not grant her the permission she seeks. Ruth addresses him once more, this time clearly driving her point home by reminding Boaz that she is being treated as a *shipḥāh*, a "maidservant," although she does not belong to that category of protected women.

VII. Boaz now understands the implication of Ruth's request and speeches. He does not reply immediately but waits until noon to make up his mind. His actions then toward Ruth clarify the nature of his decision. He seats her among his workers, invites her to share in the communal meal, and publicly presents her with her first morsels. When he instructs his workers to allow her to glean wherever she wants, indeed even to litter her path with barley, Ruth's wishes were evidently fulfilled, for she becomes a *shipḥāh* in Boaz's clan.

VIII. Ruth returns home, having gathered an extraordinary amount of grain. When she triumphantly tells Naomi of her good fortune, Naomi blesses Boaz and declares him to be one of their redeemers. Chapter 2 ends with a statement that Ruth continued to live with her mother-in-law while remaining close to Boaz's maidservants.

IX. It is winnowing time, the harvest of barley and its threshing having been completed. Naomi unfolds a plan by which Ruth is to find marital security. She urges Ruth to beautify herself and to go down to the threshing-floor where, for reasons that are not elaborated, Boaz will be spending the night. Her presence was not to be noted by Boaz until after he had finished his meal. Naomi further instructs Ruth to join Boaz--her exact instructions are purposely left ambiguous--as he lies down to sleep. Naomi assures Ruth that the man will know how to deal with the situation.

X. Ruth proceeds as instructed. In the dead of the night; Boaz, shaken with fright, twists around to discover a woman close to his body. Ruth first identifies herself as his *ʾāmāh* (a "handmaiden well suited to become a man's concubine"); she then asks Boaz to take her within his household and to act as redeemer for her mother-in-law; Boaz gently chides Ruth for placing her own future ahead of that of her mother-in-law; but he is also quick to praise her for not seeking security elsewhere. He considers her twofold request in the order that Ruth proposed. Concerning her request for protection, he assures her that her credentials as a wife of a *gibbôr ḥayil* (Mahlon) will permit him to marry her, thus making her his primary wife *(ʾēšet ḥayil)* and not just a concubine. Concerning her hopes for him to become Naomi's redeemer, Boaz first makes it plain that another man stands ahead of him in that capacity, but that he would surely assume that responsibility if the other kin gives up his right of redemption. Boaz binds himself to these resolutions by pronouncing a mighty oath, and asks Ruth to remain at his side through the rest of the night.

Just before dawn, as darkness was about to give way to light, Boaz loads Ruth with a large amount of barley and sends her, unrecognized, to her mother-in-law.

XI. While Boaz is making his way to the city gate, Ruth arrives at Naomi's house. Chapter 3 takes leave of the two heroines in a scene in which Ruth recalls the *nocturnale* at the threshing-floor. Ruth declares the barley she received as Boaz's homage to Naomi. In this way, she forestalls any criticism of her unilateral decision to involve Boaz in Naomi's redemption. But Naomi is pleased and assures Ruth that Boaz will certainly resolve the matter of redemption by day's end.

XII. At the bustling city gate, where all economic and legal activities take place, Boaz assembles a forum to listen to a case he is about to present. Naomi's redeemer, "Mr. So-and-So," fortuitously appears at the scene, and is quickly hailed by Boaz. Boaz opens by declaring that Naomi has some land that she needs to have redeemed. (The matter, it may be, was not brought out previously because of the harvest and because Naomi needed a man to initiate the court proceedings.) Boaz now asks "Mr. So-

and-So" to declare, before this legal forum, whether or not he will act as a redeemer. Boaz further declares that he will be ready to assume that duty should "Mr. So-and-So" decide otherwise. "Mr. So-and-So" eagerly accepts to act in behalf of Naomi, for he knows the widow to have no hopes of issue to whom the land will have to be restored at a future date.

Boaz springs his trap. He publicly declares that on the day the land is purchased from Naomi by "Mr. So-and-So" he, Boaz, intends to acquire Ruth for the purpose of producing an heir to Mahlon. At this point, no marriage to Ruth is at stake, for Boaz was to serve merely as Mahlon's substitute in impregnating Ruth with an heir to Elimelech's property.

Faced with the prospect of paying good money to redeem Naomi's land only to return it whenever a male child is produced by Ruth, the redeemer gives up his right of redemption and attests to his decision by handing his sandal over to Boaz. Boaz thus succeeds in his attempt to become Naomi's redeemer because his decision to act in behalf of Mahlon was totally unexpected, not the least because no one knew of the protagonists' meeting the previous night.

Placing priorities in their proper sequence, Boaz first declares before a duly constituted legal assembly that he shall become Naomi's redeemer. He then announces his decision to acquire Ruth as a woman by whom to perpetuate the line of Mahlon, and does so on the authority of an injunction that prohibited the extinction of a deceased's line. It will be noted that as a result of Boaz's declaration, Ruth finds marital security while, through her husband, the redeemer of Elimelech's land, she maintains a relationship with her former mother-in-law.

The witnesses respond affirmatively to Boaz's declaration, then break into elaborate blessings, recalling the names of illustrious ancestors in order to wish the couple a future worthy of Boaz's forefathers.

XIII. Boaz marries Ruth. Their marriage is fruitful. A son is born to them who is to ensure Naomi's lifelong support. It is recalled, among the women of Bethlehem, that the child was born to Ruth, a woman who is capable of more love than that of seven sons. The story might have ended there in perfect harmony, for all the protagonists--Ruth, Naomi, Boaz, and the *gōʾēl*--and all the themes--marriage, children, redemption, and love--are gathered within three verses. Nevertheless, we are told that as Naomi places the child on her bosom, become his "foster-mother," female neighbors establish the child's reputation, declare him to be "a son born to Naomi," and call him Obed. It is stated that Obed was the grandfather of David.

XIV. A genealogy of David, ten generations from Perez to the future King of Israel, is given. It could be noted that Boaz is accorded the seventh slot in the chain.

5. INTERPRETATION

". . . the book of Ruth, an idle, bungling story, foolishly told, nobody knows by whom, about a strolling country-girl, creeping slyly to bed with her cousin Boaz. Pretty stuff indeed, to be called the Word of God! It is however, one of the best books in the Bible, for it is free from murder and rapine."

Thomas Paine, *The Age of Reason*

"Beispiels willen jedoch gedenken wir des Buches Ruth, welches bei seinem hohen Zweck, einem Könige von Israel anständige, interessante Voreltern zu verschaffen, zugleich als das lieblichste kleine Ganze betrachtet werden kann, das uns episch und idyllisch überliefert worden ist."

J. W. v. Goethe, *Noten und Abhandlungen zu besserem verständnis des west-östlichen Divans: Hebräer*

"Le livre de Ruth est resté comme la perle de cet état littéraire où il suffit de présenter la réalité telle qu'elle est, pour que tout soit inondé de doux et chauds rayons. C'est là que l'Homère des Grecs est égalé . . . Ruth et Booz sont frappés pour l'éternité à coté de Nausicaa et d'Alcinoüs."

Ernest Renan, *Histoire d'Israel*, I.

"Rabbi Ze'ira said: 'This scroll is not concerned with either purity or defilement, either prohibition or permission. Why, then, was it written? To teach you of a magnificent reward to those who practice and dispense *ḥesed*.'"

Ruth Rabba, 2:15

"I was therefore obliged to relate this history of Ruth, because I had a mind to demonstrate the power of God, who, without difficulty, can raise those that are of ordinary parentage to dignity and splendour, to which he advanced David, though he were born of such mean parents."

Flavius Josephus, *Antiquities of the Jews*, V, ix, 4

The Literary Genre of Ruth

The Need for a New Approach

Little unanimity in the choice of terminology exists in establishing the genre of *Ruth*. This is so, interestingly enough, not so much because scholars regard *Ruth* as belonging to an indefinable category, but rather because researchers generally agree only on the parameters of given categories. Witzenrath (1975: 362-65) offers a survey of opinion on the genre to which *Ruth* belongs. Met with most often are terms such as *saga*, *tale*, *romance*, *idyll*, *folktale*, *novella*. Recently Campbell (1975: 5-10) has proposed to label *Ruth* as a "short-story," which he considers to be a new form of literary creativity. Almost all who discuss the genre of *Ruth* point to a number of obvious features: its size (modest), its protagonist (human in proportions), its sphere of activity (human rather than divine), and its time frame (a distant, imprecise period).

Placing *Ruth* within a specific literary category is not merely an exercise in classification. As we shall try to show, a successful search for a form to which *Ruth* could be assigned will yield important results. Yet we cannot progress in this enterprise without raising a fundamental question concerning the basic nature of literature, be it poetry or prose, orally or scribally transmitted, to wit: Is any narrative to be considered as a series of episodes, randomly assembled by writers who are guided solely by their own genius? Or is it, on the contrary, produced by authors who, perhaps unconsciously, followed patterns with preestablished rules and regulations.

On the assumption that literature is never created in a vacuum, literary critics of the past century have begun to identify patterns in order to identify narrative elements common to a wide variety of literature. Such enterprises were essentially reductionistic even as they were integrative and holistic. We cannot hope, of course, to retell the story behind these approaches, but we would like to recommend Scholes (1974) as a convenient medium from which to pursue this topic.

Of the many models proposed by literary critics, we mention the following as having exercised some influence on Biblical studies:

1. *The atomistic school*, which isolated (plot-)motifs common to narratives of all nations and periods. Elaborate indexes of such motifs have been compiled by A. Aarne and, more recently, Stith Thompson. This approach has found ready favor with Biblical scholars ever since the days of Hermann Gunkel. Despite the refinements of later scholarship, this method still heavily relies on isolating segments of a narrative, in order to better focus on them as literary models inherited within an ethnic group and, not infrequently, shared among neighboring folk. One deficiency of such an approach, however, is that it tends to ignore both the *theme* of a given narrative and the *motivation* behind its (re)telling. On this topic, see Lüthi, 1967: 3-16.

2. *The "archetype" school*, which combined the insights of the so-called Cambridge School (e.g. J. Frazer, G. Murray, etc.) with those of Jungian psychology. It sought to identify ancient patterns, derived from the realms of myth and rituals, which were retained in man's collective subconscious. The elaborate scheme of symbolic language(s) developed by proponents of this approach (e.g. Northrop Frye, Otto Rank, Joseph Campbell, etc.) assumes that mankind shared a common development both in terms of social organizations and individual maturity.

3. *The "Simple Forms"* of A. Jolles is one approach which has, of yet, not fostered a school of Biblical scholarship. In his *Einfache Formen* (1930, translated in French as *Formes Simples:* 1972), Jolles propounds the thesis that literary creativity is reducible into nine "simple forms": legend, saga, myth, riddles, proverbs, case, memoir, tale, and joke/pun. Jolles believes that a narrator is able to string out these essentially irreducible units into a literary complex. Despite its somewhat absurd oversimplification of the literary process, Jolles's work is a mine of insights. We quote Scholes's (1974: 47) remarks on one of Jolles's simple forms, the "tale":

The tale is a progress toward justice through potentially tragic obstacles. It is ethical in its orientation, firmly insisting that the world it presents is different from ours--long ago and far away--and better than ours, for in it justice is done. Jolles [compares the "tale"] to a related form which is not simple but learned, sophisticated: the Boccaccian *novello*. Some of the same motifs appear in both forms, but always what was general, unspecific, and ideal in the tale becomes more particular, specific, and real in the *novello*.

One could easily perceive that *Ruth* falls within the range of the "tale-*novello*."

4. *The structuralist schools* supported their theories by resorting to analyses of the various modes for human communication in general, and the method of linguistics in particular. We differentiate between two approaches that are of consequence to Biblical scholarship:

a. The *paradigmatic* approach, generally advocated by Claude Lévi-Strauss, ignores the *sitz-im-leben* of a text, and the problem of its authorship in order to present synchronically the elements within the text. The text is often seen as containing information formulated at different levels of consciousness and preserved in varying levels of explicitness. A major purpose of such a scholarship is to break the "code" that, it is believed, lies deeply structured within that text. This approach, it could readily be noted, permits the researcher not only to disentangle and display the elements of a given document, but it also allows him a great amount of discretion in establishing the contours of these elements. For this reason, it is easy to understand why Biblical scholarship could suffer when left to eager and untrained hands. The works of Leach (e.g. 1969) have been severely criticized by another structuralist, Mary Douglas (cf. *sub* Emerton: 1976). But some interesting results have been obtained by Beauchamp (1972) and Lack (1973). Indeed, Rogerson (1974: 124-25) lightly applies these methods to *Ruth*.

b. The *syntagmatic* approach was first advocated by the Russian "Formalist" school. More recently, however, French scholars have been actively working to integrate it within a paradigmatic framework. Its most widely known proponent among Russian theoriticians is V. Propp, whose seminal *Morfológiya skázki* was published in 1928. His view did not become known to Western scholarship, however, until an English translation of this work was published in 1958. Since then a veritable avalanche of publications has appeared in which Propp's basic hypothesis was adapted (Dundes, 1964), refined (bibliography in Scholes, 1974: 206-11), or disputed (Nathhorst, 1969: 22-29). An excellent mise-au-point is available in Mélétinski (1972: 202-54). Since we shall adopt Propp's findings in order to analyze the structure of *Ruth*, an expanded description of Propp's method and approach will be necessary.

V. Propp's *Morphology of the Folktale*

Propp studied a great number of Russian fairy tales in order to isolate individual units that play a role in the development of the plot of a given narrative. Thus Propp's interest is focused neither on a tale's characters, nor on the manner in which they are described, but on those elements of the plot which propel the narrative from one action to another. Propp calls these elements "functions." He next observes the position of each "function" within the chain of events which constitutes a tale. Propp's morphology--a biological rather than a grammatical term--is given in a set of four points (1968: 21-23):

1. Functions of characters serve as stable, constant elements in a tale, independent of how and by whom they are fulfilled. They constitute the fundamental components of a tale.
2. The number of functions known to the fairy tale is limited.
3. The sequence of functions [in every tale] is always identical.
4. All fairy tales are of one type in respect to their structure.

Propp considers that, at a maximum, no more than thirty-one functions are possible in a tale. It is not uncommon, however, for a number of such functions not to be applicable to a given narrative. But it is essential to note that, even with the absence of a number of functions, *the sequence of those that remain in any given tale will follow the original pattern.*

Since "functions" are the smallest unit of a plot, i.e. of an action structure, characters that affect such actions are called dramatis personae by Propp. Thus, if a function concerns "villainy," the character that influences its appearance in a tale would be called the *villain;* if it concerns "departure on a search," or "marriage," the character will be known as the *hero.* This point will become clearer as we enter into an analysis of *Ruth.* Propp isolates seven such characters but is quick to warn that more than one "sphere [i.e. a cluster of functions] of action" could be devoted to one character. Alternatively, a single "sphere of influence" may be shared by more than one character at any one time. Furthermore, a tale need not possess all seven character roles.

Although I am aware of refinements proposed by other scholars (cf. Scholes, 1974: 104-6; Mélétinski, 1972), it is best to retain Propp's listing of dramatis personae. Nevertheless, it might be of interest to give below the categories of Greimas and Souriau.

	Propp	Greimas	Souriau
1.	villain	opponent	Mars--opposition
2.	donor (provider)	helper	moon--helper
3.	helper		
4a.	sought-for person	object	sun--desired object
b.	(Its father)	giver	balance--Arbiter, Rewarder
5.	dispatcher	receiver	Earth--ultimate beneficiary
6.	hero (seeker or victim)	subject	lion--will, one who desires
7.	false hero	(opponent)	(Mars--opposition)

Although Propp's work evolved from the study of fairy tales, it is clear that the listings of functions and the types of character roles are equally applicable to folk tales (Levin, 1967: 32-49). In order to assess *Ruth* in light of Propp's morphology, we first assign the character roles found in *Ruth*. Since, according to Propp's definition, the roles are determined by their *influence on the development of the plot*, we may safely dismiss for the present those personalities that contribute nothing toward that end. This does not mean, of course, that they do not play a role within Propp's scheme, but that their particular role would not be one that is crucial to the developing actions of the narrative. We shall have more to say on this within our analysis. From the outset, therefore, we shall assign no character role to the following: Mahlon, Chilion, Orpah, the women of Bethlehem, Boaz's overseer, and the women and neighbors associated with Naomi. Elimelech's role is crucial only to what Propp calls the "initial situation."

Once this "initial situation" is presented, however, we are left with only three persons whose activities will be primal to *Ruth:* Naomi, Ruth and Boaz; the roles of two others will be relatively "static." Naomi is obviously the *dispatcher*. It is the *dispatcher* who, by means of command or urging, sets the *hero* on a quest or on a search. Furthermore, it is to be noted that the *dispatcher* tends to be the ultimate beneficiary of the *hero's* activities.

According to Propp (1968: 74-77), the *hero* of a folktale tends to be present at the early moments of the tale. We have no hesitation to assign this role to Ruth. It is she whose movements are charted in almost the whole length of our narrative; it is she who sets out on journeys, quests, or searches, aiming to resolve the difficulties of the *dispatcher*, Naomi. Boaz's role is more complicated. As we shall detail below, he fulfills not one, but two roles. We leave it to our analysis to present those arguments. Finally, it will be made clear that the *sought-for person* is to be associated with the *gō'ēl* who will ultimately be called Obed, and that the *false hero* will be represented by "Mr. So-and-So."

In the following charts, we give Propp's functions on the left-hand side. This listing will follow the definitions and the sequences established by Propp. In order to avoid subjective reinterpretation of Propp's own material, we will quote, rather than merely paraphrase, his own descriptions of each function and the alternative variations that are associated with it. The page numbering refers to Propp's volume. The other two columns are self-explanatory.

Propp	*Ruth*	Comments
α. *Initial situation.* "The members of a family are enumerated, or the future hero . . . is simply introduced by mention of his name or indication of his status" (pp. 24-25).	1:1-2	
I. β. *Preparatory section.* "One of the members of a family absents himself from home." Alternative 2. *"An intensified form of absentation is represented by the death of parents* (β^2)" (p. 26).	1:3-5	We note two aspects of "absentation": *a.* that of Naomi, from Bethlehem *b.* the death of the male members of her family
[II-VIII (γ-Θ; A). Presents the functions of "villainy" which, as Propp points out, are incompatible with VIIIa: "On examining this phenomenon, we can observe that these tales proceed from a certain situation of insufficiency or lack, and it is this that leads to quests analogous to those in the case of villainy" (p. 34).]		
VIIIa. a. "One member of a family lacks something or desires to have something" (p. 35).	1:6	This verse presents a Naomi who is childless and wanting for food.
IX. B. "Misfortune or lack is made known; the hero is approached with a request or command; he is allowed to go or he is dispatched" (p. 36). ⁝ By means of this symbol, Propp refers to the phenomenon of "trebling," in which details, functions, or groups of functions are repeated	1:7-10; 11-14; 15	On three separate occasions, Naomi pleads with her daughters-in-law (with Orpah: twice; with Ruth: thrice) to desist from following her to Bethlehem. This is a crucial moment in the tale, for it will allow a *seeker-hero* to

Propp	*Ruth*	Comments
three times. It is noted that particular emphasis is placed on the third restatement		emerge.
X. C. "The seeker [*hero*] agrees to or decides upon counteraction" (p. 38).	1:16-17	With her decision to stay with Naomi, Ruth becomes the hero-subject of the tale.
XI. ↑. "The hero leaves home" (p. 39). "Departure here denotes something different from the temporary absence element, designated earlier by β. The departure of seeker-heroes and victim-heroes [cf. Propp, 1968: pp. 36-37] are also different. The departures of the former group have search as their goal, while those of the latter mark the beginning of a journey without searches, on which various adventures await the hero" (p. 39).	1:18-22 2:1-2	We believe that both accounts preserve this function: *a*. In leaving Moab to accompany Naomi, Ruth leaves "home," setting in motion a search to achieve "peace of mind": marriage. *b*. In setting out to glean in the field of Boaz, Ruth departs on her quest to fulfill a lack: food.
["Now a new character enters the tale: this personage might be termed the *donor*, or more precisely, the provider. Usually he is encountered accidentally--in the forest, along the roadway, etc. . . . It is from him that the hero . . . obtains some agent (usually magical) which permits the eventual liquidation of misfortune" (p. 39).]	[2:3c-4]	Although we have tried to show that Ruth had proceeded from home with the hope of meeting Boaz, we note that the *donor*, in this case Boaz, is chanced upon rather quickly. His appearance at the field on precisely that morning might also be considered fortuitous.
§ (cf. pp. 71-74) [Connective].	2:5-7	Connective. By these verses, Boaz is made aware of Ruth's past history. See below.

Propp	*Ruth*	Comments
XII. D^2. "The hero is tested, interrogated, attacked, etc., which prepares the way for his receiving either a magical agent or helper" (p. 39). Alternative 2. *"The donor greets and interrogates the hero* (D^2). This form may be considered as a weakened form of testing. . . . If the hero answers rudely, he receives nothing, but if he responds politely, he is rewarded with a steed, a sabre, and so on" (p. 40).	2:8-9	Boaz is what Propp terms a "friendly *donor* (p. 48). A *gibbôr ḥayil*, Boaz's overtures to Ruth, an impoverished foreigner, are delivered in a patriarchal tone.
XIII. E^2. "The hero reacts to the actions of the future donor" (p. 42). Alternative 2. *"The hero answers (or does not answer) a greeting* (E^2)" (p. 42).	2:10	Ruth responds to Boaz's statement and is quick to refer to her status of *nokriyyāh*.
($)^2$ [Reduplication].	2:11-13	These verses symmetrically reduplicate XII-XIII.
XIV. F. "The hero acquires the use of a magical agent" (p. 43).	2:14-16	We believe that the magical agent is her acceptance within Boaz's clan. But note the act of handing Ruth parched grains in the presence of other Bethlehemites. This indeed may have legal implications.
XV. G. "The hero is transferred, delivered, or led to the whereabouts of an object of search" (p. 50).	2:17a	("So Ruth gleaned in the field until dusk.")

Propp	*Ruth*	Comments
[XVI-XVIII; H-J. These functions are not relevant to *Ruth*. They deal with the struggles of the hero with villains.]		
XIX. K. "The initial misfortune or lack is liquidated" (p. 53). Alternatives 4-6 are equally applicable: 4: *"The object of a quest is obtained as the direct result of preceding actions* (K^4)." 5: *"The object of search is obtained instantly through the use of a magical agent* (K^5)." 6: *"The use of a magical agent overcomes poverty* (K^6)" (p. 54).	2:17bc	The mention of an *ʾephāh* as having resulted from Ruth's gleanings is meant to emphasize the thoroughly satisfying manner in which the lack was satisfied. As to Ruth's acceptance within Boaz's clan, note that Naomi recognizes this event as an important step towards resolving other difficulties (2:22).
XX. ↓. "The hero returns" (p. 55).	2:18aα	
[XXI-XXII; Pr., Rs. These functions, "The hero is pursued; the hero is rescued from pursuit," are not found in *Ruth*.]		
§ [Connective]	2:18aβ	These verses are "connective," since they do not contribute to the action of the plot.
[At this point, Propp notes that many tales introduce one, even several, instances of new "villainy": "This phenomenon attests to the fact that many tales are composed of two *series* of functions which may be labeled 'moves' *(xodý)*.		

Propp	*Ruth*	Comments
A new villainous act creates a new 'move,' and in this manner, sometimes a whole series of tales combine into a single tale" (p. 59).] As a result functions VIIIa-XV are repeated.		Although we repeat VIIIa-XV, their purpose here is different.
VIIIa¹ [bis]. "One member of a family either lacks something or desires to have something." (p. 35). Alternative 1. "Lack of a bride, of an individual" (p. 150).	3:1	The "lack" in this case is that of a husband for Ruth. [This "lack" should not be confused with that of Naomi, the *Dispatcher*, the fulfillment of which will allow the tale to come to an end.]
IX. B^2. [bis]. "Misfortune or lack is made known; the hero is approached with a request or command; he is allowed to go or he is dispatched" (p. 36). Alternative 2. *"The hero is dispatched directly"* (p. 37).	3:2-4	Naomi gives instruction to Ruth.
X. C. [bis]. "The seeker [*hero*] agrees to or decides upon counteraction" (p. 38).	3:5	Ruth accepts Naomi's urgings.
XI. ↑ [bis]. "The hero leaves home" (p. 39).	3:6-7	
XII. D^2. [bis]. "The hero is tested, interrogated, attacked, etc., which prepares the way for his receiving either a magical agent or helper" (p. 39).	3:8-9a	Boaz awakens and asks the identity of the visitor.

Propp	*Ruth*	Comments
Alternative 2. *"The donor . . . interrogates the hero"* (p. 40).		
XIII. E. [bis]. "The hero reacts to the actions of the future donor," (p. 42).	3:9b-d	Ruth replies with her own requests.
XIV. F^9. [bis]. "The hero acquires the use of a magical agent" (p. 43). Alternative 9. *"Various characters place themselves at the disposal of the hero* (F^9)*"* (p. 45).	3:10-13	In this case, Boaz's promise to marry Ruth and especially his willingness to act as Naomi's *gō'ēl*, could be regarded as "magical agents." With the former, he satisfies Ruth's immediate "lack" (i.e. a husband) and ultimately provides Naomi with a son. With the latter, he promises to satisfy Naomi's other "lack," i.e. sustenance. See also the extended comment below.

At this point we must interrupt our analysis for an extended note. It is crucial to realize that Boaz, who as *donor* of *Ruth* 2 gave Ruth permission to join his clan and thus allowed her (and Naomi) to resolve their "lack" of food, will once more become the *donor* of *Ruth* 3. His role, however, will differ in this context. For, as it is important to note, Ruth's search cannot end merely by the acquisition of another "magical agent" from Boaz. Indeed, a folktale does not usually end until the lack and misfortune are reversed *and* until the *sought-for person* (or *object* as Greimas calls it) is successfully obtained (cf. Propp, 1968: 67). This last character role is defined according to the requirement of the *dispatcher*, in our case Naomi. From the perspective of folktale morphology, therefore, Boaz's acceptance of Ruth's marriage entreaties is but the beginning of a new *move*, one which will be exhausted only when the *object* of the search is attained.

This new *move* will be initiated by Ruth, when she engages as a *help-er* in order to obtain a *gō'ēl*, perhaps more exactly, to provide a *child* for Naomi. In order to account for the metamorphosis of Boaz from *donor* into a *(hero's) helper*, it is necessary to quote Propp (1968: 50).

The employment of a magical agent follows its receipt by the hero; or, if the agent received is a living creature, its help is directly put to use in the command of the hero. *With this the hero outwardly loses all significance; he himself does nothing, while his helper accomplishes everything* [italics ours]. The morphological significance of the hero is nevertheless very great, since his intentions create the axis of the narrative. These intentions appear in the form of various commands which the hero gives to his helpers. At this point a more exact definition of the hero can be given than was done before. The hero of a fairy tale is that character who either directly suffers from the action of the villain in the compilation (the one who senses some kind of lack), *or who agrees to liquidate the misfortunes or lack of another person* [italics ours]. In the course of the action, the hero is the person who is supplied with a magical agent (a magical helper), and who makes use of it or is served by it.

In discussing the manner in which *moves* occur in a folktale, Propp alludes to one device that pertains to *Ruth*.

Sometimes a tale contains two *seekers*. . . . The heroes part in the middle of the first move. They usually part with omens at a road marker. This road marker serves as a *disuniting* element. (Parting at a road marker we shall designate by the sign <. Sometimes, however, the road markers amount to a simple accessory.) On parting, the heroes often give one another an object: a signaller (a spoon, a looking glass, a kerchief). We shall designate the transference of a signalling object with the sign Y. (Propp, 1968: 93-94).

We resume our analysis, reminding our readers that from this point on, Ruth practically disappears from the rest of the tale. Her role as a *hero-seeker* is now assumed by Boaz in his capacity as a *helper*.

Propp	*Ruth*	Comments
< Y. "Leave-taking at a road marker; transmission of a signaling device" (cf. p. 155).	3:14-15	We believe the "road marker" to be the threshing floor. The object transferred is probably the six measures of barley, placed in a *mitpaḥat*, a "shawl," *an object not previously mentioned in the text.* Note also that, despite 3:17, the barley was given solely to Ruth.
XV. G. [bis]. "The hero is transferred, delivered, or led to the whereabouts of an object of search" (p. 50).	3:15e	It is noteworthy that the requirement of the folktale's morphology confirms the integrity of the MT. There is no need to emend into *wattābōʾ hāʿîr*, "she [Ruth] reached the city."
§ [Connective. XV. G. (bis) completes Propp's listing of functions which are found in a new move. "From this point onward, the development of the narrative proceeds differently, and the tale gives new functions" (p. 59).]	[3:16-18]	[This passage is not properly a "function" but merely a "connective." No longer the *hero* of the tale, Ruth's act does not contribute to the action of the tale. It does, however, permit the narrator to focus once more on the *dispatcher*, Naomi.] Please note the curious question addressed to Ruth: "Who are you, my daughter?" (3:16). This may be a last vestige of function XXIII. o., on which, see below.
XXIII. o. "The hero, unrecognized,	4:1	This function, we believe,

Propp	*Ruth*	Comments
arrives home or in another country" (p. 60).		applies to Boaz, the new *hero*, inasmuch as he is now the *hero's helper*. The "unrecognized arrival" element in this function, we believe, is that he has become, secretely, Ruth's betrothed.
XXIV. L. "A false hero presents unfounded claims" (p. 60). "The false hero is sometimes not mentioned among the enumerated dramatis personae in the initial situation, and only later is it made known that he lives at court or in the house" (p. 84).	4:1e	The *false hero* is certainly "Mr. So-and-So." In no way should one confuse the *false hero* with the *villain*. As pointed out in our annotations, there is no reason to believe that "Mr. So-and-So" would have been an unhappy choice as a *gōʾēl* of Naomi.
XXV. M. "A difficult task is proposed to the hero." Propp calls this function "one of the tale's favorite elements" (p. 60). A wide typology of tasks is presented by Propp; see his analysis on p. 126 (no. 129-136). Among these are "riddle guessing" and "ordeals of choice."	4:2-4d	Boaz's disputation with "Mr. So-and-So" is certainly to be considered as a task to be fulfilled by the *hero('s helper)*. In this case, Boaz challenges "Mr. So-and So" with the ultimate aim of tricking him into giving up his prior rights of *geʾullāh*.
XXVI. *N. "The task is resolved." Preliminary solutions of this type shall be designated by the sign *N." (p. 62).	4:4e	Boaz's proposal is set before "Mr. So-and-So," who agrees to purchase the land. In the sense that he would have become Naomi's *gōʾēl*, "Mr. So-and-So" is a *false hero*.

Propp	*Ruth*	Comments
XXVII. Q. "The hero is recognized" (p. 62).	4:5	Boaz's decision to acquire Ruth *for the purpose of producing an heir to Mahlon* is made known. Thus, Boaz is recognized as the potential sirer of Naomi's future child.
XXVIII. Ex. "The false hero or villain is exposed" (p. 62).	4:6	"Mr. So-and-So" is shown to be incapable or unwilling to resolve Naomi's problem.
§ [Connective]	4:7-10	These verses containing Boaz's legal declaration are simply connectives, since they do not contribute to the action of the tale.
XXIX. T. "The hero is given a new appearance" (p. 62).	4:11-12	We propose that the elaborate blessings, couched in royal terminology (cf. annotations), give Boaz a new form. In other words, the transfiguration of Boaz, the *gibbôr ḥayil*, into the ancestor of a dynasty occurs at precisely this point.
[XXX. U. "The villain is punished" does not obtain here.]		
XXXI. W. "The hero is married and ascends the throne" (p. 63).	4:13-15 [4:16-17]	

In Propp's vocabulary, XXXI. W. resolves the following points:

1. Lack no. 1 (poverty, insecurity) is resolved: *sought-for person* (i.e. the *gō'ēl*) is obtained for the *dispatcher* (Naomi).

2. Lack no. 2 (childlessness) is resolved: *sought-for person* (i.e. a child) is pledged and eventually assigned to Naomi (4:16-17).

3. *Hero* is wedded: Ruth (or Boaz) is wedded.

We are still left to account for 4:16-22. Propp (1968: 64) recognizes several actions within a tale which cannot be located in his scheme of functions: "Such cases are rare. They are either forms which cannot be understood without comparative material, or they are forms transferred from tales of other classes (anecdotes, legends, etc). We define these unclear elements and designate them with the sign X." Below, we shall attempt to show that 4:16-17 recalls a Near Eastern motif. We shall also try to account for it as an element grafted to the end of a folktale, permitting the tale to end with Naomi having had all her "lacks" (issue as well as sustenance) totally fulfilled. Nevertheless, we should not dismiss the possibility that 4:16-22 might also represent either another *move* in the preceding folktale or the "initial situation" of another folktale. It is noted that with function XXXI. W. a folktale often sows the seed of another folktale. For in marrying, the *hero* forms a new family that often includes children remarkable in achievements. Thus 4:16-22 may have inaugurated the tale of a certain Obed, whose deeds were widely disseminated. In the form in which they are preserved, these verses conform well to one of Propp's (cf. 1968: 85, 120, no. 1-15) "initial situations" which is concerned with the birth of a *hero*. If this were indeed the case, we might venture to explain why *Ruth*, unique in Biblical literature, actually *ends* rather than *begins* with a genealogy: From a Proppian perspective, *the genealogy of 4:18-22 actually begins the tale of Obed, rather than ends that of Boaz!*

Propp (1968: 92) defines a tale as "any development proceeding from villainy (A) or lack (*a*), through intermediary functions to marriage (W*), or to other functions employed as a dénouement." He offers extensive analysis of a number of tales (pp. 128-48) by using symbols given in pages 149-55. For *Ruth*, we offer the following analytic scheme:

(1:1-2:22)	=	Move I	$\alpha\beta^{2}aB\vdots C\uparrow\S(D^{2}E^{2})^{2}$ F $GK^{4-6}\downarrow\S$
(3:1-13)	=	Move II	$a^{1}B^{2}C\uparrow D^{2}E\ F^{9}$[. . . . §o (?)]
(3:14-15ab)	=	(Transfer of character-role)	> Y
(3:15c-4:15)	=	Move III	G§oL M*N Q Ex § T W
(4:16-22)	=	Move IV (?), 'initial situation' of a new folktale (?)	...X=(...

Implications

We hope to have shown that, because it fits comfortably within Propp's model of sequential functions, the form of *Ruth* is that of a folktale. It should be noted, however, that we are careful to avoid calling *Ruth* a folktale. For in order to conform to the folklorists' definition generally agreed upon, we should reserve that label only to narratives that have lived, at least part of their life, in an orally transmitted form (Dundes, 1965: 1-3). We simply have no resources that would allow us to suppose that *Ruth* circulated orally. Recourse to formulaicity, poetics, and to other modes of stock expressions, as has been postulated recently by Campbell (1975: 18-23), can in no way establish that a given text was transmitted by word of mouth (cf. the criticism of Sasson, 1976: 416). We can add, parenthetically, that despite the recent efforts of Biblical scholars to pursue this approach (cf. Culley, 1976; with literature on 20-30), it cannot be said that orally transmitted texts have been successfully identified within the OT. Thus, it might well be that our *Ruth* was created *upon a folktale model* by scribally oriented intelligentsia, and it might well be that in its earliest moments *Ruth* was available solely among the narrowest of elite circles. For, as it is conceded by Propp (1968: 99-112), models for structuring new folktales need not have been available only to peasants living in rural areas; nor need the folktales themselves be set in writing *only* after a long period of oral transmission.

As a conclusion to this search for a genre in which to place *Ruth*, we should confess that Propp's sequence of functions, which, for methodological reasons, we have adopted without any adaptations or amelioration, will eventually have to be refined, perhaps even restructured, in order to better suit tales from both the Ancient Near East and the Bible. Such an approach, of course, lies outside the scope of our study. We might, nevertheless, point to some material that would profit from a syntagmatic analysis:

Egypt: The Doomed Prince; Horus and Seth; The Shipwrecked Sailor; Sinuhe (in part). *The Two Brothers*, interestingly enough, does not seem to yield easily to this approach.

Mesopotamia: Etana; Gilgamesh (if a complete version could be found that is datable to a single period); various segments of the *Lugalbanda* saga. Limet (1972) discusses the Sumerian epic. Alster (1975: 90-97) attempts a shallow Proppian analysis of a tale (?)

Anatolia: Keššši.

Ugarit: Aqhat; Keret.

Bible: Since the Old Testament is one of the richest repositories of tales to come out of the Near East, it would be presumptuous to assume that all those recorded belonged to the folktale genre. Moreover, even those that might ultimately be placed within that category do not necessarily have to obey Propp's articulation of what a folktale represents or, more importantly, how it is structured. However, we do want to note that a great number of OT tales do represent the "quest of the *hero*" as a dominant motif, and we do want to indicate that "villainy," "violation of an interdiction," and the "drive to resolve a lack" are factors that guide the development of many tales.

In the preceding pages, a rather elaborate attempt has been made to offer a more precise analysis of the literary genre to which *Ruth* belonged. Once this is accomplished, however, it becomes of utmost importance to explore the literary quality of a tale which we have labeled as "folkloristic." We turn to this task in the following pages, but take the occasion to conclude this section with a quotation from Northrop Frye's well-known *Anatomy of Criticism* (New York, 1957): "The purpose of criticism by genres is not so much to classify as to clarify . . . traditions and affinities, thereby bringing out a large number of literary relationships that would not be noticed as long as there were no context established for them" (pp. 247-48).

Postscript

When my manuscript was completed and submitted to Johns Hopkins Press Professor Richard Crenshaw of Vanderbilt University, was kind enough to send me a work that was written in December 1973, under the direction of A.-J. Greimas, as a "Mémoire de diplome" at the École Pratique des Hautes Études. As far as I have been able to gather, the typescript of Corina

Galland, "Ruth: Approche structural d'un récit biblique," has never been formally published and hence will remain inaccessible as long as it retains its present form. For this reason, it would be unfair to the author, who might wish to revise her study before any formal publication takes place, and to the readers of this volume, who might wish to consult Ms. Galland's work on their own, were I to engage in discussions of this work. At this point, let me just state that Ms. Galland relies on a commonly available understanding of the tale's progress but proceeds to interpret the tale in a much more hypothetical fashion than the one I present.

The Narrative Style of Ruth

Folkloristic Considerations

Once it is agreed that *Ruth* is modeled after a folktale pattern, it becomes possible to draw conclusions that are applicable to any literature of the same genre. As an artistic creation, even when it depends on factual occurrences, the folktale is completely satisfying, for it nurtures no expectation that is ultimately left unfulfilled. From its opening scene, when either "villainy" or "lack" are posed as a challenge to the *hero*, the tale progresses on a course that is precharted in the audience's consciousness. No complications are introduced which are left unresolved; no character is given a role that remains ambiguous. *Heroes* find their mates, *villains* meet their fates, *dispatchers* find their ultimate reward, and *donors* fulfill their obligations. It is not surprising, therefore, that as a tale that hews closer to folktale patterns than most Biblical narratives, *Ruth* has constantly found favor in the eyes of a variegated audience. It is not merely that Ruth is brave and loyal, for other OT heroines are equally valorous; it is not just that Boaz is kinder than other Biblical ancestors; it is not even that Naomi is more deserving of God's ultimate favor than other matriarchs; it is simply that these protagonists fully carry out assignments that were perfected generations before *Ruth*. Moreover, because a folktale leaves nothing that is unresolved, it becomes a self-contained entity. It is unnecessary, therefore, for a folktale to be burdened either by a historical background or by a sequel meant to link it with datable narratives. Thus, unlike other Biblical narratives that gain by, indeed depend on, a historical setting, *Ruth* could easily be lifted out of the period of the Judges and still be appreciated as a superb work of art.

If it is stated above that the major protagonists in *Ruth* assume predetermined roles, it does not follow that individual touches, characteristic of the Hebrew storyteller, are absent from its contents. Despite his claims that "functions" and "character roles" are, to some degree, coded within the folktale model, Propp recognizes the many opportunities for an artist freely to improvise when no material crucial to the *action* of the tale is at stake. Thus, in order for a *donor* to hand over his "magical gift" (in our case Boaz granting Ruth permission to glean by welcoming her into his clan; Boaz accepting Ruth's proposal of marriage), the *donor* must learn of the events that preceded (Propp, 1968: 72). This would explain passages such as 2:6-7 and 3:11, the first of which allows the overseer to recount Ruth's arrival at Boaz's field, the second of which permits Boaz to explain why Ruth is worthy of being a wife, not merely a concubine. Additionally, the insertion of new characters in a folktale requires that information be communicated which would place them au courant (Propp, 1968: 70). Thus, when "Mr. So-and-So" enters the scene, Boaz devotes 4:3 to inform him of the situation. Naomi's poignant statement to the Bethlehemite women (1:19-22) could be considered as a particularly brilliant effort on the part of the narrator. Not only do these verses inform the women, i.e. the whole of Bethlehem, of Naomi's cruel plight, but they also serve to emphasize those "lacks" (food, childlessness) that will soon set the *hero* (Ruth) on her quests. Finally, we might consider as "connectives" the two episodes in which Ruth informs Naomi of her successful forays into Boaz's sympathy (2:18b-22; 3:16-18). These instances, moreover, give the author the opportunity to glance backwards one last time, before proceeding into the tale's future complications. It is not clear to me whether 4:14-15, containing the "women's" congratulations on the birth of the *gōʾēl*, are meant to forecast Obed as the ultimate *sought-for person*.

Propp speaks of at least two other opportunities in which the narrator is free to improvise: in his description of characters and of their surroundings (p. 88), and in his elaborations on his protagonist's motivations (pp. 75-78). As we shall soon observe, the style of Hebrew literature is such that the opportunity to take advantage of the first category is scarce, for the Hebrew writer is rarely moved to detail the physical attributes of his leading personalities. Except for rare instances, e.g. 1 Sam. 16:12, at most he might just note that such-and-such was "attractive" or "beautiful of form." For this reason, except for what we may deduce from the content of *Ruth*, we know nothing about our protagonist's ages, looks, or even apparel. Whether Ruth is to be thought of as either a portly matron or as a striking young women; whether Boaz is to be considered as a virile man or as an aged patriarch--are issues left to the imagination of the individual listener. This ambiguity is not without its consequence, however. To turn to the threshing-floor scene for an example, it matters enormously what is recreated in one's mind; for this scene could be validly interpreted as witnessing either the entanglements of physical passion or, the other extreme, as testifying to the dignity of self-sacrifice. Such ambiguity contributes heavily toward wide-ranging interpretations of *Ruth*.

Literary Considerations

The justly famous first chapter of Auerbach's *Mimesis*, which delineates the contrasting conceptual presuppositions of Homer and the Old Testament, can provide us with a fine threshold from which to explore some aspects of Biblical narrative style.

Auerbach notes the economical nature of Hebrew prose. Digressions are few, allowing little opportunity for either audience or reader to relax attention. For this reason, argues Auerbach, Biblical narrative tends to be consistently suspenseful. This observation is certainly applicable to *Ruth*. Although our tale could easily be divided into four major scenes, "From Bethlehem and Back," "In Boaz's Field," "At the Threshing-Floor," and "At the City Gate," it is hardly possible for an audience to slacken its alertness at the end of each. This is so first because the narrative, folkloristic in its model, is propelled relentlessly until its ultimate end, and secondly because of the tendency of the Hebrew storyteller to sow the seed of the next scene at the end of each tableau. These moments, interestingly enough, tend to overlap to a very large degree with the non-"function" elements that Propp would call "connectives." We recall that these "connectives" are segments in which no *action* of import to the development of the plot occurs; hence, their content is left to the discretion of the author. This marriage of an element of a folktale's syntax as described by Propp, to an artistic device of Biblical prose as highlighted by Auerbach, accounts for the remarkable ability of *Ruth* to grip its audience from start to finish.

To Auerbach, the passage of time is hardly ever acknowledged in Hebrew prose. Whenever it is, however, it serves not so much to define a historical sequence as to highlight a particular characteristic associated with the protagonists of the tale. This observation could be sustained by the examples chosen from *Ruth.*

(1) The sojourn of Naomi's sons in Moab for ten years *after* the death of her husband adequately explains the isolation that Naomi will feel upon her return to Bethlehem.
(2) That Ruth is said to remain with Naomi until the end of the harvest (2:23), i.e. after her acceptance into Boaz's clan, might underscore the profoundness of her devotion to Naomi's welfare.
(3) Boaz's ascent to the city gate on the morrow of the threshing-floor's nocturnale with Ruth might have been explicitly stated in order to stress Boaz's qualities of steadfastness and resolve; he was, indeed, a fulfiller of promises.

Auerbach's most arresting contribution to Biblical literary criticism is his exposition of a style that he calls "fraught with background." By this singularly intuitive phrase, Auerbach is concerned with two independent issues: the "presentness" (p. 10) of human characters, and the hovering presence of God throughout the OT narratives. Auerbach believes that individuals in the OT are endowed with a deeper sense of time, fate, and consciousness than are those of the Homeric cycles. This is so precisely because the Hebrew narratives strip away needless details--contextual, descriptive, or attributive--in order to focus on the fragment of conversations attributed to individuals. Such an excluding and exclusive style of narrative actually forces an audience to extract its own clues from the sum total of utterances, in order to understand the motivation of individual characters. By this process, not only is an audience forced to contribute heavily toward the recreation of a protagonist's character, but even the characters themselves become imbued with an awareness of their own history, become "fraught with their own biographical past" (p. 14). With the tale, the audience, and the characters thus engaged in a common enterprise, it becomes possible for Auerbach not only to speak of the "psychological dimension" of Hebrew narrative, but to base such an observation on the tendency of Biblical characters to project a "will" that influences events in which their physical presence is not even recorded.

Until a relatively modern period, narrative literary style hardly ever permitted a scene to be encumbered by more than two speaking voices--more correctly, two voiced positions--at any one time. This technique, it might be noted, is not necessarily confined to "epic" literature, as it has been maintained ever since A. Olrik's formulations of 1909, but is common to a wide variety of premodern prose. Auerbach's opinion, as sketched in the preceding paragraph, allows one to note that the dialogue of Biblical texts is not merely a medium in which two characters shape the course of future action, but one in which a third character, albeit absent from a particular scene, exerts a determining influence on that development. We turn to the threshing-floor scene for one example. When Naomi urges Ruth to prepare herself for a meeting with Boaz, her intent was solely to find *menuḥāh*, "security," for her daughter-in-law. But as Ruth responds to Boaz's inquiry, she is obviously no longer motivated by her own plight but by that of her mother-in-law as well. The latter, it must be emphasized, is never mentioned either by Ruth or by Boaz; but it is quite clear, nevertheless, that their discussion would be meaningless were we to ignore Naomi's presence, guiding and directing the recorded dialogue.

If we have, so far, agreed with Auerbach's characterizations of the Hebrew narrative art, we part with him as he observes that whatever is recorded in the OT was conceived by the Hebrew as an element in a sequence of historical events which began at Creation and that this sequence of historical events is not haphazardly arrived at, but is one that fits a divine plan. In consequence, concludes Auerbach, each and every Biblical narrative that finds place in the canon is interpretable as a vehicle testifying to God's activities within history. This thesis, it could be protested, is moored in a comparison between OT texts such as the *ʿaqedat yiṣḥāq* (Gen. 22) and Homeric episodes such as those involving Odysseus's cicatrix. Methodologically speaking, far-reaching conclusions based on material so different in genre and in purpose cannot be accepted.

Yet, Auerbach's opinion on the role of God as perceived by Hebrew writers seems eminently reasonable when it is compared to that of some Biblical scholars who consider Israel's theological interpretation of history as radically different from "mythologically oriented" conceptions of its neighbors. Although such a reading of the Near Eastern evidence has been challenged recently (cf. Roberts, 1976: 1-13), it is still quite common to meet with studies that marshall evidence for the Hebrew's perceptions of a God who looms over history. It is not surprising, therefore, that some scholars have turned to *Ruth* in order to document God's interference in the affairs of humans. No doubt the frequent mention of divine names, Yahweh (eighteen times), Shadday (twice), and of the noun *ʾelōhîm* (four times) may have encouraged some to evaluate the theological presupposition of *Ruth's* narrator, and others to interpret the book as a theological tractate. But these references, it can easily be noted, are mostly set in formulaic contexts, e.g., blessings (Yahweh: 1:8, 9; 2:12 [twice], 20; 3:10; 4:11, 12, 14; *ʾelōhîm:* 2:12) and oaths (Yahweh: 1:17; 3:13). Of the remaining attestations, two are to be considered simply as nouns (*ʾelohîm:* 1:15, 16 [twice]), while five examples are linked to Naomi's explanation of her fate or of her name (Yahweh: 1:13, 21 [twice]; Shadday: 1:20, 21). Thus, of the twenty-four references to a divine figure, only two could be considered as contributing to the development of the tale. These two instances, it is interesting to note, occur at the tale's extremities: The first occurs in 1:6, in which God's grace to the Bethlehemites sets Naomi (and the story) in motion; the second is recorded in 4:13, in which Ruth's pregnancy is permitted by God.

Because of the paucity of occasions in which God's activities are of clear consequence to the narrative (as distinguished from their rhetorical impact), a number of episodes have been singled out as testifying to the activities of a "hidden God." In the annotations we criticized at some length the application of such a theory to the elucidation of 2:3 (see also Sasson, 1976: 417). We refer the reader to the same chapter, *sub* 2:4; 4:1; and to 3:18, for our understanding of other contexts that have been cited as indicative of God's "providential control" (cf. Campbell, 1975: 28-29). At this point we would like to buttress our criticism of such an approach by returning, once more, to our analysis of *Ruth* as a folktale in model. From that discussion, it should be clear that those episodes most often cited as activated by a "hidden" God fit neatly into Propp's scheme of sequential function. Interestingly enough, the famous *wayyiqer miqrehā*, "It so happened that. . . ," of 2:3 conforms remarkably to the requirement of the folktale in which a *donor* (in our case Boaz) is to be met *accidently* by the *hero-seeker* (Ruth). The appearance of "Mr. So-and-So" in 4:1, regarded by Campbell (1975: 29, 141) as a "hint of God's working behind the scene," actually fulfills the requirements of function XXIV. L. Finally, we should like it to be recalled that no *character role* needed be assigned to God, another testimony to the relatively inconsequential nature of his involvement in the narrative.

Linguistic Considerations

In recent scholarship some attention has been paid to the Hebrew style of *Ruth*, as well as to its structure. Witzenrath's (1975) massive study of *Ruth* is strongly influenced by the works of W. Richter. Since it cannot be adequately summarized in any manner that would do the approach justice, the reader is referred to its own pages for an exhaustive (and exhausting) treatment of structure and language. Our treatment of language will be confined to a few remarks concerned with the poetry and the vocabulary of *Ruth*. On the matter of structure, however, it could be noted that the efforts of Bertman (1965: 165-68) and Porten (1976: 15-16) are most successful only when a symmetrical pattern is observed for the "core" of *Ruth* (i.e. chapters 2 and 3). This is hardly surprising since the morphology of *Ruth* indicates that 3:1-13 contains functions (VIIIa-XIV.F[9]) that reduplicate those of 2:1-22 (XI. ↑-XIV. F). Bertman and Porten are much less convincing when trying to establish a design--Porten calls it "climactic"--for the outer chapters.

Poetry

Since Hebrew metrics--whether it is defined by symmetry of the syllables, or simply by counting consonants--is in no way a confident subject of scholarship, it would be quite unprofitable to extend the discussion beyond this short paragraph. Suffice it to say, that on the basis of its rhythm, its occasional twofold repetition of material within a single line *(parallelismus membrorum)*, and its frequent recourse to vocabulary and idiom with "poetical" flavor, scholars have often spoken of the poetic nature of *Ruth* (bibliography in Witzenrath, 1975: 107[n.20]). Opinions vary, however, consisting of one that presumes an orally transmitted poem set to prose by postexilic writers (e.g. Myers, 1955, legitimately criticized by Watters, 1976: 122-26), those that consider *Ruth* to be lyrical though not poetic (e.g. Lamparter, Gunkel, and Schulz), one that speaks of its ceremonial-literary style (Campbell, 1975: 12-13), and one that recognizes a style common to *Sprüche* (Segert, 1957: 190-200). Our opinion is that, with the exceptions of 1:16-17 (Ruth's soliloquy), 1:20-21 (Naomi's lament), and 4:11-12 (blessings of the elders), one cannot speak of the "poetry" of *Ruth* without embracing an elastic definition of the term.

Vocabulary and Idiom

Despite *Ruth's* brevity, the eighty-five verses of the story are lexicographically quite rich. Myers (1955: 27-32) has made observations which are worth quoting: "The vocabulary of *Ruth* appears to conform with that of the best prose of the Old Testament. . . . Spelling, morphology, syntax, vocabulary, idiomatic phrases and expressions, all appear to place *Ruth* in the same broad category with JE in the Pentateuch, Joshua, Judges Samuel, and Kings." A few words and idioms are attested nowhere else in the Old Testament. The list drawn up by Joüon (1953: 11) includes the verb *ʿāgan* (1:13), the nouns *ṣbt/ṣbṭ* (2:14, 16), the idioms *yāṣāʾ yad* (1: 13), YHWH *ʿimmakem* (2:4), *šaʿar ʿamm-* (3:11), *nāpal dābār* (3:18), and *šālap naʿal* (4:7-8).

Paronomasia

In the annotations will be found a number of observations that pertain to the vocabulary of *Ruth* and the peculiarity of some of its idioms. Here, we shall broach the subject of *paronomasia,* that is, "word play," taking our cue from the pattern established in the *Supplement* of the IDB, 968-70.

1. Of "visual" paronomasia, we might have one example of *pseudo-gematria.* In Boaz's oath, *ḥay* YHWH (3:13), the value of *ḥeth* (8) and *yôd* (10) is 18, precisely the number of times in which the name Yahweh occurs in *Ruth.*

We *hesistantly* mention at this point a number of occasions in which crucial names are repeated seven times, three times, or multiples thereof:

a. Personal names: Naomi, twenty-one times (3 x 7); Ruth, twelve times (7 + 5); Boaz, twenty times (but note his conspicuous absence from 4:16-18); Obed, Jesse, Chilion, and Perez are each mentioned three times.

b. Place names: Bethlehem and Moab are each mentioned seven times (so too *môʾabiyyāh,* "the Moabite woman"). Yehûdāh is mentioned three times.

2. *Oral word play* occurs more frequently. The following types are attested:

a. Parasonancy, a category which spans both oral and visual word plays, includes consonants of verbal and nominal roots, given in differing order. In 2:20, Boaz's name *(bʿz)* reminds one of his kindness *(ʿzb* [*ḥasdô*]) toward the living and the dead. It is not certain whether [YHWH] *ʿānāh* [*bî*] of 1:21, in which the root **ʿnh* is recalled, should be assessed as a sophisticated parasonantic pun on the name Naomi *(nʿm)* (see the annotations).

b. Etymological word play is found in the two occasions in which the root *mrr* is used to explain the name *Maraʾ* (1:14, 21). Whether or not the other personal names in *Ruth*, such as Mahlon, Chilion, Ruth, Orpah, or even Boaz, are to be interpreted symbolically is not properly a paronomastic problem. We refer to the remarks made in the annotations.

c. Assonantic word play, in which words are strung together for oral effect, is found in 1:6, *lātēt lāhem lāḥem*. The names Mahlon and Chilion, as a pair, may afford us with yet another example of assonance.

d. Farrago, a definition of which is given in the annotations, is likely in the words *pelōnî ʾalmōnî*, "Mr. So-and-So" (4:1).

3. It is in the third category of paronomasia, loosely termed *extended word play*, that *Ruth* abounds. Speaking of the *Leitwortstil* in *Ruth*, Dommershausen (1967: 394-407) isolates words crucial to each of the scroll's four chapters. Among these are *šûb*, "return," in the first; *lāqaṭ*, "glean," in the second; *gōren*, "threshing-floor," *šākab*, "to lie down," and *gāʾal*, "to redeem," in the third; *gāʾal* and *qānāh*, "to buy," in the last chapter. It has to be admitted, however, that Dommershausen's method seems to be based on a frequency-of-occurrence count of words found in *Ruth*. Furthermore, it is our opinion that one cannot consider words such as *lāqaṭ*, *šākab*, *qānāh*, and *gāʾal* as *leitworte*, since their meaning remains *constant* in all contexts in which they occur.

It may be otherwise, however, with words such as *yeled* (1:5, 4:16), *šûb* (especially in 1:21, 4:15), *dābaq* (1:14; 2:8, 21, 23), *pāgaʿ* (1:16; 2:22), *mānôaḥ/menûḥāh* (1:9; 3:1), *kānāp* (2:12; 3:18), *ʿāzab* (1:16; 2:11, 16, 20), and derivatives of the root **nkr* (2:10, 19, 3:14). These words differ slightly in their implication and application in each one of their contexts. The author of *Ruth* may have used substitutes available in Hebrew, yet he chose to recall them precisely because he hoped they would evoke a response appreciative of his paronomastic prowess.

Rauber (1970: 27-37) and Trible (1976: 251-79), respectively, concentrate on "carefully developed and ordered series of patterns" and on "deep structures of relationship" that are found within *Ruth*. The interest of both is quickened by the scroll's reliance on sets of opposite manifestations. Rauber highlights the following themes: famine/plenty, bareness/

fruitfulness, old age/youth, isolation/community, and reward/punishment. Trible refers to many of the preceeding pairs, but adds: male/female, death/life, and tradition/innovation. These themes, it is argued, need not be juxtaposed. On the contrary, it is shown that much time, space, and activity may elapse or occur before the contrast is finally fulfilled. Rauber considers many of these contrasting themes as "bracketing devices" forcing the audience to focus on material deemed important to the narrator. Campbell (1975: 13-14) prefers the term *inclusio* for the same literary phenomenon. Additionally, he speaks of "chiasm, a technique which in the order of a pair of words is reversed on the second occurrence." He gives as examples the following: husband/boys (1:3/5); go/return (1:8/12); Shadday/Yahweh (1:20/21); lament/kiss (1:9/14); elders/people (4:9/11); and Mahlon/Chilion (1:2,5/4:9).

In the article mentioned above, Rauber refers to two narrative principles that may be peculiar to *Ruth*. One consists of *centering* the verses deemed critical to the development of each major episode (i.e. chapter). These verses are given as follows: verses 11-13 for chapter 1; verse 10 for chapter 2; verse 9 for chapter 3; verse 11 for chapter 4. Rauber's other principle is a rather elaborate scheme in which each episode is seen as provided with its own symmetrical pattern. The reader is invited to read Rauber's study for further information on the matter.

The Contexts of Ruth

Under this heading, we shall discuss the following topics concerned with *Ruth:* its social context, its cultural context, and its "political" context. At the outset, we should record our indebtedness to Bascom's (1965) fine essay, "Four Functions of Folklore," whose contents helped to shape our discussion.

The Social Context of Ruth

In discussing *Ruth* above as a folktale in its model, we were cautious to presume for it neither an origin in a rural milieu, nor an orally transmitted life *before* it was set in writing. Because of the story's highly polished narrative style and its rich Hebrew vocabulary and idiom it is our opinion that a version approximating our own was set in writing within highly educated circles, ones that, moreover, responded well to patterns coded within a folktale. Nevertheless, there is some evidence internal to the text that makes it unlikely that *Ruth* was destined to please only the archivists. (Contrast the purpose and ultimate destination of annals.) On the contrary, the following evidence encourages us to suppose that, at one point after it achieved a final version, *Ruth* was either read or recited before an audience.

1. *Ruth* is replete with examples of oral word-play. Additionally, the many *leitworte* embedded within it makes sense best when understood as literary devices intended to brace a spoken narrative by constantly stimulating an audience's memory. Unlike *Ruth*, other narratives in the Bible (with the exception of *Genesis*, a text abounding in folkloristic tales) are rather poorly stocked in this type of paronomasia. On the other hand, prophetic and to some extent poetic materials that were meant to be presented orally, similarly abound with oral paronomasia (see Casanowicz, 1894: 93-94).

2. *Ruth* breaks naturally into four major episodes. At the end of the first three, the narrative devotes a verse or two to summarize previous activities and to preview forthcoming events. These occurrences might best be explained as evidence of a technique by which *an audience*'s attention is retained while its interest in forthcoming events is stimulated. By means of the same device, the *storyteller* is provided not only with an occasion in which to find relief from the tension of a preceding scene, but with a springboard furthering him toward other dramatic heights.

3a. On a number of occasions, the language of *Ruth* suggests interaction between a speaker and his audience. The famous aside of 4:7 would gain in its impact if one presumes a vocal delivery that differed in tone from those of flanking statements. This supposition might actually be confirmed by the fact that 4:8 ("So, as the redeemer was telling Boaz: 'Purchase it for yourself,' he removed his sandal.") does not merely restate the redeemer's declaration of surrender given in 4:6, but also recalls the explanatory words of the aside in 4:7. Thus, 4:8 seems to preserve an elocutionary technique aimed at renewing words that were presented in totally differing fashion.

3b. In our annotations, we defended the *ketîb* of *yigʾal* in 4:4 ("But should *he decide* not to redeem it. . . .") as a clear sign for the narrator to mime the actions of Boaz when the latter turned briefly from haranging "Mr. So-and-So" to the elders.

3c. Two other instances may be proposed as likely to have benefited from a dramatic delivery of the narrative. Naomi's last words of instruction to Ruth as she departs to the threshing-floor ("He will tell you what next to do," 3:4) might have provided a speaker with an occasion to coyly mouth words too delicate--or too coarse--to detail. Finally, without positing a melodramatic contribution, either in tone of voice or in gesture, it would be difficult to capture the full impact of a potentially comic moment in which a violent movement and a midnight shriek abruptly interrupted a tranquil scene.

4. Of all the Old Testament books, *Ruth* has the highest ratio of dialogue to narrative text. Joüon (1953: 12 [n.1]), who counts exactly fifty-five verses out of eighty-five (i.e. almost two-thirds of the scroll), remarks that the tale could easily have been told in a few verses: "But what in part constitutes the charm of the story, is that the author, rather than stating what were the characters [of the tale], or what they did, makes them speak." Although one does not have to presume that the preponderance of dialogue necessarily suggests a dramatic presentation for *Ruth*, such frequent exchanges are certainly rich in dramatic potential. The same could be said of texts, such as Genesis 23, which brilliantly mix drama and comedy in a predominantly dialogue form.

If we have some evidence, internal to the text of *Ruth*, which indicates that *Ruth* was either recited or read, we cannot easily recreate the makeup of its audience. On the analogy, albeit tenuous, to the courtly presentations of Medieval Romances, such as *Sir Gawain and the Green Knight*, we might expect this audience to be composed of the elite--be it scribal, priestly, or political. Closer to Israel are examples of (folk)-tales such as the Egyptian *Sinuhe*, *The Shipwrecked Sailor*, *The Doomed Prince*, and so on, which "come from the sphere of the educated scribe and from the ambience of the court" (Lichtheim, 1975: 210). Egyptologists in general have no problem assuming the existence of such an audience, basing their assumptions on the richness of the vocabulary found in these texts (Lefèbvre, 1949: vii). That many of these tales were written on Papyrus scrolls found in the tombs of the upper classes, must certainly ease the burden of proving this conjecture.

The Cultural Context of Ruth

In this section, we shall investigate the relationship between a folktale and the culture that created it. Therein, however, lies an intriguing paradox. For, as has been noted by a folklorist (Bascom, 1965: 298): "While [folklore] plays a vital role in transmitting and maintaining the institutions of a culture, and in forcing the individual to conform to them, at the same time, it provides socially approved outlets for the repressions which these same institutions impose upon him." Thus, while we shall briefly summarize our conclusions concerning social institutions of the Hebrews as preserved in *Ruth*, our task shall also be to isolate those activities that may be deemed socially unacceptable to the normal course of Hebraic culture.

Legal and Social Practices Preserved in Ruth

Most serious studies of Hebrew social institutions as preserved in *Ruth* discuss the interconnection of marriage, redemption, and the leviracy. Since our extensive treatment of this subject in the annotations was based largely on philological grounds, we shall take this opportunity to redefine the issues in the light of a folkloristic interpretation.

It seems to us that those who have sought to gather from *Ruth* information on the above-listed topics have imposed upon it demands that could never be satisfied. *Ruth*, after all, is not a juridical document. Despite the setting at a city gate, where legal procedures did indeed take place, it cannot be maintained that the scene in Chapter 4 was faithfully recalling activities known to us from Near Eastern documentation of actual cases. The narrator of a folktale, after all, is not expected to realistically recreate past events, but to present his tale in as dramatic a form as possible. Thus, except for "Mr. So-and-So"'s acceptance to purchase the field (4:4) and for his abrupt volte-face (4:6, 9)--occasions which were crucial to the development of the plot--Boaz is the only one to speak. It would, therefore, seem that the storyteller lavished his attention on Boaz's harangue because it contained the language with which Boaz was to best his opponent. The latter--Propp would call him a *false hero*--enters the stage already burdened by the destiny of a loser. Hence, his first statement, "I accept [to buy the land]," is important to the narrator only as a contrast to his subsequent declaration. At that point, the trap will be set (4:5) which will cause "Mr. So-and-So" to falter quickly before Boaz's superior maneuvering. It might be also noted that, during the whole procedure, the magistrates and the witnesses are silent. In an actual case, one might have expected the elders to clarify the situation by questioning Boaz as well as his opponent. Certainly Naomi, perhaps even Ruth, might have been called into the inquiry. But the elders and the witnesses were players with specific roles: (1) to witness the disconfiture of "Mr. So-and-So" as a result of Boaz's cleverness, and (2) to provide David's ancestor with a blessing worthy of a dynast.

Viewed from this perspective, our conclusions concerning *Ruth* as a witness to Hebraic institutions are as follows:

1. *Levirate marriage*. *Ruth* tells us *nothing* about the workings of this institution. Indeed, the tale does not think of its heroine as under obligation to enter the household of any Bethlehemite.

2. *Marriage*. Ruth was free to select a potential husband from any of Bethlehem's finest young men (cf. 3:10). That she married a man of superior wealth, albeit on equal status with her departed husband, is one of the tale's main concerns.

3. *Redemption (geʾullāh)*. Redemption is at issue only as it concerns the land left to Naomi after her husband's death. Naomi alone, old and without hopes of a male issue, was in need of protection from a *gōʾēl*. However she came to possess the land that was to be purchased by the *gōʾēl* is not of immediate concern to us here (but note our remarks in the annotations). The point that we should stress is that Naomi would have been well served by any prospective *gōʾēl*; had "Mr. So-and-So" not been supplanted, there is no reason to presume that his relationship with Elimelech's widow would have been anything but correct and supportive. However, had Naomi been redeemed by "Mr. So-and-So" we would lose a major theme in *Ruth:* how Ruth succeeded in marrying Boaz yet managed to retain kinship ties with her former mother-in-law by convincing her future husband to become Naomi's *gōʾēl*.

Ruth, therefore, teaches us very little on the legal position of widows, impoverished landowners, and their *gōʾēl*. It actually proceeds with the assumption that the institution of redemption was familiar to readers and audiences and expects them to delight in Boaz's ability to circumvent its requirements.

4. *Ruth* does grant us some glimpses of actual life in its Hebrew setting. One cannot but be impressed by the harvest scene of chapter 2. Thus, there is no reason for us to doubt that harvesters were visited daily by a landowner; that they worked under the direction of an overseer; that they stopped their activities at noon to partake of a common meal; that their fare included roasted grain, bread, and sour mash. Such

glimpses, however, were probably familiar to an ancient audience. Finally, *Ruth* does present us with a vocabulary of terms that define the social position of women in Hebrew society: *nokriyyāh*, "foreign woman", *šiphāh*, "maidservant," *ʾāmāh*, "handmaiden," *ʾēšet ḥayil*, "wife of a notable." This topic has been discussed in the annotations. For convenience's sake, see Sasson, 1976: 417-19.

The Trickster Motif in Ruth

While folklore in general (including folktale in particular) aims to inform as it amuses an audience, it frequently provides society with a vehicle to protest the rigidity of some of its own institutions. Frequently, this is done by having a hero, an ancestor, or a venerated personality circumvent these requirements.

As we turn to *Ruth*, the threshing-floor scene immediately strikes us as recording a most unusual event. A young lady, well groomed and bedecked, approaches a man rendered well disposed by the consumption of a good meal. No matter what the actual outcome of this tête-à-tête between Ruth and Boaz, such a nuptial method cannot have been current or encouraged in Israel. The fact that Ruth was following Naomi's advice only compounds the boldness of the act, since it is attributed to two persons rather than one.

Yet, given the genre in which *Ruth* was set, members of an ancient audience--as well as those of a modern one--might conceivably have applauded the daring act, indeed the *chutzpah*, required to bring to the protagonists happiness. After all, the previous chapter had prepared the audience to expect demonstrations of pluck on the part of Ruth ever since the latter succeeded in extracting privileges from Boaz despite her status of a foreigner. These two episodes, however, may not have constituted the breach of a community's code of behavior as much as the scene depicted in chapter 4. For not only did Ruth's deceptive activities lead to a worthy marriage, but none of the individuals involved in the tale was hurt in the process. This is not the case in the behavior of Boaz toward "Mr. So-and-So." In setting his trap to force the latter to give up his claim over Elimelech's land, Boaz struck at the roots of an institution set up precisely to minimize potential difficulties within a clan by regulating the order in which land, otherwise inalienable, was obtained. Again, in the case in which Ruth was involved, positive responses were still Boaz's to make, even possibly to break in the future. Boaz's act of trickery, on the other hand, was successful only because the choices offered "Mr. So-and-So" were limited. Moreover, the latter's responses were binding as soon as he declared them before magistrates and witnesses. No afterthoughts were permitted, no periods of reflections granted.

Trickery, successfully negotiated and ultimately glorified, is a theme well known in folkloristic accounts. This is not to be confused, however, with another motif, in which punishment is meted out to the trickster (e.g. David and Uriah). In his excellent contribution to P. Radin's book on *The Trickster*, Kerényi (1972:185) has this to say: "[The trickster's] function in an archaic society, or rather the function of his mythology, of the tales told about him, is to add disorder to order and so make a whole, to render possible within the fixed bounds of what is permissible, an experience of what is not permitted."

The trickster as a heroic character is indeed well represented in Biblical writings. Concentrating on Genesis, we note that each one of the three patriarchs was linked to a particular manifestation of trickery: one that not only recorded the manner in which the trickster achieved his goal, but invariably reported him tricked by others. In the case of Abraham, his involvement with Pharaoh and Abimelech of Gerar permitted him to benefit enormously (Gen. 12:10-20; 20). However, when his wife, who provided him with the means with which to succeed, died, the urgency with which he had to bury her allowed Ephron the Hittite to inflate the price of the burial site (Gen. 23). Isaac, who used Rebeccah to advantage in his involvement with the same King of Gerar (*sic*) (Gen. 26:1-11), was himself tricked by her into giving Jacob his choicest blessing, *berākāh* (Gen. 27). Jacob, the trickster *par excellence*, managed to obtain the rights of the *eldest son*, *bekôrāh*, from his brother Esau (Gen. 25:29-34). In his dealings with Laban, however, he was given the *eldest daughter*, Leah, rather than his choice, Rachel (Gen. 29:22-26). In turn, note how Rachel tricked her own father and acquired the idols for her husband (Gen. 31:19, 34-35). Other examples with reference to Jacob are readily available: e.g. the manner in which he increased his flock at the expense of his father-in-law (Gen. 30:25-43), and the especially cruel way in which his own sons deceived him by selling his favored son Joseph. The incident at Schechem (Gen. 34), in which a whole population was tricked into helplessness, is to be attributed to Jacob's sons rather than to Jacob. Their own well-known tribulations are recorded in the Joseph narrative. Of interest to us, however, is the manner in which the future line of David was established by a trick played upon Judah (Gen. 38). In this connection, it is interesting to note that some medieval commentators regarded Tamar's success as a retribution for Judah's role in the sale of Joseph: "The Almighty said to him [Judah]: 'You deceived your father with a goat; [by bloodying Joseph's coat], by your life! so does Tamar deceive you'" (EBI, V, 72). So too, in the book of *Ruth*, the line of David was founded, that night on the threshing-floor, when Ruth gambled daringly, and won.

A "Political" Context for Ruth?

Under this heading, we should like to propound the theory that in its present form, *Ruth* may have been intended to bolster David's claim to the throne. As such, it would have functioned as one of many other texts preserved in the Bible which shared this goal. We would, however, like to be most careful not to speak of our hypothesis as defining *the* purpose of *Ruth*. For to claim a *single purpose* for our scroll, as indeed for any literary text from the Ancient Near East, would be quite presumptuous, even totally insensitive.

We should first recall two conclusions concerning the genealogy of 4:18-22 derived from two differing exegetical methods. Our analysis of *Ruth* according to Propp's formalistic categories has suggested that verses 4:16-18 may have opened a new folktale, that of Obed, which was grafted to the body a folktale concerned with our protagonists, Ruth, Naomi and Boaz. In "The Ancestry of David" section of chapter 3 above, however, we tried to demonstrate that a number of passages--e.g. the blessings of the elders (4:11-13), the references to Boaz as a major protagonist in the tale, and the birth of Obed (verses 16-17)--link the body of the tale to the genealogy of 18-22. Thus, whether by reference to internal evidence or to folkloristic considerations, it would be difficult to maintain that the genealogy of David was an appendix originally independent of *Ruth*. Once it is accepted that the mention of David in 4:22 need not be an addition to *Ruth*, a few moments in the narrative gain in significance.

The Evidence of Vestigial Motifs

In the annotations, we pointed out that the etiological fragment we labeled the "Son" episode (4:16-17) considers Obed as the son of Naomi. We contrasted it to the *"Gō'ēl"* segment (4:13-15), which regarded the child as born to Ruth and Boaz. The "Son" episode could be broken into the following elements:

(1) Naomi places the child on her bosom (16a,b).

(2) She becomes his *'ōmenet* (16c).

(3) The *šekēnôt* established the child's reputation (17a).

(4) The child is attributed to Naomi (17b).

(5) The child is named (17c).

(6) The genealogical progeny of Obed is given (17d).

Relevant to our present inquiry is the long note (pp. 168-70) in which we listed a number of criteria allowing us to regard the "Son" episode as a less satisfying conclusion to *Ruth* than the *"Gō'ēl"* segment. In detailing the vocabulary of verse 15-16, we concluded that *wattešitēhû beḥēyqāh*, literally: "she set him on her bosom," may have deliberately promoted an ambiguous context in which Naomi's precise act could not be ascertained (element 1). In studying the usage of *'ōmenet*, we wondered whether a translation such as "wet-nurse" might yet be relevant, despite the fact that Naomi was an elderly widow (element 2). In evaluating the role of the *šekēnôt*, we puzzled over the exceptional circumstances that leave the naming of an important ancestor to "neighboring women," rather than to his immediate parents (elements 3-5). Finally, we accepted a suggestion that the fragmentary genealogy of 17c is original to the Obed episode and hence reinforces the connection between David and Naomi (element 6).

A. Our clues for developing this section come from the activities of the *šekēnôt* as detailed in elements 3-5. Unless one is predisposed to emend the text as it now stands, there is no question that these "neighboring women" established the reputation of the child, proclaimed his birth to Naomi, and, possibly at once with Naomi, gave him a name. As pointed out in our annotations, we simply have no Biblical material to parallel, either singly or as a complex of vestigial elements, the *šekēnôt*'s deeds. We are, therefore, permitted to search the literature of Israel's neighbors for evidence that might clarify the meaning and purpose of this series of activities.

Our information on the ceremony of establishing the fate/reputation of a newly born person comes mostly from literary texts. In Hittite documents, midwives (MÍ.ŠÀ.ZU) are almost always quoted as reciting incantations on behalf of the child (Beckman, 1978: 8, 10). But this is not what seems to be at stake in the *Ruth.* Whereas the Hittite midwife merely beseeches the deities for mercy and kindness toward the child, the Biblical episode suggests that the *šekēnôt* were defining the child's future (but note Beckman's opinion, 1978: 6). Hittite texts do know of female attendants, known by the sumerogram MÍ.UMMEDA (= Akkadian *tāritum?*), whose function seems limited to the (ceremonial?) duty of handing over the newborn to his father (Hoffner, 1968: 199-200). Yet a third group of females (consisting of the low-echelon deities known as Gulšeš and Kunuštalluš) is recorded present at such occasions. Although the few literary texts that preserve a birth and naming ceremony do not elaborate on the deities' specific function, other attestations make it clear that they imposed fates upon the newborn (Goetze, 1938: 55-63).

We encounter such fate deities in Egyptian literature. At times, the goddess Meshkenet is singled out within a group of birth goddesses to utter the fate of the child (*Westcar Pap.*, 10, 1-11,1; cf. Lichtheim, 1975: 220-21). At other occasions, the (seven) Hathor deities pronounce the fate of the boy "with one voice" (*Doomed Prince, 4, 3; Two Brothers, 9, 8-9*; cf., Lichtheim, 1976: 200, 207). At Ugarit of the Late Bronze Age, we encounter a group of seven (perhaps four) goddesses who assist birth, the *kotharôt.* It is a matter of discussion whether they also imposed fate as they assisted the newborn's birth (van Selms, 1954: 83-92; Margolis, 1972: 53-61 [questionable conclusions]).

The evidence from Mesopotamia is also derived from literary texts. Although the midwife (MÍ.ŠÀ.ZU = Akkad. *š/tabsūtu*) does appear in secular documentations (Von Soden, *AHw*, 1120), it is the Old Babylonian legend of *Atraḫasis* which links the midwife to fate-establishing duties. The portion that we quote dovetails a myth neatly into an incantation, probably addressed to the goddess Mami--also known as Bēlet-ilī and Nintu. We could presume that this incantation was mouthed by a midwife as she extracted a child from his mother's womb (Lambert, 1969: 63, lines 8-20):

The wise and learned/ Twice seven birth-goddesses had assembled, Seven produced males,/ [Seven] produced females./ The birth-goddess, creatures of destiny (*bānāt šimtu*)--/ They completed them in pairs,/ They completed them in pairs in her presence,/ Since Mami conceived the regulations for the human race.// In the house of the pregnant woman in confinement/ Let the brick be in place for seven days,/ That Bēlet-ilī, the Wise Mami, may be honoured./ Let the midwife rejoice in the house of the woman in confinement,/ And when the pregnant woman gives birth/ Let the mother of the babe sever herself.

A Sumerian hymn is even more precise on the role of birth deities: "I [a goddess] assist Nintu in lifting the child [or: extracting the child]. I know how to cut the umbilical cord and how to say good things when determining the fate (of the child)." See the text that is quoted and translated by Jacobsen (1970: 322) and, further, the incantation studied by van Dijk (1973: 504-5).

Further information that makes it clear that such attention was quite special, is available to us from an Old Babylonian (Nippur?) Sumerian composition. Although dubbed *Enki and the World Order* by its editors, this document is meant to explain the great powers of the goddess Inanna (Benito, 1969: 77ff.). In lines 409-10 of this text, the goddess Ninmug is said: ". . . to help (the mother) to give birth to the king, to tie (around his head) the MÙŠ [cf. Sjöberg and Bergmann, 1969: 46-47], to help (the mother) to give birth to the [EN]-lord; (and) to place the crown on his head is indeed in her hand" (cf. Benito, 1969: 134; Sjöberg and Bergmann, 1969: 142-43; Jacobsen, 1973: 294). In other contexts, different avatars of the great birth goddess (Mami, Ninhursanga Ninmah, Aruru, Ninmenna, and so on) are said to fulfill similar functions (Jacobsen, 1973; 1976a: 107-10). The point for us to remember, as we move to another motif that seems vestigial to the last lines of *Ruth*, is that *Ancient Near Eastern literature assigns female deities the task of establishing the fate, hence the future, of a newborn male; and that such a newborn, if human, is invariably a future king.*

B. We turn next to the activities of Naomi as recorded in 4:16. She is said to take the child, place (verb: *šyt*) him on/at her "breast" (noun: *ḥēq*), and become his *ʾōmenet.* In our annotations, we have shown that these activities cannot be easily interpreted as adoptive or legitimating. To better understand them, we further explore Near Eastern materials.

Cuneiform literature knows of many texts in which kings claim divine parentage. Most recently, Sjöberg (1973: 87-112) assembled a wide spectrum of evidence on this topic from the third and the first half of the second millennium B.C. We allude to the following items in order to bring this collection through the second millennium: Edzard, 1957: 58 (Isin-Larsa period); Machinist, 1976: 465-68 (Middle Assyrian period); Brinkman, 1968: 135-44 (Post Kassite, Isin Dynasty). Kraus (1971: 241-50) offers a balanced evaluation of this evidence.

We are interested in pursuing the instances in which a royal child is said to have been placed on the lap of a deity, and is suckled by her. An excellent example of these motifs could be gathered from Sollberger, 1971: 48. There, Eanatum, King of Lagash at around 2450 B.C., commemorates his own birth as follows: "[The god] Ningirsu planted the seed, Eanatum, in Ninhursanga. Ninhursanga bore him, and was pleased over him. Inanna took him by the arm and named him (by his throne name). . . . She placed him on the sacred knees of Ninhursanga. Ninhursanga suckled him from her sacred breast. [Alternative translations: Sjöberg and Bergmann, 1969: 143: "Inanna sat him on the right knee of Ninhursanga. Ninhursanga reached out her right breast to him"; Jacobsen, 1976: 251: ". . . and Ninhursanga fed him at her right breast."]

This motif appears on a number of other occasions. We limit our examples here to the following: Entemena of Lagash (at around 2400) was also suckled by Ninhursanga (Sollberger, 1971: 68); Lugalzaggesi of Umma (at around 2350) is suckled by the same deity (Sollberger, 1971: 94). The statement of the goddess Ninsunna on behalf of Shulgi or Ur, ca. 2090, deserves its own quotation: "Shulgi, you sacred seed to which I gave birth,/ you holy semen of the [divinized king] Lugalbanda;/ on my holy lap I raised you,/ at my holy breast I determined the destiny for you,/ you are the best that fell to my portion" (Jacobsen, 1976a: 158-59).

From subsequent periods, this motif may have been kept alive, for we find it invoked by the Assyrian king Esarhaddon (680-669 B.C.): "I am the great midwife who delivered you," says Ishtar, "I am your good wet-nurse" *(sabsuttaka* [*sic*] *rabītu anāku mušēniqtaka dēqtu anāku)*. On another occasion, this goddess says: "I have raised you on my chest [literally: between my wings]." (Cf., conveniently, the literature collected in Ishida, 1977: 91). Similarly, Esarhaddon's successor Assurbanipal, ca. 668-627 B.C., is said to have suckled the breasts of Ishtar. (Cf. the passage quoted in CAD, *E*, 165 [*sub enēqu*]. Note also the passages mentioned in CAD, *Z*, 149 [*sub zīzu* B]; *H*, 36, 187 [*sub ḫalāpu* B; *ḫilpu*]. For other examples of the child placed on divine lap, see Von Soden, AHw, 1095 [*sub sūnu(m)*, 1c].)

Such motifs are also known from plastic and epigraphic sources found in Egypt and Ugarit. We refrain from elaborating further since the appropriate materials have been conveniently assembled by Montet (1964: 58-63) (Egypt) and van Selms (1954: 91-93) (Ugarit). Our discussion shall, henceforth, center on (1) the relevance of the above-mentioned motifs to *Ruth* 4:16-17, and (2) their implications.

1. We have gathered a series of symbolic acts and utterances from Near Eastern documents which allude to divine interference in the course of human affairs, with the aim of singling out a future king as a particular favorite of the gods. In some cases, those thus blessed were likely to call themselves "divine" (e.g. Pharaoh, Shulgi, Tukulti-Ninurta, Adad-apla-iddina). At other times, they were addressed as mortals. Rather strikingly, we find these acts--visitation for the purpose of establishing fate, placement on a woman's lap for the purpose of breast feeding, conferring a name on the child--gathered within the compass of two verses in *Ruth*. Furthermore, one of these occurrences, the involvement of *šekēnôt* in a naming/fate-establishing ceremony, is unique in Biblical texts. We should like to propose, therefore, that the activities preserved in 4:16-17 be considered as vestigial motifs, with meanings decipherable according to Near Eastern symbolism. To be sure, the *šekēnôt* and Naomi are nowhere addressed as divinities in *Ruth*. Nevertheless, there are two hints with regard to the latter which might betray her Near Eastern antecedence: *a*. the doublet *Naomi/Maraʾ*, both of which are reminiscent of epithets applied to divine or mythical females in Ugaritic texts (see above); *b*. the lack of interest in resolving the apparent dual maternity of Obed (Ruth; Naomi), which may reflect a situation in which Near Eastern kings sometimes attributed their own birth to divine as well as to human parents (Gordon, 1977: 101).

2. The motifs we have gathered above, together with texts that explicitly speak of a king as a descendent of divine parentage, have elicited a large literature whose purpose is to evaluate ancient man's concept of a "divine" or, more precisely perhaps, "divinized" kingship. Whereas few scholars are willing to deny that this concept did obtain among Israel's neighbors, few are categorical in attributing it to Hebrew thinkers. We do not intend to tackle the subject fully here; nor to parade Biblical texts often promoted in the debate (e.g. 2 Sam. 7; Ps. 2; 45:7; 89; 110; and so on). After referring the reader to the latest substantial discussion on this matter, that of Mettinger (1976: 254-65), we should merely

like to bring into sharper focus some of the issues involved, and to advance conclusions useful to our discussion of *Ruth* 4:16-17.

Whether one considers the motifs discussed above, either singly or in combination, as indicative of a theology that erased the boundary between kings and gods (i.e. in terms of a mythological category), or as attesting to a concept that considered the king as the god's adoptee (i.e. in terms of an adoptive category), it is nevertheless observable that ancient Near Eastern man rarely confused the respective realms in which they existed. The actual status of the king was not altered, whether these texts spoke of him as being "divinized" or as adopted by the gods. He remained human in all his activities, and was treated as such by his contemporaries. We would say this even about Pharaoh, despite the large literature that attributes to the ancient Egyptian an inability to differentiate between kings and gods (cf. even with its modifications, Barta's volume, 1977). In this respect, we find Posener's study most convincing. In his *De la divinité du Pharaon* he points out that the Egyptians were able to distinguish between the monarchy, which was permanent, and Pharaoh, who was not (1960: 20-21). For this reason, when Pharaoh represented the majesty and eternity of his office, religious and hymnic texts accorded him divine functions. As an individual, however, a mortal who succeeded another and will inevitably be succeeded by yet another, Pharaoh was treated, mostly by the "popular" literature, with irreverent affection, even with sarcastic disapproval. Thus, concludes Posener (p. 103), ". . . les Égyptiens tout en portant leur souverain aux nues, étaient capables de le voir tel qu'il était, avec lucidité et détachement."

Posener's approach, recently echoed by Lorton (1976) and Wildung (1977), allows us to question alleged "Egyptian" influences whenever the subject of divine kingship in Israel is broached (lastly by Mettinger, 1976: 262-66). Indeed, as we turn to the Asiatic Near East, we discover sporadic evidence that its concept of kingship was but a step removed from that of Egypt. Thus, in Mesopotamia, the king's divinity was not personal, but one that was conferred upon his office, an office which was *patterned after a heavenly prototype*. Thus, whereas in Egypt kingship was divine because it was eternal and because it simply continued in a pattern established on earth by the gods, in Mesopotamia kingship acquired a touch of divinity because it was a gift brought down from above. The difference between the two positions is important. Consequently, the king in Sumer and Akkad might sporadically inspire his scribes to utter statements such as those alluded to above; but, nevertheless, his divinity was not conceived as seriously approaching that of the gods; it was at least twice removed from the world of the immortal:

Gods → Celestial monarchy / / Human monarchy → kings.

If our proposal appears too arithmetical to suit ancient Near Eastern sensibilities, let it be recalled that the Mesopotamians were quite precise in ranking their deities. This is most obviously reflected in their plastic arts, where the higher gods were depicted wearing multiple pairs of horns while those of lower rank had to be satisfied with as few as one pair. Interesting in this respect is the observation that kings who preceded their names with the divine determinative, Sumerian: DINGIR (= Akkadian *ilum*), were accorded the minimum exhibited by deities: one set of horns (Boehmer, in RIA, III, 431-34; on the figure of a horned Moses, see Bailey, IDB, *Supplement*, 419-20; on that of a horned Pharaoh, see Wildung, 1977: 3-8).

We should not extend our discussion on a topic that merits its own monograph. What we do wish to stress, however, is that Near Eastern man was reasonable and rational. He would no more consider a king sitting on the throne, obviously governed by human needs, as a full-fledged deity than would his modern counterpart. Thus, when his kings called themselves divine, he understood their statements in the same spirit as other utterances that seriously challenged reason: statements such as those of Eanatum of Lagash (ca. 2450 B.C.) in which he declared himself over *eight feet tall* (Sollberger, 1971: 48; Jacobsen, 1976: 252 [cf. n. 19]) and of Pharaoh, who repeatedly decimated battalions of "wretched Asiatics" singlehandedly. These attestations of monarchs suckling divine breasts, receiving their fates from visiting goddesses, and so forth, should be regarded as no more than metaphors that translate the legitimacy conferred by the gods on the office of kingship into a statement of their personal solicitude for the welfare of a single individual.

A Hypothesis

We conclude this speculative segment by gathering the various points made above in order to posit a "political" context for *Ruth*. Activities are assigned to the *šekēnôt* and to Naomi in 4:16-17. These activities are strongly reminiscent of divine acts and utterances used in the Ancient Near East as metaphores for the legitimacy of royal figures. Attributed to human personalities, these symbolic gestures formed a conclusion that was grafted to *Ruth*, ending the tale in a less satisfying manner than it would have otherwise. Nevertheless, because those involved either played exceptional roles (the *šekēnôt*) or bore evocative names (*noʿomî/ marāʾ*). the audience may have been alerted to the unfolding of an unusual scene. Those in a position to decipher the code would have understood *Ruth* as a vehicle to support David's claim to the throne of Saul, by showing that, decades previously, David's grandfather had already enjoyed divine protection.

Of course, *Ruth* did not rely solely on esoteric symbolism to advance David's legitimacy. For those not inclined to decode complicated iconographies, divine affirmation of David's legitimacy had already been expressed through the elegant blessings addressed to Obed's father (4:11-12):

ʿaśēh-ḥayil beʾeprātāh
ûqerāʾ-šēm bebēyt lāḥem.

We never find in folktales an accurate memory of a particular stage in culture; cultural styles and historical cycles are telescoped in them. All that remains is the structure of examplary behavior--that is, one that can be virtually experienced in a great number of cultural cycles and at many historical moments.

Mircea Eliade, *Myth and Reality*, 196-97

The Dating of Ruth

Few Old Testament books have elicited as wide a range of opinion on the matter of dating as has the book of *Ruth*. Some scholars have proposed an origin for the scroll in either the "early," "middle," or "late" Monarchic period. Others have defended positions which would place *Ruth* in either 'preexilic,' 'exilic,' or 'postexilic' times. A few have insisted on dates as late as the fourth century B.C. With "oral" composition as a subject of research, some scholars have theorized a number of stages from the tale, including an early "oral" phase generally conceived as "premonarchical," and a "late" written phase generally regarded as postexilic. We refer the reader to the following bibliographies on the question: Witzenrath, 1975: 359 (n. 27) (the most complete); Rowley, 1965: 172 (n. 1); Glanzman, 1959: 201-7; Campbell, 1975: 23-28; Vesco, 1967: 235-47.

Survey of Previous Literature

We shall entertain the various positions under the following headings: Onomastics; Anthropology; History; Genealogy; Linguistics; Context; Theology; Folklore. We do not undertake this survey merely to enshrine positions that may no longer be acceptable to the consensus of scholars, but to gather a wide selection of opinions on *Ruth*'s function and purpose, an assessment of which often forms the basis for dating for the scroll.

Onomastic Considerations

Glanzman (1959) points out that, apart from the names Obed and Boaz, the appellatives found in *Ruth* are unique to the Old Testament. Searching for equivalents within West Semitic onomastica, Glanzman locates many in the Ugaritic documents. Because he thinks it unlikely that a Hebrew writer in the first millennium B.C. would have invented names common to a population that lived in the latter half of the second millennium B.C., Glanzman reconstructs three stages in which *Ruth* achieved its final form: first, a Canaanite poetic tale borrowed by the Israelites sometime after they arrived in Canaan; second, a prose version adapted to an Israelite setting of the eighth and ninth centuries; third, a final draft of the tale in the postexilic period.

Uneven criticism of Glanzman's position has been voiced by Loretz (1960: 397[n.23]: "Glanzman . . . does not take into account [the] tenacity of tradition among the Semites") and by Vesco (1967: 245-46: "Whatever may be thought of the original meaning for the personal names, the author of [*Ruth*] obviously gives them a symbolic meaning. . . . Any attempt to find in the book of *Ruth* various literary stages, does not take into account the unity of the book"). Our own onomastic research (see chapter 3, *sub voce*) has indicated that a West Semitic equivalent for each person's name need not be restricted to documents from the second millennium B.C., but could be found in those from a much later period. With its basic premise undermined, therefore, Glanzman's theory cannot be maintained.

Anthropological Considerations

Custom and Law (cf. Vesco, 1967: 240-43; Leggett, 1974)

The relationship among the institutions of marriage, redemption, and the levirate has stimulated much discussion concerning the dating of *Ruth*. In particular, Biblical formulations on levirate marriage, culled from Gen. 38 and Deut. 25:5-10, are often considered as "earlier" than those preserved in *Ruth* 4. The fact that Boaz was evidently not the brother of Mahlon, Ruth's deceased spouse, is often cited as an indication that the requirements of leviratic legislations were relaxed, in the course of time, to include members of a clan in addition to those belonging to one family. Further, the narrator's aside in 4:7 is often interpreted to indicate the passage of a long stretch of time between Deut. 25:5-10 and *Ruth* 4. Carmichael (1977: 335-36), who is convinced that the Deuteronomist enacted laws after surveying Israelite traditions, posits the opposite: *Ruth* is earlier than Deuteronomy.

In our annotations to these particular moments in *Ruth*, we have found no trace of levirate marriage as formulated in Deut. 25. Hence, this issue cannot, in our opinion, be used to date our scroll. Additionally, our understanding of *Ruth* as a folktale inhibits its use as a source for Biblical legal practices.

"Patriarchal" Themes

Porten (1976: 16) finds fifteen parallels linking *Ruth* to Genesis. Similar evaluations are expressed by Weinfeld (1972: 518-19) and Vesco (1967: 246-47). See also Carmichael, 1977: 335. We have added a few more observations above. Porten derives no conclusion on dating *Ruth* from his findings. His caution is admirable, since dating the patriarchal narratives is itself a difficult enterprise.

Social Purposes (Witzenrath, 1975: 354[n. 18])

(1) Vellas (1954: 209) believes that *Ruth* was written to encourage family solidarity in an age when the family was no longer unified. He believes that Malachi, writing slightly before Ezra-Nehemiah, i.e. early to middle fifth century B.C., bemoans precisely such a condition. Vellas, therefore, would make *Ruth* contemporaneous with *Malachi*.

(2) A number of writers share the opinion that the purpose of *Ruth* is to further social bonds either by glorifying the virtues of *ḥesed*, "loyalty, loving kindness," or by extolling the accomplishments of love. According to Humbert (1958: 109): "Ruth, c'est donc le poème biblique de la fidélitè. C'est une fugue à trois voix sur le thème de la *pietas* [Humbert's rendering for *ḥesed*]." Brichto (1973: 11-12) believes that *Ruth* was written to celebrate the continuity of a family line. No specific dating of *Ruth* is provided by either of these approaches.

Historical Considerations

Although almost all scholars credit *Ruth* with some historical worth, few are certain about the precise setting in which to place the events narrated in the text. Crook (1948), however, believes that *Ruth* could be separated into two strands, the later one of which was composed by Jehoiada the priest, as a polemic against the pagan reign of Athaliah (ca. 842-837 B.C.) (cf. 2 Kings 11 and 2 Chron. 22-23). In Crook's opinion, the miraculous survival of the infant Joash, last of David's line, to become king of Israel is reminiscent of the birth of a Obed to a family on the point of extinction.

Genealogical Considerations (Rowley, 1965: 13[n. 5])

We refer the reader to our extensive discussion on the importance of the genealogy of 4:18-22 to the dating of *Ruth*. To most scholars, these verses are but an appendix; hence they contribute nothing to the dating of the tale itself. Wellhausen, cited by Rowley (1965: 173[n. 5]), however, is one of those who believes that the entire tale, along with the genealogy, is datable to the postexilic period. See our annotations.

Literary and Linguistic Considerations

Poetics

The arguments for and against the presence of a poetic (sub)stratum in *Ruth* have been delineated above. Scholars who postulate an orally circulating poetic version of *Ruth* are wont to consider it as "earlier" than the written version. Just why poetic forms are necessarily "earlier" than prose forms, an unwarranted asumption with wide credence ever since the days of Herder, is rarely made clear. Note, further, the remarks of Hurvitz (1972: 56-58)

Vocabulary and idioms

Arguments for a "Late" Dating. Much has been written concerning literary material deemed "late" by scholars. This includes words and expressions which have parallels only in "later" books of the Old Testament, i.e. books composed in exilic and postexilic periods. Additionally the evidence of "aramaicism" is often cited to declare *Ruth* as a later product of Hebrew literature.

Our objections to the invocation of "aramaisms" to date *Ruth* (bibliography in Witzenrath, 1975: 361[n. 33]) parallel those of Hurvitz (1968: 234-40). Noting that many certifiably "early" texts preserve "aramaisms," Hurvitz proposes that a text be assigned to a "late" period only if it contains a preponderance of such aramaisms. In the case of *Ruth*, aramaisms are very few. In our annotations, *sub voce*, we had occasion to remove *halāhēn* of 1:13, *qiyyēm* of 4:7, and *śibbēr* of 1:13 from the roster of aramaisms. Since *ʿāgan* of 1:13 is a *hapax legomenon* in the Old Testament, it would be rather bold to consider it as an Aramaic verb.

Campbell (1975: 24-25) is one of many recent commentators who regards such an approach as essentially unproductive. We agree with many of his conclusions and take this opportunity to recall that many Akkadian words and idioms span millennia between attestations (see above). Thus, it is our opinion that, despite an enormous literature on the subject, dating a Hebrew text on literary and linguistic bases will continue to be a most unreliable approach as long as our extrabiblical corpus of Hebrew vocabulary remains as sparse as it is presently.

Arguments for an "Early" Dating. If we are weary of assigning the composition of *Ruth* to a postexilic period because of linguistic usage deemed "late," we are equally unimpressed by references to allegedly "archaic" features in order to secure an early date for *Ruth* (Glanzman, 1959: 205-7; Gray, 1967: 400). Weinfeld (1972: 521-22) adopts a relative "early" dating of *Ruth* on precisely the same grounds as those who promote a "late" dating.

The book abounds with expressions of gracious manners which are characteristic of the patriarchal narratives and the Books of Samuel. . . . All these pnrases and expressions [listed above] are not found after the period of Elisha [ca. second half of the ninth century B.C.]. . . . This may give us an approximate clue for the date of the composition . . . and may also indicate the possibility that it was composed in Northern Israel.

Campbell (1975: 26) is equally impressed by evidence for an earlier period in which to set the composition of Ruth:

In sum, no linguistic datum points unerringly toward a late date. Indeed, the impact is just the opposite. While a number of features may be conscious archaisms, they are not used randomly or unknowingly; there is nothing artificial about them. The language of *Ruth* is the language of the monarchic period, tinged with the archaic. The archaic features may be due to "cultural lag" in the countryside, but the overall impression is one of close relationship to stories stemming from the tenth and ninth centuries, the time of *J* and *E* and the Court History. On language alone, one would be justified in leaning toward the earlier part of our spread 950-700 B.C.

But the arguments often adduced for archaisms, conscious or stylized, are not terribly convincing:

(1) *The use of the "paragogic" nûn, suffixed to imperfect forms.* However, this particle, whose morphology cannot be separated in function from that of the "energic" *nûn*, is known to all phases of Biblical Hebrew. On this point, see GKC, 47m (pp. 128-29); Joüon, *Grammaire*, 44e-f (pp. 103-4).

(2) *The use of -tî as a second person feminine singular suffixed to a perfect conjunction,* is hardly a convincing argument for archaisms in *Ruth*, for GKC (44n [p. 121]) indicates its presence in Jeremiah and Ezekiel. Incidentally, the occurrence of these sufformatives in 3:3 and 3:4 have permitted some to retain a first person singular translation of the verbs ("*I* shall go down . . . *I* shall lie by his 'legs'") and to conjecture that Naomi was originally the bearer of Obed (cf. Volz, 1901: 348-49; somewhat similar Gunkel, 1930: 2180-82).

(3) Other criteria, such as pleonastic writing in 2:8, orthographic details, and so forth, have been used with less than complete enthusiasm by Myers (1955: 10, 11, 17) and Campbell (1975: 26-27). We need not pursue the details.

Arguments for a Late Date with Archaic Features. Gordis (1974: 245) is wont to date *Ruth* to the fifth century (i.e. "late") by allowing the tale features that are at once "late" and "early"! We quote: "The author . . . was a late writer who was consciously archaising and using colloquial speech, in order to give an antique flavor to his narrative, which he set [*sic*] in the period of the Judges." Gordis's opinion thus underscores the hazards of resorting to linguistic evidence in order to fix the composition of *Ruth* to a specific period.

Contextual Considerations

A number of opinions on the dating of *Ruth* are formulated by establishing the context that would best explain its presence in the Old Testament canon. The examples listed below are not without a manifest tendency to reason circularly.

Universalism (bibliography in Witzenrath, 1975: 349[n. 5]; Rowley, 1965: 173[n. 1]).

Once widely disseminated is the opinion that *Ruth* was a polemical tract, written to combat the narrow vision of a closed community as propounded by Ezra (9-10) and Nehemiah (13:23-29). The author of *Ruth*, espousing universalistic ideals that rival those of Deutero-Isaiah and Jonah, would have punctured the presumptions of exclusivity.

Two variations on this theme are evident in the scholarly literature on *Ruth*. First, *Ruth* is considered as a polemic against the legislations of Deut. 23:4-8 which exclude Ammonites and Moabites from the "Assembly of God." Whether or not the mention of *qəhal YHWH*, "Assembly of God," indicates that this exclusion is limited to the participation of males in the divine cult is not seen as an issue. On the basis of this passage, a dating for *Ruth* is offered which is slightly earlier than the one proposed above. Ap-Thomas (1967-68: 373) represents a good example of this second variation on the theme of "universalism versus exclusivism": "The Book of Ruth . . . puts forward the same positive policy that we find in the Book of Jonah: those who take the opportunity to become believers, when it is offered, are not to be refused fellowship, or denied their right to God's grace. God himself accepts them, blesses them and uses them." See also the opinions of Eissfeldt (1965: 483), and Gordis

(1974: 244-46). And, secondly, Gerleman (1965: 4-11) proceeds from the position that a Moabite ancestry could not have been invented for David after the exile, since it would have been rejected by the virulent xenophobia of the postexilic period. Moreover, the ancestry of David must have been available to the Chronicler, who used it in his transfiguration of David into the ideal king. Hence, it is Gerleman's belief that *Ruth's* purpose is to "Judaize" an already available tradition that claimed a Moabite as David's ancestress. *Ruth* is a *Führungsgeschichte* of a type similar in function as that attached to the patriarchal narratives. Both, it is claimed, precede the theocratic covenants of Sinai and David; hence, Gerleman would place *Ruth* in the early Monarchic period. Meinhold (1976: 129-37) thinks of a pre-Deuteronomic Bethlehemite tradition, of which he finds echoes also in Ps. 132.

Rowley (1965: 173) is one of many scholars of recent times to challenge the tendency to read polemical sentiments into a tale utterly devoid of factious discord. Campbell (1965: 27) notes that "the entire proposal has far too modern a ring." In our notes above, we observed that the Hebrews were not ashamed to attribute foreign ancestresses to Israel's royal lines. Since it does not seem exceptional within Israel's traditions to have a heroine born outside Israel, *Ruth* could not have become a medium for an internal conflict on the issue of exclusivism.

Moab

If the above-mentioned theories referring to a conflict between advocates of an "open" and "closed" society have proved to be unconvincing, it remains impossible to account persuasively for the mention of Moab in *Ruth*. Shearman and Curtis (1969: 239-40) recently resurrected a proposal that considers Moab, home of the chtonic deity Chemosh, as a symbol of the Netherworld. Interpreting *Ruth* as an allegorical drama, this theory pits Yahweh's Bethlehem, "House of Bread/Food," against Chemosh's Netherworld.

Often cited to account for the initial setting is the occasion in which, according to 1 Sam. 22:3ff., David's parents were given refuge in Moab. Thus, it is argued, the tale establishes Israel's primacy over a land in which David may have found welcoming kinsmen. On this topic, see Grønbaek's discussion (1971: 149-50). A venerable hypothesis linked Ruth's Moabite ancestry to Gen. 19:30-38, in which Moab was said to have been founded through Lot's incestuous marriage with his eldest daughter. Thus

Boaz and Ruth would be credited with beginning the reunification of Terah's line, a reunification that would be completed when Solomon marries Naamah (*sic*) the Ammonitess and, through her, fathers Rehoboam (1 Kings 14:21). Finally, we might point out that folkloristic considerations along Propp's categories require the *hero* of a tale, in our case Ruth, to depart from one country and cross into another before accomplishing heroic deeds. Because of its proximity to Bethlehem, Moab might have offered a convenient locale from which Ruth could proceed into her adventures.

Theological Considerations
Cultic and "Mythological"

(1) Practically extinct are the many elaborations on *Ruth* as a fictionalized liturgy for Tammuz to be dated to the Neo-Babylonian period (ca. 625-540 B.C.). Following Winckler (1902: 65-78), Staples (1937: 145-57; 1938: 62-65) codified this theory. It has recently been resurrected by Shearman and Curtis (1969: 235-40) and by Sheehan (1973: 40-43). May (1939: 75-78) proceeds with the assumption that, in Boaz's time, no prophets had yet risen in Israel. To May (1939: 78), *Ruth* relates how a sacred prostitute from Moab was sent by Naomi to Bethlehem's sacred "high places" in order to become impregnated with Obed: "Naomi and Ruth, as the source of the Davidic line, are represented according to the pattern of the mother-goddess who gives birth to a son who rules as a divine king and brings prosperity to the land." Both of the above hypotheses have been severely criticized by Rowley (1965: 189[n. 2]), among many other scholars. Gunkel (1913: 90-92) believes that the story is based on a reworking of the Egyptian Isis and Osiris legend.

(2) Astour (1965: 278-79) believes that *Ruth* "tells--in a fully euhemerized form--the Hebrew version of the Eleusis myth." Thus, an agrarian tale relates how Naomi (= Demeter) arrives to Bethlehem (= Eleusis) after she experiences losses in Moab (= Hades [cf., Chemosh = Nergal, god of the Underworld]). A sacred marriage is consumated between Boaz (= Iason?) and Ruth (= Core [a double of Demeter]). The offspring (= Triptolemos) is considered Naomi's (i.e. Demeter's) child. Triptolemos, ultimately teaches mankind agriculture ("Obed" = "the Tiller"). Astour's reconstruction has not been discussed in the scholarly literature on *Ruth*. It may be that the Eleusian myth shares many motifs with the story of *Ruth* precisely because both fit neatly into a folktale pattern.

Yahwistic (Witzenrath, 1975: 355[n. 19])

A good deal of recent scholarship has focused on the role Yahweh plays in *Ruth*. Rudolph (1962: 32), as one example, claims: "Like much of the Old Testament literature, Ruth does not speak of people, but of God; we are not to admire a group of noble personages, but to learn how God acts." Loretz (1960: 397-98) speaks of God's interference in history to provide an heir, divinely chosen to be the ancestor of a royal line. Similar sentiments are expressed in Gerleman, 1960: 8-10; von Rad, 1962: 52; and, in America, Hals, 1969 (cf. IDB, *Supplement*, 758-59); Campbell, 1975: 28-29; Trible, 1976.

A context for Yahweh's interference in history, often presented in discreetly "hidden" fashion, is obtained by comparing *Ruth* to other narratives in which His involvement is similarly motivated and expressed. The "Succession History of David," told in 2 Sam. 9-20, and the story of Joseph, recounted in Gen. 37-48, are considered as similar in ideology. Since many scholars nowadays are wont to date these accounts to the period of "Solomonic enlightenment," the composition of *Ruth* is placed at around 950-700 B.C.

It might be objected, however, that we know nothing about the "Solomonic enlightenment." Almost all our information on the subject is derived from Old Testament materials that are assigned to the reign of Solomon on vague, humanistic grounds. We refer, further, to chapter 3 and pages 220-21 above where we disputed the tendency to exaggerate the theological context of *Ruth*. It seems to us that Lucien Gautier's opinion of almost a century ago on this matter is still relevant: "Au point de vue religieux, la portée du livre de Ruth est à peu près nulle" (quoted disapprovingly by Humbert, 1958: 102).

Folkloristic Considerations

An analogy could be drawn from observing the manner in which folklore is used to promote ideological positions. For our purposes, we could distinguish between two such positions: nationalistic and dynastic/royal.

Nationalistic (Dorson, 1966: 277-98)

Not infrequently in the last centuries, a handful of patriotic scholars would avidly collect, edit, and rearrange the folk literature of their native land in order to produce a national scripture which would be shared by a fragmented, often a defeated, population. These scholars were aware that, in order to fuse disparate elements into a unified nation, a past must be reconstructed which would be worthy of emulation by the present. The following bibliography discusses this process as it occurs in specific nations: Wilson, 1976 (Finland); Fernandez, 1962 (Africa); Wang, 1965 (Communist China); Falnes, 1933 (Norway); Kamenetsky, 1977 (Nazi Germany); Dorson, 1966; Coffin, 1961 (Ireland and United States).

From the above perspective, it might be possible to regard the folkloristic materials preserved in Genesis-Judges (e.g. the saga of the Patriarchs, the escape from Egypt, the conquest of the land) as the work of intellectuals who, beginning with the second half of the Monarchic period, sought to present a defeated and fragmented nation edifying models worthy of imitation. These models defined the goals of Hebraic society in terms of repeated covenants between its ancestors and God, and reawakened nationalistic fervor by alluding to the heroic deeds of a conquering tribal confederacy.

Dynastic/Royal

Folkloristic embellishments could promote a specific individual as a prototypical personality, foremost representative of his age, and actualizer of his people's destiny. Such individuals help to recall a Golden Age by deeds that barely stretch human credulity. Dynasts and eponymous ancestors are good candidates for such honors. Focusing on the Ancient Near East, we might place in this category Enmerkar, Lugalbanda and Gilgamesh (Sumer), Sargon of Agade (as recalled by the Assyrians), Keret (Ugarit), Djoser, Amenemhet I (Egypt), and Khattushilish I (Hatti). We offer the following short bibliography for those who would pursue this topic beyond the confines of the Middle East: OCD^2, 1970: 521-23 (Greece); Hadas, 1959: 115-29 (Hellenistic Greece); Stover, 1967: 378-82 (Western prototypes).

In Israel, no other personality--with the possible exception of the aretalogized figures of Moses and Elijah--equalled David as the subject of a historicizing literature. In consonance with Hebraic artistic as well as humanistic tenets, this paradigmatic king was not drawn without human weaknesses and pettiness. Nevertheless, his deeds and accomplishments were detailed, even to the point of assigning him a legendary youth. In chapter 3 we interpreted a number of vestigial motifs in *Ruth* 4:15-17 as indicative of Obed's unusual infancy. For those capable of interpreting these motifs, *Ruth*, therefore, might have formed part of a large literature on the rise of David to kingship. This literature was not without a perceptible apologistic strain, for it depicted David as eager to preserve God's anointed, Saul, and his dynasty on the throne of Israel (Kapelrud, 1959: 294-301). But as God's choice ever since the birth of his grandfather Obed, David could only acquiesce to the will of God. It is quite unlikely that such a glorification of David and his ancestry occurred in David's own life time or in that of his immediate successors. Rather, an appreciably later period might be sought, one in which the activities of David might be recalled as precedent to those of a monarch eager to introduce reforms that either lacked popularity or required harsh readjustments. Without totally dismissing the era of Hezekiah (715-687/6 B.C.), we think that the reign of Josiah (640-609 B.C.) might well have provided a setting in which *Ruth*, a folktale, became a vehicle for the glorification of David. It might be noted that the reign of Josiah was recalled in terminology that was matched only by that of David (cf. 2 Kings 23:25). Furthermore, modern Biblical scholarship has increasingly assigned the codification of the *Geste* of David, as preserved in Samuel, to precisely that period (cf. IDB,S, 188-92, 226-28).

Conclusion

It is clear that none of the approaches summarized above, taken either singly or in combination, could be expected to yield a convincing date in which *Ruth* was set in writing. For neither "internal" (i.e. onomastic, anthropological, theological, linguistic) nor "external" (i.e. historical, contextual, folkloristic, genealogical) evidence is compelling enough to establish a credible period in which our scroll was either authored or committed to writing. Our own contribution, inspired by folkloristic considerations, should be considered as no less conjectural than any of the other proposals. Moreover, were one to admit the possibility that *Ruth* may have circulated in an oral form before it achieved its present shape, the search for a suitable date of composition would become hopelessly complicated.

In order to avoid ending this study on such a negative note, I propose that our failure to establish a date for *Ruth* is not of calamitous consequence. Even if our formalistic and folkloristic exposition of *Ruth* is deemed unconvincing by readers, the fact that the scroll is primarily a literary creation cannot be seriously questioned. Were the aim of promoting a date for a literary text limited to placing it chronologically within a sequence of other compositions, the recompenses for the enormous outlay of creative energy needed to fulfill that narrow goal would be few indeed. To "date" a literary text, however, is to permit us to say something about it beyond the narrow issue of its original purpose at the moment of composition. For when such a text earns a place among other literary creations, it obviously responds to needs that transcend momentary gratifications. Therefore, in approaching the task of "dating" any text, it might be better to try to "locate" it within specific frames of references. In discussing the social and cultural contexts of *Ruth*, in establishing the literary merits that have made the scroll immortal, even in methodically challenging the approaches taken to secure for it a "date," we hope to have outlined the nature and the parameters of these frames of reference. To that degree, we hope to have satisfied much of the curiosity which impels scholars to fix *Ruth*'s origins in a specific moment of the past.

BIBLIOGRAPHY

Extensive as it may seem, the bibliography presented below does not fully represent the literature on *Ruth*. Only those studies that are cited in the text have been recorded. Additional references can be gathered from the following items:

Witzenrath, 1975: 396-407 (with additional data throughout the text).

Campbell, 1975: 42-45.

Gerleman, 1965: 11-12.

Rudolph, 1962: 33-36, 60-61 (on levirate marriage).

Myers, 1955: 65-69.

For up-to-date bibliographical data, the index of the yearly *Elenchus Bibliographicus Biblicus* (Rome) should be consulted, *sub. Ruth*.

Aharoni, Y.
1967: *The Land of the Bible*, trans. A. F. Rainey (Philadelphia, 1967).

Albright, W. F.
1968: *Archaeology and the Religion of Israel*, 5th ed. (Baltimore, 1968).

Alster, Bendt
1975: *Studies in Sumerian Proverbs* (Copenhagen, 1975).

Andersen, Francis I., and Forbes, A. Dean
1976: *A Linguistic Concordance of Ruth and Jonah: Hebrew Vocabulary and Idiom*, Biblical Research Associates (1976).

Ap-Thomas, D. R.
1967-68: "The Book of Ruth," ET 79(1967-68): 369-73.

Astour, Michael C.
1965: *Hellenosemitica* (Leiden, 1965).

Auerbach, Erich
1953: *Mimesis*, trans. W. R. Trask (Princeton, 1953).

Baillet, M., Milik, J. T., and de Vaux, R.
1962: *Les "petites grottes" de Qumrân (Discoveries in the Judaean Desert)* 3 (Oxford, 1962).

Barta, Winfried
1975: *Untersuchungen zur Göttlichkeit des regierenden Königs, (Münchener Ägyptologische Studien* 32 (Munich, 1975).

Bascom, William R.
1965: "Four Functions of Folklore," in A. Dundes, 1965: 277-98; *Journal of American Folklore* 67 (1954): 333-49.

Batto, B.F.
1974: *Studies on Women at Mari* (Baltimore, 1974).

Bauer, H.
1932: *Das Alphabet von Ras Schamra* (Halle, 1932).

Baumgartner, Albert
1973: "A Note on the Book of Ruth," JANES 5 (1973; *Gaster Festshrift*): 11-15.

Beattie, D. R. G.
1971: "Ketibh and Qere in Ruth IV 5," VT, 21 (1971): 490-94.

1974: "The Book of Ruth as evidence for Israelite legal practice," VT, 24 (1974): 251-67.

1977a: "A Midrashic Gloss in Ruth 2 7," ZAW, 89 (1977): 122-24.

1977b: *Jewish Exegesis of the Book of Ruth*, JSOT, Supplement Series, 2 (Sheffield, 1977).

Beauchamp, Paul
1972: "L'analyse structurale et l'exégèse biblique," VTS, 22 (1972): 113-28.

Beckman, Gary
1978: *Hittite Birth Rituals: An Introduction, Sources from the Ancient Near East* 1-4 (Malibu, 1978).

Benito, Carlos A.
1969: *"Enki and Ninmaḫ" and "Enki and the World Order"* (Ann Arbor, 1969).

Benz, Frank L.
1972: *Personal Names in the Phoenician and Punic Inscriptions*, Studia Pohl 8 (Rome, 1972).

Bertholet, A.
1923: "Das Buch Ruth," HSAT 2, 4th ed. (1923).

1929: "Leviratsehe," RGG III, 2nd ed. (1929): 1603.

Bertman, Stephen
1965: "Symmetrical Design in the Book of Ruth," JBL 84 (1965): 165-68.

Bertram, G.
1959: "Zur Prägung der biblischen Gottesvorstellung in der griechischen Übersetzung des AT. Die Wiedergabe von *schadad* und *schaddaj* im Griechischen," *Welt des Orients* 2 (1959): 502-13.

Bewer, Julius A.
1902-3: "The *Ge*ʾ*ullāh* in the Book of Ruth," AJSL 19 (1902-3): 143-48.

1903-4: "The *Goël* in Ruth 4:14, 15," AJSL 20 (1903-4): 202-6.

Biblia Rabbinica
1972: *Biblia Rabbinica,* ed. Jacob ben Hayim (Venice, 1952 and Jerusalem, 1972).

Biggs, R. D.
1967: *ŠÀ.ZI.GA: Ancient Mesopotamian Potency Incantations, Texts from Cuneiform Sources* II (Locust Valley, N.Y., 1967).

Boehmer, R. M.
no date: "Hörnerkrone," RLA IV, 431-34.

Boling, Robert G.
1975: *Judges,* AB (Garden City, N.Y., 1975).

Bottéro, Jean
1958: *Textes économiques et administratifs,* ARMT VII (Paris, 1958).

1975: "Antiquités assyro-babyloniennes," École Practique des Hautes Études, *Annuaire* (1975/76); ive section; sciences historiques et philologiques (Paris, 1975).

Brichto, Herbert Chanan
1963: *The Problem of "curse" in the Hebrew Bible* (Philadelphia, 1963).

1969: "Taking-off of the shoe(s) in the Bible," *Proceedings of the 5th World Congress of Jewish Studies* (1969), pp. 225-26.

1973: "Kin, Cult, Land, and Afterlife--A Biblical Complex," HUCA 44 (1973): 1-54.

Bright, John
1965: *Jeremiah,* AB 21 (Garden City, N.Y., 1965).

Brinkman, John A.
1968: *A Political History of Post-Kassite Babylonia: 1158-722 B.C., Analecta Orientalia* 43 (Rome, 1968).

Brongers, Hendrik Antonie
1965: "Bemerkungen zum Gebrauch des adverbialen *w*[ec]*attā* im Alten Testament," VT 15 (1965): 289-99.

Bruppacher, Hans
1966: "Die Bedeutung des Namens Ruth," ThZ 22 (1966): 12-18.

Burrows, Millar
1938: *The Basis of Israelite Marriage* (New Haven, 1938).

1940: "The Marriage of Boaz and Ruth," JBL 59 (1940): 445-54.

Campbell, Edward F., Jr.
1975: *Ruth,* AB 7 (Garden City, N.Y., 1975).

Caquot, André
1971: "Anges et démons en Israël," *Sources Orientales* 8 (Paris, 1971): 113-52.

Carmichael, Calum M.
1977: "A Ceremonial Crux: Removing a Man's Sandal as a Female Gesture of Contempt," JBL 96 (1977): 321-36.

Caspari, Wilhelm
1908: "Erbtochter und Ersatzehe in Ruth 4," NKZ 19 (1908): 115-29.

Casanowicz, Immanuel M.
1894: *Paronomasia in the Old Testament* (Boston, 1894).

Coffin, Tristram P.
1961: "Folklore in the American Twentieth Century," *American Quarterly* 13 (1961): 526-33.

Cohen, Ch.
1973: "The 'Widowed' City," JANES 5 (1973; *Gaster Festschrift*): 75-81.

Cooke, G. A.
1918: "Ruth and Judges," in *Cambridge Bible* (1918).

Crook, Margaret B.
1948: "The Book of Ruth: a New Solution," JBR 16 (1948): 155-60.

Cross, Frank M.
1973: *Canaanite Myth and Hebrew Epic* (Cambridge, Mass., 1973).

Cross Frank M., and Saley, R.J.
1970: "Phoenician Incantations on a Plaque of the Seventh Century B.C. from Arslan Tash in Upper Syria," BASOR 197 (1970): 42-49.

Cross, F. M., and Talmon, Sh., eds.
1975: *Qumran and the History of the Biblical Text* (Cambridge, 1975).

Culley, Robert C.
1976: *Studies in the Structure of Hebrew Narrative* (Missoula, Mont., 1976).

Curtis, E. L.
1952: *Chronicles,* ICC 11, 2nd printing, (Edinburgh, 1952).

Dahood, Mitchell
1965: "Hebrew-Ugaritic Lexicography III," *Biblica* 46 (1965): 311-32.

1966: *Psalms I*, AB 16 (Garden City, N.Y., 1966).

1968: *Psalms II*, AB 17 (Garden City, N.Y., 1968).

1970: *Psalms III*, AB 17A (Garden City, N.Y., 1970).

1972: *Ras Shamra Parallels I, Analecta Orientalia* 49 (Rome, 1972).

Dalley, Stephanie, Walker, C. B. F., and Hawkins, J. D.
1976: *The Old Babylonian Tablets from Tell Al Rimah* (London, 1976).

Daube, D.
1947: *Studies in Biblical Law* (Cambridge, 1947).

David, M.
1942: "The Date of the Book of Ruth," OTS 1 (1942): 55-63.

Deroy, Louis
1961: "Un symbolisme juridique de la chaussure," *L'Antiquité Classique* 30 (1961): 371-80.

Dhorme, E.
1923: *L'Emploi métaphorique des noms de parties du corps en hébreu et en akkadien* (Paris, 1923).

Dietrich, M., Loretz, O., and Sammartin, J.
1973: "Die Ugaritischen Verben MRR I, MRR II, und MRR III," UF 5 (1973): 119-22.

Dijk, J. van
1978: "Une incantation accompagnant la naissance de l'homme," *Orientalia* 42 (1973): 502-7.

Dombrowski, B. W.
1971: "The Meaning of the Qumran *Terms 'T'WDH' and 'MDH',*" *Revue de Qumran 7* (1971): 567-74.

Dommershausen, Werner
1967: "Leitwortstil in der Ruthrolle," in *Theologie im Wandel: Festschrift zum 150 jährigen bestehen der Katholisch-Theologischen Fakultät Tübingen 1817-1967* (Munich and Freiburg, 1967).

Donner, H., and Röllig, W.
1964: *Kanaanäische und Aramäische Inschriften,* 3 vols. (Wiesbaden, 1962-1964).

Dorson, Richard M.
1966: "The Question of Folklore in a New Nation," *Folklore Institute Journal* 3 (1966): 277-98.

Driver, G. R.
1959: "Lilith, heb *lîlîth* "goat-sucker, night-jar," PEQ 91 (1959): 55-58.

1967: "Hebrew Homonyms," VTS 16 (1967; *Festschrift Baumgartner*): 50-64.

1973: "Affirmation by Exclamatory Negation," JANES 5 (1973): 107-14.

Driver, S. R.
1951: *Deuteronomy*, ICC, 3rd ed. (Edinburgh, 1951).

Dundes, Alan
1964: *The Morphology of North American Indian Folktales*, F.F. Communications 195 (Helsinki, 1964).

1965: *The Study of Folklore* (Englewood Cliffs, N.J., 1965).

Edzard, Otto Dietz
1957: *Die "Zweite Zwischenzeit" Babyloniens* (Wiesbaden, 1957).

Ehrlich, A. B. E.
1900: *Mikrâ kî-Pheshutô*, 3 vols. (Berlin, 1900; reprinted Jerusalem, 1969).

Eissfeldt, Otto
1965: *The Old Testament, An Introduction*, trans. P. R. Ackroyd (New York, 1965).

Emerton, J. A.
1976: "An Examination of a Recent Structuralist Interpretation of Gen. 38," VT 26 (1976): 79-98.

1977: "The Etymology of *HIŠTAḤAWĀH*," OTS 20 (1977): 41-55.

Epstein, L. M.
1927: *Jewish Marriage Contract* (New York, 1927).

1942: *Marriage Laws in the Bible and in the Talmud*, HSS XII (Cambridge, Mass., 1942).

Falkenstein, A.
1950: Review of S. Kramer, *Sumerian Literary Texts from Nippur* (New Haven, 1944) in ZA NF 15 (49) (1950): 325-28.

Falnes, Oscar J.
1933: *National Romanticism in Norway* (New York, 1933).

Fernandez, James W.
1962: "Folklore as an Agent of Nationalism," *African Studies Bulletin* 5 (1962): 3-8.

Fichtner, J.
1956: "Die etymologische Ätiologie in den Namengebungen der geschichtlichen Bücher des Alten Testaments," VT 6 (1956): 372-96.

Fohrer, G.
1969: *"nios,"* ThW 8 (1969): 340-54.

Fraine, J. de
1955: *Ruth* in *De Boeken van het oude Testament* III (Roermond, 1955).

Frankena, Rintje
1974: "Dit zij u een teken," *Vruchten van de Uithof: Studies opgedragen aan Dr. H. A. Brongers ter gelengenheid van zijn afscheid (16 mei 1974)* (Utrecht, 1974), pp 28-36.

Freedman, D. N.
1973: "God Almighty in Psalm 78,59," *Biblica* 54 (1973): 268.

Frey, Jean Baptiste
1936-52: *Corpus Inscriptionum Iudaicarum*, 2 vols. (Rome, 1936-52).

Friedrich, J.
1950: "Churritische Märchen und Sagen in hethitischen Sprache," ZA NF 15 (49) (1950): 213-55.

Gelb, I. J.
1965: "Ancient Mesopotamian Ration System," JNES 24 (1965): 230-43.

Gerleman, Gillis
1965: *Ruth*, in BK XVIII (Neukirchen, 1965).

Ginzberg, Louis
1909-47: *The Legends of the Jews* I-VII (Philadelphia, 1909-47).

1961: *The Legends of the Jews*, one vol. ed. (New York, 1961).

Glanzman, George S.
1959: "The Origin and Date of the Book of Ruth," CBQ 21 (1959): 201-7.

Glueck, N.
1967: *Ḥesed in the Bible*, trans. A. Gottschalk (Cincinnati, 1967).

Goetze, Albrecht
1938: *The Hittite Ritual of Tunnawi*, American Oriental Series 14 (New Haven, 1938).

Gordis, R.
1970: "On Methodology in Biblical Exegesis," JQR 61 (1970): 93-118.

1974: "Love, Marriage, and Business in the Book of Ruth: A Chapter in Hebrew Customary Law," in *A Light unto my Path: Old Testament Studies in Honor of Jacob M. Myers*, eds. Bream, Heim, and Moore (Philadelphia, 1974), pp. 241-64.

Gordon, C. H.
1965: *The Common Background of Greek and Hebrew Civilizations*, 2nd ed. (New York, 1965).

1977: "Paternity at Two Levels," JBL 96 (1977): 101.

Gray, G. B.
1896: *Studies in Hebrew Proper Names* (London, 1896).

Gray, John
1967: *Joshua, Judges and Ruth*, Century Bible, new ed. (London, 1967).

Grayson, Albert Kirk
1976: *Assyrian Royal Inscriptions, Part II,* Records of the Ancient Near East II (Wiesbaden, 1976).

Greenberg, M.
1957: "The Hebrew Oath Particle Ḥay/Ḥē," JBL 76 (1957): 34-39.

Greengus, S.
1966: "Old Babylonian Marriage Ceremonies and Rites," JCS 20 (1966): 55-72.

Grønbaek, J. H.
1971: *Die Geschichte vom Aufstieg Davids (1 Sam. 15-2 Sam. 5): Tradition und Komposition,* Acta Theologica Danica 10 (Copenhagen, 1971).

Gröndahl, Frauke
1967: *Die Personennamen der Texte aus Ugarit,* Studia Pohl 1 (Rome, 1967).

Gunkel, Herman
1913: "Ruth," in *Reden und Aufsätze* (Göttingen, 1913), pp. 65-92.

1930: RGG IV 2180-82, 2nd ed. (Tübingen, 1930).

Hadas, Moses
1959: *Hellenistic Culture* (New York, 1959).

Hals, R. M.
1969: *The Theology of the Book of Ruth* (Philadelphia, 1969).

Hartmann, D.
1901: *Das Buch Ruth im der Midrasch-Literature* (Leipzig, 1901).

Heide, A. van der
1974: "A Biblical Fragment with Palestinian-Tiberian ('Pseudo-Ben Naftali') Punctuation in the Leyden University Library (Hebr. ?59-I)," *Muséon* 87 (1974): 415-23.

Heltzer, M. L.
1976: "Mortgage of Land Property ... In Ugarit," JESHO 19 (1976): 89-95.

Hirsch, H.
1961: *Untersuchungen zur altassyrischen Religion* AfO Beihefte 13-14 (Graz, 1961).

Hoffner, H. A., Jr.
1968: "Birth and Name-Giving in Hittite Texts," JNES 27 (1968): 198-203.

1974: *Alimenta Hethaeorum* (New Haven, 1974).

Hoftijzer, J.
1965: "Remarks Concerning the Use of the Particle ʾ*T* in Classical Hebrew," OTS 14 (1965): 1-99.

1970: "David and the Tekoite Woman," VT 20 (1970): 419-44.

Horst, F.
1961: "Zwei Begriffe für Eigentum (Besitz): *naḥalāh* und *ʾaḥuzāh*," in *Verbannung und Heimkehr*, Festschrift W. Rudolph, ed. A. Kuschke (Tübingen, 1961), pp. 135-56.

Huffmon, Herbert B.
1965: *Amorite Personal Names in the Mari Texts; A Structural and Lexical Study* (Baltimore, 1965).

1966a: "The Treaty Background of Hebrew *YĀDAʿ*," BASOR 181 (1966): 31-37.

1966b: "A Further Note on the Treaty Background of Hebrew *Yādaʿ*," BASOR 184 (1966): 36-38 (with S. Parker).

Hulst, A. R.
1970: "De Beteknis van het woord *menûḥah*," in *Festschrift W. H. Gispen* (Kampen, 1970), pp. 62-78.

Humbert, Paul
1949-50: "En marge du dictionnaire hebraïque," ZAW 62 (1949-50): 199-207.

1958: "Art et leçon de l'histoire de Ruth," in *Opuscules d'un Hébraïsant* (Neuchâtel, 1958), pp. 83-110.

1958b: "Les Adjectifs *zār* et *nŏkrī* et "la femme étrangère" des Proverbes bibliques," in *Opuscules d'un Hébraïsant* (Neuchâtel, 1958), pp. 111-18.

Hurvitz, A.
1968: "The Chronological Significance of 'Aramaisms' in Biblical Hebrew," IEJ 18 (1968): 234-40.

1972: *Bēyn lašōn lelašōn* [*The Transition Period in Biblical Hebrew*] (Jerusalem, 1972).

1975: "ʿal'šelipat-hannaʿal' šebemgillat rût [On 'Casting the Shoe' the Scroll of Ruth]," *Shnaton* 1 (1975); 45-49.

Irvin, D.
1976: *Mytharion: The Comparison of Tales of the Old Testament and the Ancient Near East*, AOAT 32 (Neukirchen-Vluyn, 1978).

Ishida, Tommo
1977: *The Royal Dynasties in Ancient Israel* (Berlin, 1977).

Jacobsen, Thorkild
1970: *Toward the Image of Tammuz and Other Essays*, Harvard Semitic Series 21 (Cambridge, Mass., 1970).

1973: "Notes on Nintur," *Orientalia* 42 (1973): 274-98.

1976a: *Treasures of Darkness: A Study of Mesopotamian Religion* (New Haven, 1976).

1976b: "The stele of the Vultures Col I-X," in *Kramer Anniversary Volume: Cuneiform Studies in Honor of Samuel Noah Kramer*, Alter Orient und Altes Testament 25 (Neukirchen-Vluyn, 1976), pp. 247-59.

Jastrow, Marcus
1950: *Dictionary of the Targumim, the Talmud Babli and Jerushalmi, and the Midraschic Literature*, 2 vols. (New York [Reprint], 1950).

Jepsen, A
1937-38: "Das Buch Ruth," TSK 108, NF 3 (1937-38): 416-28.

1958: "*Amah* und *Schiphchah*," VT 8 (1958): 293-97.

Jeremias, Alfred
1931: *Der Schleier von Sumer bis Heute*, Der Alte Orient 31 (Leipzig, 1931).

Jeremias, J.
1963: *The Parables of Jesus*, trans. S. H. Hooke (New York, 1963).

1969: *Jerusalem in the Time of Jesus*, trans. F. H. and C. H. Cave (Philadelphia, 1969).

Johnson, M. D.
1969: *The Purpose of the Biblical Genealogies* (London, 1969).

Jolles, André
1930: *Einfache Formen* (Halle, 1930).

Joüon, Paul
1947: *Grammaire de l'Hébreu biblique*, 2nd ed. (Rome, 1947).

1953: *Ruth: commentaire philologique et exégétique* (Rome, 1953).

Kamenetsky, Christa
1977: "Folktale and Ideology in the Third Reich," *Journal of Am. Folk.* 90 (1977): 168-78.

Kapelrud, A.
1959: "King David and the Sons of Saul," in *The Sacral Kingship*, Studies in History of Religion IV (Leiden, 1959), pp. 294-301.

1969: *The Violent Goddess* (Oslo, 1969).

Kaufmann, Yehezkel
1960: *The Religion of Israel*, trans. and abridged by Moshe Greenberg (Chicago, 1960).

Keil, C. F., and Delitzsch F.
1876: *Joshua, Judges and Ruth* (Edinburgh, 1876).

Kerényi, Karl
1972: "The Trickster in relation to Greek Mythology," in Paul Radin, *The Trickster: A Study in American Indian Mythology* (New York, 1972), pp. 173-91.

Kilmer, A. D.
1974: "Symbolic Gestures in Akkadian Contracts from Alalakh and Ugarit," JOAS 94 (1974): 177-83.

Köhler, L.
1909: "Die Adoptionsform von Rt 4[16]," ZAW 29 (1909): 312-14.

Kramer, S. N.
1963: "Cuneiform Studies and the History of Literature: The Sumerian Sacred Marriage Texts," *Proceedings of the American Philosophical Society* 107/6, December 20, 1963, pp. 485-527.

Kraus, F. R.
1971: "Das Altbabylonische Königtum," in *Le Palais et la Royauté*, XIXe Recontre Assyriologique Internationale, 1971 (Paris, appeared 1973), pp. 235-61.

Kretschmar, Georg
1955: "Himmelfahrt und Pfingsten," *Zeitschrift für Kirchengeschichte* 66 (1955): 209-53.

Labuschagne, C. J.
1967: "The Crux in Ruth 4 11," ZAW 79 (1967): 364-67.

Lacheman, E. R.
1937: "Note on Ruth 4 7-8," JBL 56 (1937): 53-56.

Lack, Rémi
1973: *La symbolique du livre d'Isaïe* (Rome, 1973).

Lackenbacher, S.
1971: "Note sur l'*ardat-lilî*," RA 65 (1971): 119-54.

Lambert, W. G., and Millard, A. R.
1969: *Atra-ḫasīs: The Babylonian Story of the Flood* (Oxford, 1969).

Leach, Edmund
1969: *Genesis as Myth and Other Essays* (London, 1969).

Lefèbvre, Gustave
1949: *Romans et contes égyptiens de l'époque pharaonique* (Paris, 1949).

Leggett, Donald A.
1974: *The Levirate and Goel Institutions in the Old Testament, With Special Attention to the Book of Ruth* (Cherry Hill, N.J., 1974).

Leibovici, Marcel
1971: "Génies et Démons en Babylonie," in *Sources Orientales* 8 (Paris, 1971): 85-112.

Leiman, Sid Z.
1976: *The Canonization of Hebrew Scriptures: The Talmudic and Midrashic Evidence* (Hamden, Conn., 1976).

Lerner, M. B.
1971: *ʾaggadat rût ûmidraš rût rabbah* (Jerusalem, 1971).

Levin, Isidore
1967: "Vladimir Propp: An Evaluation on his Seventieth Birthday," *Journal of the Folklore Institute* 1 (1967): 32-49.

Levine, Étan
1973: *The Aramaic Version of Ruth*, Analecta Biblica 58 (Rome, 1973).

1976: "On Intra-familial Institutions of the Bible (Review of Leggett, 1974]," *Biblica* 57 (1976): 554-59.

Lewy, Hildegard
1965: "Anatolia in the Old Assyrian Period," in CAH^2, I, xxiv, VII-X (facs. no.40).

1966: "Assyria c. 2600-1816 B.C.," in CAH^2, I, xxv (facs. no.53).

Lichtheim, Miriam
1975: *Ancient Egyptian Literature* I: *The Old and Middle Kingdoms* (Berkeley, 1975).

1976: *Ancient Egyptian Literature* II: *The New Kingdom* (Berkeley, 1976).

Limet, Henri
1972: "Les Chants épiques sumériens," *Revue belge de philologie et d'histoire (Bruxelles)* 50 (1972): 3-24.

Lipiński, E.
1976: "Le mariage de Ruth," VT 26 (1976): 124-27.

Long, B. O.
1968: *The Problem of Etiological Narrative in the Old Testament* (Berlin, 1968).

Loretz, Oswald
1960: "The Theme of the Ruth Story," CBQ 22 (1960): 391-99.

1964: "Das Hebräische Verbum *LPT*," *Studies Presented to A. Leo Oppenheim* (Chicago, 1964), pp. 155-58.

1974: "Die Umpunktierung von *m'd* zu *mā'ēd* in den Psalmen," UF (1974): 481-84.

1975: "Poetische Abschnitte im Rut-Buch," UF 7 (1975): 580-82.

1977: "Das Verhältnis zwischen Rut-Story und David-Genealogie im Rut-Buch," ZAW 89 (1977): 124-26.

Lorton, David
1976: "Legitimate and Illegitimate Kingship in Egypt," unpublished paper read at the 1976 meeting of the American Oriental Society.

Lüthi, M.
1967: "Parallel Themes in Folk Narrative and in Art Literature," *Journal of the Folklore Institute* 4 (1967): 3-16.

Lys, D.
1971: "Résidence ou Repos? Notule sur Ruth ii 7," VT 21 (1971): 497-501.

McCurley, E. R.
1969: "A Semantic Study of Anatomical Terms in Akkadian, Ugaritic, and Biblical Hebrew" (Dissertation, Dropsie College, 1969).

MacDonald, J.
1975: "Some Distinctive Characteristics of Israelite Spoken Hebrew," BiOr 32 (1975): 162-75.

McIntosh, A. A.
1969: "A Consideration of Hebrew *gʿr*," VT 19 (1969): 471-79.

McKane, W.
1961-62: "Ruth and Boaz," *Transactions of the Glasgow University Oriental Society* 19 (1961-62): 29-40.

Machinist, Peter
1976: "Literature as Politics: The Tukulti-Ninurta Epic and the Bible," CBQ 38 (1976): 455-82.

Malamat, A.
1968: "King Lists of the Old Babylonian Period and Biblical Genealogies," JAOS 88 (1968; *Essays in Memory of E. A. Speiser*): 163-73.

Mandelkern, S.
1971: *Veteris Testamenti Concordantiae* (Jerusalem-Tel Aviv, 1971).

Marcus, D.
1974: "Ugaritic Evidence for "The Almighty/The Grand One"?" *Biblica* 55 (1974): 404-7.

Margulis, Baruch
1970: "A Ugaritic Psalm (RŠ 24.252)," JBL 89 (1970): 292-304.

1972: "The Kôšārôt/kṯrt Patroness-saints of Women," JANES 4 (1972): 52-61.

May, H. G.
1939: "Ruth's visit to the High Place at Bethlehem," JRAS (1939), pp. 75-8.

Meek, Th. J.
1960: "Translating the Hebrew Bible," JBL 79 (1960): 328-35.

Meinhold, A.
1976: "Theologische Schwerpunkte im Buch Ruth und ihr Gewicht für seine Datierung," ThZ 32 (1976): 129-37.

Mélétinski, É.
1972: "L'étude structurale et typologique du conte," in V. Propp, *La Morphologie du Conte* (Paris, 1970), pp. 202-54.

Mendenhall, George E.
1973: *The Tenth Generation: The Origins of the Biblical Tradition* (Baltimore, 1973).

Mettinger, Tryggve N. D.
1976: *King and Messiah: The Civil and Sacral Legitimation of the Israelite Kings*, Coniectania Biblica 8 (Lund, 1976).

Midrash Rabbah: Ruth
Trans. Louis I. Rabinowitz (Soncino, 1939).

Minc, R.
1967: "Le rôle du choeur féminin dans le livre de Ruth," *Bible et vie Chrêtienne* 77 (1967): 71-76.

Montet, Pierre
1964: *Eternal Egypt* (New York, 1964).

Moor, J. C. de
1969: "Ugaritic *hm*--Never 'Behold,'" UF 1 (1969): 201-2.

1971: *Seasonal Pattern in the Ugaritic Myth of Ba^{c}lu*, AOAT 16 (Neukirchen-Vluyn, 1971).

Moren, S. M.
1977: "A Lost 'Omen' Tablet," JCS 29 (1977): 65-72.

Myers, Jacob M.
1955: *The Linguistic and Literary Form of the Book of Ruth* (Leiden, 1955).

1965b: *I Chronicles*, AB 12 (Garden City, N.Y., 1965).

1965b: *II Chronicles*, AB 13 (Garden City, N.Y., 1965).

Nathhorst, Berthel
1969: *Formal or Structural Studies of Traditional Tales*, Stockholm Studies in Comparative Literature 9 (Stockholm, 1969).

Neufeld, Ephraim
1944: *Ancient Hebrew Marriage Laws* (London, 1944).

Nims, Charles F.
1976: Review of Cyril Aldred, *Akhenaten and Nefertiti* (New York, 1973), JNES 35 (1976): 279-81.

Noth, Martin
1928: *Die Israelitischen Personennamen im Rahmen der gemeinsemitischen Namengebung* (Stuttgart, 1928).

Nötscher, F.
1953: "Zum emphatischen Lamed," VT 3 (1953): 372-80.

Olrik, Axel
1909: "Epische Gesetze der Volksdichtung," *Zeitschrift für Deutsches Altertum* 51 (1909): 1-12. Translated as "Epic Laws of Folk Narrative," in Dundes, 1965: 129-41.

Onians, R. B.
1954: *The Origins of European Thought* 2nd ed. (Cambridge, 1954).

Oxford Classical Dictionary
Ed. N. G. L. Hammond and H. H. Scullard 2nd ed. (Oxford, 1970).

Page, S.
1968: "The Tablets from Tell Al-Rimah 1967: A Preliminary Report," *Iraq* 30 (1968): 87-97.

Pardee, Dennis
1975: "The Preposition in Ugaritic," UF 7 (1975): 329-78.

Parker, S. B.
1976: "The Marriage Blessing in Israelite and Ugaritic Literature," JBL 95 (1976): 23-30.

Patai, Raphael
1964: "Lilith," *Journal of American Folklore* 77 (1964): 295-314.

Paul, Shalom M.
1969: "Exod. 21:10: A Threefold Maintenance Clause," JNES 28 (1969): 48-53.

Peters, N.
1914: Review of Gunkel, 1913 *Theologische Rundschau* 13 (1914): 449.

Pope, Marvin H.
1965: *Job*, AB (Garden City, N.Y., 1965).

Porten, Bezalel
1976: "Structure, Style, and Theme of the Scroll of Ruth," Association for Jewish Studies *Newsletter* 17 (1976): 15-16.

Posener, Georges
1960: *De la Divinité du Pharaon*, Cahiers de la Société Asiatique 15 (Paris, 1960).

Propp, Vladimir
1968: *Morphology of the Folktale*, 2nd ed., revised and edited with a preface by L. A. Wagner; new introduction by A. Dundes (Austin, 1968).

Rad, Gerhard von
1962: *Old Testament Theology* I: *The Theology of Israel's Historical Tradition* (London, 1962).

Rahlfs, Alfred
1922: *Das Buch Ruth griechisch, als Probe einer kritischen Handausgabe der Septuaginta* (Stuttgart, 1922).

Rahmani, Y.
1973: Review of Eric M. Meyers, *Jewish Ossuaries: Reburial and Re-Birth*, in IEJ 23 (1973): 121-26.

Rauber, D. F.
1970: "Literary Values in the Bible: The Book of Ruth," JBL 89 (1970): 27-37.

Rinaldi, G.
1963: "L'Ostracon di Samaria C. 1101," *Bibbia et Oriente* 6 (1963): 117-18.

1967: "Nota," *Bibbia et Oriente* 9 (1967): 118.

Roberts, J. J. M.
1971: "The Hand of Yahweh," VT 21 (1971): 244-51.

1976: "Myth *Versus* History: Relaying the Comparative Foundations," CBQ 38 (1976): 1-13.

Robertson, Edward
1949-50: "The Plot of the Book of Ruth," *The Bulletin of the John Rylands Library. Manchester* 32 (1949-50): 207-28.

Rogerson, J. W.
1974: *Myth in Old Testament Interpretation*, BZAW 134 (Berlin, 1974).

Rowley, H. H.
1965: *The Servant of the Lord and other Essays on the Old Testament*, 2nd ed. (Oxford, 1965).

Rudolph, Wilhelm
1955: *Chronikbücher, Handbuch zum Alten Testament*, Hg, von O. Eissfeldt 1/21 (Tübingen, 1955).

1962: *Das Buch Ruth, Das Hohe Lied, Die Klagelieder, Kommentar zum Alten Testament* XVII 2nd ed. (Mohn, 1962), pp. 23-72.

Sasson, J. M.
1972: "Numbers 5 and the 'Waters of Judgement,'" BZ 16 (1972): 249-51.

1976: "Divine Providence or Human Plan," review of Campbell (1975), *Interpretation* 30 (1976): 415-19.

Scholes, Robert
1974: *Structuralism in Literature* (New Haven, 1974).

Schorr, M.
1913: *Urkunden des altbabylonischen Zivil- und Prozessrechts* (Leipzig, 1913).

Schulz, A.
1926: *Das Buch der Richter und das Buch Ruth*, in HSAT 2 (1926).

Segert, S.
1957: "Vorarbeiten zur hebräischen Metrik, III: zum Problem der metrischen Elemente im Buche Ruth," *Archiv Orientální* 25 (1957): 190-200.

Selms, A. van
1954: *Marriage and Family Life in Ugaritic Literature* (London, 1954).

Seux, M. J.
1967: *Epithètes royales akkadiennes et sumériennes* (Paris, 1967).

Shearman, S. L., and Curtis, J. B.
1969: "Divine-Human Conflicts in the Old Testament," JNES 28 (1969): 231-42.

Sheehan, John F. X.
1973: "The Word of God as Myth: The Book of Ruth," in *Word in the World, Essays in Honor of Frederick L. Moriarty, S.J.* (Weston College, 1973), pp. 35-46.

Sheppard, H. W.
1918: "Ruth iii:13b: An Explanation of B's inserted Words," JTS 19 (1918): 277.

Shibayama, S.
1966: "Notes on *Yārad* and *ʿĀlāh:* Hints on Translating," JBR 34 (1966): 358-62.

Sjöberg, Åke W.
1973: "Die göttliche Abstammung der sumerisch-babylonischen Herrscher," *Orientalia Suecana* 21 (1972): 87-112.

Sjöberg, Åke W. and Bergmann, E.
1969: *The Collection of the Sumerian Temple Hymns, Texts from Cuneiform Sources* 3 (Locust Valley, N.Y., 1969).

Skinner, J.
1930: *Genesis,* ICC 2nd ed. (Edinburgh, 1930).

Smith, L. P.
1953: "Introduction and Exegesis of the Book of Ruth," IB (Nashville, 1953).

Soden, W. von
1957a: "Zum akkadischen Wörterbuch," *Orientalia* 26 (1957): 127-38.

1957b: "Zu einigen altbabylonischen Dichtungen," *Orientalia* 26 (1957): 306-20.

1957-58: "Die Hebamme in Babylonien und Assyrien," AfO 18 (1957-58): 119-21.

Sollberger, Edmond (and Kupper, Jean-Robert)
1971: *Inscriptions royales sumériennes et akkadiennes,* Littératures anciennes du Proche-Orient (Paris, 1971).

Speiser, E. A.
1940: "Of Shoes and Shekels," BASOR 77 (1940): 15-20.

Sperber, Alexander
1968: *The Bible in Aramaic* IVa: the Hagiographa (Leiden, 1968).

Staples, W. E.
1937: "The Book of Ruth," AJSL 53 (1937): 145-57.

1938: "Notes on Ruth 2:20 and 3:12," AJSL 54 (1938): 62-65.

Stark, Jürgen Kurt
1971: *Personal Names in Palmyrene Inscriptions* (Oxford, 1971).

Stinespring, W. F.
1944: "Note on Ruth 2:19." JNES 3 (1944): 101.

Stover, Robert
1967: "Great Man Theory of History," in the *Encyclopedia of Philosophy* III (New York, 1967): 378-82.

Thompson, Thomas L.
1974: *The Historicity of the Patriarchal Narratives*, BZAW 133 (Berlin, 1974).

Thompson, Thomas and Dorothy
1968: "Some Legal Problems in the Book of Ruth," VT 18 (1968): 79-99.

Thornhill, Raymond
1953: "The Greek Text of the Book of Ruth: A Grouping of Manuscripts according to Origen's Hexapla," VT 3 (1953): 236-49.

Tomkins, H. G.
1885: "The Name Beth-lehem," PEQ (1885), p. 112.

Trible, Phyllis
1976: "Two Women in a Man's World: A Reading of the Book of Ruth," *Soundings* 49 (1976): 251-79.

Tucker, G. M.
1966: "Witnesses and 'Dates' In Israelite Contracts," CBQ 28 (1966): 43-45.

Vaux, Roland de
1961: *Ancient Israel: Its Life and Institutions*, trans. J. McHugh (London, 1961).

1971: *Histoire ancienne d'Israël*, I (Paris, 1971).

Veenhof, K. R.
1973: "Een Ammonieische inscriptie," *Phoenix* 19 (1973): 299-301.

Vellas, B. M.
1954: "The Book of Ruth and its Purpose," *Theologia (Athens)* 25 (1954): 201-10.

Vermeule, C.
1964: "Greek, Etruscan and Roman Sculptures in the Museum of Fine Arts, Boston," AJA 68 (1964): 323-41.

Vesco, J.-L.
1967: "La date du livre de Ruth," RB 74 (1967): 235-47.

Vincent, Albert
1952: *Le Livre des Juges/Le Livre de Ruth*, BJ (Paris, 1952).

Volz, P.
1901: Review of D. W. Nowack, *Richter-Ruth* (HAT I/4, 1900), in *Theologische Literaturzeitung* 26 (1901): 348-49.

Vriezen, Th. C.
1948: "Two Old Cruces," OTS 5 (1948): 80-88.

Waard, Jan de
1973: "Translation Techniques Used by the Greed Translators of Ruth," *Biblica* 54 (1973): 499-515.

Wambacq, B. N.
1964: "Le mariage de Ruth," *Studi e testi* 231 (1964; *Mélanges Tisserant I*): 449-59.

Wang, Betty
1965: "Folksongs as Regulators of Politics," in Dundes (1965: 308-13).

Watters, William R.
1976: *Formula Criticism and the Poetry of the Old Testament* (BZAW, 138; Berlin, 1976).

Weinfeld, Moshe
1972: "Ruth, Book of," *Encyclopaedia Judaica* (Jerusalem, 1972).

Weiss, David Halivini
1964: "The Use of *qnh* in Connection with Marriage," HThR 57 (1964): 244-48.

Wellhausen, J.
1885: *Prolegomena to the History of Israel*, trans. Black and McKenzie (Edinburgh, 1885).

Westbrook, Raymond
1971: "Redemption of Land," *Israel Law Review* 6 (1971): 367-75.

Wildung, Dietrich
1977: *Egyptian Saints: Deification in Pharaonic Egypt*, Hagop Kevorkian Series on Near Eastern Art and Civilization (New York, 1977).

Wilson, R. W.
1975: "The Old Testament Genealogies in Recent Research," JBL 94 (1975): 169-89.

Wilson, William A.
1976: *Folklore and Nationalism in Modern Finland* (Bloomington, Ind., 1976).

Winckler, Hugo
1902: "Rut," *Altorientalische Forschungen* 3 (1902): 65-78.

Witzenrath, Hagia Hildegard
1975: *Das Buch Rut: eine literaturwissenschaftliche Untersuchung*, Studien zum Alten und Neuen Testament 40 (Munich, 1975).

Wolfenson, Louis B.
1911: "The Character, Contents, and Date of Ruth," AJSL 27 (1911): 285-300.

1924: "Implications of the Place of the Book of Ruth in Editions, Manuscripts, and Canon of the Old Testament," HUCA 1 (1924): 151-78.

Wolff, H. W.
1974: *Hosea*, Hermeneia Series (Philadelphia, 1974).

Würthwein, E.
1969: *Die Fünf Megilloth*, HAT I, 18 (1969).

Yamauchi, Edwin
1965: "Aramaic Magic Bowls," JAOS 85 (1965): 511-23.

Yeivin, S.
1959: "Jachin and Boaz," PEQ 91 (1959): 6-22.

Zewit, Ziony
1975: "The So-called Interchangeability of the Prepositions *b*, *l*, and *m(n)* in Northwest Semitic," JANES 7 (1975): 103-12.

Zijl, Peter J. van
1972: *Baal: A Study of Texts in Connexion with Baal in the Ugaritic Epics* AOAT 10 (Neukirchen-Vluyn, 1972).

Zlotowitz, Meir
1976: *The Book of Ruth/Megillas Ruth. A New Translation with a Commentary Anthologized from Talmudic, Midrashic and Rabbinic Sources*, With "An Overview/ Ruth and the Seeds of Mashiach" by Nosson Scherman (New York, 1976).

Zyl, A. H. van
1960: *The Moabites* (Leiden, 1960).

INDEXES

INDEX TO BIBLICAL REFERENCES

Genesis

2:4a, 179
3:16, 26
4:17-24, 181
5:3-31, 181
11:10-26, 181
12:1-9, 52
12:10, 16
12:10-20, 231
15:14, 26
16, 21
19, 16
19:30-38, 247
20, 231
20:11, 94
20-21, 17
21:33, 53
22, 220
22:21, 18
23, 227; 231
23:3, 21
23:10, 107
23:17-20, 149
23:18, 107
24:5, 85
24:12, 45
24:27, 60; 162
24:28, 23
24:30, 80
24:54, 90
25:10, 120
25:29-34, 231
26, 17
26:1-11, 231
26:3, 16
26:9, 94
26:12, 97
27, 231
29:22-26, 231
29:34, 110
30:3-8, 170
30:25-34, 231
31:14-16, 123
31:15, 51
31:19, 231
31:34-35, 231
31:48, 110
32:18, 46
33:6, 100
34, 231
35:17, 173
35:19, 19; 154
36, 181
36:26, 18
36:35, 16

Genesis

37:2a, 179
37:15, 80
37-48, 249
38, 28; 129; 132; 145; 232; 242
38:1, 42
38:2, 42
38:8, 126; 156
38:11, 23
38:28, 173
38:29, 187
46, 181
46:21, 18
47:4, 16
48:5-12, 170
48:7, 19
48:20, 151
49:28, 147
50:23, 170

Exodus

1:14, 33
1:15-22, 173
2:1, 161
2:10, 171
6:19, 179
9:3, 26
11:4, 74
12:29, 74
13:4, 26
14:8, 26
21:8, 51
21:10, 26; 161
32:20, 65
34:16, 161

Leviticus

15:33, 64
18:16, 127; 133
19:9, 42
20:21, 127; 133
21:3, 24
22:12, 24
22:13, 23
23:22, 42
25, 138-39
25:14-15, 120
25:25, 114
25:25-28, 110
25:54, 26
27:4-7, 98
27:10, 141
27:24, 120
27:33, 141

Numbers

1:7, 188
11:12, 172
13:4-15, 181
13:6, 19
13:7, 159
21:20, 16
22:9, 101
22:25, 79
26:5-51, 181
27:8-11, 112
30:7, 24
30:17, 23
31:36, 26
33:3, 26

Deuteronomy

2:10, 141
2:12, 141
2:20, 141
3:11, 20

Deuteronomy
4:7, 47
4:44, 147
6:1, 147
8:2, 35
8:3, 35
8:16, 35
15:12, 110
22:21, 23
23:1, 81
23:4-5, 137
23:4-8, 246
24:2, 24
24:4, 43
24:5, 26
24:19, 42
25:128; 132; 145
25:5, 28; 132
25:5-6, 125
25:5-10, 28; 144
25:6, 137; 151
25:7, 28; 107
25:8, 107
25:10, 165
32:3, 176
34:6, 16

Joshua
3:9, 55
7:8, 43
9:4, 142
9:16, 43
11:10, 141
13:12, 20
14:15, 141
15:15, 141
19:15, 15
23:1, 43
24:20, 43
24:22, 149

Judges
1:10, 141
1:11, 141
1:23:141
2:15, 26
3:2, 141
3:8, 110
4:21, 74
6:19, 57
8:31ff., 17
9:28, 47
11:34, 80
11:36, 43
12:8, 15
12:8-10, 15; 40
13:17, 100
16:3, 74
16:29, 78
18:11, 40
18:25, 33
19:2, 23
19:3, 23
19:6, 90
19:23, 43
21:23, 20

1 Samuel
1:8, 167
2:5, 167
4:5, 32
4:20, 173
9:9, 141; 143
9:12, 181
10:2, 19
12:3, 35

1 Samuel
12:15, 26
14:38, 55
16:22, 217
17:17, 56; 57
18:6-7, 32
20:21, 92
20:29, 40
21:2, 105
21:3, 105
22:3ff., 247
24:4, 74
25:18, 56
25:42, 85
30:6, 115
30:13, 46

2 Samuel
1:16, 35
2:5, 60
4:3, 16
4:4, 42; 172
7, 237
9-20, 249
12:20, 67
12:25, 173; 174
13:28, 73
17:25, 42
17:28, 56
19:31, 43
20:1, 41
23:36, 159

1 Kings
1:45, 32
3:20, 74; 170
5:1, 177
7:21, 41
8:66, 73
14:21, 248
17:20, 35
20:39, 26
21:11, 107
22:23, 115

2 Kings
4:14, 112
5:23, 68
6:8, 105
7:1, 98
7:1-20, 64
7:16-18, 98
8:1, 16
8:1-6, 112
10:1, 172
10:5, 172
10:11, 83
11, 243
11:9, 73
14:27, 115

Isaiah
3:9, 35
3:22, 68
4:1, 81
5:8, 138
8:1, 106
8:3, 106
8:16, 146
8:20, 146
9:5, 177
14:26, 147
16:11, 24
25:10, 26
34:4, 77
43:7, 176

Isaiah
47:2, 70
48:1, 176
48:19, 151
49:21, 177
49:23, 172
51:19, 100
56:5, 151
64:11, 35

Jeremiah
3:1, 24
8:3, 20
14:7, 35
20:15, 173
31:20, 24
32:7, 147
32:7-8, 141
32:8, 118
32:8-15, 138-39
32:9, 120
34:14, 110
37:13, 41
43:12, 26
44:19, 167
44:26, 165; 176
49:9, 136
49:19, 107

Ezekiel
16:8-13, 66; 81
16:9, 67
40:1, 43

Hosea
3:2, 98; 123
3:3, 24
5:5, 35
7:10, 35
9:1, 97

Joel
1:8, 26
2:2, 31
2:22, 155

Amos
7:2, 100
7:5, 100

Obadiah
13, 87

Micah
1:5, 47; 100
2:2, 138
5:1, 19
6:3, 35
6:8, 106

Nahum
3:4, 109

Zechariah
14:9, 41

Malachi
3:2, 167
3:17, 177

Psalms
2, 237
9:10, 39
10:1, 39
15:3, 39
19:5, 26

Psalms

19:8, 166
23:3, 166
31:22, 162
38:12, 39
44:10, 26
45:7, 237
45:17, 151
55:23, 95
66:20, 162
69:9, 51
73:25, 100
76:4, 78
89, 237
99:6, 176
102:26, 141
110, 237
132, 247

Job

3:3, 78
6:18, 78
13:18, 107
15:31, 141
19:14, 39
19:15, 51
19:21, 26
20:18, 141
21:7-8, 155
27:2, 34
28:17, 141
29:7, 107
34:20, 74
42:11, 141

Proverbs

7:4, 39
7:6-23, 26
11:2, 106
15:15, 73
18:24, 28
24:7, 107
25:13, 166
31:3, 155
31:10-31, 88
31:23, 107

Ruth

1:1, 14
1:2, 16; 149; 225
1:3, 20; 225
1:4, 52; 149
1:5, 20; 58; 149; 170; 224; 225
1:6, 21; 113; 221; 224
1:6a, 16
1:6b, 16
1:8, 8; 23; 60; 221; 225
1:8-9, 23
1:9, 87; 221; 224; 225
1:10, 8
1:10-13, 24
1:11, 129
1:11-13, 225
1:12, 225
1:13, 34; 36; 221; 223; 244
1:14, 8; 27; 28; 50; 224; 225
1:15, 28
1:15-17, 28
1:16, 62; 224
1:16-17, 119; 222
1:17, 221
1:18, 31
1:19, 22
1:19b, 32
1:19-22, 217
1:20, 8; 34; 221; 225

Ruth
1:20-21, 32; 162; 222
1:21, 33; 34; 58; 101; 166; 221; 224; 225
1:22, 16; 36; 115
2:1, 8; 38; 41; 43; 87
2:1-22, 222
2:2, 42; 43; 59; 101
2:3, 43; 221
2:4, 45; 64; 104; 221; 223
2:5, 46; 56; 94
2:6, 16; 36
2:6-7, 47; 217
2:7, 10; 56; 101
2:8, 28; 80; 105; 224
2:8-9, 49
2:9, 50; 55
2:10, 43; 51; 94; 224; 225
2:11, 8; 23; 64; 224
2:11-12, 52
2:12, 81; 221; 224
2:13, 43; 52; 119
2:14, 8; 10; 44; 223
2:14-18a, 54
2:15, 44; 47
2:15-16, 56
2:16, 55; 223
2:17, 57; 96; 97
2:18, 9; 64
2:18b-22, 217
2:18b-23, 99
2:19, 58; 94; 101; 224
2:20, 29; 43; 60; 83; 92; 163; 221; 223; 224
2:21, 9; 28; 50; 63
2:21-22, 61
2:21-23, 100
2:22, 9; 61; 62; 224
2:23, 9; 28; 50; 64; 102; 130; 131; 219; 224
3:1, 24; 224
3:1-2, 63
3:1-13, 222
3:2, 39; 130
3:3, 8; 9; 64; 68; 163; 245
3:4, 8; 69-71; 245
3:5, 8
3:6-7, 72
3:7, 69
3:8, 69; 70; 74; 95; 104
3:9, 52; 80; 81; 86; 100; 101; 114; 119; 163; 225
3:10, 23; 60; 127; 128; 142; 221; 229
3:10-13, 55; 82; 148
3:11, 80; 90; 151; 217; 223
3:11-13, 92
3:12, 8; 163
3:12-13, 88; 90
3:13, 8; 91; 163; 221; 223
3:14, 8; 9; 69; 70; 93; 95; 224
3:15, 8; 9; 10; 68; 95; 104
3:15e, 210
3:16, 9; 100
3:16-18, 99; 217
3:17, 8; 58; 71; 98; 210
3:18, 105; 221; 223; 224
4, 228
4:1, 8; 64; 87; 104; 221; 224
4:2, 107
4:3, 16; 36; 40; 42; 108-10; 217
4:3-4, 91; 107; 148
4:4, xii; 8; 115; 148; 153; 226; 228
4:4-5, 124
4:5, 8; 10; 28; 65; 67; 90; 91; 119; 123; 126; 129; 137; 156; 228

Ruth
4:6, 8; 90; 136; 226; 228
4:7, 140; 141; 226; 242; 244
4:7-8, 223
4:8, 147; 226
4:9, 110; 129; 153; 225; 228
4:9-10, 123; 124; 148
4:10, 17; 87; 122; 134; 163; 182
4:11, 19; 153; 156; 164; 165; 166; 221; 225
4:11-12, 151; 180; 222; 240
4:11-13, 232
4:12, 126; 158; 169; 180; 181; 221
4:13, 221
4:13-15, 161; 168; 182
4:13-17, 91
4:14, 32; 92; 163; 165; 166; 175; 183; 221
4:14c, 182
4:14-15, 162; 217
4:14-17, 150; 163
4:15, 91; 224
4:16, 21; 172; 224; 235
4:16-17, 168; 174; 182; 232; 237-40
4:16-18, 223, 232
4:17, 173, 175
4:17a, 165
4:17c, 165
4:17c-22, 172
4:18, 8
4:18-22, 156; 158; 170; 178; 182; 184; 232; 243
4:19b-22, 188
4:21, 150
4:22, 8; 232

Canticles
3:4, 23
5:4, 24
5:6, 26
6:12, 189
7:2, 189
7:3, 65
8:2, 23

Ecclesiastes
2:24, 26
9:4, 85
9:7, 73

Lamentations
1:11, 166
1:16, 166
1:19, 166

Esther
2:7, 172
2:12, 66
2:14, 176
2:15, 43

Daniel
2:6, 25
2:9, 25
4:24, 25
8:13, 105
10:3, 66
10:6, 69
11:44, 26

Nehemiah
1:3, 20
13:5, 141

1 Chronicles
1:46, 16
2:3-9, 19
2:5-15, 184
2:12-13a, 157; 188
2:18, 19
2:19, 19
2:36-46, 188
2:50, 19
3:5, 169
3:22, 159
4:3-4, 19
4:40, 141
5:30-36, 188
5:37-40, 188
8:8, 16
8:28, 179
9:20, 141
9:34, 179

2 Chronicles
3:17, 41
13:3, 85
22-23, 243
23:8, 73
30:12, 26

Tobit
3:7-9, 137

Judith
10:3, 66

2 Maccabees
7:27, 172

Matthew
1:2-16, 181
1:5, 169; 190
1:6, 190
22:23-38, 137
25:1-13, 74

Mark
12:18-23, 137

Luke
1:57-66, 173
2:21, 174
3:23-38, 181
20:27-33, 137

1 Corinthians
7:1-11, 26

CITATION OF SCHOLARS

Aarne, A., 198
Aharoni, Y., 19
Albertz, R., 70
Albright, W. F., 41
Alster, B., 215
Amsler, S., 131
Andersen, F.I., 23, 176
Ap-Thomas, D. R., 108-9; 110; 175; 180; 246
Astour, M. C., 41; 248
Auerbach, E., 11; 218ff

Bachrach, Y., 11
Bailey, L. R., 239
Baillet, M., 9
Barsotti, D., 11
Barta, W., 238
Bascom, W. R., 225; 228
Bauer, H., 41
Beattie, D.R.G., 11; 48; 112; 122; 128; 129; 138
Beauchamp, P., 199
Beckman, G., 234
Benito, C. A., 235
Benz, F. L., 18; 19; 33; 177; 183; 187; 189
Bergmann, E., 235; 236
Bertholet, A., 51; 75; 128; 151
Bertman, S., 22
Bertram, G., 34
Bewer, J. A., 127; 128; 131; 163
Biggs, R. D., 26
Boehmer, R. M., 239
Boling, R. G., 39
Bottéro, J., 57, 76
Brichto, H. C., 24; 27; 31; 81; 107; 110; 111; 117; 128; 137; 142; 144; 154; 160; 243
Bright, J., 165
Brinkman, J. A., 236
Brongers, H. A., 86
Bruppacher, H., 21
Burrows, M., 111; 112; 123

Campbell, E. F., Jr., 9; 11; *passim* in commentary; 198; 214; 222; 225; 241; 244; 245; 247; 249
Caquot, A., 77
Carmichael, C. M., 71; 144; 242
Casanowicz, I. M., 226
Caspari, W., 112
Cassel, P., 41; 75
Cheyne, T. K., 41; 46
Coffin, T. P., 250
Cohen, Ch., 123

Conrad, J., 107
Cook, S. A., 41
Cooke, G. A., 175
Crenshaw, R., 215
Crook, M. B., 243
Cross, F. M., Jr., 9; 78
Culley, R. C., 214
Curtis, E. L., 188
Curtis, J. B., 94; 247; 248

Dahood, M., 27; 35; 54; 70; 82; 100
Dalman, G., 56
Daube, D., 138
David, M., 129
Delitzsch, F., 121; 129
Deroy, L., 144
Dhorme, E., 24; 73
Dietrich, M., 33
Dijk, J. van, 235
Dombrowski, B. W., 146
Dommershausen, W., 224
Donner, H., 38
Dorson, R. M., 249; 250
Douglas, M., 199
Driver, G. R., 52; 75; 77
Driver, S. R., 133; 151
Dundes, A., 199; 214

Edzard, D. O., 236
Ehrlich, A. B., 37; 75
Eissfeldt, O., 77; 152; 175; 179; 180; 182; 246
Eliade, M., 240
Emerton, J. A., 51; 199
Epstein, L. M., 21

Falkenstein, A., 67
Falnes, O. J., 250
Fernandez, J. W., 250
Fichtner, J., 158
Fohrer, G., 171
Fraine, J. de, 41; 84
Frankena, R., 102
Frazer, J., 198
Freedman, D. N., 27; 37; 72
Friedrich, J., 73
Frye, N., 198; 215

Galland, C., 216
Gautier, L., 249
Gelb, I. J., 57
Gerleman, G., 10; 92; 106; 137; 171; 175; 247; 249
Ginsberg, H. L., 34
Ginzberg, L., 10; 20; 75
Gitay, Y., 37; 101
Glanzman, G. S., 18; 241; 244
Glueck, N., 23; 60
Goethe, J. W. von., 196
Goettsberger, J., 185
Goetze, A., 234
Gordis, R., 109; 110; 116-18; 125; 126; 141; 246
Gordon, C. H., 33; 35; 88; 121; 122; 127; 130; 237
Gray, G. B., 17; 244
Gray, J., 122; 152
Grayson, A. K., 52
Greenberg, M., 92
Greengus, S., 67
Greimas, A. J., 200; 208; 215
Gressmann, H., 48
Grønbaek, J. H., 247
Gröndahl, F., 17; 18; 19; 283; 187
Gunkel, H., 97; 175; 198; 222; 245; 248

Hadas, M., 250
Halperin, D. J., 45
Hals, R. M., 44; 154; 249
Hartmann, D., 10
Heide, A. van der, 8
Heltzer, M. L., 138
Herder, J. G. van, 244
Hoffner, H. A., Jr., 56; 171; 234
Hoftijzer, J., 24; 64
Horst, F., 140
Huffmon, H. B., 17; 19; 33; 39; 190
Hulst, A. R., 24
Humbert, P., 23; 31; 51; 56; 58; 66; 84; 97; 101; 123; 154; 155; 243; 249
Hurvitz, A., 144, 244

Irvin, D., 174
Ishida, T., 236

Jacobsen, T., 235; 236; 239
Jastrow, M., 78; 79
Jenni, E., 108; 119
Jepsen, A., 53; 112; 172
Jeremias, A., 68
Jeremias, J., 74; 123; 131
Johnson, M. D., 169; 178; 190
Jolles, A., 198
Joüon, P., *passim* in commentary; 223; 227
Jung, C., 198

Kamenetsky, C., 250
Kaufmann, Y., 35
Keil, C. F., 121; 129
Keller, C. A., 162
Kerényi, K., 231
Kilmer, A. D., 116
Klostermann, E., 41
Köhler, L., 120; 171
Kosmala, H., 39
Kramer, S. N., 67
Kraus, F. R., 236
Kretschmar, G., 13

Labuschagne, C. J., 35; 155-56; 165; 166
Lacheman, E. R., 144
Lack, R., 199
Lackenbacher, S., 76
Lambert, W. G., 234
Lamparter, H., 22
Leach, E., 170; 199
Lefèbvre, G., 227
Leggett, D. A., 242
Leibovici, M., 76
Leiman, S., 11
Lerner, M. B., 10
Levin, I., 201
Levine, E., 10; 16; *passim* in commentary
Leeuwen, C. van, 146; 149
Lewy, H., 15
Lichtheim, M., 56; 227; 234
Limet, H., 215
Lipiński, E., 92; 108; 110; 121-22
Long, B. O., 158-59; 171; 174
Loretz, O., 27; 51; 78-79; 131; 156; 178; 241; 249
Lorton, D., 238
Lüthi, M., 198
Lys, D., 48

MacDonald, J., 26; 60; 64; 92

Machinist, P., 236
Malamat, A., 183
Marcus, D., 27
Margulis, B., 34; 234
Martin-Achard, R., 51
May, H. G., 97-98; 248
McCurley, E. R., 73; 170
McIntosh, A. A., 57
McKane, W., 111; 128; 130
Meek, Th. J., 61; 84
Meinhold, A., 247
Mélétinski, E., 199; 200
Mendenhall, G. E., 21
Mettinger, T.N.D., 237; 238
Milik, J. T., 9
Minc, R., 162
Montet, P., 237
Moor, J. C. De, 38; 65; 100
Moren, S. M., 77
Murray, G., 198
Myers, J. M., 15; *passim* in commentary; 222; 223; 245

Nathhorst, B., 199
Neufeld, E., 112; 127
Noth, M., 17; 41; 187; 189
Nötscher, F., 54

Onians, R. B., 171
Orlik, A., 220

Paine, Th., 196
Parker, S. B., 152-53; 154; 156; 158; 181
Peters, N., 175
Pope, M. H., 34; 141
Porten, B., 60; 222; 242
Posener, G., 238
Propp, V., xiii; 199; 200; *passim* in the interpretation

Rad, G. von, 249
Radin, P., 231
Rahlfs, A., 9
Rahmani, Y., 31
Rank, O., 198
Rauber, D. F., 224-25
Renan, E., 196
Richter, W., 222
Ringgren, K.V.H., 108
Roberts, J.J.M., 26; 220
Robertson, E., 98
Rogerson, J. W., 199
Röllig, W., 38
Rowley, H. H., 61; 86; 112; 113; 119; 126; 127; 132; 137; 160; 179-80; 241; 243; 246; 247; 248
Rudolph, W., 8; *passim* in commentary; 249

Saley, R. J., 78
Sasson, J. M., 33; 214; 221; 230
Scholes, R., 198; 199; 200
Schorr, M., 45
Schottroff, W., 118
Schulz, A., 175; 222
Scott, R.B.Y., 41
Seebass, H., 85
Segert, S., 222
Selms, A. van, 234; 237
Shearman, S. L., 94; 247; 248
Sheehan, J.F.X., 16; 248
Sheppard, H. W., 93
Shibayama, S., 104
Sjöberg, Å. W., 235; 236

Skinner, J., 23; 119
Smith, L. P., 27; 46; 156; 179; 186
Soden, W. von, 234; 236
Sollberger, E., 236; 239
Souriau, É., 200
Speiser, E. A., 144
Staples, W. E., 61; 88; 97-98; 248
Stark, J. K., 18; 19
Stinespring, W. F., 58
Stolz, F., 24; 162
Stover, R., 250

Thompson, D. I., 129; 131; 144
Thompson, S., 198
Thompson, Th. L., 17; 129; 131; 144
Thornhill, R., 9
Tomkins, H. G., 15
Trible, P., 224-25; 249
Tucker, G. M., 146; 149

Vaux, R. De, 9; 19; 34; 40; 76; 107; 120; 169; 170
Veenhof, K. R., 189
Vellas, B. M., 242
Vermeule, C., 80
Vesco, J.-L. 154; 241; 242
Vetter, D., 136
Vincent, A., 8
Volz, P., 245
Vriezen, C., 121

Waard, J. De, 9; 87
Wallis, G., 27
Wang, B., 250
Wanke, G., 132
Watters, W. R., 222
Weinfeld, M., 242; 244
Weippert, M., 34
Weiss, D. H., 123
Wellhausen, J., 185; 243
Westbrook, R., 109; 111
Westermann, C., 70; 166
Wildberger, H., 20; 85; 172
Wildung, D., 238; 239
Wilson, R. W., 183; 250
Winckler, H., 248
Witzenrath, H. H., 155; 164; 165; 170; 173; 175; 176; 178; 180; 185; 197; 222; 241; 242; 244; 246; 249
Wolfenson, L. B., 11-12; 131
Wolff, H. W., 53; 98
Woude, A. S. van der, 81; 131-32; 133; 165
Würthwein, E., 152

Yamauchi, E., 77
Yeivin, S., 41

Zijl, P. J. van, 100
Zlotowitz, M., 11
Zobel, H. -J., 70; 116
Zyl, A. H. van, 15; 29-30

SUBJECT INDEX

Abimelech, 17; 231
Abishag, 157
Adad-apla-iddina, 237
Adaption, 170-71
Age of protagonist, 218
ʾ*almānāh* (widow), 20; 123-24; 132-33; 145
ʾ*āmāh* (handmaid), 80-81; 192-93; 230
Amenemhet I, 250
Amenemope, 56
Anat, 17; 29
Appu, 73
Aqhat, 3; 33; 215
Aramaism, 25; 32-33
Arslan Tash, 77-78
Asenath, 169
Asherah, 18
Assurbanipal, 236
Assyrian Law code, 123
Athalia, 243
Atrahasis, 234

Bethlehem (Judah), 15; *passim*
Bethlehem (Zebulun), 15
Bezalel, 19
Boaz, etymology of, 40-41

Caleb, 19
Canon, *Ruth* in, 11-12
Chelubai, 19
Chemosh, 29; 247
Chilion (etymology), 19
Context: cultural, 227-32; political, 232-40; social, 225-27

Danel, 33
David, 154; 157; 179; 231; 232; 240; 250-51
Demons, 76
Deutero-Isaiah, 246
Djoser, 250
Doomed Prince, The, 215; 227; 234
Dumuzi, 67

Eanatum, 236; 239
Edom, 19; 77
Eglon, 15; 21
Ehud, 15
Eleusis myth, 248
Elimelech: etymology of, 17; 92; land of, 110-15
Enki and the World Order, 235
Enmerkar, 250
Entemena, 236

Ephraim, 169
Ephron, 231
Esarhaddon, 236
Esau, 231
ʾēšet-ḥayil, 87; 192-93; 230
Etana, 215

Famine, 15
Festivals, 75
Folktale, 215ff
Formalism, 199ff

Genre, literary, 197ff
gēr, 16
geʾullāh/gōʾēl, 60-61; 82-84; 91-92; 114; 136-40; 162-64; 208; 209; 211; 213; 217; 229
Gilgamesh, 215; 250
Gulšes, 234

'Hand of God,' 26-27
Harvest, 130-31; 229
Hathor, 234
ḥesed, 23
Hezron, 19
Horus and Seth, 215
Hur, 19
Hurriya, 152

Ibn-Ezra, 11; 43; 46
Ibzan (Bethlehem), 15; 40
Idioms in *Ruth*, 223; 244
Inanna (Ishtar), 67; 235; 236
Interpretation, criteria for, xii-xiii
Isaac, 231
Isis and Osiris, 248

Jacob, 231
Jehoiada, 243
Jephtah, 15
Joash, 243
Jonah, 246
Joseph, 169
Josephus, 10; 12; 38-42; 114; 177; 197
Judah, 19; 126; 153; 155; 169; 174; 232

Keret, 17; 152; 181; 215; 250
Keššši, 215
Khattushilish I, 250
Kunuštalluš, 234

Laban, 231
Laḫḫmu/laḫ(a)mu, 15
Laḥmi, 16
Leah, 154; 231
Legitimation, 170-71
Levi, 33
Levirate marriage *(yibbûm)*, 24, 28-29; 125; 128-29; 132; 144-45; 229
Lilith, 75-78
Lugalbanda, 215; 236; 250
Lugalzaggesi, 236

Mahlon, etymology of, 18; 180
Maraʾ, etymology of, 32-34
Marital rights, 26
Marriage: ceremony, 66; of Ruth, 91-92; 124; 229
mem (enclitic), 35; 122
Mephiboshet, 172
Merari, 33
Merismus, 60; 86

Meshkenet, 234
Midwives, 234-35
Migration, 16
Moab, 15; 80; 247-48
Moses, 177

Naamah, 248
Name-giving, 172-75; 234
Naomi, etymology of, 17
Nehemiah, 246
Ninhursanga, 236
Ninsunna, 236
nokriyyāh, 51; 192-93; 230

Oath taking, 30; 92
Obed, etymology of, 175-78
Octagenarian, 8
Odysseus, 220
Onan, 137; 145
'Oral' literature, 214
Orpah, etymology of, 20

Paronomasia. *See* Word-play
Perez, 19; 154; 155; 156; 157; 158; 169; 170; 174; 180; 181
Poetry, xii; 222; 243-44
Pughat, 33

Rachel, 154; 231
Rahab, 169
Ram, 186; 187-89
Rashi, 11
Redemption/Redeemer. *(See ge'ullāh/gō'ēl)*
Rhyming names, 18
Ruth, etymology of, 20-21

Šadday, 34

Salma'/Salmon, 169; 189-90
Samson, 78
Sargon of Agade, 250
Saul, 240
Shelah, 145
Shipwrecked Sailor, The, 215; 227
Shoe transfer, 143-44
Shulgi, 236; 237
Simeon b. Johai, 11
Sinuhe, 215; 227
šipḥāh (maidservant), 53-54; 80; 192-93; 230
Sir Gawain and the Green Knight, 227
Sister-in-law *(yebēmet)*, 28-29
Solomon, 248
Structuralsim, 199

Tamar, 19; 126; 132; 145; 154; 156; 169; 174; 181; 232
Tammuz, 248
Terah, 248
Theology, *Ruth's*, 44-45; 220-21
Tiglath-Pileser I, 52
Translation criteria, xi-xii
Trickster, 230-31
Tukulti-Ninurta, 237
Two Brothers, The, 215; 234

Universalism, 246
Uriah, 231

Vestigial motifs, 233-39
Vocabulary in *Ruth*, 223; 244

Winnowing, 65

Word-play, 19; 33; 36; 43; 51; 52; 58; 60; 64; 79; 81; 106; 116; 142; 150; 156; 159; 167; 223; 226

Yaphet Ben-ʿAli, 11
yigʾāl, 166; 183

Zebulon tribe, 40